THE NEW SPIES

JAMES ADAMS

THE NEW SPIES

EXPLORING THE FRONTIERS OF ESPIONAGE

HUTCHINSON

London

© James Adams 1994

The right of James Adams to be
identified as Author of this work has been asserted
by James Adams in accordance with the
Copyright, Designs and Patents Act, 1988

This edition first published in 1994 by
Hutchinson

Random House (UK) Ltd
20 Vauxhall Bridge Road, London SW1V 2SA

Random House Australia (Pty) Ltd
20 Alfred Street, Milsons Point, Sydney, NSW 2061, Australia

Random House New Zealand Ltd
18 Poland Road, Glenfield, Auckland 10, New Zealand

Random House South Africa (Pty) Ltd
PO Box 337, Bergvlei, 2012, South Africa

A CIP catalogue record for this book is available from the British Library

1 3 5 7 9 8 6 4 2

ISBN: 0 09 174063 0

Set in Bembo by Pure Tech Corporation, Pondicherry, India
Printed and bound in Great Britain by
Clays Ltd, St. Ives PLC

CONTENTS

CONTENTS

To
Grace

Acknowledgements

Daria Antonucci conducted some of the early research and I am grateful for her help. She has now moved on to another position where her experience of the intelligence world should be of considerable assistance.

Jaimie Seaton, an outstanding researcher, filled in many of the gaps and cheerfully answered all those nagging questions that hit an author just when he thinks he has most of the answers. She also put up with my periodic bouts of frustration with great good humour.

Steve Flynn, who has done some pioneering work on combating illegal drugs, was generous with his time and his research. Gordon Witkin, a reporter with *US News and World Report* kindly shared some information on the same subject.

I am also very grateful to a number of current and past members of the intelligence community who took the trouble to read the manuscript and offer helpful suggestions that have improved the final version. No intelligence service would wish to be publicly thanked and then blamed for the errors and omissions which remain and so I merely acknowledge their assistance and they have my thanks.

Delivery of this book was delayed by a month while I coped with the arrival of a new daughter, Grace, a sister to Ella. My wife, René, found the time and the energy to encourage me down the home straight and to read and improve the first draft. As always I am very grateful to her for the support and faith which make it all possible and worthwhile.

Glossary

ANO	Abu Nidal Organization
AWAC	Airborne Warning and Control Aircraft
BDA	Battle Damage Assessment
BND	Bundesnachrichtendienst
BOX	slang for the Security Service
BW	Biological Weapons
CIA	Central Intelligence Agency
CIO	Central Imagery Office
CIS	Commonwealth of Independent States
CW	Chemical Weapons
DEA	Drug Enforcement Administration
DI	Directorate of Intelligence
DIA	Defense Intelligence Agency
DIS	Defence Intelligence Staff (UK)
DO	Directorate of Operations
DST	Direction de la Surveillance du Territoire
ELINT	Electronic Intelligence
FBI	Federal Bureau of Investigation
FCS	Federal Counterintelligence Service
GCHQ	Government Communications Headquarters
GRU	Glavnoye Razvedyvatelnoye Upravleniye
HUMINT	Human Intelligence
IAEA	International Atomic Energy Authority
ICBM	Intercontinental Ballistic Missile
INM	Bureau for International Narcotics Matters
ISA	Intelligence Support Activity
JCS	Joint Chiefs of Staff
JIC	Joint Intelligence Center (US)
JIC	Joint Intelligence Committee (UK)
JSO	Jamahirya Security Organization
KGB	Komitet Gosudarstvennoi Bezopasnosti
MB	Ministerstvo Bezopasnosti

MoD	Ministry of Defence
MTCR	Missile Technology Control Regime
NATO	North Atlantic Treaty Organization
NHITC	National Human Intelligence Tasking Center
NIC	National Intelligence Council
NIE	National Intelligence Estimate
NPC	Non Proliferation Center
NPT	Non Proliferation Treaty
NSA	National Security Agency
NSTL	National Security Threat List
ONDCP	Office of National Drug Control Policy
PFLP-GC	Popular Front for the Liberation of Palestine – General Command
PLO	Palestine Liberation Organization
RUC	Royal Ulster Constabulary
SAS	Special Air Service
SEAL	Sea Air Land Team (US Navy)
SIGINT	Signals Intelligence
SIS	Secret Intelligence Service
SNIE	Special National Intelligence Estimate
SS	Security Service
SVR	Sluzhba Vneshnei Razvedaki
UNDCP	United Nations Drug Control Program

Author's Note

I first became interested in the world of espionage when researching *The Financing of Terror*, a book that was published in 1986. The thesis of the book, that terrorists could be more effectively countered if we understood their finances better, caused some interest in the intelligence community. I was invited to talk to the Defense Intelligence Agency and began a series of lectures to the British Special Branch and met with senior British intelligence officials. Later books, which dealt with covert warfare, the arms business and terrorism, expanded my knowledge of the intelligence community.

In addition, ten years as the defence correspondent of *The Sunday Times* brought me into frequent contact with both military and civilian intelligence agencies all over the world. I covered both the Iran-Iraq War and the Gulf War as well as a number of guerrilla wars and terrorist campaigns and so had ample opportunity to see both the effectiveness of good intelligence and the consequences of shoddy work.

In the beginning, I, perhaps like many others, was of the view that spies were a combination of Borgia and Bond; the 'buggers and burglars' of Peter Wright fame. The reality, I discovered, is much more prosaic. Intelligence officers are primarily government servants working in a vast bureaucracy where the swashbuckling behaviour of the James Bond is frowned upon as dangerous and largely unhelpful. Most intelligence work is very boring, frequently lonely and with little of the glamour or excitement portrayed in books and films. Of course, there are moments of high drama – the brush pass with a source, the high speed chase or the perfect piece of intelligence that helps stop an act of terrorism – but these are rare indeed.

The idea for this book actually began with the rise of Mikhail Gorbachev and the revolution he brought with him to the Soviet Union. As the target that has obsessed every Western intelligence agency since the end of the Second World War gradually became more accessible, the principal reason for the existence of many intelligence agencies and agents was vanishing. In this time of uncertainty, it was fascinating to observe the reactions of different members of the community. Some were enthralled, thrilled and challenged by the opportunities that would come with the end of the Cold War. Others saw it as another example of a Soviet plot, the beginning of a new era when we would let down our defences only to have them assaulted by a new version of the aggressive Russian bear. The vast majority were disturbed and threatened by the changes which removed all the certainties that had marked their careers to date. With no Soviet threat and no communist bloc to oppose, the bedrock of their existence had been removed and a new world had to be carved from the old.

As the Soviet bloc collapsed so did the accepted rationale behind the existence of nearly every intelligence service. With the Cold War replacing the fight against fascism, organizations like the OSS were able to swiftly evolve into the CIA, or MI6 become the Secret Intelligence Service, without any serious questioning of the need for such organizations to defend national security both by fighting foreign spies and spying to find out the enemy's intentions. But the end of the superpower conflict changed all that. With the Soviet Union gone, the critics asked, what possible justification could there be for intelligence services and their budgets? That perfectly legitimate question sent a collective shudder through the worldwide intelligence body. Each organization scrambled to see the new challenges for the future, to define the new roles and to ensure, like all bureaucracies, that whatever the apparent changes, there would be a job for everyone and a budget to pay for them.

Within three years, intelligence services all over the world had done their analysis and come up with remarkably similar conclusions. The new world, they say, will be an unstable place without the certainties of the Cold War, which was at least predictable in its causes and effects. The new world will be filled with terrorism, international financial crime, ambitious dictators and ethnic conflicts. All were agreed about the main priorities (national security, terrorism, proliferation, drugs) and most argued that more people and money would be needed to meet the challenge. Few policy makers bought this line and most intelligence agencies have had their budgets cut in line with cutbacks in the armed forces.

Much of the thinking about the reorganization of intelligence is still being done but some clear patterns have emerged. The most important of these is that the radical surgery that some argued for is not going to happen. By and large the old institutions have simply evolved to absorb the new roles assigned to them. This is hardly surprising. No bureaucracy yields power willingly and few democratic countries have policy makers with sufficient courage and muscle to force through revolutionary change. What has been striking about the reform process so far is that it has largely been organized from within. In a country like Britain, for example, there has been no debate at all and the public remain almost entirely ignorant about where £800m of their money goes each year. In America, even with its more effective oversight system, there has been little overt debate and very little information has been made public outside of the closed world of the Congressional intelligence committees and the community itself.

The research for this book proved the most challenging that I have had to do on any subject. Understandably, the intelligence community is wary of outsiders asking questions and particularly nervous when, as now, they are still searching for some of the answers. But that very uncertainty seems to have helped open some doors, as individuals and agencies have been anxious to explain themselves as they confront the challenges of the post-Cold War world. To my surprise, I ended up with some stunning access and in the course of six months in 1992 I interviewed Bob Gates, then director of the CIA, William Sessions, then director of the FBI, Yevgeni Primakov, the head of the SVR which used to be the First Chief Directorate of the KGB, and three heads of Western intelligence agencies. I do not believe any outsider has ever had such access, particularly as when I met Primakov it was his first interview to anyone since his appointment, and for both Gates and Sessions, it was the first time that a foreign journalist had interviewed the serving heads of the CIA and FBI.

Those individuals talked not about operations but about policy and the changes that have been made or will be made in the near future to cope with the challenges facing the intelligence community into the next century. I went to others for the stories which I hope bring this book to life and make it an interesting factual account of the current and future problems and successes of spies around the world. It is the nature of the intelligence world that very few officials will talk on the record. This book is footnoted so the reader can check published sources. Where I have conducted an interview with a source who does not wish to be named, the footnote makes that clear. There are also some instances where information has been given by senior intelligence officials on the condition that it remains unsourced. These requests were made either to protect sources and methods or to prevent political retribution. In every case, I have checked the information and was satisfied about its accuracy before including it.

This book will help frame the debate that has gone on inside the intelligence community since the end of the Cold War so that both the professionals and those outside the community who are interested in the subject will have a better understanding of the issues. This is not intended as a completely comprehensive manual of every intelligence service or every nuance of the debate. That would not only be very boring but it would also be thousands of pages long. In examining recent history, current changes and plans for the future, I have highlighted the main issues facing the intelligence community and looked at them from the perspective of the old principal protagonists – the Americans and the Russians – while looking in detail at British intelligence because it is one of those that has been forced to change dramatically by the end of the Cold War.

It has become clear to me that some changes that have been made are inadequate while others have not been addressed properly. This book, therefore, will try to shed light on the debate and to provide a framework for the ongoing discussions about the future of intelligence into the next century.

DEFINING INTELLIGENCE

At the outset, it is worth looking at the most basic question confronting all those who have been wrestling with the reforms over the past four years: what is intelligence? *The Random House Dictionary* describes intelligence as 'the gathering or distribution of information especially secret information; information about an enemy or potential enemy'.[1] *The Encyclopedia of the US Military* quotes the Joint Chiefs of Staff definition as 'the product resulting from the collection, processing, integration, analysis, evaluation and interpretation of available information concerning foreign countries or areas'.[2]

While this is more useful than the simple dictionary definition, a more comprehensive version appears in *United States Intelligence, an Encyclopedia*: 'To begin, intelligence should be differentiated from information and intelligence information. Information is unevaluated material of every type. Intelligence information is information that has not been processed into intelligence, but may be of intelligence value. Finally, intelligence is the product that results or the knowledge that is derived from the cyclical processing of information. Shaman Kent maintains that intelligence has three definitional subsets: knowledge (the knowledge that our nation must have the proper decision making); institution (the physical organization of people who are pursuing a certain type of knowledge); and activity (the actions of collection, evaluation, research, analysis, study, presentation, and more).'[3]

What these definitions tend to forget and what the intelligence community all too frequently ignores is that the gathering of information is not performed in isolation but in response to requirements articulated by the decision makers in government. Therefore, a fourth definition set out by Jennifer Sims, a staff member of the US Senate Select Committee on Intelligence, is perhaps more appropriate: 'Intelligence is best defined as information collected, organized, or analyzed on behalf of actors or decision makers. Such information may include technical data, trends, rumors, pictures or hardware.'[4]

An understanding of the scope of intelligence is important because it defines how the community sees itself and how in turn it is seen by the policy makers who provide the resources and consume the product. In the past, the intelligence community has frequently operated in a vacuum, gathering information because it is there and not because there is a consumer who wants it. At the same time, all intelligence services are obsessed with secrecy, determined to protect at all costs the sources and methods that produce the most difficult information that is often the most dangerous to obtain. Over the years the cult of secrecy has cast a pall over all aspects of the intelligence world. Intelligence officers are reluctant communicators, seeing anyone outside their narrow world as an intrusive threat. But all too often the information they collect and guard so assiduously is either irrelevant to the needs of any policy maker, or collected from open sources, or collected by clandestine methods but available from other, less sensitive areas. For example, there have been a number of occasions in the past where after considerable difficulty I have obtained a briefing from someone in the intelligence community only to find that the information passed over has either come from something I have written or from published sources that I have in my files.

In the same way, definitions bedevilled the whole process of countering terrorism in the 1970s – one man's terrorist is another man's freedom fighter. In the case of intelligence, the definitions are both too confusing and too confining to be used as a way to restrict the current debate. Intelligence is simply the information which somebody in government decides he or she needs. The issue then comes down to how that intelligence should be gathered and who should do the collecting. Too often in the past, these issues have been masked by the very secrecy with which the intelligence community tends to cloak itself.

For many years there has been an automatic assumption that any and all work carried out by an intelligence service is secret. In fact, like all gatherers of information, intelligence agencies rely on overt sources – newspapers, magazines, speeches, contract bulletins – for their data as they do on satellites and the sensitive human source. Classifying all this information as secret is unnecessary as much of the product is neither secret nor sensitive but is readily available to those interested in following the same avenue of inquiry. Both governments and intelligence agencies have been reluctant to confront this issue. The agencies benefit from the mystique of intelligence, the idea that everything they do is somehow so delicate that it cannot be talked about in an open way. Governments are often so ignorant about the workings of intelligence that they are unable to distinguish between secret and overt sources. Finally, it is the natural inclination of all bureaucracies to hide methods and information from public scrutiny and any move to change the methods of classification will be resisted. But the fact remains that much of what the intelligence community does and the product it delivers are classified as secret because of where it comes from and not because of what it is, says or does.

The exact role of intelligence into the next century – the sources and methods of gathering information, the likely requirements of policy makers – is still being debated. But some common themes have emerged and although there will be more changes in the future, it is clear that in general the intelligence services that exist today will be around in the future and the roles they have defined for themselves in the past four years will remain.

One study, completed in August 1992 by the Institute for the Study of Diplomacy at Georgetown University in Washington DC, published a detailed post-Cold War analysis of the future of American diplomacy into the next century. Aside from recommending widespread reforms of the existing structure and its tasks, the study had this to say about intelligence:

> The traditional rule of thumb in intelligence gathering was that 90 per cent of the information policy makers needed was openly available. Diplomatic reporting was charged with both gathering and analyzing this 'overt' intelligence. The remaining ten per cent, it was argued, could only be obtained covertly by the intelligence community.
>
> The dramatic softening of hard intelligence targets and the willingness, even eagerness, of former adversaries to share once jealously guarded information has changed that rule-of-thumb ratio. Information on munitions factories and oil fields once obtainable only with expensive satellites or eavesdropping equipment might now be had for the price of a train ticket for an embassy reporting officer or for a lunch with a Western businessman. The recent 'Open Skies' agreement dramatically simplifies photographic intelligence collection, while the demise of the Warsaw Pact reduced the frequency with which photos need be taken. The abolition of the East German

and Czech intelligence agencies and the retrenchment in the KGB and others eliminates whole sets of targets and threats.[5]

This change in the nature of intelligence has affected some agencies more than others. In the American intelligence community, for example, 'intelligence' has always been taken to mean information gathered from both open and secret sources. This in turn has meant that an inordinate amount of resources has been spent on gathering information that is readily available. In the new world, a flood of previously secret information has appeared which, in theory, should make redundant some of the work that used to be carried out by the intelligence community. There is little evidence that these changes are reflected in the current structure of American intelligence which has retained most of the old trappings of the Cold War. To do otherwise would be to accept a reduced role and smaller budgets which in turn would mean fewer employees and less power, consequences that no head of any organization would accept without a fight.

The situation in British intelligence is different. SIS has always worked on the principle that all intelligence is secret intelligence and that effort should only be expended on gathering information that is not available to other agencies or from open sources. Of course, SIS uses information gathered by other government departments in researching different subjects but this information is in addition to, or complementary to, the intelligence gathered by covert means. This focus has allowed SIS to remain small and effective and has helped mitigate the consequences of the recent changes.

No one doubts that the world has changed dramatically. The confusion arises when attempts are made to understand what those changes mean: do they hold promise or peril for the future? For every intelligence agency the questions that are being asked about them internally and externally are fundamental to their future. Some, which have been dragged along by the transformation of the society they have helped control – as in the former Soviet Union – have undergone a revolution imposed from outside which has been resisted with vigour. Others, such as the CIA or the SIS, which have been captive observers of a restructuring of a familiar world into a new and disturbing planet, have had to evolve to meet the new challenges.

To the sceptical outsider, it may seem that the intelligence community has no role at all. With the end of the Cold War, arguably there is no justification for it, for the scale of global intelligence operations no longer exists. On the contrary, the changes that have taken place provide an opportunity to transform the intelligence community – a symbol of a bygone era – into a force for good. Instead of watching each other, former enemies can guard the environment, instead of counting tanks they can count crop yields.

CHAPTER ONE

THE BELLY OF THE BEAST

Hidden deep inside a birchwood forest just off the ring road south-east of Moscow at Yasenevo lies the house known as Ten Ash Trees. Reached by a single-lane bumpy track, it is invisible from the road and lies in the heart of what is perhaps the most secure complex in Russia. For twenty years, Ten Ash Trees was where the KGB held court, entertaining spies from all over the world to grand dinners before escorting them upstairs to one of the comfortable suites with the hidden microphones and concealed cameras.

Furnished in 1960s kitsch, the building is decorated with contributions from foreign intelligence agencies who once came to stay as honoured guests. A stuffed turtle head – an endangered species – is on one wall, courtesy of the DGI, Cuba's intelligence service; a cheap etching from Vietnam is on another wall; a grotesque clock from President Assad of Syria sits alongside a stuffed blowfish from an unnamed donor.

Today, like the KGB itself, Ten Ash Trees is a hollow shell, a monument to another age when the KGB was the most feared spy agency and half the world was coloured red. The rooms are empty, the Swedish furniture is unused and the house smells of disinfectant and decay. Only a single caretaker remains to monitor the security cameras that surround the building. But there is nothing to see, no guests and nobody interested in penetrating the security screen to find the few tawdry secrets left.

Just outside the red-brick confines of Ten Ash Trees stands a luxurious dacha which also lies empty. This was where Yuri Andropov used to stay when he was head of the KGB and before he became president. In these more democratic times, the head of the former KGB refuses to stay here. He is sensitive to criticism from the Russian parliament about the exotic lifestyle of the intelligence services.[1]

Just over a mile away through the trees lies the headquarters of the foreign intelligence division of the former KGB. This complex, built in 1972 by a Finnish architect, is dominated by the twenty-two-storey white main building which in turn is surrounded by car parks and an ornamental lake. This top secret complex has never before been visited by a Westerner and it is a sign of the new times that even this is now open for inspection.

Unlike the CIA headquarters at Langley, an air of decay surrounds these buildings too. The guardhouse, a single wooden structure, looks like a relic from Stalag Luft VI and the car park – reputed to be the busiest in Russia – is dominated by ancient Volgas. Security is tight but even the feared red KGB identity card has been replaced by an anonymous green plastic laminated card. Inside, the plain offices appear almost empty, a reflection of the recent cutbacks.

How times have changed. Five years ago the KGB had an army of 300,000 men, kept files on millions of Soviet citizens and had absolute power to enforce one of the most ruthless tyrannies ever seen. It was the KGB that placed neighbour against neighbour, committed dissidents to 'psychiatric' hospitals and ordered the assassination of opponents of communism at home and abroad. The KGB was feared and respected as the most ruthless and effective intelligence agency the world has ever known.

Today, the old organization has been destroyed. The twenty former directorates which formed the KGB have been disbanded, thousands of agents have been fired and – if the new spymasters are to be believed – the new KGB wants to come in from the cold.

In this new wilderness of mirrors, every image has changed. The former KGB now wants to cooperate with the West in combating terrorism, proliferation and drugs and is actively courting Western intelligence agencies. This new era has produced some extraordinary images: Stella Rimington, head of the British Security Service, or MI5, travelling to Moscow to meet the very people she has fought against for years; Bob Gates, former head of the CIA, making the same pilgrimage; a director of Britain's Secret Intelligence Service, or MI6, flying to Hungary to discuss with his counterparts how Britan can help introduce democratic controls into that country's intelligence service.

With all the certainties of the Cold War gone forever, intelligence is now a new game with new rules and many new players. The key enigma remains of just what form the new KGB is taking.

Yevgeny Primakov is the public face of the new KGB. Appointed by Boris Yeltsin in October 1991, Primakov heads what was once the First

Chief Directorate of the KGB and is now known as the Sluzhba Vnesh-nei Razvedaki or SVR. He controls all Russia's spies abroad, deciding their targets and approving their methods. What he thinks and how he translates that thought into action is of critical importance to the West and to other spy agencies such as Britain's MI5 and MI6 or America's CIA and FBI.

Since his appointment, Primakov has consistently refused to be interviewed by Russian or American journalists, preferring to keep his counsel as he tries to reform the agency against strong opposition from hardliners in the Russian parliament and from within the KGB itself. But Primakov and Yeltsin need allies in the West and so they have launched a charm offensive to try and convince the world that the new KGB is an organization with which everyone can do business. For his first interview, we meet in a house not far from Red Square which used to be a secret base for Lavrentia Beria, Stalin's confidant and one of the most ruthless leaders of the Russian secret service. The house is now a mixture of beautiful old wood panelling, baroque gilt scrollwork and modern plush red velour couches.

Born in the Ukraine in 1929 and brought up in Georgia, Primakov trained as a journalist with *Pravda* and served for many years in the Middle East where Western intelligence believes he first started working for the KGB – an allegation he denies. A full member of the Academy of Scientists, a member of the Central Committee and a former director of the Institute of Oriental Studies, his establishment credentials are impeccable. But he is a long-standing friend of Yeltsin and was one of those who denounced the August 1990 coup.

Opinion in Western intelligence circles is divided about just where his loyalties lie. Some say he got his current job because his old friends in the KGB orchestrated it and needed a man at the head whom they could trust. Others argue he is a genuine reformer, a man determined to shrug off the shackles of the past and bring the KGB into a more democratic world. Wearing a well-cut grey suit, his small round body bounces into the room. Although he speaks fluent English, he insists on working through an interpreter which gives him time to consider his answers, which appear as a deep rumble from inside the jowls that almost hide his small chin.

The mere fact that I was sitting in Moscow with the head of the former KGB was a mark of how things had changed. Five years earlier, when Russia was part of the Soviet Union, I had been introduced to a military attaché from the Soviet embassy in London. He was a member of the

GRU, the military's branch of Soviet intelligence. It was an opportunity to try and get to see the Soviet armed forces in action and at his suggestion we met at the Connaught Hotel, one of London's most expensive restaurants, to discuss the matter over lunch. At the end of the meal, when I raised the question of visiting the Soviet Union, the reply was simple: 'We know that you are a spy. All you defence correspondents are spies and a visa is impossible. Even for me to ask would cause me trouble.'

This time there were no such difficulties and aside from frequent feeble jokes about 'your friends in MI6' it was an extraordinarily frank and open Russian intelligence service that was made available for my inspection.

'Things really are changing,' Primakov insisted. 'First of all we have repudiated the old ideological model we had before, which predetermined that there are permanent enemies and permanent friends. The old model predetermined confrontations and pushed to the background our country's national interests, which were sometimes sacrificed in order to give ideological support to our allies. Now, we are not working against someone. We are working in defence of the national interest.'

This is not the language of the head of the hated KGB; this could be spoken by any head of Western intelligence. The priorities Primakov went on to set out for his organization – gathering military secrets, preventing arms proliferation, countering terrorism and drug trafficking – are identical to those spelled out in the months preceding this interview by Bob Gates, Bill Sessions and other heads of Western intelligence.

The new reality has in part been imposed by the Yeltsin regime and the new democracy in Russia and in part by financial realities. Primakov claims that his organization has shut thirty offices abroad, including withdrawing from most countries in Africa and large parts of the Far East. By the end of 1992, staff operating abroad will have been cut by around 50 per cent. This revolution means that any pretence that Russia has of influencing foreign governments through covert operations has gone. Today Primakov claims that the kind of mission associated with the KGB – fomenting revolution in Latin America, helping the spread of communism in southern Africa – is history.

'Before, we were very seriously engaged in the internal political situation in a certain country, even concentrating on such ambitious aims as changing its government. As history shows, we were not always very successful in this respect, even in those countries where we sent our troops, like Afghanistan. Now we have stopped all attempts at subversion and we do not support specific political forces inside a country.'

Even Directorate A has been disbanded by Primakov. For years this was in the front line of the propaganda war with the Glavnyi Protivnik, or Main Enemy, as the United States was known to the KGB. Directorate A claimed that AIDS was designed by the CIA and that America had developed a bomb that would kill only black people. Now there is no black propaganda, there are no KGB agents with poisoned umbrellas assassinating dissidents abroad, no Leylas seducing innocent British businessmen in hotel rooms wired to record every slap and tickle for use as blackmail. There are even regular meetings between the new SVR and the CIA to talk over any issues the people at Langley feel might suggest the SVR was slipping back to its old ways.

'Our latest assessment is that the old KGB was represented in virtually all the countries in which there was a Soviet mission,' said one Western intelligence source. 'Cutting thirty overseas stations would therefore not necessarily be as significant as it might seem. The 50 per cent reduction mentioned by Primakov probably represents a target to be achieved over the medium term. Reductions of this order have been made in some countries, but certainly not on a worldwide basis.'[2]

Visits to Moscow by senior British, American, French and German intelligence officials among others suggest that, despite the public protestations, the new KGB has some way to go before being fully welcomed into the brotherhood of acceptable spies. For example, the new KGB has refused to supply details of arms supplied to countries such as Libya, or to provide a list of terrorists trained in the former Soviet Union, claiming that such lists do not exist.

'They may have learned the language but they still have a long way to go to demonstrate by practical means that they have changed for the better,' said one senior Western intelligence official.[3]

This cautious view is mirrored in every Western agency where for generations careers have been made or broken on the Soviet target. But since the collapse of communism the very foundations of the intelligence world have disintegrated along with the Berlin Wall. While the professionals inside Western intelligence maintain today that the Soviets were a relatively small part of their total work, the fact remains that success against the Soviets was the most important goal. Years were spent trying to discover the tiniest detail of the workings of the Kremlin so that each apparently insignificant piece of information could be slotted into the largely blank mosaic which was the Soviet Union.

Now, the intelligence community is overwhelmed by the information that is pouring out of the former Soviet Union. Defectors are coming out at the rate of more than one a month and both MI6 and the CIA have had to turn away dozens of potential recruits.

'Our problem is that there simply are not enough people to debrief all the people who want to come across,' said one intelligence source. 'Not only do we have defectors but there are literally thousands of pages of documents that you can get from the governments in the former Soviet Union. Five years ago, we would have spent thousands of dollars and years of effort trying to get sight of just a single page.'[4]

This flood of information has forced change in organizations like MI6. Analysts whose careers have been spent digesting the trivia of the Politburo's rubbish bins have been told that history is now largely irrelevant, that the targets have changed and that while Russia is a threat, it is a timid beast compared with the bullying bear of a few years ago.

The intelligence community initially divided into the believers and the sceptics. The latter argued that the Russian bear was very much alive, and a military coup or even a takeover orchestrated by the former KGB could see the communists revert to type. Today, the sceptics have either left or been forced to revise their thinking, as the reforms in the former Soviet Union have remained in place and it has become clear that the old Communist Party structure is finished. Now, the community has divided between those who truly believe the old guard have gone forever and the cynics who claim that much of the old intelligence structure remains. That group says that the KGB may have changed its name and its missions but it will remain active against Western interests for the foreseeable future, particularly in the former Soviet republics.

But, for the most part, Western agencies have been revamped with new staff and new priorities. In MI6, for example, there has been a palace revolution with a whole generation of older, senior staff taking early retirement or being moved aside as a new breed of men and women in their forties moves into top management. These are the people who were educated in the 1960s and came of age in the 1970s when passions had cooled from the first stages of the Cold War; people able to understand and adapt to the new realities.

General Vadim Alexeevitch Kirpitchenko is one of the reasons why the old guard say that nothing has really changed at the KGB. He made his mark recruiting spies in the Middle East, eventually becoming No 2 in the First Chief Directorate, sitting at the right hand of many of the ogres of the intelligence business, and counted hardliners such as Yuri

Andropov and Vladimir Kryuchkov as close friends. Prematurely killed off in Frederick Forsyth's novel *The Fourth Protocol*, Kirpitchenko has survived the recent turbulence in Russia to emerge as a 'consultant' to Primakov. Whether he means them or not, he has learned the new lines well and speaks convincingly about the new democratic KGB.

'In the field of operational activity, we have now given up all forms of pressure and if we work with anybody, it is on a purely voluntary basis. We no longer make use of compromising material and we are categorically against the use of psychotropic substances or any special medicinal products. We are against the use of intimidation, nor do we get involved in someone's private or personal life.'

For an organization that used to pride itself on the personal files it held on millions of Soviet citizens and which made liberal use of psychiatric hospitals to silence dissidents, these are extraordinary changes.

'If you see us simply as a bear with a dagger in its teeth, then it is difficult to understand what really happened. The fact is that we, the veterans of intelligence, have always seen the shortcomings in our own service. We do have people with brains, people who had worked abroad and who see life in the West as it really is, with all its pluses and minuses. That is why there was this aspiration to work within a legal framework, and to know that what you are doing is lawful.'

Today, the SVR and the other branches of the former KGB that still exist are controlled by a complex oversight system which allows various committees of the Russian parliament to control what they do and how the work is carried out. In theory, this oversight system is both more visible and more effective than anything that exists in Britain today, something that every senior officer in Russian intelligence is quick to point out.

'We have outstripped many Western countries in the openness and democratization of our intelligence services,' said Kirpitchenko. 'But while we have done this your beloved intelligence has no such laws, it publishes nothing and your British intelligence operate outside the law.'

This may be a real propaganda point but not even the most ardent democrat in the Russian parliament would claim that he has control over the SVR. To date, the Russian oversight system has been little more than a façade; nevertheless, it is true that some Western countries, such as France, do not even have a façade.

Tatyana Samolis is the new face of Russian intelligence. For seventeen years she worked at *Pravda*, rising to become the deputy letters editor.

Then in 1991 she got a call from Primakov to head up the new press office which was being established to orchestrate the former KGB's charm offensive to a sceptical world. Two years later she remains almost entirely ignorant about the workings of Russian intelligence, unable to answer even the simplest questions about policy, numbers or missions.

'It is still a secret to me whether I am a representative of the media in intelligence or a representative of intelligence in the media,' she said.

The real work of the press office falls to the KGB's equivalent of British comedians Morecambe and Wise: Yuri Koboladze, tall, gangling, congenial and amusing, is the bureau chief of the public affairs office. He goes everywhere with Oleg Tsarev, a slim, dapper and serious man who acts as a 'consultant' to the SVR and organizes the publication of documents from the archives. They appear as comfortable and confident entertainers, both fluent in English and perfect foils for the Western press who are satisfied merely to have someone to provide answers, however superficial.

These two devised the publicity stunt of the Miss KGB competition and orchestrated the selective release of archive material that appeared to show that the British had helped prolong the war with Germany by rejecting the overtures of Rudolf Hess; that Alger Hiss was not a Soviet spy; and that British intelligence was totally penetrated by the KGB, even after the discovery of the Cambridge spy ring.

As examples of smart propaganda these are in the best tradition of the old KGB and have been greeted with impotent fury in British intelligence, where outdated secrecy rules prevent any detailed rebuttal.

What is not generally known is that both men cut their KGB teeth on the English desk of the First Chief Directorate. They also worked undercover in England as journalists during the 1970s and 1980s, living in Bayswater and cultivating friends on the *Guardian* and in the House of Commons. By their account, their careers were virtual failures.

'I loved England and I made many friends there,' recalls Koboladze, whose conversation is bizarrely sprinkled with the words 'actually' and 'Jesus' spoken in a rehearsed upper-class English accent. 'Honestly, I would do nothing to harm the British people or Britain. It was all a great game and 90 per cent of my time was spent on simple political reporting.'

But forty-three-year-old Koboladze is now a colonel in the SVR, a rank given only to those who have done exceptional service. Oleg Gordievsky, a KGB colonel who defected to Britain in 1985, described Koboladze during his debriefing by MI6 as 'one of the best line officers I ever knew.'[5]

Tsarev, too, was a colonel before he retired to become a consultant to the SVR. Tsarev is now persona non grata in the UK and is described by one British intelligence source as 'a thoroughly professional and very experienced active measures man'.

Koboladze is still allowed in England and with considerable relish tells the story of arriving in England for the 1991 G7 economic summit hosted by Prime Minister John Major. As the summit concluded, Koboladze asked a friend in the No 10 press office to get Major to answer his question first.

'Major didn't know what I looked like so could only look around calling for the man in the grey suit. When I stepped forward there we were, the British prime minister and the KGB man face to face.'

Both men profess a total acceptance of the new order. Koboladze makes a joke of the old days and laughs at how stupid the communists were. But as the jokes flow more freely it is Tsarev whose laugh becomes strained. While his lips smile, his eyes say clearly that he expects his time to come again − a sentiment widely shared in the new KGB.

But even if there are some reservations, the new intelligence service is determined to show how different their world has become.

The Lubyanka is one of the most feared buildings in Soviet mythology. It sits menacingly up the road from the Bolshoi at the top of Okhotny Ryad, a huge red building whose top floors have a stunning view of the Kremlin. Before the revolution, a statue of Feliks Dzerzhinsky, the founder of Russian intelligence, stood in front of the building. Today, the statue has been torn down to be replaced by a simple wooden cross. Along the base has been daubed in Russian the inscription 'By This We Conquered', a reminder to those going to work each day that for the moment the people have taken their power.

The Lubyanka used to be the headquarters of the Second Chief Directorate of the KGB, which was responsible for internal security. Today, the MBR or Ministry of Security has replaced the old order in substance and form and the headquarters controls a staff of 135,000, a reduction of around 30 per cent.

The guards of the Lubyanka are two young conscripts dressed in the standard light olive uniform with dirty shoes, dirty hands and cigarettes burning in the filthy ashtray. There is one security camera producing a crackly image on a small black-and-white screen. Inside, the halls are cavernous with high ceilings and stone floors. Curiously, MI5 and the MBR seem to have shared an interior decorator. The furniture is identical 1970s Scandinavian utilitarian. The only difference is that the

Russian telephone system is so antiquated that each extension requires a separate phone and so offices tend to be short of working space. The once famous cells in the building have been converted to offices and a restaurant, symbols of the changes since the revolution.

'We are no longer allowed to bug telephones without legal authority and we no longer spy on people for ideological reasons,' said Alexei Kondaurov, the chief of public affairs for the MBR. 'We no longer watch over journalists. In fact, they are now so free that I, personally, am terrified.'

This new breed of policeman is trained in an enormous, nine-storey, drab brown building on the outskirts of Moscow. The Academy is in much better condition than the training centre for MI6, with a massive indoor sports complex, language schools, a forensic laboratory and a computer centre. In the basement, Colonel Viktor Pavlov, the deputy chief of the Academy, shows off the underground shooting range. Four recruits display their shooting skills before a smiling Pavlov challenges me to a competition; 10 shots in under 60 seconds at 25 metres with an automatic pistol. Clearly this is an opportunity to demonstrate his prowess in front of the students.

Though I have not fired a pistol in years, I accept. On the command, I adopt the approved Miami Vice position and fire away. When the paper targets are brought back, Pavlov's face darkens. I have scored six bulls and four outers, a rather better score than he managed. I feel sure the exchange convinces them that I have been sent by my masters at British intelligence.

Strolling through the echoing corridors of the Academy, Pavlov repeats the common litany. That the old order is finished and that the new spies of today and tomorrow are a different breed. We must cooperate, he says, because we all share a common enemy in the terrorists and the drug traffickers. It is a convincing line, but just how true is it?

To the immigration officer at Helsinki airport, the young couple approaching the desk on the morning of April 23, 1992 seemed ordinary enough. Both dark-haired, slim and in their mid-twenties, they looked like any other couple touring Europe. He handed over a passport in the name of James Tristan Peatfield which showed he had been born on 23 February, 1968 in Croydon. The woman was Anna Marie Nemeth who had been born on 14 July, 1968 in Wembley.[6]

Two things sounded a vague alarm bell: they seemed nervous, the hands and eyes giving away the tell-tale signs of a drug smuggler or a criminal on the run. Also, they had no luggage except a single vinyl sports bag.

The couple said they were on a summer holiday in Europe and had just flown from Austria to Moscow where they had stayed for a week and they now planned to stay in Helsinki for a few days before moving on. His suspicions aroused, the immigration officer asked them who had won the recent British general election, which had brought in John Major as Britain's prime minister. Neither was able to answer this simple question. The immigration officer then asked to look in their bag and found a few items of clothing, a Sony world band shortwave receiver and $30,000 in cash rolled in an old shirt.

Peatfield told the immigration officer that he had moved to the USA before 1974, lived in New York and then worked in Canada before coming home to set up his own business in Fulham. Nemeth had returned to the UK in 1991 after emigrating to Canada with her parents twenty years earlier. She was now working as a secretary with an advertising agency in London and was living with Peatfield.

Under examination it turned out that their passports were false, simple copies of originals that had probably been 'borrowed' while their owners were travelling in the Eastern bloc. Helsinki police then contacted the British Security Service who checked out their story and discovered that the real people existed and were safely in their homes in England. The couple's jobs were fake.

With their story exposed, the two immediately confessed that they were Russians, a husband and wife who had decided to emigrate illegally. Peatfield was Igor Ivanovich Lutskov, born in 1965 in Chelyabinsk. For some time he had been living with relatives near Moscow and had worked in a number of cooperatives as a commercial agent. Nemeth was really Nataliya Valeryevna Lutskova, born in Sverdlovsk in 1965, a technical interpreter at a building factory.

This story might have been more believable if the couple had been able to explain just why they had needed to enter the West illegally when travel restrictions had been relaxed under President Yeltsin. They claimed to have purchased the passports on the Moscow black market and to have made the $30,000 by selling Chinese jackets and women's underwear. For a time it appeared to their interrogators that the woman might be turned to work for the West and the questioning was halted. This was a false hope and the couple were expelled to Moscow.

11

News of the arrest flashed around the world to the heads of Western counter-intelligence agencies, where it was seen as confirmation that despite their protestations, the KGB was up to its old tricks.

'It was a classic illegals operation,' said one British intelligence source. 'A false identity, a second identity if discovered and actually they were working for the KGB the whole time.'

A month earlier, police in New Zealand announced they had discovered a man using a forged British passport trying to obtain a second passport using a technique borrowed from the novel *The Day of the Jackal* by Frederick Forsyth. The man had arrived in New Zealand six months earlier and had applied for a New Zealand passport using the birth certificate of a New Zealander who had died as a child.[7]

Under questioning, the man confessed that he was an agent for Russian intelligence. His real name was Anvar Kadyrov, born in Uzbekistan in 1959. He had been trying to obtain a New Zealand identity to establish a 'legend' that would allow him to move on to a third country with a watertight history.

Exactly what these people were supposed to do remains a mystery. Both the FBI and MI5 say that a major focus of Russian intelligence these days is on scientific and technical secrets, known in the trade as S and T.

'As their economy has collapsed so they need to steal our economic secrets rather than trying to develop their own innovations,' said one intelligence source. 'This is even more of a priority for them now and we have seen a huge increase in their efforts in this area.'

Exactly how the SVR can afford to pay its men in the field and who decides their priorities remains unclear.

'Sometimes I wonder whether there is any direction coming from the centre or whether we have something comparable to the Energizer rabbit that just keeps coming along without any central nervous system,' said Bob Gates, the CIA Director under President George Bush. 'The KGB has gone through dramatic changes. It's basically a Russian organization now. The Union KGB, for all practical purposes, has ceased to exist. And I think we have to wait and see how that develops.'[8]

While the new KGB may have reduced its activities, the GRU, Russian military intelligence, remains as active as ever. They are spearheading the assault on Western industrial and military secrets, apparently determined to steal a march on their old enemies in the KGB. In the complex political maelstrom that is Russia today, the organization with the most secrets is the one that can be assured of greatest political influence.

In both the United States and Britain the GRU has actually increased its activities in the past year. Boris Yeltsin has been told personally about Western concerns but has been unable or unwilling to rein in his troops.

'The real situation is that he is probably powerless,' said one Western source. 'The military need all the muscle they can get and stealing our secrets could give them a lot of leverage. They are fighting to survive so they will ignore any orders to curb their activities.'

Around the corner from the Lubyanka, in part of what used to be the KGB officer's club, is the new Intelligence Museum. By appointment only, visitors can get a guided tour of the triumphs of Soviet intelligence since the Russian Revolution. It is a unique display which makes the CIA's efforts at Langley appear feeble (Britain has no intelligence museum).

There are the usual pictures of the great spies such as Philby and Blake. But more surprisingly there are pictures of American and British spies caught in the act of passing or receiving messages; an American device disguised as a tree stump which could intercept messages, record them and send them in bursts to a satellite; a camera disguised as an electric razor; a pair of spectacles issued by the CIA to one of their Russian agents with poison concealed in the stems; and secret messages embedded in the pages of a copy of the *National Geographic*.

The exhibition ends with examples of the new direction of Russian intelligence: the fight against corruption, drugs and terrorism.

The museum is supposed to serve as an illustration of the long journey undertaken by the Russian intelligence services. Beginning as heroes of the Revolution they went through the darkness of the Stalin era, through the Cold War and the fight against Western attacks and have now entered the uplands of the new democracy. It sounds fine but the picture is neither as simple as the Russians would have it nor as forbidding as some Western experts portray it.

There is no doubt that the new KGB continues to spy on Britain, America and any other countries where secrets useful to the new Russian state may be hidden. Members of British and American intelligence confirm that many of the practices so reviled during the Cold War have stopped. Today the new KGB is indistinguishable from its Western counterparts in most areas of its work. The Israelis spy on America to gather military and business secrets, so do the Russians. The British spy on the Russians to gather military and economic secrets and the SVR do what they can to spy on us.

At the same time as that level of spying continues, there are degrees of cooperation emerging between former enemies. MI6 has been very active in eastern Europe, working with intelligence agencies in the new democracies to help create structures that work for and not against the people. The CIA has been active in Russia to achieve the same thing. All parties appear to have accepted that behind the propaganda, the world really has changed for the better.

Perhaps the biggest change is that today it is possible to telephone or fax the press office of the former KGB and get a prompt answer to any question. That is still not possible in Britain where government indolence has given a telling advantage to our former enemies in the secret world of intelligence.

A month after my visit to the former KGB, Bob Gates, the director of Central Intelligence, made the same journey. For months the Russians had been pressing the CIA to formalize their relations with a trip which could provide the opportunity to discuss 'matters of mutual interest' including proliferation, terrorism and drugs. Gates had resisted the requests, fearing that the 'exchange' would actually be a one-way street which would allow the KGB to make propaganda use of the apparent normalizing of relations; he doubted whether they would be ready to hand over any real information.[9]

His previous experience of direct contact with the KGB had coloured his views about the prospects of success this time around. He had had three secret meetings with Vladimir Kryuchkov when he was head of the KGB under Mikhail Gorbachev and Gates had been first on the National Security Council and then deputy director of Central Intelligence. The first meeting had taken place in Washington in December 1987 when Gorbachev was on a state visit to meet President Reagan.

The official party included Gorbachev's wife Raisa; Anatoly F. Dobrynin, the Communist Party secretary in charge of foreign policy; Foreign Minister Eduard Shevardnadze; Yuri Dubinin, the Soviet ambassador to Washington; Marshal Sergei Akhromeyev, the Soviet military chief of staff, and Aleksandr Yakovlev, the Communist Party propaganda chief. An unaccounted member of the delegation was Kryuchkov, the KGB chief, who had been brought along as part of Gorbachev's efforts to convince the West that the Soviet Union really had changed. Who better to present the argument than the chief of the world's most feared secret police and who better to meet him than Bob Gates, a lifelong Soviet analyst and one who had regularly cautioned against accepting the Gorbachev revolution at face value?

Kryuchkov was, like Gates, a career intelligence officer, a product of the Cold War who had done nothing to change the West's view of the KGB as the most predatory intelligence organization in the world. Indeed, since he had taken over, the KGB had actually increased its quest for scientific and technical intelligence in the West. The CIA believed that Kryuchkov had been a compromise appointment by Gorbachev, who owed much of his power base to the covert support of the KGB. Exactly how much power Gorbachev had in the Soviet Union was unclear but the Agency was convinced that Kryuchkov controlled some or all of the short rein on which he was kept.

Both Gates and Kryuchkov wanted their first meeting to be secret, but with every aspect of the Gorbachev visit receiving the undivided attention of hundreds of Washington journalists, such a covert meeting was difficult to arrange. Gates did not want the KGB to come to the White House or even to Langley as both venues would have suggested a formality and structure that did not exist. He did not want to go to the Russian embassy as this would undoubtedly have been picked up by the media and awkward questions asked. So they decided on a bold approach and booked a table at Maison Blanche, one of Washington's most expensive and fashionable restaurants, just a few hundred yards from the White House.

Colin Powell, chairman of the Joint Chiefs of Staff, joined them at the lunch which remained a complete secret from the Washington press corps and, with the exception of the President and a few of his close advisors, from the rest of the American government.

That first meeting was a tentative affair with neither side willing to volunteer information or make concessions. Powell was a more enthusiastic participant in the lunch than Gates. The first black chairman of the JCS, Powell was a strong military commander whose views had been formed in the crucible of the Vietnam war. But he was also a consummate politician, attuned to every nuance of the pitfalls that waited every officer serving the Pentagon and clever enough to have risen above them and prospered in the snakepit of Washington politics. He had been an enthusiastic supporter of Gorbachev and believed that every opportunity to embrace the Soviets should be explored. The closer they came, the better understanding there was on all sides, the less chance there would be of a war or even an accidental conventional or nuclear exchange.

Gates viewed the situation differently. In the darker world of intelligence he had fought against the excesses of the KGB all his life. He had seen their overtures to Western governments turn to dust and watched as their public protestations of decent behaviour were matched by increased spying, subversion and support for terrorism. Gates had lost good friends in the silent war and he could neither forgive nor forget the years of duplicity.

Kryuchkov came to the meeting determined to convince the sceptical Gates that the KGB had changed. He offered Gates a gift of a first edition of Marshal Georgi Zhukov's autobiography. Zhukov was a Soviet hero who played a key role in the Kryuchkov coup that resulted in the arrest of Lavrenti Beria, the hated chief of the secret police. The coup marked the end of the Stalin era and the beginning of a new period in Soviet politics with some liberalization in domestic and foreign policy. If Kryuchkov thought the Zhukov memoirs were appropriate, Gates also recalled that Khruschev himself was purged, and that throughout his rule the KGB remained the most powerful instrument of state.

The trio spent most of the meal talking about the tumultuous events taking place in the Soviet Union. The Gorbachev reforms were beginning to take their toll. The heady wind of freedom was sweeping through the Soviet empire, the people were demanding change and Gorbachev was being forced to make concession after concession both at home and abroad.

The language that Kryuchkov brought to the table was clearly his master's voice. He talked enthusiastically about the progress of reform and reassured his listeners that not only did he and the KGB leadership support the changes but also that the course the Soviet Union had taken was irreversible.

Gates used the opportunity to raise the case of Oleg Gordievsky's family, who were being held virtual prisoners in their Moscow apartment. Gordievsky, a British spy in the KGB, had defected in 1985 and done enormous damage to Soviet covert operations around the world. Since his defection, he had been trying to arrange for his wife Leila and two daughters, Maria and Anna, to join him at his safe house in England. Both Margaret Thatcher and Ronald Reagan had raised the issue with Gorbachev but he had been unwilling to do anything about it. Gates understood from other sources that it was the KGB which was blocking their release. Gordievsky's defection had badly affected morale in the organization and there was a determination to exact revenge by holding on to his family.

'I told him that we would never behave like this,' said Gates. 'If Russia wanted to join the family of civilized nations then they would have to let Gordievsky's family go.'

Leila and the children did not reach England until 1991 after the coup that brought Yeltsin to power.

Only once during the meal did a glimpse of the old KGB emerge. Since the arrival of Gorbachev and the gradual collapse of communism, Western agencies had received a flood of applications for asylum from KGB operatives. Some were cynically trying to jump ship before it sank while others were genuinely trying to speed up the reform process by providing information to the former enemy. Whatever the motive, defectors had been coming over to British, French and American intelligence at such a rate that it was impossible to accept them all or to process all the information they had. Kryuchkov wanted to use the lunch to pass on the KGB's interpretation of these events.

'He was convinced that we were drugging and kidnapping their people,' said Gates. 'There were just so many defectors he could not believe they were coming over under their own volition.'

The allegations were ridiculous and were laughed off by both Gates and Powell. But it was a measure of Kryuchkov that despite his protestations about reform, he still thought and talked about the CIA and America generally in ways more appropriate to the Cold War.

Gates met twice more with Kryuchkov, in February 1989 and May 1990, in Moscow. In February, they met in the KGB safe house once owned by Beria, the same building that later housed the SVR's public relations operation. Again Kryuchkov went out of his way to underline his support for Gorbachev, and stressed his conviction that the reforms would work while underlining the difficulties of implementing them.

By the third meeting, everything had changed. Kryuchkov insisted that Gates come to KGB headquarters at Yasenevo. Kryuchkov was wearing his KGB uniform rather than the civilian suit he had worn to previous meetings and it was clear to Gates as soon as he walked in to the KGB chairman's office that the changes wrought by *perestroika* and *glasnost* had come to an end.

'At the first meeting Kryuchkov had been a strong partisan on behalf of Gorbachev and reform,' said Gates. 'But now it was clear he had totally fallen off the bandwagon. The language had changed and aside from the formality and the coldness, he referred to people being "dizzy with change" and a need to restore stability.'

This marked the end of Gates's flirtation with the KGB leadership. Over the next few months Kryuchkov attempted to woo him back with gifts of caviar passed in the diplomatic bag via the Russian embassy in Washington. But Gates had been critically influenced by that final meeting. He had watched the transformation of the KGB leader from an ardent supporter of the Gorbachev reforms to a harsh critic – not so much of the President but of the people for wanting too much too quickly. To Gates the signals were quite clear and that final secret meeting with Kryuchkov helps explain why among all the Bush administration's senior officials he was the most pessimistic about the future of the Soviet Union while many others, including the President, remained strongly allied to Gorbachev. From that May meeting, Gates was firmly of the conviction that Gorbachev's days were numbered. The only debate challenging the intelligence community and the administration was about when the change would occur and how violent it would be.

He believed that the mood of the country had changed irrevocably and that, without the support of the KGB, Gorbachev's grip on power was slipping away. Almost a year later, the CIA's Office of Soviet Analysis produced a report for the President entitled 'The Soviet Cauldron' which set out in stark terms how the traditionalist vultures were gathering around what increasingly appeared to be the corpse of Mikhail Gorbachev. Vladimir Kryuchkov was identified as one of the leaders of the traditionalist movement who could be expected to take a prominent part in any attempted putsch.

On Sunday August 18 the coup happened, Boris Yeltsin triumphed and the Soviet Union disintegrated shortly afterwards. Over the next two years the KGB was transformed as the forces of democracy insisted on change in the world's most notorious secret police. The rise of Yeltsin coincided with Bob Gates's elevation to DCI. Gates had watched as the promise of reform had gradually been replaced with the compromises of Russian *realpolitik*; though Yevgeni Primakov had replaced Kryuchkov as head of the newly reformed First Chief Directorate, now known as the SVR, for Gates these changes meant very little.

Since Primakov's appointment in September 1991 he had made many overtures to the CIA in an attempt to win new friends. While the British Secret Intelligence Service, or SIS, had discussed cooperating with the SVR, as had the Germans, Finns, Swedes and French, the CIA had kept its distance and Gates wanted it to stay that way until there were more visible signs of change.

'I am very sceptical of Primakov. He has been around a long time; he is a remarkable survivor and he played a very unconstructive role leading up to the Gulf War. And there's no doubt in my mind that one of the purposes of putting him there was to try and bring some respectability to the organization.

'Here's a guy that a lot of Westerners know, a guy who was especially close to Gorbachev. But you basically still have the same cast of characters and we know that they consider the US still their number one priority. And we know that they still consider the theft of US technology to be the number one priority within that framework. So, they asked for a lot and I was determined that we should give very little.'

However, after initially writing off Boris Yeltsin as a Philistine and a drunken boor compared with his friend Gorbachev, President Bush had decided that Yeltsin the Democrat deserved to be given every chance to prove himself. In the late summer of 1992, Gates was instructed, or 'encouraged' as he puts it, to accept the invitation to go to Moscow to meet with Primakov.

In the preliminary discussions with the CIA station chief in Moscow, the SVR had made clear that they wanted all areas of cooperation to be on the agenda: drugs, nuclear and conventional arms proliferation, terrorism, and chemical and biological weapons. Gates was just as determined that in this first exploratory meeting the talks would be kept very focused.

'The problem with our people is that they want to say too much,' recalled Gates. 'At the slightest prompting they want to show off how much they know and how they know it. So I had agreed a very limited agenda and a clear structure to the meeting so that we would give a little and if they responded then we would give a little more. But if we gave a little and got nothing then we would leave.'

Gates arrived in Moscow on October 15, 1992 and was driven to Spaso House, the official residence of Bob Strauss, then the American ambassador to Russia. The SVR had leaked the fact that the trip was being planned but had not revealed the exact date. The Russians had wanted to hold a private session which would be followed by a joint press conference, but the Americans saw this as an obvious propaganda ploy designed to make it appear as if the CIA approved of the new SVR, which very definitely was not the case. So it had been agreed that there would be no publicity and that the meetings would be held in secret. So Gates's arrival in Moscow coincided with a trip by Secretary of State Jim Baker.

As with the first meeting with Kryuchkov five years earlier the attentions of the media were very unwelcome. The journalists and their cameras were camped in a small park opposite Spaso House and Gates was determined to avoid their scrutiny. At five o'clock in the morning he got up for his usual early morning run and set off on a five-mile jog along the banks of the Moskva River. An armed Russian Olympic runner who was also a member of the Russian internal security service, the MBR, kept Gates and his CIA security detail company. That run by the head of the CIA in the heart of Moscow with former KGB men providing security was one of the DCI's more extraordinary memories from that unique trip.

Later that morning, Primakov sent a Zil limousine to Spaso House. It collected Gates and drove straight past the assembled media without any of them noticing who the passenger was. News of the visit had clearly leaked inside the SVR headquarters and when the small motorcade pulled up at the main building Gates got out of the car and looked up to see hundreds of faces pressed against the windows.

In Primakov's sparsely furnished office, Boris Yeltsin, Yevgeni Primakov and Gennadi Barranikov, the head of the MBR, waited for him. The meeting began with Primakov arguing that now that the Cold War had ended there were new opportunities for cooperation to combat drugs, proliferation, organized crime and terrorism. Gates agreed that these were common areas but was noncommittal about the opportunities for sharing information.

As a gesture of goodwill, Gates had asked his staff to come up with something which might show the Russians that he was prepared to make a contribution to the new relationship. The Agency had selected a long dead CIA operation against the Soviets as a peace offering. For the first time the CIA director admitted that the CIA had run a covert operation in 1974, code named Project Jennifer, to try and raise a sunken Soviet Golf-2 diesel-powered submarine. Using a specially designed salvage ship, the *Glomar Explorer*, leased from the tycoon Howard Hughes, the CIA worked for months to try and lift the submarine and its nuclear missiles off the seabed. The submarine broke in half and only the fore section was recovered, but this contained two nuclear torpedoes and a great deal of information was gained about the capability of Soviet nuclear submarines. Gates reported that the CIA had recovered the bodies of six Soviet sailors, and had buried them at sea with full honours. They had also recovered the Soviet flag from the vessel and Gates promised this would be handed over to Yeltsin. None of this should have been news to any student of KGB history as the story of Project Jennifer had been told often enough, not least by William Colby who was CIA Director at the time. Nonetheless, an admission of CIA participation to the Russian head of state was an historic event.[10]

Rather than the general discussion that Primakov wanted, Gates had decided to keep the focus of the meeting very narrow by limiting it to an area of mutual interest where he knew the Russians had a great deal of intelligence: North Korea.

The CIA briefer had brought a comprehensive dossier on North Korea's nuclear programme which included information gathered by agents and satellites. He began with an overview of North Korea's nuclear programme and expressed the CIA view that the Pyongyang government was only a few years away from making its own nuclear weapon. To Gates's surprise, the Russian response was not to detail what they knew about the nuclear issues – in part perhaps because they did not know as much as the CIA. Instead, the SVR briefer replied with a detailed breakdown of North Korea's chemical and biological weapons programme which was far more extensive than the CIA had believed.

This information was the most detailed piece of intelligence ever shared by the Russians with the Americans. It accounted for an increase in the intelligence devoted to the North Koreans and a series of warnings that were issued to Western governments over the next six months about the dangers posed by its nuclear, chemical and biological weapons programmes.

Despite this, Gates left the meeting unconvinced that cooperation with the SVR could amount to much. He had watched the interplay between Yeltsin and Primakov and reached some pessimistic conclusions. 'Primakov's a guy that a lot of Westerners, a lot of foreigners know. He's a guy who was especially close to Gorbachev and so that provided some continuity for us,' said Gates.

'Although Primakov sat next to Yeltsin in our meeting and Barranikov sat one seat away, I think that was because Primakov was doing his damnedest to make sure that he was my host, and we were doing our damnedest to make sure that he and Barranikov were co-equal hosts. I had the sense from the body language and everything else that there was a much deeper relationship between Barranikov and Yeltsin than between Primakov and Yeltsin. There has never been any doubt in my mind that Barranikov was behind Yeltsin but I have the sense of Primakov just riding the crest of the wave. He is welcomed in the KGB because he gives them an in to Yeltsin and he offers them some personal protection in terms of getting resources because of respectability. My own sense of it is that most of them are just biding their time, trying to figure out where things are heading, but in a peculiarly personal way. In other words, each of them is very much looking out for himself.'

Throughout the tumultuous Gorbachev years and even into the Yeltsin presidency, Bob Gates, first as national security advisor, then deputy DCI and finally as DCI, took a very cautious, even pessimistic view about the extent of the changes in Russia. He does not accept that all the reforms are permanent and argues that the situation is so unstable that a return to some kind of undemocratic and authoritarian regime is possible. If that happens, the SVR is waiting to reform and carry on as before with the backing of a still strong military. It is hardly surprising that he came away from Moscow sceptical about the value of further cooperation.

The day of his departure, the Russians announced that the meetings had taken place and that 'the two sides discussed the possibilities of cooperation in the fields of ensuring the non-proliferation of nuclear weapons, fighting international terrorism and preventing drug trafficking and organized crime.' Gates, angry that the Russians had broken their agreement to keep the meetings confidential, authorized the US embassy to release a one-line statement acknowledging that the meetings had occurred.[11]

From Russia, Gates travelled to the Ukraine and St Petersburg. Among his security detail, Gates has a reputation for speedwalking artistic sites around the world. Twenty minutes for the Louvre, fifteen for the National Gallery in London, thirty for the Top Kapi museum in Istanbul. It is a measure of his fascination with Soviet history that he spent a full hour in the Hermitage. From there he was driven to what used to be the Czar's summer palace on the outskirts of the city in a Zil once owned by the local Communist Party chief. When he arrived at the palace, he was greeted by a band dressed in the uniform of the Czar's royal guard playing the 'Star Spangled Banner'. He was piped out of the museum by another band playing an off-key rendering of the 'St Louis Blues'. Even to a sceptical Bob Gates it was clear that some things really had changed.

THE NEW WORLD:
AMERICA

CHAPTER TWO

CHASING THE TIGER

Within the United States, the FBI is responsible for counter-intelligence in the same way that the Security Service in Britain tracks down spies. In the decades following the Second World War, the FBI's primary responsibility was to combat the efforts of the Soviet Union and its allies, either to gather secrets in America or to subvert the country from within through the sponsorship of the Communist Party or through hidden subsidies to individuals and groups. The threat was known and the policy of containment easily understood. But, with the effort so focused on the Soviets, other less important countries received no attention at all unless they happened to commit an act so outrageous that the FBI noticed.

The end of the Cold War came at a time when the FBI had just completed a decade of extraordinary growth. The FBI's budget has grown from $622 million in 1980 to around $2 billion in 1993, while the number of FBI special agents has risen from 7,857 to 10,366 over the same period. The Bureau is now responsible for investigating 281 criminal activities, up from 229 in 1982.[1]

By early 1990, with the revolution in the Soviet Union well under way, it became clear that the old strategy of combating the Soviets and their allies was redundant, not least because many of her allies who had acted as surrogate spies in America such as the Czechs, Poles and Bulgars had either cut their ties with Moscow or were about to do so. The FBI formed a committee at their Washington headquarters to examine the future and devise a new strategy. Over the next two years, the committee consulted with the CIA, the DIA and the State Department and called in field officers for discussions.

The study concluded that while some of the traditional threats against the US had reduced (the East Germans for example, once one of the most active group of spies in America, had abandoned espionage) there remained a strategic threat posed by some of the old enemies. The KGB was still active but less effective; the GRU, Soviet military intelligence, was operating as if nothing had changed; the Chinese remained very active and some countries such as Libya and Syria continued to sponsor terrorists who saw America as a prime target.

As the bipolar world of superpower rivalry disintegrated, so old alliances fragmented and individual nations stopped gathering intelligence and began to look at the world from a narrow, national perspective. Cuba, for instance, which during the Cold War was very active in the US on behalf of the Soviet Union, now had little contact with Moscow and was working in isolation. This pattern was repeated throughout the former Warsaw Pact. Even though the intelligence agencies in those countries were being radically altered or even destroyed by the revolution sweeping through eastern Europe, new nations would certainly rise from the old and like every other country they would need good intelligence. It was likely, though, that the nature of that intelligence would change. A country like Poland would have no interest in gathering information about military capabilities or preparations for war. Poland would remain concerned about possible problems with her neighbours but would turn to the US for intelligence on economic or technological developments and perhaps for some military secrets to help her own arms industry, rather than to defend the Warsaw Pact from an attack by Nato.

'All the traditional threats had to be re-evaluated,' said Bill Sessions, the FBI director. 'We had to be sure that we analyze without the old forms or old inhibitions or old views that maybe no longer apply.'

By the beginning of 1991, the FBI had ceased all covert activities against the countries of the former Eastern bloc with the single exception of Russia. The reason for this was simple: each nation had either disbanded its intelligence services or had no money available to maintain active operations against American targets. This was the first time since the Bureau began that the communist threat was essentially disregarded. It was a dramatic reflection of just how quickly the intelligence world was changing.

The Bureau discovered that while their eye had been fixed on the Soviet ball, a large number of countries had mounted successful recruitment and penetration operations against the US to steal economic and military secrets. Countries the FBI had never examined were suddenly found to have very effective intelligence operations in the US.

'The counterintelligence program that we had been so comfortable

24

with for so long should probably have been examined before 1990. But it took a real jolt like the fall of the Soviet Union to get the bureaucracy to take action,' said Patrick Watson, Deputy Assistant Director, Intelligence Division of the FBI.

Among those countries that had been most successful in this area were India, Brazil, China, Japan, Taiwan and Israel.

From the outset it became clear that the FBI needed to widen the definition of its targets to take in these new countries. Today, the FBI no longer refers to a 'hostile intelligence service', which suggested targeting only those countries known to be hostile to the States which, in Cold War language, meant the Soviet Union and her allies. Now, the FBI refers to 'foreign intelligence service', which can embrace any country, a recognition that friend or foe might mount aggressive operations against the US.

The result of these deliberations was a two-part strategy called the National Security Threat List (NSTL), completed at the end of 1991. The List combines two elements. First, it includes national security issues that the FBI believes need to be addressed no matter where the threat comes from or what country is involved. Second, it includes those countries that pose a continuing and serious intelligence threat to American security interests.

In deciding which states should be put on the country-specific threat list, the FBI considers four criteria. The first is the level of intelligence or terrorist activity associated with a country. This is based on the FBI's own records and information gathered from other agencies. Second is the nature of the intelligence a country is trying to gather. If that intelligence is of little interest to American national security then clearly the country remains a low priority. Third is the capability of the country concerned. If it has high ambitions but no effective intelligence apparatus then there is no threat worth countering. Finally, the political, military and economic status of the country is considered.

After the four criteria have been examined, the completed threat list is passed to the Attorney General for his approval and he in turn consults with the State Department and a final list is approved which is revised annually.

Included in the list of issue threats were the following:

First, foreign intelligence directed at United States critical technologies as identified by the National Critical Technologies Panel. In the past the FBI had seen this problem in terms of the officials and intelligence organizations that were part of the communist structure. What that meant was that the counterintelligence effort focused on thwarting

25

anything the Soviets or their allies might do to gather information in the US. The Russian embassy in Washington, for example, was under permanent photographic and electronic surveillance to detect the movement of diplomats as well as any contacts between American citizens and the Soviets.

In Silicon Valley, the centre of computer manufacturing and development in the US, the Soviets maintained a consulate that was so heavily monitored that they were effectively prevented from doing any serious spying. What the FBI study discovered was that, frustrated in the US, the Soviets had begun to target key people who were travelling or working in foreign countries. So the FBI began to look at the likely targets of intelligence gathering efforts rather than at the intelligence officer himself. That appreciation led to the Bureau devoting more resources to security and countermeasures, an area which, in the past, had been left to industry.

Second, foreign intelligence activities directed at the collection of United States industrial proprietary economic information and technology, the loss of which would undermine the US strategic industrial position. This is the 'level playing field' argument brought to the world of counter-intelligence. Industry argues that it is unfair for foreign countries, such as the Japanese, to have restrictions on foreign imports while the US has a policy of free trade. In the same way, US intelligence does not gather economic intelligence that can be used for its national industrial base whether in the private or public sector. Therefore, the FBI will now target any country which uses its intelligence organizations to gather that kind of information.

Third, clandestine foreign intelligence activity in the US. A large number of countries which have intelligence agencies were never watched by the FBI and were able to operate almost with impunity in the US. Now, the Bureau has made an effort to identify every country with intelligence officers working undercover in America and they will all be watched to try and understand what kinds of intelligence they are obtaining and whether it matters.

Fourth, foreign intelligence activities directed at the collection of information concerning defence establishments and related activities of national preparedness. Obviously, the ability of America to defend itself and mobilize for wars both big and small is of critical importance. In concert with other agencies, the FBI has always been involved in trying to protect such national secrets and this task remains unchanged.

Fifth, foreign intelligence activities involved in the proliferation of special weapons of mass destruction to delivery systems of those weapons of mass destruction. Although this has been given a higher profile since the end of the Cold War, this was always an FBI task. Because of the failures in Iraq and the concern of all governments to stop the spread of nuclear, chemical and biological weapons, the FBI sees this as a fruitful area in which to expand.

Sixth, foreign intelligence activities involving the targeting of US intelligence and foreign affairs information and US government officials. Clearly, the recruitment of American government officials to spy for foreign countries has always been a priority area and will continue to be one.

Finally, foreign intelligence activities involving perception management and active measures. The days when the Soviets would spread rumours in the developing world that AIDS was an American invention have passed, but there is some residual concern that there will be attempts, perhaps by terrorist organizations with access to satellite communications systems, to manipulate public opinion. But this is a low priority and absorbs few resources.

'We are no longer looking at the same group of countries, we are looking at the whole world,' said Watson. 'Any country that engages in these collection activities will be investigated. This is a substantial change from the past where we did not have an aggressive program to look at countries that were not on the basic list.'

One of the first results of the reorganization was the shifting of 300 counter-intelligence agents to combat violent street gangs in 39 cities. Describing the changes as a 'peace dividend', Attorney General William Barr said: 'This large scale reallocation of FBI resources has been made possible by changes that have taken place in Eastern Europe and the Soviet Union, changes which, for the time being at least, have modified the espionage threat against the United States.'[2]

While the FBI would like to see greater cooperation with the former Soviet Union, there seems little prospect of any breakthrough in the near future as long as both the former KGB and the GRU continue aggressively to pursue US targets.

'If you translate the shift in [our priorities] into our relationship with law enforcement with the former Soviet Union, what might be the dividend?' said Bill Sessions. 'The dividend might be better, more tangible cooperation in the areas that concern them now which are counter-terrorism, organized crime, drugs, some white-collar crime. If they were to deal with their intelligence gathering in a way that would allow us to reduce our reaction to it, we could obviously provide more capability to deal with real crime in that country.'

The establishment of the NSTL gave the FBI a framework for future operations and a method of looking at potential targets. Under that umbrella they continued to counter terrorism in the same way they had done before, on the assumption that the problems would continue as before. The Pentagon, which is also responsible for gathering intelligence on terrorism via the DIA and individual service intelligence structures, treated the terrorist threat differently. A series of reviews began immediately after the collapse of the Soviet Union with the aim of matching future reduced budgets with requirements and force structures. Different models, accompanied by dozens of complex war games, resulted in recommendations for downsizing in almost every area. One of the most interesting studies was organized by the Office of the Assistant Secretary of Defense for Special Operations and Low Intensity Conflict. With a budget of $500,000, they tried to develop a model for the US in the years 2000, 2010 and 2025 so that resources and training can be changed to meet the new environment. That review has not been completed but the preliminary results were discussed at a conference at Virginia Beach in June 1993.

The initial research to try and predict what the future will look like was carried out by Forecasting International, a company which works extensively with government agencies to develop future models on everything from population growth to the likely gross national product of developing nations. In this instance, after months of canvassing the intelligence and special forces community, the company came up with four likely scenarios which will form the basis of future American counter-terrorist policy:

1. Blade Runner (Holy Terror): The reemergence of traditional socio-cultural animosities that were muted by the Cold War. The international order is in a state of anarchy, as peoples seek to redefine themselves along ethnic, religious, and cultural lines rather than as national groups. The Soviet Union fragments into states that are armed with nuclear weapons and are driven by ethnic passions. China collapses into feuding provinces. Japan's growing assertiveness antagonizes its neighbors. There is an enormous potential for conflict when tensions and hostilities are organized not by an ideology but by pluralistic cultural, ethnic, and religious differences.

In this world there are few guideposts to action but there are numerous occasions on which a conflict could emerge.

In this context, there will be an increasing assertiveness of Islam across the globe in several regions that share ethnic backgrounds. A religious schism between the Islamic and non-Islamic worlds transcends cultural and geographic boundaries. Hence, religion strongly colors politics in this world and the militant Islamicists reject the standards of international behavior as a Western artifice.

Should the internecine Arab conflict abate, militant Islamic nation-states might unite for a common struggle against the West. This modern Jihad, like the old tension between Communism and pluralism, has the potential to create rifts in international politics that are as violent and enduring as those that we have experienced during the Cold War.

This scenario illustrates the role of trans-national ideology whose domination of international politics encompasses a variety of political, economic and socio-cultural domains. It also highlights the dangers for the United States in a world in which adversaries are hostile for religious, as well as cultural and ethnic reasons and some are equipped with weapons of mass destruction.

US national political leaders advocate a strong welfare, social investment economy. Information and data are manipulated so as to create the impression of universal affluence. The military is seen as the same size as or even larger than it is today, with a mission of internal security control, and is perceived by the public as a police force.

2. Haves and Have Nots (Economic Competition). The rise of economic tensions between states that have been staunch allies for nearly half a century. Cold War politics is replaced by a redefinition of traditional balance-of-power politics, based on economic power and market forces. A unified European community and an American community attempt to preserve economic stability in a world where the Asian countries experience recession and political-military struggles. International politics stresses the ability to dominate trade blocs rather than the ability to become a local military hegemony. Thus, it is not military alliances but rather trans-regional trade blocs which vie for world power. In this world, the actions of states are driven by essentially economic calculations. Although the reasons for conflict are different from traditional causes of war, the

collapse of ideological hostility and the emergence of economic motivations do not create a pacifist world. Wars are fought not only to protect ideological allies but to secure trade rights and discourage protectionism as well. This world does not reflect schisms between the developed and developing worlds alone, but involves frictions among the developed nations, including the United States, Europe and Japan. The rise of nationalism worldwide has suppressed US international influence and has precluded US military presence overseas.

Nation-states lose ground to economic blocs and multinational corporations. In this world of broad cooperation among industrial regions, international competition is keenest between industrial regions and developing regions. Military threats derive not from major powers but from developing world maverick states and terrorists. The preferred means of enforcing international laws and conventions is the United Nations, which enforces its bans on arms sales and nuclear weapons. The US military is assumed to be the same size or smaller than it is today. Its mission is global and largely economic – to protect the international economy and promote economic development. Its structure is largely management orientated. The major threat to our military is that it is becoming totally absorbed into the UN. US community infrastructures (economics, politics, demographics, resources, attitudes and values etc.) inhibit military stationing requirements and reduce installation investments.

In this world, US technological development shifts from a military focus to a commercial focus as national security becomes defined in economic terms. The new technologies provide opportunities for those who can use them, but they also widen the gap between social classes in the industrial societies and between industrial societies and developing ones. Emphasis on privatization of social functions produces a Social Darwinian struggle between the various elements of society. The intellectual basis of society is shifting from a paradigm of control, based on machine and computer logic, to one of mutual adaptation, based on organic models. Military is perceived as guardian of the nation.

3. Same Old Stuff (Status Quo). This scenario represents only a marginal departure from today's world. In this world, the prospect for global war is slightly lessened, but the need for powerful defensive forces remain. This world evolved from the post World War II

order that existed at the end of the 1980s to a multipolar one. The United States will exercise leadership as part of the 'Americas' bloc. It will compete with five other blocs. However, these blocs are unstable, shifting economic alliances. The nation-state remains the basic political organization but sovereignty and freedom of action are constrained by increasingly interdependent societies that, on balance, have become more cooperative and homogeneous. The United States is drawn into close cooperation with other major actors, yet it must compete against other economic power centers in the developed world. At the same time, the United States will have to cope with challenges from the less developed world. There, a rapidly expanding population spawns social unrest and migration to other regions. Even so, conventional military conflicts will be less frequent, although also more lethal; and costly. The most taxing challenges to US security will flow from economic competition, a rapid influx of illegal immigrants, terrorism, and the proliferation of advanced weapons systems to dictators in the developing world.

The key to national security will be the development and protection of economic and technological strength. Arms control monitoring through remote sensing will be the first line of defense. Offensive operations, conducted collectively with other major powers, will be the last line of defense.

In sum, barring unlikely but possible 'wild cards' – such as malevolent leaders successfully exploiting tensions, cataclysmic natural disasters, devastation from plagues, or industrial calamities such as nuclear reactor meltdowns – this world will provide a safer, more secure, environment for the United States in terms of overt military threats.

4. Rose Colored Glasses (Green/Benign). In this scenario, the world's most salient threat to humankind is of its own making. It stems from significant, world-scale ecological problems (water, food, pollution, global warming, etc.); the AIDS epidemic in Africa; the increasing cost of protecting Middle Eastern oil; and the decline in the number of biological species. In response, the United States abandons its frontier mentality (as an outmoded image of limitless possibilities) and settles down to lead a mature management of what it has left on the planet. Military resources are redirected to attack environmental problems, paralleling a trend to encourage decentralized means of providing basic necessities. All Americans serve

two years of compulsory military service in the newly-created National Planetary Service, with the mission of protecting the global ecosystem. There is a concomitant rise in the importance of non-governmental organizations that monitor indicators of environmental well-being. The primary driver for these changes is the increasing cost of extraction and disposing of resources in a world where low cost sources and sinks have already been exploited.

This vision of the future represents a world in which change is revolutionary, not evolutionary. The world order as we know it is breaking up, driven by growing interdependence, accelerating technological change, and mounting stresses on traditional authority structures. A new ideology or reinterpretation of existing ideologies will emerge out of the breakup of the late 20th century world order. Its chief tenets will include the following:

1. Emphasis on managing disagreements and avoiding armed conflict;
2. Restrictions on nation-state sovereignty;
3. A new stress on cooperation;
4. A determination to link rapid technological development with an ethical framework that advances the human condition.

The nation-state will not be the primary locus of authority. Instead the regional association, based on geographic proximity and commonality of interest, will be the basic unit of the international system. Dominant players will take the lead in bringing regional groupings together and playing an integrative role across regions. An authoritative international legal framework will be emerging. Global acceptance of human rights standards will effectively inhibit states from engaging in wholesale repression of their citizens. Regional or international associations will decide the use of military force. Defense sufficiency will be the watchword of these associations, primarily because of economic costs. Military power will be applied selectively, because of the potential for damage to increasingly interdependent systems as well as the lethality of new weaponry. The world will have moved beyond the nuclear age.

In the scramble for a reduced federal budget, the FBI has argued that although the final make up of the counterintelligence effort is not yet clear, there is an expanded need for a large Bureau counterintelligence role. That in turn will mean more analysts, an expanded data base and greater liaison with other intelligence organizations.

The Bureau took a similar approach to this reorganization as other intelligence organizations, not just in America but all over the world. Each took the broad range of issues that could be embraced under the intelligence umbrella, including all those previously ignored because of lack of resources, and made a case for covering as many as possible. Of the three cases examined here, the weakest is the FBI's. Since the Second World War, they have done a good job protecting the national security interests of the US, primarily against the Soviet Union and her allies. Now that the Cold War is over, it is very difficult to accept the argument that roles which were unnecessary during the Cold War have suddenly become a high priority. Yet these arguments, with minor variations, are the same ones being produced by every intelligence agency around the world that is trying to maintain budgets and influence.

There is a clear justification for increasing the anti-proliferation effort. There were failures with numerous countries over the past ten years including Libya, Argentina, Pakistan, Iran and Iraq. That some of those countries and others wish to acquire weapons of mass destruction, or even more sophisticated conventional weapons, is unarguable. That more resources should be devoted to ensure that they do not is also unarguable. What is more debatable is whether countries like India and Brazil, both of which have become a higher priority under the FBI's new criteria, pose any kind of threat to the security or economic interests of the US. It is also difficult to imagine that active measures by any of the countries that have emerged as powers after the Cold War could endanger the security of the US.

If the studies conducted by the FBI are to be accepted at face value, it is clear that during the Cold War whole geographic and subject areas were left untouched by the intelligence community while the focus was on the Soviet Union and her allies. Now, suddenly, these areas and subjects are found to be critical to the future of the United States and her allies. The logic of this is flawed, suggesting that bureaucracy, threatened with severe cutbacks, has created reasons to justify its continued existence. Such a cynical view would hardly be surprising given that it is unreasonable to expect any organization to recommend making itself extinct. Instead, systems tend to evolve in a way that either justifies the status quo or produces apparently coherent arguments for expansion. The situation is exacerbated when the debate goes ahead hidden from the public gaze. It is striking that both the FBI reforms and the proposed changes at the Pentagon have not been debated publicly at all. That is not the case with the CIA, where the debate has been more public and exhaustive.

CHAPTER THREE

THE GUESSING GAME

The intelligence business stands or falls not just by the quality of the information it gathers but by what it does with it. The KGB made a massive worldwide effort to gather information of all kinds. It was in Moscow that the most serious pitfalls of biased or faulty analysis could be seen, where information was used to confirm prejudices or to pander to the known preferences of policy makers. The result was often farcical.

A case in point was Raketno Yadernoye Napadeniye or Nuclear Missile Attack, also known as Operation Ryan, which began with a telegram circulated in November 1981 to all KGB offices in Nato countries and other key countries by Moscow Centre. The origin of the telegrams was a growing paranoia in the Politburo based apparently on the belief that America was preparing a first strike nuclear attack against the Soviet Union. President Carter's decision to create a global rapid deployment force following the 1979 Iranian hostage crisis, plus the arrival of a belligerent President Reagan in the White House, combined to convince the Soviets that a new, much more aggressive American foreign policy was in the works.[1]

Although the serious intelligence professionals in the field did not support the Politburo analysis and could detect no signs of a change in policy that might indicate a planned nuclear attack, the KGB and GRU men were too craven to argue the issue. In Britain, for example, the KGB were required to keep watch on government offices, including 10 Downing Street and the Ministry of Defence, to see if there were any changes in work patterns (lights burning at night was one thing to look for). They were also told to report stockpiling of food, unusual traffic between government officials and Buckingham Palace and any increased movement of troops or preparations to use nuclear bunkers. The KGB resident in London delegated much of this work to a junior official who had to travel around London by public transport (he had no car) to gather what information he could.

As the data flooded in to Moscow from all over the world, the paranoia reached dangerous levels, with fifty KGB analysts preparing regular briefings for senior officials. This figment of the Russian leadership's collective imagination almost produced a nuclear war in November 1983 when Nato practised a routine command post exercise, codenamed Able Archer. The exercise was designed to test Nato's nuclear release procedures and was, as is normal, carefully monitored by Soviet intelligence. They in turn were watched by the NSA and others to see how they responded to what they learned. To the surprise of Nato commanders, a significant increase in the amount of coded signals traffic in the Eastern bloc was detected and Moscow Centre sent a flash message indicating that US bases had been placed on a higher state of alert. This message, which was untrue, was followed by a request for any details which might suggest that a first strike was imminent. Able Archer ended three days after this message was sent and the crisis wound down.

Western intelligence was able to follow the drama in unusual detail because a senior KGB officer, Oleg Gordievsky, was keeping his controllers in SIS briefed throughout. When he finally defected in 1985, he had already handed over dozens of documents relating to Operation Ryan, which revealed the extent of Moscow's misunderstandings about Western policy towards the Soviet Union. In September 1985, SIS distributed details of Gordievsky's information about Operation Ryan and Soviet perceptions of the Reagan presidency. It was a fifty-page briefing entitled 'Soviet Perceptions of Nuclear Warfare', which President Reagan read in its entirety. He was shocked by its contents and as a result toned down the 'evil empire' rhetoric, one of the principal reasons for the Soviet paranoia.

Many of Reagan's perceptions about the expansionist and threatening nature of that evil empire had been framed by the CIA. Over several years, the Agency reinforced the President's prejudices with alarmist reports about massive increases in defence spending in the Soviet Union, plans to destabilize governments friendly to the US and aggressive activities of Soviet intelligence agencies. In 1980, the CIA announced that over the previous five years the annual rate of growth of Soviet military expenditure had been maintained at 4.5% despite a decline in gross national product to about 2%. This led the Agency to increase the ratio of military expenditure to GNP from 12% to 14%. Three years later, the

CIA admitted that the total cost of Soviet defence had risen at about 2% a year since 1975, the same increase as in the economy generally.[2]

Ironically, it was the CIA, once viewed as overly conservative on the question of Soviet military expenditure, who, in 1975, under pressure from the DIA (which had always taken a more alarmist view of the Soviets), were forced to revise their estimates of Soviet defence spending up from around 6% of GNP to around 20% of GNP. A series of studies known as National Intelligence Estimates, or NIEs, had been prepared by the Agency for distribution to the policy makers. NIEs are the CIA's best product and are generally used to help form government policy.

The change in the CIA's estimates for the Soviet Union – an apparent admission of failure – was compounded the following year when George Bush, then DCI, ordered a competitive analysis of Soviet intentions. The CIA team, designated Team A, reported that the Soviets were engaged in a steady build-up of military forces but that their intentions were essentially defensive. The Team B report, which was prepared by outsiders, was a blistering attack on the Agency's analytical procedures and much more alarmist in its conclusions.[3] Team B found that:

The NIE . . . series through 1975 had substantially misperceived the motivations behind Soviet strategic programs, and thereby tended consistently to underestimate their intensity, scope and implicit threat.

This misperception has been due in considerable measure to concentration on the so-called hard data, that is data collected by technical means, and the resultant tendency to interpret these data in a manner reflecting basic US concepts while slighting or misinterpreting the large body of 'soft' data concerning Soviet strategic concepts. The failure to take into account or accurately to assess such soft data sources has resulted in the NIEs not addressing themselves systematically to the broader political purposes which underlie and explain Soviet strategic objectives. Since, however, the political context cannot altogether be avoided, the drafters of the NIEs have fallen into the habit of injecting into key judgments of the executive summaries impressionistic assessments based on 'mirror imaging', i.e. the attribution to Soviet decision-makers of such forms of behavior as might be expected from their US counterparts under analogous circumstances. This conceptual flaw is perhaps the single gravest cause of the misunderstanding of Soviet strategic objectives found in past and current NIEs . . .

Analysis of Soviet past and present behavior, combined with what is known of Soviet political and military doctrines, indicates that these judgments are seriously flawed. The evidence suggests that the Soviet leaders are first and foremost offensively rather than defensively minded. They think not in terms of nuclear stability, mutual assured destruction, or strategic sufficiency, but of an effective nuclear war fighting capability . . .

Team B feels the USSR *strives for effective strategic superiority in all the branches of the military, nuclear forces included* . . . Their military doctrine is measured not in Western terms of assured destruction but in those of a *war-fighting and war-winning capability*; it also posits a clear and substantial Soviet predominance following a general nuclear conflict.

We believe the Russians place high priority on the attainment of such a capability and that they may feel it is within their grasp. If, however, that capability should not prove attainable, they intend to secure so substantial a nuclear war-fighting advantage that, as a last resort, they would *be less deterred than we from initiating the use of nuclear weapons*. In this context both détente and SALT are seen by Soviet leaders not as cooperative efforts to ensure global peace, but as means more effectively to compete with the United States.

Although the Team B report appeared at the end of the Ford administration and was largely ignored by President Carter, it reflected a more conservative view that gained much wider currency when President Reagan arrived in the White House. One of the Team B authors, Paul Nitze, became Reagan's chief arms control negotiator; another, Paul Wolfowitz, became undersecretary for policy in the Pentagon, while the chairman of the team, Richard Pipes, became one of the Soviet Union's staunchest critics during the Reagan years. It is difficult to estimate just what effect the Team A and Team B exercise had on the analytical process in the Agency. Successive DCIs maintain that the analytical process is politically independent but, outside of the community, this is believed by no one. Certainly it is a striking coincidence that while presidents Reagan and Bush were warning of the threat posed by an expansionist Soviet Union, the CIA invariably tended to support that view with analysis which now is seen as inaccurate in many material regards.

These statistics matter because they were used as the measure on which American and indeed Nato defence expenditure was based. During the

1970s and 1980s, it was the perceived gap that existed between allied and Soviet defence spending that was used to justify the large increases in defence programmes in the West. Both President Reagan and Prime Minister Thatcher used these statistics to illustrate just how far behind the communist bloc the West was, just how dangerous the Russian bear was and how necessary the Western defence build-up. The result was what many have referred to as a new arms race, the most visible symbol of which was Star Wars, the space based defence programme.

There were other failures too: the DIA claimed in the early 1970s that the Soviet Backfire bomber was designed to hit targets on US soil while the CIA disagreed. The process stymied arms control talks for some years; in the late 1970s the DIA claimed that the Soviets were deploying nuclear artillery in Europe while the CIA disagreed, seriously underestimating Soviet capability until 1983 when they agreed with the DIA. In Afghanistan the Agency predicted that the Soviet invaders would defeat the guerrillas and it was only ten years later, after a Soviet withdrawal, that the CIA forecast a mujahedeen victory.[4]

The most damaging recent criticism is that because of the constantly skewed analyses of the economy and the nature of defence spending within it, the CIA failed to predict the disintegration of the Soviet Union or the August 1990 coup that eventually toppled Mikhail Gorbachev. Today Bob Gates defends the Agency's record at the time and claims that, in a series of NIEs, the CIA did warn policy makers of impending disaster. In a speech to the Foreign Policy Association in New York on May 20, 1992, Gates made a lengthy and detailed defence of the CIA's recent record, quoting from a number of NIEs which warned of the imminent collapse of the Soviet Union and the possibility of a coup against Gorbachev.

He is undoubtedly right that the Agency did pass on some warnings, but the fact that these warnings were made but not heard by the policy makers is an illustration of one of the major flaws of the reporting system that existed at the time. NIEs tended to be so long and so filled with caveats as each part of the bureaucracy covered its back that it was frequently difficult to discern just where the hard conclusions lay. As Gates admitted, there were also some errors of judgement.

First, until early 1989 we did not contemplate that a Soviet communist apparatchik – Gorbachev – once in power would unintentionally set in motion forces that would pull the props from under an already steadily declining economic system and bring down the entire political and imperial system in the process. We wrote many assessments describing the growing crisis in the Soviet Union – describing a steady but gradual and open-ended decline – but only in early 1989 did we begin to think the entire edifice might well collapse. Even so, we saw it in time to warn policy makers more than two years in advance.

Second our statistical analysis, while the best available East or West in absolute terms, described a stronger, larger economy than our own analysis portrayed and than existed in reality. Our economic model of the Soviet economy and statistical methodologies – both developed with extensive academic and private sector help – were analytical constructs the output of which increasingly diverged from the portrayal of a collapsing economy and political system we were presenting to policy makers. CIA invited criticism of the model and methodologies but – again like our own analysis – the criticism was usually data-poor and thus hard to integrate into quantitative analysis. Further, our quantitative data failed adequately to capture the growing qualitative disparity between the Soviet economy and economies in the West. We were aware of this and repeatedly emphasized the point to our readers. Moreover, the data did not deflect us from the warnings I have described. Finally, despite clear deficiencies in our statistical approach, this work did over time allow us correctly to identify, isolate and analyze areas of strength and weakness in the economy and to portray trends accurately. Also, to be fair, it is hard to overstate the difficulty of the task of trying to measure an economy where data is inaccurate, falsified or non-existent . . . But the contrast between the numbers and the warnings we were sending senior policy makers was significant.

Third, from a personal standpoint, I would contend also that our quantitative analysis always considerably understated the real burden economically of the Soviet military.

Fourth we did not remind policy makers, and ourselves, often enough that, from time to time, some things are simply unknowable – even to the protagonists.

What then, were the lessons learned? First, when assessing events or developments where the outcome is truly unknowable, we must do better in exposing the policy maker to uncertainty, to alternative possibilities, and to different points of view – even while providing a 'best estimate'. Second, we should learn from our Soviet experience the broader lesson not to allow ourselves to adhere single-mindedly to quantitative models or approaches that are increasingly at odds with the reality we observe. We must also avoid having such models – often used for measuring trends – take on a life of their own as notional data or numbers that become treated as real. The changes we are making in the Intelligence Community will incorporate all of these lessons.

For a man who had spent all of his intelligence career in the intelligence or analytical branch of the CIA, these were extraordinary admissions of failure, failure which was shared by other Western intelligence agencies. In part this was because they shared much of the same data, but it was also a reflection of the 'mirror imaging' that the Team B report had complained about in 1976.

But the CIA was not alone in overestimating the scale of the Soviet economy or the influence of the military and the share that defence spending took of GNP. The British, the French, the Germans and the Japanese all concurred in general terms. 'For years we had really only been concerned with the military threat. Who cared how many loaves of bread were being baked,' said one British intelligence officer. 'We knew that the military was taking the best of the Research and Development in terms of both money and people but we had no idea just how wide the gap was between the military and civilian sector.'[5]

Senator Dennis de Concini, chairman of the Senate Select Committee on Intelligence, believes that the CIA's analysis has been wrong on the two most important issues confronting the US in recent years, the strength of the Soviet economy and of the Iraqi army.

'They told us the Soviets had a world class economy,' he said. 'That was absurd, and I question whether that was really professional intelligence or something put together at the behest of high-ups to build public support for our foreign policy.' He also argued that the CIA had predicted that allied forces would take tens of thousands of casualties during Operation Desert Storm while the total casualties numbered a few hundred.[6]

Critics, of course, have the benefit of hindsight and it is easy to say why and how things should have been better. It is important to remember, too, that the Cold War was won by America with the help of her allies. By any standards, it was a resounding victory which was won in part because the Western countries managed to outspend the Soviet Union and drive the communist economy into bankruptcy. So, the CIA may have overestimated the scale of Soviet defence spending and the strength of its economic base, but the net effect was positive in that it encouraged the West to spend more and thus accelerated the collapse of communism.

The idea that the analytical process is somehow tainted by politics is something that all CIA professionals claim is untrue. But despite such denials, both foreign and national consumers of intelligence claim that the American analytical process does suffer from a number of different biases, not least of which is the rivalry between the CIA and the DIA. Over the years, the DIA, as the military's intelligence arm, has tended to take a more hawkish view of the threat while the CIA has always been more cautious. As part of his overhaul of the American intelligence process, Bob Gates set up a review of the analytical process under the chairmanship of Edward Proctor, a deputy director of intelligence at the Agency during the 1970s. Gates was moved to defend the Agency after he was attacked during his confirmation hearings for allegedly inserting political bias into CIA assessments, something he always denied. After interviewing over 100 Agency managers and analysts and examining over 250 anonymous questionnaires, the panel gave the CIA a fairly clean bill of health.[7]

'Distortion was not perceived as pervasive and had much to do with poor people-management skills and misconceptions arising from the review, coordination and editing of an analyst's work,' said an Agency official.[8]

The report was typical of many CIA ventures which ended up too anxious to please all those concerned. The vast majority of the criticisms came from analysts complaining about unfair interference in their work or editing of their texts. Those disagreements are little different from complaints heard every day in newspapers, magazines and television networks, and form a routine part of the creative process, where egos suffer from an overly strong commitment to a project or to self. The fact that there are such complaints is a healthy sign that the analysts and managers hold strong views about their work, and reveal that work does not get routinely slanted.

But the bigger and more rigid the bureaucracy, the more difficult it is to eliminate the tendency to curry favour with superiors who hold known political views. There is no doubt that an ambitious manager or analyst might feel more tempted to write a robustly anti-Soviet assessment under President Reagan with Bill Casey as DCI, than under President Clinton with Jim Woolsey as DCI. That is human nature, and can only be addressed by divorcing the analytical process from the political. However, the structure of the American intelligence community is so rigid and so overwhelmed by a highly structured bureaucracy that it is difficult to make the analytical process leaner and more independent.

In Britain the structure is much simpler. At the tip of a fairly narrow pyramid embracing SIS, the Security Service, GCHQ and DIS sits the Joint Intelligence Committee. This is housed in the cabinet office and is chaired by an independent 'wise man' (currently Paul Lever) who reports to the cabinet secretary and thus to the prime minister. In recent years, it has become customary for the chairman also to be personal foreign affairs advisor to the prime minister. The chairman is a powerful figurehead with the political muscle to ensure that the JIC remains independent of the warring factions in the different branches of the intelligence community. His power is directly related to the influence of the prime minister and to the strength of the individual in the position. Under Margaret Thatcher, Sir Percy Cradock proved a powerful and effective chairman of the JIC. Under the less demanding John Major, some senior intelligence officials say that Rodric Braithwaite, the former chairman of the JIC, was less effective. Paul Lever, the current JIC head, is a tough Whitehall operator who will restore intellectual rigour to the JIC.

The JIC, which numbers around twenty, is staffed with people drawn almost entirely from the Foreign Office and the Ministry of Defence who serve on secondment for periods of up to four years. The JIC is divided into geographic areas (Middle East, Russia etc.) and functions (energy, trade, arms control, proliferation). The JIC meets every Thursday, when requests for assessments from different government departments are reviewed and assigned. At the same time, the assessment staff can suggest their own subjects for review. This process means that the intelligence community and the JIC is almost entirely task oriented and delivers product that is tailored to the consumer. There is no time and there are not enough people for the independent generation of assessments which the community thinks that policy makers might want. This keeps the JIC lean and helps to make it responsive.

The assessment staff begin their working week on Friday following the Thursday meeting. The first task of each desk officer is to produce a draft report which is then discussed at the meeting of the Current Intelligence Group for each area, which is made up of some members of the JIC plus representatives from all the other interested agencies, usually including the CIA. The CIG discuss the draft and a finished version is agreed which is generally no longer than five or six paragraphs and represents the distillation of all the available intelligence as well as a recommendation for action or a firm conclusion. 'The key to the assessments is how tightly written they are,' said one JIC member. 'The more it meanders, the less chance it has for survival.'[9]

Two different assessments are produced by the JIC. One is national; it might perhaps deal with the future of Northern Ireland, and is not shared with Britain's allies. The second will be international, perhaps on the future of the Ukraine, drawing on intelligence from other countries and being shared with those who have contributed. Both kinds are reviewed one final time at the next meeting of the JIC and then distributed.

For the national assessments, all the intelligence agencies and any other relevant government departments produce what information they have and pass it to the JIC official charged with drafting the report. If it is an international report, almost invariably the Americans make a contribution, and under existing agreements, the Canadians and the Australians share some intelligence with the British and Americans. New Zealand, which used to be party to this agreement, was excluded after declaring itself a nuclear free zone.

The JIC may produce eight reports a week on a variety of subjects. If there is a crisis, the production rate may go up to one a day on a particular subject. Long-range assessments can take several weeks, but the emphasis is on speed and brevity. Unlike the American system, where reports tend to run to many pages with each contributing agency insisting on having its point of view represented, there is almost no competitive analysis done by the JIC. The product is the sum of the best analysis the staff can produce and it is a single product from a single agency with no dissenting voice allowed. The finished product is therefore not lowest common denominator but a fairly forthright view from independent analysts. In talking to analysts, producers and senior directors in different agencies, there is agreement that in the areas where it works, the JIC analysis is as good and frequently better than anything produced by the CIA. And yet American intelligence has thousands of analysts who do essentially the same job as the twenty-strong JIC staff. For example, the Intelligence and Research Department at the State Department produces a twenty-page intelligence bulletin every day, which goes to press around 4.00 am for circulation to policy makers. It is only a single agency, among at least four in the government that do similar jobs.

Members of the JIC portray themselves as the lean, mean end of the intelligence business, able to take on the Americans at their own game and beat them. There may be some truth to this, but the JIC can get it wrong too. The system completely failed to warn about the Argentinian invasion of the Falklands in 1982, despite the availability of a considerable amount of intelligence. After the Falklands War, the Franks Committee recommended that the JIC be removed from the control of the Foreign Office to make its assessments more independent. It was then that it came under the control of the cabinet office with its chairman reporting to the cabinet secretary and thus to the prime minister.[10]

The JIC also failed to understand the nature of Saddam's preparations to invade Kuwait or correctly to predict the consequences or the extent of his massive military build-up during the 1980s. Despite these failings, it is surprising that the JIC with its tiny staff can produce assessments that are even comparable to those delivered by the American intelligence community with its thousands of analysts.

Identifying the reasons for this difference is difficult, as opinions differ. One study, completed in 1992, frames the debate about analysis in this way:

> Intelligence analysis is important. But what do we mean by 'analysis' and what, exactly are analysts supposed to do? If the task of analysis is to synthesize everything we know about another country or an international issue and present a crisp summary, together with dissenting opinions and an account of what we don't know, then it is not clear why analysis is an intelligence activity at all. Universities, consulting firms, and the National Academy of Sciences do exactly this all of the time; what can intelligence analysis add to that, especially since most of the sources for any summary are publicly available? The answer seems to be that an analytical unit adds information from secret sources to that from open sources. But that answer is only valid if the information gleaned from secret sources is materially different from or better than information gleaned from public sources. It is not clear how often that is the case. Thinking through this issue is important, because to the extent that analysis is a government function, especially a classified one, there will be enormous pressures to produce consensus estimates or to tell policy makers what they want to hear. It usually takes something akin to a coup d'état to produce competitive estimates internally. [Recall the bitter legacy of Team A/Team B exercise.] But it is business as usual to produce competitive estimates externally. Should we try to have the best of both worlds by relying on competitive external sources for most of the analytical world, using an internal unit only for the specialized task of adding to these estimates information too secret to be shared outside a small number of people?[11]

Bob Gates attributes the difference in performance to the structure of the JIC. 'Many people in the JIC come from the military and the Foreign Office and so combine the best of our analytical capability with some direct experience of the place or subject being examined.'[12]

By contrast, the analysts in the DI tend to spend their career doing straightforward analysis and there is infrequent crossover with the DO. This division means that the people with the experience on the ground are never used. But even within the DI there is an extraordinary level of expertise. The sheer size of the American intelligence bureaucracy allows for specialists in almost every area imaginable to carve out a niche and a career. In Britain, with the emphasis on switching people around to different jobs every few years, there is a tendency to have a larger number of generalists who know a little about a great deal rather than to tap into a vast reservoir of knowledge about a very small area. In Britain, the analysts tend not to be intelligence officers but intelligence generalists who have an understanding of the issues but little knowledge of the minutiae that obsess so many analysts. The single exception to this is the Defence Intelligence Staff who tend to encourage the kind of specialists that can recognize every type of gun in the Russian armoury or can describe in minute detail the Libyan chemical warfare capability.

Being able to stand back from the subject, they make objective judgements. In the American analytical community, the process and the product are treated in the same way as research for a PhD. Every item must be sourced and cross-checked so that the final scrutiny will stand the most rigorous peer review. This obsession with the details inevitably makes for the kind of bureaucratic 'mush' that General Schwarzkopf complained about during the Gulf War. That such a process has been allowed to evolve over the years suggests a lack of tough leadership in the analytical community that has allowed the worst trends towards verbosity and waffle in the academic community to flourish in an environment where tougher, hard hitting substance is required.

Others argue that a more serious issue is that the analysts are themselves part of the intelligence community and that their reports are the result of analysts from different agencies squaring off against each other. It is inevitable in such circumstances that individual agencies fight to justify their own position and that a final product is so hedged with caveats that discerning recommendations or judgements is often difficult. A third area of difference strikes to the heart of the American political process. Some senior officials in the American intelligence community – beginning with the DCI himself – are political appointees whose attitudes change at the whim of a different administration. The independence of the analytical process is something every DCI and most intelligence professionals swear to. But those same professionals will readily acknowledge that they are serving politicians and, clearly, both the subjects examined and the way that examination is done depends on the people giving the orders.

By contrast, the JIC staff are anonymous civil servants, and the heads of British intelligence serve out their time irrespective of which political party is in power. That system produces greater independence and so may produce better analysis.

However fallible, the JIC's record is a serious condemnation of the American method of producing intelligence and was one of the main targets for the reforms planned for the early 1990s. But the community did not accept that there was anything fundamentally wrong with the process as it stands. For their part, Congress argued that the mistakes of the past highlighted the need for radical reform if the community is to address the needs of the future.

Everyone inside the American intelligence community and all those outside who share its analysis, recognize that the process that distills the intelligence is faulty. But however often the faults may be highlighted in crisis after crisis, or simply through the day-to-day management of the intelligence business, there will never be change from within. While the community makes mistakes, there is an inbuilt inertia in the process that tolerates those mistakes and shuns reform. Indeed, even close intelligence allies such as Britain have done little to push for reform while privately being the most critical of the American intelligence product.

The only way the analytical process in American intelligence will change is by downward budgetary pressures which will force a reduction in the vast duplication of analysis. Already, these pressures are evident in Europe and Russia. As governments demand cuts, so each national agency has been forced to defend itself and as each nation depends to a greater or lesser extent on the American analytical process, for many agencies continued business in America is actually a threat to their own positions. So there have been calls to American intelligence leaders from their foreign counterparts, but with little result.

It is Congress that will drive this process rather than foreign or internal criticism. Already it is clear that Congress is determined to make significant inroads into the American intelligence budget and if those moves are successful then the reforms that have taken place so far will simply be the beginning.

CHAPTER FOUR

CIRCLING THE WAGONS

The lion's share of the $27 billion US intelligence budget is swallowed up not by the CIA but by TIARA, the Tactical Intelligence and Related Activities budget allocated to the Defense Intelligence Agency. This little known portion of the American intelligence community actually swallows some $10 billion of the annual budget in developing intelligence and systems to help manage a full conventional war. By comparison, the CIA takes around $3 billion of the budget; nevertheless it is at Langley where intelligence policy is made by the DCI.

The problem of identifying the threats, then justifying the Agency's response to those threats, was addressed by Bob Gates in what, for the intelligence community, was a novel approach. He went to all the major government agencies and asked what they wanted from the intelligence community. This assumption that the Agency had first to respond to the customer and then devise solutions around defined budget limits was one that had never been heard of before. In the past, the community paid lip service to the needs of the policy makers but essentially operated an autonomous operation which might, on occasion, produce information of interest to the Commerce Department or the Environmental Protection Agency or the State Department. But the meshing of requirements, capabilities and resources was never properly addressed, which is one of the reasons why so many policy makers are frequently so critical of the poor performance of the intelligence community. Gates understood that if the policy makers could be gathered closer into the process as consumers of the product they would be more likely to be supportive.

The review was set against a background not just of criticism over predicting the collapse of the Soviet Union and of wrongly estimating the size of the economy, but also of the community's performance during the Gulf War. While some of the technical intelligence was superb (the coalition forces were listening to and transcribing just about every conversation that occurred on the Iraqi front line), there was no worthwhile human intelligence from inside Iraq. Despite a lengthy intelligence relationship between the CIA and the Iraqi high command during the 1980s, when intelligence was passed over to help bolster Saddam in his war with Iran, there had been no successful recruiting of important Iraqi agents. The British, too, had little success in gathering HUMINT from inside Iraq.

'You're not going to have too much of it in the right place when you have a guy like Saddam Hussein who killed or deported the whole opposition, and anybody who looked cross-eyed was apt to die. He killed twenty-six people once to get one person he knew was among the twenty-six. That's not an easy environment in which to work,' recalled Judge William Webster, who was DCI at the time of the war.[1]

That deficiency was exacerbated by squabbling between the intelligence agencies in Washington and a lack of useful tactical intelligence delivered to the ground force commanders in Saudi Arabia. General Norman Schwarzkopf, the coalition commander, described many of the intelligence estimates he received as 'mush'.[2] At the start of the crisis, the Pentagon set up the Joint Intelligence Center to bring together all the information gathered by different branches of the armed forces and intelligence agencies. This system worked reasonably well in that it compressed a wide range of data into a single source. (The problem was that all the information was dumped into the computer, and commanders in the field had no method of filtering out what they did not want. As a result, all the intelligence officers with the coalition forces had to read millions of bits of irrelevant information to get at the few nuggets, a time-consuming task in a war zone.) But the CIA chose to remain outside the JIC, not wishing to compromise its independence from the military. This added an additional layer to the intelligence bureaucracy, which was already overloaded with data.

'No commander is ever fully satisfied with intelligence,' said Schwarzkopf. 'At best what you do is guessing. It's called estimating, and if you're right 50 per cent of the time you're a hero as far as I'm concerned. Our frustration with intelligence was that rather than estimating, rather than being willing to stick the neck out, they were safe-sighting to the point that their information was of little use to me as a commander.

'Let me give you a very good example: the chemical capability of a Scud missile. Six months prior to the crisis even erupting, I was asking, do the Iraqis have a chemical capability on a Scud missile? I was told absolutely not. Every test we've ever made, everything they've ever made that we have monitored shows they don't have a chemical capability. They do not have it.

'Well, then along comes a crisis and we went from "definitely do not have" to "maybe they have" to "they might have" to "they probably have". Yet not one damn thing changed in the interim as far as the information that was being collected.'[3]

After the air war began, the air force reported that they were doing considerable damage to the Iraqi military and to the command, control and communications system. For day after day, the pilots produced assessments that showed a high rate of success. But when this information was fed back to the intelligence community in Washington for analysis, the reports showed that very few targets were being destroyed. By early February, with the ground phase just two weeks away, Schwarzkopf's staff were reporting that up to 40% of the Iraqi tanks and artillery had been destroyed, the French and British put the figure at around 30% while the CIA put the figure at 10–15%. The situation became so bad that the joke in Riyadh was that if a CIA man saw a satellite picture of an Iraqi tank lying on one bank of a river with its turret on the other he would note it down as 'possible damage' because both parts appeared to be intact.[4]

This difference in approach to the question of Battle Damage Assessment (BDA) infuriated Schwarzkopf and caused a great deal of frustration in his headquarters.

'We had a very strict set of criteria and we did not want to launch a ground war until we had accomplished those criteria. But we were out there, wreaking havoc on the Iraqi military and pilots were coming back in reporting what they had done and the reports I was getting from the intelligence agencies that were charged with giving us the definitive information was that we weren't doing any damage. It didn't compute. My statistics at my headquarters were showing that we were doing very, very well and then the official reports would come out saying we weren't doing a damn thing.'

The BDA problem was resolved when Schwarzkopf designed a different analytical model which allowed for a compromise between the very conservative CIA estimates and the more optimistic reports from the pilots. Immediately after the new system was imposed, 'The CIA were sort of the thorn in my side because they were the one agency that kept on saying that we weren't doing what we knew we were doing.'

A later assessment of intelligence performance during the Gulf War singled out the BDA process as one of the most glaring failures. 'The body count given by General Schwarzkopf on Iraqi tanks destroyed during the air campaign was, in all likelihood, exaggerated. A careful analysis of units involving 22% of the claimed kills shows an overestimation of tanks killed by 100% and, perhaps, by as much as 134%.'[5]

After the war, Congress moved swiftly to consolidate the changes in the Pentagon's intelligence structure. The JIC was established as the permanent and single collection centre for tactical intelligence gathered by both the services and the DIA. It was also given responsibility for issuing warnings of any military threat to the military, performing the same function that the CIA's Warning Center does for the policy makers. Responsible to the DIA, the JIC is supposed to cut across individual services' intelligence functions and to have automatic access to all relevant national and operational intelligence. This structure was supposed to eliminate the hoarding of information by the single services but it failed to eliminate the analytical functions of all the different service intelligence organizations. This significant failure – a compromise between the reformers and the conservatives – has meant that there remains a very large amount of unnecessary duplication.[6]

For the CIA, the Gulf War posed different challenges. Aside from BDA, there had been problems getting intelligence to the troops on the ground in timely fashion; much of the satellite imagery was useless; and the distinction between tactical and strategic intelligence difficult to discern, which resulted in slow responses by the intelligence analysts who frequently delivered the wrong type of information in a form that was of little value to the commanders on the ground.

It was clear that, with the perceived problems in analyzing the Soviet Union, apparent failures in Iraq and a climate of change sweeping through government, the intelligence community was certain to be a target of cost cutting and reform by a Congress determined to show the people some tangible benefits from the American victory in the Cold War.

It was to fall to Bob Gates, the consummate CIA insider, to implement the reforms demanded by the changed world circumstances. Gates had first been nominated for the position of DCI by President Reagan in 1987 but was forced to withdraw his nomination because of Senate opposition. Gates, who had been deputy DCI under Bill Casey, had been tainted by the Iran-Contra affair and, although he had no direct involvement in either the operation to smuggle arms to the Contras or the subsequent cover-up, the Senate were not satisfied he had answered all their questions frankly. Gates had then moved to become deputy national security advisor under Brent Scowcroft while Judge William Webster moved in as DCI in what was essentially a caretaker appointment.

Gates is a small, dapper man whose official persona is at odds with his private life. Professionally, he is cold, hard and incisive with little of the warmth he can display privately. To his friends, he shows a quick sense of humour, a liking for Bond movies and hiking in the mountains of Oregon. He was forty-eight when he was nominated to be DCI for the second time, and this time around Iran-Contra was less of an issue. His nomination passed the Senate without any serious trouble.

Almost all Gates's professional life has been spent in the intelligence or analysis branch of the Agency. His cautious approach to his job and the cynical way others see him is demonstrated by the old adage told of him that 'when an intelligence officer smells flowers, he turns around and looks for the coffin'. On his desk at CIA headquarters, Gates kept a small plaque which read: 'As a general rule, the easiest way to achieve complete strategic surprise is to commit an act that makes no sense or is even self-destructive.'

He moved swiftly to undercut Congress's plans to reorganize the intelligence community, which by the end of 1991 were beginning to take shape. He realized that if matters were wrested from him, the whole structure of the community would change forever and he would have little control of the process. Instead of waiting for Congress, he decided on a preemptive strike which had the effect of drawing the intelligence wagons into a circle and forcing the reformers to try and penetrate a very effective defence. A brilliant bureaucratic infighter, within three days of being sworn in as DCI in November 1991, Gates had a plan in place which would allow him to conduct his own detailed review designed not only to be as comprehensive as the Congressional proposals but to blunt them. President Bush was a staunch Gates ally, and the DCI had no trouble persuading him to support his review plan. In November 1991, Bush signed National Security Review Directive 29, which called for a comprehensive review by the executive branch of its future requirements for the intelligence community. The results of this survey, due to be delivered to the President by March 20, 1992, would provide a framework for the reorganization of the intelligence community to meet the new challenges up to the year 2005.

For the first time, twenty different government agencies from the

Department of Environment to Commerce, State and the Department of Defense were to give their priority requirements from the intelligence community into the next century. They were asked not simply to look at past product from the CIA or any other intelligence agency but what they would like to receive in the future. The purpose of this was not only to embrace the different government departments in the reform process but to help convince the CIA's enemies in and out of government that real reform was taking place; that the Agency was going to respond to the needs of the consumer rather than remain isolated at Langley indiscriminately shovelling information.

There were two other reasons for engaging in this dialogue. First, each government agency was asked to list its priority needs. They would then be matched against the available resources. It was certain that the list of requirements would far outstrip the money available to meet them. Gates would then be in the fortunate position of going to Congress, demonstrating a clear need for increased intelligence and being able to present some tough arguments, largely generated outside the intelligence community, about why the budgets should remain intact.

Second, the intelligence community needed help in deciding just where the priorities for the future lay. While the Threat, in the shape of the Soviet Union, still existed, there was no difficulty in working out the requirements. Each year would be simply an evolution of the year before. Now, new enemies needed to be identified and priorities assigned to them. It was here that the consumer of intelligence could play a part. At the beginning of 1992, Gates defined the problem this way:

'I think that enemy might not be the right word in all cases, but clearly we're interested in the activities of countries that don't abide by international agreements, whether they have to do with economic affairs, or the surreptitious sale of nuclear reactors or ballistic missiles. We're clearly interested in the activities of drug kingpins and the governments that allow them to operate, or in the activities of governments that are resisting them, to see where we can help. I think the regime of Saddam Hussein is an enemy. I think that the government of a country and its leader that will brutally and ruthlessly destroy a passenger airliner in flight is an enemy of civilized nations. So I think that there are certain categories of behaviour on the part of certain governments that certainly make them the focus of attention – those who support terrorism and the terrorist groups themselves for example. On the other hand, there are other areas in which there is a collective sense of the need to know more. I think Congress is interested in our doing more on some issues like the social and economic implications of things like pandemics like AIDS, or in doing more on the environment.'[7]

While policy makers were charged with identifying their needs, Gates also set up fourteen task forces to examine imagery, HUMINT, management, coordination overseas, openness, real time electronic intelligence, support for military operations, publications, coordination with law enforcement agencies, politicized intelligence and internal communications. They were given two months to report their findings. The reports began flowing in at the end of December 1991 and were immediately distributed to all members of staff likely to be affected by the recommendations – an unheard of example of employee relations within the community. For five days after the distribution of each report people were asked for their comments. Then the DCI amended the recommendations or agreed them and passed them to the President for approval.

At the beginning of January, he approved the recommendations of the task force on coordination with law enforcement agencies. The proposal was for a new set of systems by which intelligence routinely gathered, which might not be relevant to a particular Agency requirement, should be reviewed to see if it might be of use to outside agencies such as Justice or the Treasury.

This issue had become controversial as a result of the intelligence gathered by different agencies including the CIA, the State Department and the NSA during the 1980s about the Bank of Credit and Commerce International, the corrupt financial empire which became the bank of choice for terrorists, drug money launderers, arms dealers and intelligence men. The CIA had used BCCI as a convenient channel for funds to support the mujahedeen in Afghanistan, while Abu Nidal had used the bank to support his terrorist networks through its London branch. The fact that the bank had been operating shady and illegal financial practices for over a decade before legislators moved against it in 1991 was known to the intelligence community, yet nothing was done to shut it down.[8]

The Agency had been criticized for its involvement in the cover up, but information had been passed to both the Treasury and the Comptroller of the Currency, who had apparently not understood the data they were getting. The Agency acknowledged that more should have been done to alert other departments and the task force's recommendations addressed this issue.

'There was some concern that that reporting should also have gone to law enforcement agencies such as the Justice Department, the Federal Reserve or whatever,' said Gates. 'So what we've been looking at is how to change our procedures to ensure that these reports get to all of the agencies that ought to see them, when we come across the potential of wrongdoing in some of the reporting we gather.

'That has gotten very complicated in recent years, as we have gotten into issues like proliferation, technology transfer and monitoring of export controls, because the law gets very intricate. Some case officer sitting out in some little foreign capital isn't going to know that a three-axial gizmo, the export of that is a violation of American law. So we're trying to put into process some flags that can be raised so that these things can be sent to the lawyers or to whoever is expert on them, to get a reading and then get them to the right people.'9

These changes, which were a reasonable response to legitimate concerns raised by the BCCI case, revealed a disturbing trend within the American intelligence community. The Agency, and indeed the community generally, is already heavily constrained not just by the law but by lawyers. In 1990, Elizabeth Rindskopf, then aged forty-six, was appointed general counsel at the CIA. She moved from a similar job at NSA where she had been embroiled in the Iran-Contra affair and had refused to hand over a number of documents to special prosecutor Lawrence Walsh. It was her determination to keep the secrets secret that in part led to the dropping of several major charges against Marine Colonel Oliver North. But Rindskopf is no bastion of conservatism, coming from a background as a Southern civil rights lawyer who represented Vietnam draft dodgers among others. Convinced of the need for intelligence, she also believes that espionage must be conducted within the law.

'We do misrepresent, lie, steal on occasion,' she said. 'But once you get beyond the question of whether we ought to do espionage, this is as ethical a group of people as you'll find.'10

Since she arrived at the Agency, the number of lawyers has increased considerably, reflecting both her and Gates's determination to do everything by the letter and the spirit of the law. There are now some sixty lawyers working at CIA and every single covert action is reviewed by them. Today, the sequence of planning for a covert action works like this: a proposal is written detailing the plan; this is reviewed by the Agency's lawyers who approve it for presentation to the NSC committee which reviews all such activities. If the NSC approves the plan, the report is presented to the President. If he approves, it then goes before the intelligence committees. This very detailed review process is designed to ensure that no more freelance activities along the lines of Iran-Contra can slip through the net. So far the process has worked well,

54

but as the need for more rather than less covert action arises, the creeping influence of the lawyers will undoubtedly confine freedom of movement within the Agency, and fewer creative decisions will be taken.

On January 14, 1992, Gates held a meeting in his office with the six other senior officials of the Agency to announce that he had also accepted the recommendations of the Openness task force which recommended declassifying large amounts of historical information and making senior members of the Agency more accessible to the media and to Congress. These recommendations reflected concerns common to all intelligence agencies in the new era; that they move to help elected officials, and that the public become better informed about the work they do. Without such information, the community recognized that there could be no guarantee of public support for their continued existence.

'With the proper concern for sources and methods, I think we can be more open as an institution about what we do and what we are about,' said Gates. 'What is this business of intelligence? How do we carry it out? What is this process about? And it seems to me that there is, shall we say, a somewhat deficient understanding on the part of almost everybody on what it's all about. I think we can be more open about that, and I'm prepared to have senior officials of this agency, if they wish to, be more available to people in the press, to people in public groups and so on, talking about the process of intelligence.'

While the task force reports flowed in, Gates began a public relations blitz with regular appearances on television talk shows and a series of important speeches designed to keep the Agency's profile high. He talked in unusually frank terms about the problems facing the world in an uncertain time and also pointed out specific threats that the CIA knew about, such as the targeting of the US by Chinese nuclear ICBMs.[11] This flurry of public activity was designed to show people in general, and Congress in particular, that the world was still a dangerous place and only the intelligence community understood just how dangerous.

Despite all these moves, Congress remained determined to take action. In February 1992, both the House and Senate introduced their own bills. These would create a new post of director of national intelligence, with authority over both military and civilian intelligence agencies. They would give the new intelligence czar the power to make the agencies work together at less cost. More importantly, the new supremo would have control over the intelligence budget and be able to disburse the funds as he saw fit. The bills would also create a national intelligence Center run by a new director, responsible for all intelligence analysis across the community. Predictably, the Pentagon opposed the changes, as they would have destroyed the autonomy of the DIA, the NSA and the NRO, all of which were funded by the Defense Department. There was also strong resistance to bringing analysis under one roof as this would have meant a reduction of influence by individual agencies and a loss of control and status by some departments. The CIA in particular would have been reduced to a simple gatherer of intelligence and organizer of covert operations, not unlike SIS in Britain. The changes were opposed, on grounds both of cost and efficiency, and it was clear from the outset that they had little chance of passing. But they did, as Senator David Boren, chairman of the Senate Intelligence Committee, suggested, administer 'an electric shock' to the agencies.

In earlier hearings when Congress was still formulating its plans, David Boren outlined the need for change like this:

'Our own interest in reorganization was born out of a concern that, despite a sizeable growth in development in intelligence during the 1980s, military commanders were not receiving timely and relevant intelligence regarding the threats and contingencies they perceived as most threatening. The members of this committee became concerned that national and tactical intelligence bureaucracies were isolated from each other resulting in duplication, waste and poor performance. In the report accompanying the Fiscal Year 1991 Intelligence Authorization Bill, this committee stated: ". . . the tactical and national intelligence communities appear to be excessively isolated from one another, leaving each free to pursue self-sufficiency in their particular realms. Military commanders seek self-sufficiency through organic systems and organizations on the argument that national systems cannot be relied upon for support. The national community, likewise, emphasizes its peacetime missions and pays scant attention to the commander's need."'[12]

The intelligence community was united in its opposition to Congress's proposals. A typical reaction came from Frank Carlucci, the former national security advisor in the Reagan administration.

'As a practical matter, none of these changes will happen; they are politically impractical and in my judgement managerially questionable. The intent seems to be to create a strong line organization, but this is of necessity done at the expense of other line organizations that have legitimate requirements and powerful constituencies. The end result is likely to be a compromise where the DNI emerges as an equal with the Secretaries of Defense and State with regard to their intelligence activities and nobody is in charge. This is, of course, a formula for paralysis.'[13]

'There was considerable merit to the Congressional proposals, which would have eliminated large amounts of unnecessary duplication, improved the analytical process and saved large sums of money (the opposite was argued in opposing the changes). But whatever the merits of the argument, the intelligence bureaucracy is so large in the United States that the kind of revolutionary change proposed by Congress is almost unthinkable unless it had the full backing of the White House.'[14]

On March 17, Dick Cheney, the defense secretary, wrote to Les Aspin, chairman of the House Armed Services Committee, to express his reservations about the proposals.

I would recommend that the President veto these bills if either were presented to him in its current form.

Both bills are unnecessary and so severely flawed that selective amendments would not make either of them acceptable. They contain a number of provisions which needlessly duplicate actions already underway, or compelled, to improve the functioning of the Intelligence Community, without legislation. Moreover, both bills would unwisely create a single, national intelligence 'czar'. Departmental requirements for intelligence vary widely within the Federal government because mission needs are so different.

The roles of the Secretary of Defense and the Director of Central Intelligence have evolved in a fashion that meets national, departmental and tactical intelligence needs. Each of the reorganization bills would seriously impair the effectiveness of this arrangement by assigning inappropriate authority to the proposed Director of National Intelligence (DNI), who would become the director and manager of internal DOD activities that in the interest of efficiency and effectiveness must remain under the authority, direction, and control of the Secretary of Defense. Of major concern, the reorganization bills hold the prospect of reducing the effectiveness of intelligence support to our war fighting commanders.

For these reasons, I strongly oppose this proposed legislation. We appreciate support for US intelligence efforts but, regrettably, this legislation hurts, not helps, those efforts.

The climax to all the lobbying came at a joint session of the House and Senate intelligence committes on April 1, 1992 where Gates arrived to defend his position.

Senator David Boren set the tone: 'Our legislation was based on a number of sound and important principles; namely, there should be clear lines of accountability; we should, whenever possible, eliminate duplication; cost effectiveness in the current budgetary climate is absolutely essential; the independence of analysis and broad based analysis, is crucial for a changed world environment; and enhanced support to unified and specified commanders in time of crisis by the national intelligence community is also essential. If we're ill-prepared for crisis, billions of dollars spent on peacetime intelligence is of little value.'[15]

Gates began his testimony by explaining just how much the intelligence world had changed in recent months:

On the eve of a new century, of a new millennium, we see a world where, as never before, people are demanding and making progress towards peace, democracy and an economic system that works. The Soviet Union has disappeared. The Cold War is over. The major military threat to the United States has receded dramatically. Many regional conflicts are coming to an end. Where a decade ago 90 per cent of the people of Latin America lived under authoritarian governments, now more than 90 per cent live under governments that are democratically elected. Apartheid is being dismantled in Southern Africa. Peace talks, however difficult, are under way in the Middle East. Eastern Europe is liberated. Germany has been peacefully united. And the United Nations is finally playing the role its founders envisioned. It is truly a time of revolutionary change, a time of great hope, promise and opportunity. Yet the opportunity is fragile and perhaps transitory. In places familiar and remote, whether we like it or not, problems and dangers all over the world will continue to engage America's attention . . .

In such a revolutionary and turbulent world, and one so transformed from the last two generations, our national security institutions, especially defense and intelligence, must change, and they must change dramatically to meet new and different challenges. But our changes should be evolutionary, conforming to the reality of an unstable, unpredictable, dangerously over-armed, and still transforming world, not yet the world of our hopes and dreams.

Among the major decisions outlined by Gates were the following:

To increase the value of intelligence provided to policy makers, there would be greater discussion of alternative scenarios, greater autonomy for parts of the Directorate of Intelligence to respond directly to policy makers' requests, and systems put in place to try and improve the contact between analysts and outside agencies so that the intelligence product was relevant to their needs.

To address the sensitive concerns about the politicization of intelligence, Gates approved a study of management practices in the Intelligence Directorate, measures to reduce the seemingly infinite layers of the review process, an allowance for alternative views in the product, the appointment of an ombudsman to deal with complaints of politicization and the erection of Chinese walls between the analysts in the DI and the covert action people in the DO.

To improve communications between the community and policy makers, it was agreed to transfer to a computer and video based information system that would allow those with clearance to access information without the need to generate volumes of paper.

The National Human Intelligence Tasking Center, managed by the DO, was established to coordinate all human intelligence requirements across every intelligence agency. With representatives from DOD and the State Department, the Center is supposed to decide which agency is best suited to achieve a particular task at the minimum risk.

Agency employees had complained for years about the stifling nature of the intelligence bureaucracy. Annual evaluations would now take account of how much effort each manager had made to encourage employees to speak out about ways to improve the collection and management of intelligence.

To strengthen centralized coordination and management, the intelligence community staff was abolished and replaced by a new management staff directly responsible to the DCI and headed by an executive director of community affairs. This new position carries with it broad responsibility for managing both programmes and budgets on a community-wide basis to establish clear divisions of labour, cut out duplication and improve coordination. The consequence of this was to bring under the DCI responsibility for the funding of different agencies and this was approved in the 1993 Intelligence Authorization Act.

Until the reforms, the National Intelligence Council was responsible for carrying out long range assessment for the CIA. Gates moved the NIC outside the CIA along with all the National Intelligence officers responsible for producing the National Intelligence Estimates which help form the foundation of American foreign policy. To further enhance the independence and status of the NIC, other agencies responsible for producing analysis such as the Joint Atomic Energy Intelligence Committee, the Weapons and Space Intelligence Committee, and the Science and Technology Intelligence Committee were also transferred out of the CIA to the NIC. The Intelligence Producers Council, which formerly reported to the National Intelligence Production Board, was renamed the National Intelligence Production Board and also placed under the NIC.

Within the NIC itself, the chairman is now a member of the National Foreign Intelligence Council, which is responsible for allocating resources within the community. A new position of vice chairman for evaluation was established to act as an overseer of the assessment and NIE process. His job is similar to that of the chairman of the Joint Intelligence Committee in Britain: to oversee the final product, look at past assessments and make sure that lessons are learned and improvements made.

A second vice chairman for estimates was created to take charge of the estimating process and to implement the changes in the analytical process which the other task forces had recommended. In particular, he or she ensures that different points of view are canvassed and incorporated into every assessment so that a clear distinction is made between estimates and fact, the known and the unknown. From now on, there would be regular use of the Team A/Team B approach that Bush had ordered fifteen years earlier to produce different estimates of the Soviet threat. The idea behind these changes was to reduce criticism of the intelligence community for being too bold in its analysis when the factual information does not support the conclusion.

These changes may refine the product but will still not produce the kind of certainties that policy makers tend to demand. As Judge Webster puts it: 'We in the intelligence community often talk about the difference between mysteries and secrets. Secrets are knowable. If you're good, you can find out what the secret is. The mystery is a little more difficult if not impossible. You can't know what someone is going to do before they know what they are going to do. And that's a mystery. The mysteries are part of the area of limitation. The users of intelligence should not look to us for the kinds of things we don't do as well. We are not a 'not for prophet' agency.'[16]

For the first time, with the appointment of an open source coordinator, the community recognized the critical role that open source material plays in intelligence gathering. The coordinator's job is to prepare a catalogue of all open source holdings and to design a system that will allow everyone across the community to have access to a database.

The task force on imagery was particularly critical of the way satellite imagery is gathered and dispersed. 'A major shortfall is the piecemeal planning, separate organizations . . . concentrating on specific segments . . . no single entity in charge of overall process . . . no firm mechanism to coordinate between them . . . relatively limited knowledge of many operational military users of what capabilities are available . . . lack of effective access by operational commanders . . . limited ability to disseminate imagery to field echelon commanders . . . need for a single architect . . .'

This damning report recommended establishing a National Imagery Agency which would absorb the Defense Mapping Agency, the National Photographic Interpretation Center and the National Reconnaissance Office. This was vehemently opposed by the Pentagon who did not want one of their most valuable and resource-rich assets taken away. After tough negotiations between the CIA and the Pentagon, the Central Imagery Office was set up to control all US satellite operations. Under the deal, the CIA got lead responsibility for designing satellites that use images, including both photography and radar satellites, while the air force retained the lead responsibility for electronic eavesdropping systems. All other agencies with an interest in overhead acquisition systems, including the DIA and the NSA, have now ceded control in these areas to the CIO. However, existing agencies such as the Defense Mapping Agency survived the changes.[17]

To address the concerns about lack of intelligence raised during the Gulf War, the Agency established a new post of associate deputy director for Operations for Military Affairs and an associated Office of Military Affairs. This office will coordinate work between the CIA and the Pentagon down to an operational level to ensure that the intelligence community has a better understanding of the military's needs. Equally, the military are now in a position to know more about the Agency's capabilities. One of the first tasks for the new CIO was to create a new Comprehensive Operational Image Architecture which would integrate satellite and other imagery to allow battlefield commanders to keep up to date with developments on the ground.

The fact that President Bush had already approved all these changes by the time Gates came to the Hill to testify about them effectively stopped Congressional legislation dead. There was no serious attempt to put through either the Senate or the House plan, and Gates had succeeded in keeping the reform process inside the intelligence community and out of the hands of the legislators.

Gates had hoped to stay on as DCI after the election of President Clinton but his image among Democrats had been tarnished by his association with Bill Casey and with Iran-Contra. President Clinton appointed James Woolsey, a conservative Democrat who had served both as undersecretary of the navy and a key arms control negotiator. Like Clinton, he is a Rhodes scholar and a Yale law school graduate, and he has a very good understanding of the workings of both intelligence and the Washington political world. He had also served as chairman of the panel established by Gates to examine reform of the gathering and processing of satellite imagery, which had resulted in the establishment of the Central Imagery Office. So Woolsey came to the job with some familiarity with current issues and the reform process that was already under way.

During his confirmation hearings before the Senate Select Committee on Intelligence, Woolsey described the post-Cold War world in graphic terms. 'Yes, we have slain a large dragon, but we live now in a jungle filled with a bewildering variety of poisonous snakes, and in many ways the dragon was easier to keep track of. You have a right to expect that the Director of Central Intelligence will take a strong lead in reorienting the intelligence community to deal with this new world of . . . 1,000 points of darkness.'[18]

In his first appearance before the Permanent Select Committee on Intelligence, the new director appeared to endorse much of his predecessor's work:

The disappearance of the Soviet Union's oppressive presence has revealed a world in some ways more dangerous, more perplexing, more uncertain and more challenging than it was before. The threat of annihilation in an all-out nuclear exchange has receded, but nuclear weapons have not become museum pieces, and we can't stop being concerned about their use, including against the United States.

We must be sharply attentive to the spread of modern military technology, especially weapons of mass destruction, to countries all over the world. This proliferation of weapons increases both the probability of local wars and their destructive potential. And whether we are directly involved in any of these wars or not, we are likely to suffer.

We watch daily the violence that nationalism and ethnic hatred breed – the most vivid example being in the former Yugoslavia, the country that not long ago sponsored a lovely winter Olympics at Sarajevo. We see the real possibility of that violence spreading to the rest of the Balkans and the further possibility that it could lead to conflict between US allies.

We also witness daily the nationalistic conflicts that smolder and sometimes flare along Russia's periphery, especially in the south.

There are other examples of cultural and religious intolerance, fanned by extremists in Africa, the Middle East, and South Asia. The Soviet Union smothered, or the Cold War obscured, some of these ethnic and nationalist frictions. Today they are leading to new violations of human rights, both by governments and by extremists, to wars, and to world wide terrorism.

While welcoming its new freedoms, we all wish that the 'new world order' was not so short on 'order'. But, 'Stop the world, I want to get off' is a fantasy, especially for those who govern the world's only remaining superpower. Like it or not, the information age, modern transportation, the dependence of our economy upon international trade, and modern weapon systems all narrow the Atlantic and Pacific radically. We are enmeshed in the international arena and thus entangled in its crises. It is critical for us, and for all those with whom we share this planet, that we have the knowledge and understanding to respond appropriately.[19]

These statements rehearsed the familiar arguments which Gates had been articulating for the previous two years. Woolsey went on to mark up the American intelligence community's successes in Bosnia, Haiti, Iraq and on proliferation. It seemed as if there was hardly a chink of light between one administration and the next. But this was very misleading. Immediately after his confirmation hearings, Woolsey received a memorandum from the White House setting out what President Clinton wanted to get from the intelligence community during his administration. According to sources familiar with the correspondence, it had three main points:

First, there must be a greater focus on the environment. This was something that had emerged as a priority during Gates's studies. It did not fall in the list of top priorities but he had included it as a subject of interest for the community because it was clear that there was a strong sentiment for action in that area both in Congress and among the general public. Now, President Clinton wanted more resources devoted to the monitoring of environmental treaties and to use satellite technology more effectively to monitor food production and to detect areas where land and water might be used more effectively.

This was a personal initiative of Vice President Al Gore. In response Woolsey set up an environmental panel which included representatives from the Central Imagery Office and fifty scientists from academia. The preliminary findings of this group suggested that the millions of satellite photographs stored in the community's archives could be used to establish baselines for global climate changes through, for example, studies of deforestation, Arctic ice and coastal changes, shifting tundra boundaries and desertification. As a more active measure, the data bank could also be applied to US and global environmental clean up and reforestation programmes.

Second, as part of his general desire to produce a 'level playing field' in trade relations, the President asked for a re-examination of the potential of economic espionage. Although this had already been looked at by Gates and any further action rejected, the President clearly believed that the CIA had been dragging its heels. A new study, completed in the summer of 1993, essentially reaffirmed the previous study and argued that any further involvement by the intelligence community in economic espionage would be very costly on resources, had the potential for tying up the community in endless and costly litigation and would be of little advantage to American business.

The third area in which the President expressed an interest was the most startling. He wanted, the memo said, the Agency to establish a new interest in 'democratization'. This word, which brought back old memories of the active measures which resulted in the Bay of Pigs, Panama and Grenada, sent a wave of concern through the upper echelons of the Agency. A request for clarification followed and the reply did little to settle the disquiet. The White House explained that, if there was a country of which the US disapproved, then the Agency was to seek ways of overthrowing its government. On the other hand, if there was a government of which the US approved and a strong opposition was threatening the democracy, then the Agency should find ways to undermine that opposition.

For the Agency, where the Church Committee and Iran-Contra among other major incidents had left scars and a huge and restraining legal structure, the orders came as a shock. At a stroke, President Clinton wanted the intelligence community to adopt aggressive new policies the like of which had not been seen since the dark days of the Cold War. The idea of overthrowing governments and undermining political opponents in friendly countries was the equivalent in CIA terms of unleashing the dogs of war. There is little appetite for such activities in the intelligence community and it is striking that such instructions should be issued by a President who is so firmly committed to the democratic process, a child of the 1960s who opposed the Vietnam War and who has repeatedly made clear his respect for national sovereignty.[20]

While demanding these extra activities, the administration also made clear to Woolsey that it would be seeking deeper cuts in the intelligence budget than those envisaged by the Bush administration. The intention is to achieve a 25% cut by 1997 from around $29 billion to $22.5 billion in current dollars, which compares with a 20% overall cut proposed by President Bush.[21]

Recognizing the new reality, Gates had offered the Congressional budget authorization committes a 15% cut in staff over five years beginning in fiscal year 1993. He thought he had a deal, so was surprised when the 1993 budget mandated a 17.5% cut in staff which would require redundancies, the first time any pink slips have been handed out since the end of the Vietnam War. As part of this process, the CIA has introduced an early retirement scheme which offers employees a $25,000 one-time payment with full pension for leaving early. This small cash sum is designed to encourage the departure of the 'tail', or administrative staff, rather than the 'teeth', from operations.

While this must come as a major culture shock, the idea that any employee should have a job for life is one reason why the intelligence community has become so conservative and bureaucratic. If the economies are used as a method to make the community more competitive and more product-driven then the changes should improve the process of gathering and analyzing.

Gates describes many of the changes he made while DCI as revolutionary. Certainly, he took steps to open up the musty corridors by releasing some old files for inspection. He also helped give the Agency a more public face by allowing some of his officials to appear in public and speak to the media, a practice that Jim Woolsey plans to continue. But these are cosmetic changes designed to improve image rather than substance. What really matters is what Gates and his successors have done to improve performance.

It is still not clear if the changes have gone far enough. All the reforms assumed that the underlying structure of the intelligence community should remain intact, despite the collapse of communism. With the primary threat no longer credible, identifying new areas of interest was not a problem. Gates cleverly engaged the policy making community who were only too eager to come up with their priorities. Gates winnowed these down, but nevertheless there has been a significant shift in priorities so that today the Agency looks at environmental issues, trade and AIDS as well as the threat posed by nuclear proliferation or conventional conflict.

The reforms that are in place are evolutionary, rather than revolutionary as Congress wanted. Instead of establishing an intelligence czar with control over all intelligence agencies, Gates opted for enhanced powers for the DCI but little real change to existing working arrangements. Instead of setting up a coordinating national intelligence center, the National Intelligence Committee was given increased authority to produce its own assessments, but the individual agencies will continue to handle their own analysis.

Gates and his supporters argued that there is real value in the fragmented structure of the intelligence community, that its very diversity is its strength. It is difficult to see either the management or the practical logic in this. A single leader is generally considered to be more effective than several; a single analytical centre must similarly be more effective. It is argued that competition is necessary to produce good analysis, and indeed the Gates reforms increased the competition between analysts rather than decreased it. But in other countries such as Britain, it is the people and the product that make the difference rather than the complexity of the process.

However, the assumption is that the intelligence community can continue business pretty much as usual with some modest changes to keep Congress happy. This complacency is not likely to be borne out in the years to come. Already, the budget for the intelligence community is due to fall by 25% by 1997 which will mean that large numbers in every branch of the community will lose their jobs. At present, the reforms largely preserve the existing structures. As the cuts begin to bite, each department will have to make sacrifices.

This process of 'salami slicing' will result in a degradation of the capability of every department, as each area struggles to do the same or more with less. It is a fact of life that there is no appetite in Congress nor among the general public to approve any increases, so the cuts are here to stay. Unless radical reform is carried out by this administration to allow for the budget reductions, the CIA and the rest of American intelligence face the prospect of going down the same grim road as their former enemies in the KGB.

CHAPTER FIVE

DRAWING THE CLAWS

In December 1991, Robert Strauss, the US ambassador in Moscow, received a telephone call from Vadim Bakatin, the head of the KGB appointed after the failed coup against Mikhail Gorbachev the previous August. The two men had become quite friendly in recent months. Bakatin was a committed reformer and close to President Boris Yeltsin. He had indicated that he wanted to transform the KGB and repair some of the damage done to Russian-American relations by years of aggression by the intelligence organization. Strauss and Bakatin had enjoyed several dinners together but the American ambassador had made it clear that he remained sceptical about the promises of change.

This time, Bakatin invited Strauss to his office where he said he had 'a present' for the American. Strauss immediately drove to Bakatin's office in the Kremlin, and after a few minutes of pleasant chat over coffee, Bakatin turned to the subject of the gift.

'And with that,' Strauss said, 'he went over to his safe and pulled out a big file like this, six or eight inches thick, and with it a suitcase, bag, looked like a suitcase. And he opened the kit, and it had mechanical devices in it, high-tech devices. And he flipped over the plans and they were – it looked like the plans for a high-tech plant of some kind.

'And he said, Mr Ambassador, these are the plans that disclose how the bugging of your embassy took place, and these are the instruments that were used. And I want to give them to you and I want them turned over to your government, no strings attached, no quid pro quo, in the hope that maybe we can repay you, save you some money, maybe you can use that building again someday.'

Fearing some kind of attempt at entrapment, Strauss refused to accept the bag, which contained twenty bugs, or the two thick books 'which looked like the plans for a rocket to get to the moon'. Instead, he returned to the embassy, consulted with the CIA in Langley and three days later made another appointment with Bakatin at his office. When Bakatin tried once again to hand the bag and the documents over, Strauss found they were too heavy to carry and went back to the embassy empty handed. Later that day two diplomats made a third trip to Bakatin's office and this time returned with the goods which were immediately sent over to Langley in the diplomatic bag.[1]

Over the next few months the plans and the bugs were matched with what knowledge Langley had already gleaned about the attempts to bug the embassy.

Strauss later described the meeting as 'the most amazing thing that's happened to me in my life'. The CIA, who examined both the documents and the bugs, pronounced the gift genuine although there remains some uncertainty about whether the KGB has revealed all their embassy secrets. As far as the Agency and Congress are concerned, Bakatin's gift has come too late to save the embassy. In November 1992, Congress voted to build a new embassy costing $220 million, as the old building is still considered too insecure for use by the CIA or the State Department.

The Strauss experience was a practical demonstration of just how much the old and feared KGB has changed since the second Russian revolution. Not only has the name disappeared – Gorbachev abolished the KGB in October 1991 – but the structure and purpose of what was once the world's most powerful secret police has altered also. The visible faces of the present intelligence structure in Russia are enthusiastic disciples of the new order, men and women who profess to have always been on the side of democracy while fighting for the survival and growth of communism. To believe that these individuals can have changed their basic philosophy so radically and accepted defeat so graciously takes a strong leap of faith. The KGB in all its manifestations has always been the real instrument of power in the Soviet Union, the one unchanging structure that makes or breaks governments.

The original KGB was founded in 1917 after the Russian revolution, and went through a number of name changes as the Soviet Union evolved, beginning with the Cheka then the GPU, OGPU, GUGB, NKVD, NKGB, MGB, and finally the KGB in March 1954. In all its different forms its mission remained the same: as the 'Sword and Shield of the Party' to gather intelligence and spread the revolution abroad while controlling all aspects of Soviet life and thought at home.[2]

The old structure, which employed close to 750,000 men and women, was organized into four chief directorates and eight directorates. The most important of these, from a Western perspective, was the First Chief Directorate, responsible for HUMINT, active measures, counter-intelligence and analysis. The Second Chief Directorate was responsible for domestic counter-intelligence and control of the Soviet civilian population. The Border Guards Chief Directorate administered the KGB troops who patrol the frontiers and form an elite military force. The Eighth Chief Directorate was responsible for Communications and Cryptography. The Third (Armed Forces) Directorate carried out counter-intelligence and counter-subversion within the armed forces. The Fourth was responsible for transport. The Fifth Chief Directorate was charged with the suppression of all dissent within the Soviet Union. The Sixth Directorate carried out counter-intelligence and was responsible for industrial security. The Seventh Directorate carried out surveillance. The Operational and Technical Directorate handled the research and development of technical systems. The Sixteenth Chief Directorate was responsible for communications security and signals intelligence. The Military Construction Directorate was responsible for KGB buildings and the Ninth (Guards) Directorate was responsible for guarding the leadership and protecting sensitive installations.[3]

Under the reforms begun by Gorbachev and continued under Yeltsin, the old KGB structure has been dismantled. Today, the First Chief Directorate has been renamed the Sluzhba Vneshnei Razvedaki and remains responsible for all espionage abroad. (Confusingly, the SVR operators sometimes refer to themselves as the RIS or Russian Intelligence Service, the name by which the SIS knew the old KGB and GRU combined.) The Second Chief Directorate has absorbed the fourth and sixth directorates and now deals with fraud, corruption and organized crime rather than with political threats to the state. The Third Directorate has been transferred to the control of the armed forces and essentially will be folded in to the GRU. The Fifth Directorate, also known as Department Z, which was responsible for suppressing internal dissent, was abolished in September 1991. The Ninth Directorate has been renamed the Bodyguard Service and placed under the direct control of the President.[4]

Oleg Kalugin, a former head of First Chief Directorate operations in America, who retired a KGB general and is now the favourite and acceptable face of the reformed KGB in the West, describes his former employers as having 'no programme, no platform and no compass . . . The power of Russian intelligence was based on ideology. That doesn't exist any more. They get no money and they feel neglected, unwanted and confused.'[5]

It seems clear to even the most diehard Cold Warriors that the old KGB is gone forever. It is inconceivable that unless there is a violent revolution which brings another authoritarian regime to power, there will never again be the kind of repression that was routine before the Gorbachev era. Even if that happened, there is some doubt that whatever the wishes of a new dictator, the people and the members of the secret services would allow a new KGB modelled on the old to reemerge.

Vladimir Kryuchkov was the last head of the old-style KGB. A hardline intelligence operative with fourteen years' experience in the First Chief Directorate, he was one of the reasons that many observers in the West believed that the Gorbachev regime was doomed. The appointment of Kryuchkov was the price Gorbachev had to pay to keep the KGB alongside his reform movement. It soon became clear to those who knew Kryuchkov that he and his fellow hardliners were gradually turning against the man they had helped create. In the secret meetings that Bob Gates had with him, the KGB chief revealed himself to be increasingly disenchanted with the Gorbachev regime but it was only in August 1991 when the coup attempt unfolded that it became evident how far Kryuchkov was prepared to go to restore the old values.

But Kryuchkov's orders to the KGB's elite Group Alpha to attack the Russian parliament building and capture Boris Yeltsin were ignored and the KGB remained on the sidelines throughout the attempted coup, recognizing perhaps that times really had changed.

Afterwards, Kryuchkov was replaced by Vadim Bakatin, a leader of the reform movement and a former head of the Interior Ministry. One of his first acts was to release the wife and daughters of Oleg Gordievsky, the British agent who had defected to the West in 1985. This gesture was a response to a quiet and lengthy campaign that had involved President Reagan, Prime Minister Thatcher and senior diplomats and intelligence agencies over a number of years. The Gordievsky defection had caused consternation within the KGB and the damage he did to the organization was immense. The old guard were determined that he and his family should pay a heavy price for his betrayal. The fact that Bakatin was able to move against the old guard and release Gordievsky's family was a clear message to the West that it was no longer business as usual. At last, it seemed as if the KGB everyone had fought for so many years was changing for the better.

Under financial and political pressure, Bakatin oversaw the disintegration of the KGB and the formation of the new agencies that exist today. He stated that the KGB should only deal with intelligence and counter-intelligence, not border security, executive protection, government communications or the bugging of dissidents. Within two months, the KGB border guards had been removed from the intelligence service. The directorates charged with protecting the leadership were also taken away, and Bakatin was committed to reducing the KGB to a rump of around 35,000. These changes were too much for the still powerful security agency and Yeltsin was persuaded to fire him in order to maintain the loyalty of the hardliners. After he was fired Bakatin was offered the post of ambassador to the Netherlands or Bulgaria. He turned both down. Bakatin was replaced by Viktor Barranikov who assumed responsibility for the Interior Ministry while handing over control of the former First Chief Directorate to Yevgeni Primakov.

Barranikov was the architect of a decree published in December 1991 which created a new superministry of internal affairs and public security, something last heard of in Stalin's time. The constitutional court ruled that move illegal but Barranikov soon reabsorbed the KGB border guards back into the MB, creating once again a very powerful internal intelligence structure. Barranikov himself was dismissed in late 1993 and he later joined the anti-Yeltsin forces in the failed September coup. After the December elections produced significant gains for the anti-reformers, Yeltsin disbanded the MB, claiming the organisation had failed to warn him about the growing opposition. The new Federal Counterintelligence Service is headed by Viktor Golushko, the serving Security Minister and a 56-year-old former KGB agent and a political conservative. It is unclear just how much the MB will really change under the same leader but a new name.

The dismissal of Bakatin and his replacement by Primakov raised fears in Western intelligence that the KGB was reestablishing its power base in Russia after a period of lying low after the coup. Primakov was born in 1929 in the Ukraine and brought up in Georgia. He is half Jewish but changed his surname from Kirshblat to avoid the anti-Semitism that was prevalent in the Soviet Union.

Primakov was the perfect establishment communist, a Moscow insider who enjoyed all the privileges of the elite. He was also, according to Western intelligence sources, through much of his career an agent for the KGB.

'He was a KGB agent of long standing, particularly when with *Pravda* in the Middle East, and he did active measures work,' said one such source. 'He was appointed to head the SVR because his old KGB friends needed a new head who appeared to have nothing to do with the KGB, but whom they knew they could trust.'

This cynical interpretation is flatly denied by Primakov. In his first full interview given since he was appointed head of the SVR, Primakov set out his views of the future of Russian intelligence. They are worth quoting at length because they mark a dramatic shift in the operations and priorities of Russian intelligence. This is the first time such views have been made public.[6]

Things are really changing. First of all, we have repudiated the old ideological model . . . which predetermined that there are permanent enemies and permanent friends, and maybe not only friends, but also permanent allies. The old model predetermined confrontations and, in general, pushed to the background our country's national interests, which were sometimes even sacrificed in order to give ideological support to our allies; or they were sometimes produced as a trump card for confrontation with the enemy. We have repudiated all this.

We are now working not against someone, we are now working in defence of the national interest. Thus, the definition of our national interests has acquired a special importance. What do these national interests consist of? A stabilization of the situation, of course, especially a stabilization in the regions surrounding our country. We can see the very great danger which arises from the proliferation of weapons of mass destruction and we feel we must monitor the activities of those crazy circles which now and always represent a danger for Russia.

We have become very active in giving positive constructive support to measures taken in the economic sphere, measures which correspond to the defence of our interests. In other words there is now a change of direction but this does not mean that we won't be active in intelligence work because we don't want to be faced with an unexpected possible move by this or that country to destabilize the existing armaments system. But now our work in the political military field is not aimed at strengthening our position in confrontation with somebody.

We do not now undertake intelligence work with the aim of supporting specific political forces inside a country. It is not the job of intelligence to help one party or another [in a foreign country]. It's not our business.

Scientific technical intelligence must monitor the development of technology, technology of dual use, monitor how it is developing, in what way it is developing, and if any breakthroughs are possible. As you know, up to now, many secrets are still being kept from us by many countries. If this information were openly available to us then there would be no need to engage in intelligence in this direction. But I fully agree with Gates as regards economic intelligence; one must know how economic obligations supported by economic agreements are being fulfilled. But, we shall not provide it [to companies]. We shall only provide it [to] government bodies. I am categorically against allowing intelligence to work for, say, the Raw Materials Commodity Exchange or any other private concern. We are a budget organization, budgeted from public money and therefore we must only work for the government.

Primakov claims that some thirty intelligence stations have been shut down, mostly in countries like Papua New Guinea or Cameroon that have no strategic interest for the new Russia. But this is the first reduction in the intelligence presence of Russia or the former Soviet Union since the start of the Cold War. At the same time, the SVR has reduced its overseas staff by 50 per cent. Both these reductions have been confirmed by Western intelligence which generally accepts that the SVR is operating in a very different way from the old KGB.

But while these cosmetic changes have been under way, the old intelligence apparat has been repositioning itself in more sinister ways to consolidate its influence in the new democratic Russia. Seventy-five per cent of the new Russian Stock Commodities Exchange Centre are former KGB officials; dozens of former KGB men have emerged running joint ventures with Western businessmen. Others have taken influential non-commercial jobs such as Alexandr Drozdov, a former First Chief Directorate operator in Japan who is now editor of *Rossiya*, the Russian parliament's weekly newspaper.[7]

If the former KGB has moved to retain its influence internally, it is having more difficulty continuing its role as an influential player abroad. Whatever Primakov may say, there is ample evidence that the new SVR is trying to be as active as before in gathering secrets in foreign countries, especially those that are part of Nato. They may have stopped supporting revolutionary movements and trying to subvert governments, but they still need the military and business secrets that over the past twenty years helped a bankrupt Soviet economy survive.

One of the many defectors who came over in late 1991 was Vladimir Konoplyov, the first secretary of the Russian embassy in Brussels. He brought with him details of a massive spy network that was still operating in Belgium and France. For several weeks after his defection, Belgium's military intelligence unit (the SGR) and the counter-espionage service, the Sûreté de l'Etat, kept surveillance on those suspected of involvement in an operation ironically codenamed Glasnost. At the beginning of April 1992, the Belgian police raided twenty houses across the country and arrested three industrialists, a journalist and a civil servant and expelled two diplomats from the Russian embassy and two Russian trade officials.[8]

Two weeks later, several French nationals were also arrested after the Belgians had been interrogated and documents taken from the offices of the spies had led to another ring in France.

What was striking about the Belgian ring was that it had been in operation since 1967, and had spread to include a prominent journalist, a manager at the Union Chimique Belge and a reservist in the Belgian army. The target of the group was industrial and military secrets, with their biggest success being the apparent transfer of plans for a Nato battlefield communications system codenamed Rita.

The spy ring had continued to operate after the collapse of the Berlin Wall and the disintegration of the Soviet Union. In fact, as the police pounced, the ring had launched a major recruiting drive to find new spies who were being hired with cash supplied by the Russian embassy.

With the exposure of the Belgian spy ring, and the information that other defectors brought with them, it has become clear to Western agencies that the new KGB is as active as money and people will allow. But whatever the ambitions of the SVR or GRU, they have been hampered by the loosening of the central control of Moscow on a system that survived for generations by oppression or through convincing people to espouse the communist philosophy. Now, there is less oppression and no ideology so it has proved exceptionally difficult to keep the loyalty of those who remain in intelligence.

Since the collapse of the Soviet Union, every Western intelligence agency, but in particular the British and American services, has been inundated with requests for asylum from former KGB members. This wealth of defectors has led to a very selective policy being adopted in Washington and London where the majority of requests for asylum are turned down. Even so, high grade defectors have been leaving at the rate of more than one a month for over three years, causing a serious decline in morale in every branch of Russian intelligence, civilian and military.

During the Cold War, the KGB was seen as a centrally controlled monolith. The activities of all the different areas of Soviet intelligence were guided by a central hand in the Politburo. Now that is not the case, with President Yeltsin having only a delicate hand on the intelligence tiller. The GRU appears to be operating as a completely independent entity, a clear sign of the increased power of the military since the revolution.

The new leaders of Russian intelligence point with pride to the strength of the parliamentary oversight system which is now in place. Superficially, this is as strong as the American version and certainly much tougher than anything in Britain, although, as I have said, this oversight is little more than a fig leaf to cover what business as usual they can afford or manage without being caught. The parliament was elected before the abortive coup and the rise of Boris Yeltsin. Many members owe their allegiance to the old guard, not to the new democrats. In fact, the KGB organized the candidate lists in republican and local elections in 1990 and nearly 2,800 former members of the KGB were elected to local and republican legislatures, giving the intelligence structure a valuable new power base.

It is, of course, too early to say just what influence this penetration of the new democratic structures by the old intelligence services will have. Even they have accepted that the days of bugging, tailing and commitment to psychiatric wards are over. But it would be naive to assume that a simple issue like elections or democracy will give such an ingrained organization much pause for thought. For generations, the intelligence services have embedded themselves deep inside Russian (and Soviet) society where they have frequently played the role of kingmaker in both national and local politics. That is not going to change, and while the KGB has been destroyed, the influence of the experienced intelligence professionals will continue to be felt inside Russia.

What matters to the new pragmatists in the Kremlin is opening up their lines of communication with their former enemies in the West. The charm offensive that began in the Gorbachev era has continued and even increased under Yeltsin. The German, American, British and Finnish intelligence heads, among others, have visited Moscow or been visited by Primakov and at each meeting the message is the same: we have common interests so let us cooperate to fight drugs, terrorism, organized crime and proliferation. Senior officials of the former Second Chief

Directorate have visited the US several times in the past two years seeking cooperation from the FBI on issues that range from the transfer of forensic technology and crime fighting techniques to sharing intelligence on drugs and organized crime. So far, the response in America has been very reserved.

'We have told them: You can't come to the dinner table then steal the silverware,' said Pat Watson, deputy assistant director of the FBI's intelligence division.

The Russians have everything to gain from a deal. Their economy is in tatters. Law and order are collapsing and control from Moscow of the outlying Russian countryside is increasingly fragmentary. Clearly, Western intelligence and police agencies could help to improve the situation. But for the former KGB there is another agenda, which is to try and maintain a seat at the top political tables in Moscow. Having dominated the scene since the revolution, the KGB is unaccustomed to being a secondary influence. As the ideological struggle with the West has been replaced by a more introspective role defending national security, so the former KGB's influence has dwindled. The battle now is over who can bring the most important scientific and technical secrets back home to help the struggling Russian economy. So far, the competition has been won by the GRU, the military's intelligence arm. They have survived the turmoil of the past few years relatively intact and are now able to exploit the years they spent building up effective S and T networks while leaving political analysis to the KGB. This has turned out to be a solid investment and the GRU is able to bring a regular stream of valuable information back to Moscow.

By contrast, the KGB has been emasculated over the past three years. There are still networks and spies, trying to replace those who have defected or been blown. But with political analysis less relevant and subversion no longer an option, the KGB has found itself short of product. As a result, the SVR has had to try and evolve new methods of doing business.

One of the most difficult phenomena to combat has been the move by some KGB officers from spying to business. Several thousand KGB men and women have moved to the private sector and many have used their official contacts to set up joint ventures with Western countries. Until 1990, the KGB leadership broadly opposed the use of joint venture cover on the grounds that its officers might be corrupted by any association with capitalism. But with the arrival of democracy and the worsening economic climate, the SVR has come under pressure to lose staff, earn hard currency to pay its way and to improve operational security.

In early 1992, SVR officers were instructed to find alternative cover slots in order to become financially self-sufficient and to compensate in part for the loss of slots in trade missions and embassies. Many of those who have established themselves in business are now happily working for themselves, rather than the SVR, thus confirming the worst fears of the old KGB leadership. But often it is difficult to distinguish between the genuine entrepreneur who may maintain some links with the SVR and the real SVR operative. For example, there is an ongoing operation in Sweden where a former KGB officer involved in a joint venture came under observation. It was known that the man was putting half his income through the books and pocketing the rest. He was also using his position to gather political information. What was not clear was whether he was using all his old skills to make himself rich or whether he had been deliberately sent to Sweden by Primakov to gather data and pass it back to Moscow while making money to fund SVR operations abroad. Western intelligence is now satisfied that the man is working under orders and he is still under surveillance to see if his contacts comprise a new agent network in the West.

Joint ventures are just one example of the changed nature of SVR spying. More complex is a general move by SVR agents away from operating under diplomatic cover. More and more agents leave Russia or the republics as businessmen, scientists or even musicians and are allowed to move freely in the West in ways that would have been impossible a few years ago. Without sources inside the SVR, it is virtually impossible for counter-intelligence agencies to keep track of these people, many of whom are perfectly innocent. The result is that once the SVR refines its operational techniques, the flow of intelligence back to Moscow will resume, if not to previous levels, at least to a level that will make the SVR a significant political player once again.

Meanwhile, the best it can do is to try and cut a deal with agencies like the CIA and the SIS in an attempt to bring back some of the influence it has lost.

There is now a kind of weary tolerance of the SVR, as if it is an old friend who hasn't yet realized its days are over. The attitude to the GRU is altogether more professional.

'The level of KGB activity is not high,' said one senior member of British intelligence in June 1992. 'I think it's fair to say that there is not a serious threat from the KGB today. But the GRU are still very active and there has been no serious reduction of their activities worldwide.'

Western agencies have viewed the performance of the GRU with increasing concern. Three examples are used by Western intelligence to illustrate its activities.

In November 1991, Colonel Viktor Sherdov was arrested while meeting a potential recruit in Saxony-Anhalt in Germany. At his trial in August 1992, the prosecution showed that he was a senior GRU officer who had been operating overseas since 1980. At the time of his arrest, he was head of the GRU's office in Magdeberg, responsible for spying on the German army and its Nato allies in an area that stretched from Holland to France. He was jailed for three years, the first Russian officer to be sent to prison since German reunification.

Viktor Vasilyevich Fedik was another GRU officer working under cover as third secretary at the Russian embassy in Oslo. He had been discovered by Norwegian intelligence trying to recruit a student to spy on other foreign students in Norway and was expelled on October 6, 1992.

On January 2, 1993, a Russian military officer working at the embassy in Washington in the military attaché's office was expelled from the United States. He was the first Russian to be declared persona non grata since the collapse of the Soviet Union in 1991 and his expulsion reflected growing frustration with the continued activities of the eighteen GRU officers based at the Russian embassy. Some of these men had been videotaped servicing dead letter boxes and meeting with agents, and the videos were shown to President Yeltsin as part of the American campaign to persuade Russia to curb the GRU.[9]

At each of these confrontations, which also took place with the British, Yeltsin either denied everything or claimed there was little he could do. While he is clearly limited in the amount of action he can take against the military, the continued activities of the GRU will prevent a full normalization of relations between Russia and Western countries.

If the GRU continues with business as usual, the KGB has been transformed in the past five years from one of the most feared intelligence organizations to a shadow of its former self. No longer spying on dissidents at home or assassinating enemies abroad, no longer subverting governments and fomenting revolution, no longer bugging journalists and entrapping visitors with seductive men and women, it is now a different, less threatening organization. But the new SVR still employs more people than the CIA's DO and the SIS combined, it is still active in over a hundred countries and is trying wherever it can to recruit new spies and keep the old ones active.

For the Western nations trying to evolve a policy for dealing with an old enemy who now wants to be a friend, it is difficult if not impossible to distinguish the actions of one agency from another and treat them as if they were part of a different country. For example, if the DIA mounted an aggressive intelligence gathering effort in Russia while the CIA were asking the SVR to cooperate in combating drugs, the SVR would see the CIA overtures as a ploy to gather intelligence or gain credibility at home. That is exactly the response of Western agencies to the approaches that have been made by Primakov and others.

'We have to decide who will fill that role, who will cooperate with them, who will train with them, who will share intelligence with them, who will come back primed internationally and locally with them,' said Bill Sessions, the former FBI director. 'But when we reach out and if we find that some other part of the government is actually causing us great pain, it does not make great good sense to try to further the cooperation and enhance your relationship when another agency holds a knife to your ribs.'[10]

Despite such reservations, overall the charm offensive by the Russian intelligence services has worked. America, France and Germany have now accepted SVR station chiefs in their capitals who are formally declared to the host nation. They act as liaisons and are free to visit the intelligence headquarters of what, until recently, was a sworn enemy. In the space of twelve months, France, Germany and America all accepted visits from Primakov, which have been reciprocated by trips to Moscow by Western chiefs.

The only holdout in this new arrangement has been Britain where there remains a great deal of residual distrust of the new KGB.

'As far as we are concerned, very little has changed in Russia with regard to intelligence,' said one intelligence official. 'It is the same people running the same desks doing the same thing. They are still actively spying on the West, still trying to recruit agents and insert illegals.'[11]

Two working groups from the SVR did visit London in October 1992. They were led by General Gennadi Yestaviev, a former First Chief Directorate officer who served four years in New York, served in Geneva and is currently head of the non-proliferation unit in the SVR. Each working group had six members and they discussed terrorism, proliferation, counter-narcotics, organized crime and money laundering. Yestaviev also asked for permission to establish a permanent and overt SVR presence in Britain.

Before the meetings, SIS had decided to test the promises of a new era with some tough questions. The meeting began with SIS naming a number of Iranians, part of the Tehran government's procurement network, who had travelled to Russia recently to buy weapons. What did the Russians know about them? After promising to find out the information, none has been forthcoming and the October visit has been dismissed as 'long on atmosphere, short on substance'.

The CIA have been less cautious and official working groups have been set up to tackle proliferation and terrorism. But at Langley these groups are not considered significant as they have produced no operational information and the Russians clearly have no plans to offer any hard intelligence.

Contacts will continue and there will be some sharing of information on a case-by-case basis but too many of the old suspicions remain for there to be any great sea change in the intelligence relationships of agencies that have fought each other for so long. If the former KGB starts to cooperate by supplying the kind of intelligence that the Libyans passed over to SIS on the IRA in 1992 then the talk of shared information and operations may be viewed more positively in Western capitals.

This new kind of relationship between Russia and her former enemies has another side which has been hampering the work of Western spy agencies. The more open the work of the CIA station chief in Moscow has become, the more difficult it is for him aggressively to seek intelligence targets. In political terms, Russia is now perceived to be neutral, even a friend – whatever may be happening on the ground between the spies. It is now very difficult for the CIA to try and recruit a senior aide to Boris Yeltsin because if such an approach was discovered it would be politically embarrassing, even damaging. The result of this nervousness, particularly for the CIA, has been a toning down of some recruitment operations in Russia. Britain has less to lose politically so SIS has been able to continue with a more cautious recruitment campaign. This in turn has helped keep the British position at the top table of spies as SIS now has some of the best sources inside the new Russia.

Whatever the public protestations about a new working relationship, the spy business between Russia and the West continues pretty much as usual. In some areas, the collapse of the Soviet Union has provided new opportunities for the West and new challenges for Russia. The republics that now surround Russia are a new battleground between her and the West. As Russia struggles to maintain influence, Western spy agencies are doing their best to surround her with an invisible but vast array of systems and people to gather intelligence on the new Russia.

THE NEW WORLD:
RUSSIA

CHAPTER SIX

REAPING THE HARVEST

In December 1990, three officials, two from SIS and one from MI5, flew from London to Budapest. They were led by a man we will call Peter who had made a career of spying in the former communist bloc. It was his first visit to Hungary under his own name. He had operated under cover in a number of communist countries, always under the watchful eye of the KGB or their satellite agencies. Yet, Peter had been able to carry out covert operations almost at will. With that background, he flew in to Budapest sceptical of many of the changes that had occurred since the election of President Yeltsin.

The invitation to SIS had come some weeks earlier after the British ambassador in Hungary had suggested to local officials that there might be some common ground to explore. Hungarian intelligence had been reformed by the new government which had appointed Kalman Kocsis, a former station chief in Athens, as its head. The team were met at Budapest airport by a limousine and driven to the headquarters of Hungarian intelligence in the wooded hills ten kilometres outside the city. This was the British team's first visit inside an intelligence HQ of a former Warsaw Pact country and they looked around them, excited and fascinated. Parts of the building appeared to have been looted with signs hanging off doors, others torn off altogether. But in other areas, people continued to work as if nothing had changed.

'It was eerie, a feeling of, Christ, is this really happening?' recalled Peter. 'But the mere fact that we were there was a sign of the victory we had won. An extraordinary feeling.'

The three men were escorted with great formality into a room where three men sat on one side of a long wooden table, bottles of alcohol and glasses in front of them. After brief introductions, Peter stood up and made a short formal speech.

'It's a pleasure to be here under such interesting circumstances,' he began. 'Our countries were kept apart by the unfortunate episodes of the Cold War. We grieved with you in 1956, and we felt solidarity with the Czechs in 1968. We should all be relieved that we can now meet together under such different circumstances.

'We would like to base a station chief in Budapest, in an open way, so that we can have a reasonable dialogue with you. This is not diplomacy, this is intelligence. We want to work with you to seek the common ground for dealing with the problems of the new world and the new order.'

The formalities over, the six men retired to à dacha, once a favourite haunt of the old Communist Party bosses, a magnificent building which had been turned into a luxury hotel. At the end of that first evening, after endless toasts to cement the new relationship, there were hugs and tears among these hard-bitten professionals, each moved by the extraordinary circumstances that had brought them together to mark a new era.

The Hungarian experience was repeated in a number of former communist countries which have decided to retain or rebuild their intelligence structures. This has given rise to a new word in the intelligence lexicon: lustration, which is derived from the Latin word *lustrum* and means washing clean, purification. All the former communist countries are going through lustration or are lustrating as they struggle to destroy the old intelligence apparatus that was used as a tool of repression. At the same time, each government wants to retain enough of the old system so that there is some continuity. It has been a difficult balancing act which each country has resolved in its own way.

The Estonians and the Czechs, for example, started from scratch, while Lithuania and Latvia drew on some of the old local KGB people but mostly rebuilt using new staff. At the other extreme, the Poles simply changed the name on the door and continued with business. The new head of the Polish External Services is Gromek Chimpinski, a tough, able and Westernized officer of Department 1 of the MSW, the intelligence service of communist Poland, who was accepted by the new government on the pragmatic grounds that all along his heart was almost certainly in the right democratic place. At heart, he was judged to be a nationalist, rather than a communist, who would always put loyalty to country above personal political beliefs.

In the middle are countries like East Germany, which may have vanished in the reforms, but which left behind an intelligence legacy the dimensions of which are still uncertain. The Stasi, the East German secret police, has been disbanded but it is clear that many of the agents who worked for one of the communist bloc's most effective intelligence services have simply transferred their allegiance to new masters. Alexander von Stahl, the German attorney general, claims that up to 80 per cent of the old Stasi network operating in Germany has been taken over and reactivated by the SVR. That means that up to 500 Stasi agents are currently working for the SVR in Germany while others have sold their services to nations such as Iran and Syria. It is estimated that over 1,000 KGB and GRU officers remain on East German territory, ostensibly to ensure the smooth evacuation of Russian forces.[1]

Of the old services, only Romania continues to behave as if nothing has changed. All the others have adapted to some extent, and have tried to distance themselves from their old Soviet masters. But there is no doubt that, whatever the agreements, Russia continues to operate agents in all these countries. That is neither surprising nor a particular point of criticism as other agencies such as SIS and the CIA do the same. The difference with Russia is that their agents operate covertly while Western agencies maintain an overt, and therefore less threatening, presence.

The new contacts that have been developed between the new intelligence services in the former communist countries and their Western counterparts have provided ample opportunity for new kinds of spying. While the Russians have continued their spying on the Western countries, the CIA and SIS have been trying to establish new eyes and ears in the former Soviet Union. As the KGB has a 'no spying' agreement with the Baltic states, these have become the centre of intelligence activity by the CIA and SIS who use them as a recruiting base and the heart of operations, in the same way as Finland and Austria used to be important centres during the Cold War. The CIA, NSA and SIS have moved in to the Baltic states to try and recruit sources or to install listening posts to monitor both Russia and the Ukraine, as well as Russians who regularly travel to the new countries.

'The way this works is that the ambassador goes to talk to the head of an infant intelligence organization and offers contacts with the intelligence service and the lines are then opened,' explained one senior intelligence official.

'We see significant advantages in making links with these countries, particularly in the Baltics. By doing so we have been able to establish listening posts, to take advantage of the free flow of people from Russia to the Baltic countries and back, and we have been able to recruit large numbers of agents in place. This has allowed us to gather really a stunning amount of intelligence in the last couple of years.'[2]

By pushing back the borders of the Russian empire in this way and bringing American and British spies in large numbers to Moscow's doorstep, British and American intelligence services have infuriated Yeltsin and his government.

'At present, we have no intelligence activities in the Baltic republics, but I cannot guarantee that this will be so in the future because we are receiving a lot of information that the Baltic republics and the Eastern European countries are being used as platforms for intelligence activities against Russia,' said Primakov. 'For instance, we have even identified meetings by foreign intelligence services with their agents there, on the territory of these countries. If that continues, then we will be obliged to have our own people there to monitor this process.'

This public statement is the first official acknowledgement from a senior SVR official of the existence of this new underground war that has been going on since the collapse of the Soviet Union. On the one hand are the spies from countries like Britain, France and America who see the opportunity both to make an investment in the new republics and to reap a rich intelligence harvest from a now vulnerable Russia. On the other side are the Russians, encircled by potential enemies, all of whom are trying to gather the few secrets that remain unexposed and to consolidate positions in the heart of what until recently was the Soviet empire. It has been a difficult pill for the Russians to swallow, and they have begun to fight back.

According to Leonid Shebarshin, a senior intelligence officer who resigned rather than change the KGB, the CIA began setting up a new network in the Baltics in early 1992 with a headquarters in Vilnius, the capital of Lithuania.

'I know that foreign intelligence services have not only not ceased their activity against Russia, but on the contrary have increased it,' said Shebarshin. 'Already in early 1992, after I had resigned, the US intelligence services began creating a bridgehead in the Baltics for work against Russia. The Baltic republics' authorities were quite receptive.

'At the beginning of 1992, the CIA station in Vilnius had about fifty people. The main activity of this office was not so much work in the Baltics but in Russia, Belarus and Ukraine. And it is not only what is happening today, but what could happen in the future. One must not allow foreigners the run of the place with impunity on the territory of

Russia, whether their intentions are good or bad. One must not allow them to interfere in our internal affairs, form their own lobbies and recruit their agents from among us.'[3]

The MBR, the Russian internal security service, has set up a special department for problems relating to the former Soviet republics and to promote Moscow's interests in the 'near abroad', as the republics are known. There is concern, particularly among the Russian military, that unfriendly governments in power in the fourteen republics could have serious political and economic consequences. In part this is because the new republics have been developing their own trading links with countries such as China and Iran to further weaken the Russian economy. But there is also the worry that ethnic tension, especially among the seventy million Muslims living in the Asian republics might spread to Russia and destabilize the whole region.[4]

To address these problems, the MBR, in concert with the SVR and the GRU, has orchestrated an extensive campaign in some of the republics to promote pro-Moscow leaders and to destabilize those who are seen as a potential threat to Russia. In Azerbaijan, for example, President Abdulfaz Elchibey was forced to flee the country after a rebel army led by Gaidar Aliyev, a former member of the Politburo, marched on the capital. Elchibey had upset Moscow by withdrawing from the Commonwealth of Independent States and planning to export oil not through Russia but to Turkey.

Russian troops pulled out of Azerbaijan ahead of schedule and left behind enough weapons to equip a 20,000-man army under the control of Colonel Suret Guseinov, an Aliyev ally who was later appointed prime minister.

In Georgia, Eduard Shevardnadze, who is hated by many in Moscow for his pro-West leanings during the Gorbachev era, has been targeted by both the GRU and the SVR. This led the CIA to send a team to the country at the beginning of 1993 to try and bolster the Shevardnadze government and to provide training to the local intelligence service in surveillance and counter-insurgency methods. The CIA team was led by forty-five-year-old Freddy Woodruff who became a regular feature at the bar of the Metechi Palace Hotel in Tiblisi where he enjoyed drinking with Eldar Gogoladze, the head of Georgian intelligence.

On August 6, 1993 it was Gogoladze who was driving a jeep with Woodruff and two women as passengers on a sightseeing trip in the Caucasus Mountains when the vehicle was ambushed by highway robbers. When Gogoladze refused to stop, one of the bandits fired a single round from his Kalashnikov rifle which hit Woodruff in the head, killing him instantly. He was the first casualty of this new war and his death left Georgia awash with rumours that he had been gunned down by a Russian hit squad.[5]

While this was untrue, Georgian intelligence told the CIA during August that they were convinced Russia was planning a coup against Shevardnadze. In December 1992, thirteen billion roubles were transferred from a private bank in Moscow to banks in Gaduata, the main city in the breakaway Georgian province of Abkhazia. According to the Georgians, the money has been used to pay for equipment and training for a rebel army. At the same time, several hundred men from the 345th Guards Parachute Regiment of Russia's 104th Guards Division, which is normally stationed in Azerbaijan, were secretly moved to Abkhazia. Other Russian special forces are training the rebels to use weapons supplied by Moscow.

During July and August, Georgian intelligence recorded a number of meetings and conversations between officials from the Russian embassy in Tiblisi and opposition figures around the country. On two occasions, the conversations involved two members of the GRU, which keeps a staff of eight at the embassy. In the talks the Russians suggested the dissidents organize demonstrations against the government in the hope that Shevardnadze's position would weaken.

Russian Spetsnaz forces have been training forces loyal to Zviad Gamsakhurdia, the former president of Georgia who was fired by Shevardnadze. At the same time, Russian intelligence officers have been acting as a bridge between Gamsakhurdia and other opposition leaders in an attempt to form a united front against Shevardnadze.

The listening posts and spy missions that are now firmly established in the new republics will be a focus for Western efforts to underpin the new democracies. They will also be a running sore for the Russian government which has still not got used to the idea of having such a prominent Western presence so close to their border. What particularly infuriates the Russians is not just the lack of influence they now have in countries where they once held total sway but also the fact that now they feel every conversation is being overheard and every traveller outside Russia's borders is being targeted for recruitment. The Russians have always had a paranoid view of their own vulnerability; this constant attrition is wearing them down and provoking the aggressive policies which are now evident in Azerbaijan and Georgia.

These policies would undoubtedly continue even if the CIA and SIS were not so prominent in the region. To Russia, simple economics are as much a policy driver as security concerns. As these new nations become more independent so they will cut their traditional economic ties with Moscow and the Russian economy will slide even further into chaos. But Russia is in no position to dictate the terms of this new war. As long as the SVR and the GRU remain active trying to destabilize democratic governments in the new republics, Russia will not be able to discard the old image of the aggressive and expansionist Russian bear.

THE NEW WORLD: BRITAIN

CHAPTER SEVEN

OUT OF THE SHADOWS

It was one of those parties where the glitterati go to be seen, where politicians rub shoulders with actors, and tycoons actually talk to television presenters over white wine and delicate canapés of shrimp and smoked salmon. The occasion was the farewell party for Sir David Nicholas, the retiring chairman of Independent Television News, held in October 1991 at the Savoy Hotel in London. David Frost, John Smith, then shadow chancellor, and Richard Branson, head of Virgin Atlantic, were among the guests.

For one guest, the invitation to the party had posed a serious dilemma. Although he had known Nicholas for some years, he had never been introduced to any of Nicholas's friends. It was not because he was shy or even because he disliked such entertaining company. Rather, he was the heir to generations of British tradition that ensured he lived his professional life in darkness, forever hidden from public and parliamentary scrutiny. But that evening, after months of agonized debate, he had decided to come out, to reveal his true self.

It was with some nervousness that he went to the Savoy that night and with some pride that he introduced himself with the words: 'My name is Sir Patrick Walker. I am the director-general of the Security Service.'

Thus the head of MI5, one of Britain's top spies, broke with tradition and marked the beginning of a new era for the Security Service. Until the party, Walker had been almost completely anonymous. Until he was knighted in 1991, he did not appear in *Who's Who*, and even now there is only a two-line entry stating that he was born in 1935 and works in the Ministry of Defence, until now the usual hideout for spies. Kenneth Baker, the Home Secretary, who sanctioned Walker's outing, was also at the party and must have watched with interest to see how the British establishment reacted to this brave step into the new world. According to friends of Walker, the reaction both at the party and since has been typically British. Some people have never heard of the Security Service, others believe it is a private company like Securicor and the remainder shuffle their feet and change the subject.

(A similar reaction occurred after Prime Minister John Major acknowledged the existence of SIS and its chief Sir Colin McColl in the House of Commons on May 6, 1992. Later that week, the SIS station chief in Washington, who had been operating under cover as a counsellor, turned up at the weekly meeting of senior staff which is chaired by the ambassador. 'I have something to say,' he announced. 'I am now able to tell you that I am the SIS representative here.' This statement was greeted with neither a handclap nor a cheer as everyone around the table had known exactly who he was and what he did from the moment he arrived, a measure of how farcical the policy of secrecy regarding British intelligence had been.)

But whatever the disappointment within MI5 about the reaction to the new openness, the Savoy party was important and marked the beginning of a new policy in the Security Service. In future, the director-general will no longer be a mystery figure and his name can be published without fear of a D notice or arrest under the Official Secrets Act.

In fact even before Walker's emergence into the limelight, the intelligence community had been tentatively opening lines to the outside world. The new era really began with the appointment of Sir Anthony Duff as director-general of the Service in 1985 by Margaret Thatcher. This was an extraordinary appointment as Duff was a liberal and not from the tough Tory mould of many other Thatcher appointments. (He spent some of his retirement working in a food kitchen serving London's homeless.) But Duff was always both forthright and courteous in his dealings with Thatcher, two attributes she respected.

By appointing an outsider, the Prime Minister was sending a signal that she wanted changes and Duff immediately set about trying to deliver. He was shocked to find that the organization was extraordinarily old-fashioned, with traditions and structures that owed more to the old boy network and the fears generated at the height of the Cold War than the realities of the late twentieth century. Duff began with simple measures: he personally toured every department, meeting staff who had never before met the director-general; he instituted an internal monthly newsletter and required every department to contribute articles about their work. This met strong resistance from many who had hidden inefficiency behind anonymity, using secrecy to disguise failure. Today the newsletter is read by everyone and is even used to air grievances such as the justification for the firing of two homosexuals.

He made moves, too, to broaden the recruiting network of MI5. Traditionally, the organization had relied on graduates, with a bias towards Oxford and Cambridge. Unlike SIS, which is more elitist, the Service also draws on the army and the police for its recruits as well as taking in others from what remains of the Empire. It was clear, however, that if the modern terrorist was to be combated effectively, the recruiting base would have to be broadened to include men and women from all walks of life, both graduates and non-graduates. Today, out of the 2,000 members of the Security Service, 40% are under thirty and the majority of these were recruited outside the narrow Oxbridge net.

Duff made no secret of the fact that he questioned the value of much intelligence work. He was appalled by the traditional methods which seemed cumbersome and frequently unjustified, and the traditional enemies targeted by MI5, often, he felt, for no reason other than that they had always been there and were a threat many years ago.

'The internal threat to the state is virtually dead,' he said. 'People did believe in it at one time and perhaps they were right to do so. But the Labour Party have shown themselves to be quite capable of taking care of the most serious threat today which was Militant Tendency. Now it is hard to conceive of any organization that could actually threaten the stability of the nation. But I suppose you have to keep an eye on things in case a political organization turns to terrorism.'[1]

A number of defectors, notably Oleg Gordievsky, the designated KGB head of station in London, had provided a wealth of detail about the work of the KGB against the West. (Duff spent many hours talking to Gordievsky, a man he came to admire and respect as a true idealist. In the autumn of 1988, Gordon Brook Shepherd published *The Storm Birds*, which gave the first detailed account of Gordievsky's contribution to the end of the Cold War. To celebrate the publication and as a mark of their friendship, Gordievsky inscribed a copy of the book and put it in a plain brown envelope. SIS, who were looking after Gordievsky and still had him in hiding, put a Carrickfergus stamp on it and posted the book to Duff at his home in Devon. With an Irish stamp, a handwritten address and a book shape, it had all the hallmarks of an IRA letter bomb and Duff called the police. Since he lived in a remote country village, the nearest bomb squad was at an army base in the next county, and arrived two hours later. The army propped the package against the compost heap at the bottom of the garden and blew it up. Only by piecing the bits together did they learn the nature of the gift.)[2]

The evidence of people like Gordievsky was that the KGB was far from being the all-seeing, all-knowing intelligence organization the West had feared for so long. It still managed occasional coups but generally achieved little. It made Western intelligence bureaucracies appear monuments to modern management.

'The vast amount of material gathered by the KGB was really pretty unimportant,' said Duff. 'They were not working to politically undermine the state but were trying to learn what is confidential and secret,' he explained.

Even with that reality, continued Soviet/Russian attempts to recruit sources in Britain to gather political, economic and technological secrets were clear. At the time of Duff's review there were around thirty KGB agents active in Britain along with some ten GRU agents.

'If the other side insist on sending in vast numbers of people to spy then it really is unacceptable to allow them to operate freely however puerile their efforts may be. It is also absolutely crucial that you should be secure enough that your signals should be safe.'

With that as background, Duff ordered a major reduction in the counter-subversion efforts of the Service. Already there was little effort expended on trade unionists or members of what in the 1960s and 1970s would have been described as 'left-wing' groups. There were no organizations left that could be considered a threat to the state. However, work continued on watching those groups who could pose either an economic threat or provide support for terrorist groups, such as the Animal Liberation Front. This narrowing of the remit allowed the service to focus more attention on countering terrorism, and Duff ordered a major recruiting drive to hire agent-runners and to recruit agents to counter that threat.

That recruiting drive was accompanied by a more general attempt to bring some new blood into the organization. Demographics and poor management had led the Service to have a serious shortage of high grade people to promote to director level. To improve the management, an additional deputy director-general was appointed to handle personnel and administration. There was ample talent to fill the assistant director slots at the middle management level but no people readily available for promotion from the ranks below. So, efforts were made to find mature recruits in the armed forces and the police, which proved successful. One of the new directors appointed in 1992 to head G Branch, for example, is a former policeman.

MI5 continues with its traditional role of vetting and providing security advice to government officials and departments. But the actual expenditure is small compared with other departments such as the Ministry of Defence ('A grain of salt on a peanut compared to what is spent on security generally,' is how Duff describes it).

To underline the changes, Duff appointed Stella Rimington to head up Directorate G, which is responsible for counter-terrorism. The position was also elevated literally and figuratively to the top table. She became one of four directors invited to Duff's private dining room at MI5's headquarters in Gower Street near King's Cross for a buffet lunch which has become known inside the building as Directors' Buns. To improve the dialogue between departments there is now a meeting every three months with the fifty assistant directors and directors to discuss matters of mutual interest and to generate ideas.

When Duff first arrived, the private lunches were served by an ancient retainer whose heavy smoking prevented him from moving at more than a snail's pace. An equally ancient cook prepared the worst kind of English public school food with duffs and sponges a regular feature on the dessert menu. He was replaced by a cordon bleu cook called Henrietta who produced less school food and a few more quiches. To complete the culinary reform, Duff insisted that the restaurants in Gower Street and Curzon Street be changed to produce food that people wanted to eat, telling friends that 'there is no communication between branches, but to be effective we must have good inter-departmental gossip and therefore there need to be good restaurants where people can talk freely.'

These were largely cosmetic changes. They certainly helped improve morale within the organization, which had begun to suffocate on its own obsession with secrecy. At the same time, the reforms broke through the barriers that had been built up between MI5 personnel and the world outside the confines of Gower Street. These changes were essential if normal, well-adjusted people were to join the service, rather than those who wanted to live, work and play within the very narrow confines of the Service ethos. While the cosmetics made a difference, of more serious interest were the efforts Duff made to have MI5 placed on a legal footing for the first time.

Following the *Spycatcher* débâcle, when former MI5 employee Peter Wright alleged widespread illegal activities by the Security Service, MI5 had been both embarrassed and furious at the bad publicity the case generated. It was felt that public confidence in the intelligence community was being undermined, in part by the repeating of the Wright allegations without any attempt to check them – in part because no such checking mechanism existed. It was also recognized that, without any legal standing, it was difficult for government ministers to defend MI5, which could apparently operate outside the law. In fact, it is difficult to imagine a more bureaucratic organization than the Security Service, far removed from the image created by Wright of a bunch of right-wing 'buggers and burglars'. The almost universal criticism of the Security Service from other security agencies and branches of government is not that they are too aggressive but that they have allowed the most conservative aspects of government bureaucracy to dominate everything they do. All decisions have to be accompanied by endless memos and seem to take forever. Doing nothing is preferred to doing something, and the results frequently fall far short of expectation. To members of SIS, their counterparts in the Security Service are known as the 'Leaden Footed', a clear indictment of one professional group by another.

But the public and political perception was what mattered. So Duff, who favoured public accountability for MI5, began to steer the organization for the first time towards daylight.

When Tony Duff took over at MI5 he inherited Bernard Sheldon as the Legal Advisor. This position is a unique Security Service appointment, where the official is both a lawyer and the organization's conscience, as well as a counsellor to the director-general. Sheldon had endorsed the prosecution of Peter Wright; with hindsight, a bad decision which achieved nothing except to increase sales of the book. Sheldon was felt to be part of an old regime, and when he retired David Bickford, a foreign office lawyer with considerable experience in tackling money laundering around the world, was appointed. Bickford, a congenial but tough collector of Gilbert and Sullivan first edition scores, came from a different generation than his predecessor. In his early forties at the time of his appointment, he had little time for the old restrictions and recognized that changes were vital if MI5 was to survive intact.

There were some serious practical reasons, too, why MI5 had to be legalized. The British government was being taken to the European Court of Human Rights over allegations by the Campaign for Nuclear Disarmament and the National Council for Civil Liberties that MI5 had operated illegally against them. While the case would not be heard for some years, the European court had made clear in past judgements that there must be effective oversight of a security service to protect the rights of an individual. A defeat for the government in court would add yet another embarrassment to MI5's record and would open the door for further suits from other groups who feared they had been targeted.

While Duff wanted the new act legalizing MI5 to allow for visible and effective oversight of the Security Service, the Prime Minister, Margaret Thatcher, was fiercely opposed. She proved a defender of the old guard, reluctantly conceding that some change was needed but resisting any attempt to make the Service more publicly accountable. Throughout the last four years of her leadership, senior civil servants, led by Sir Clive Whitmore, then permanent undersecretary in the Home Office, and senior intelligence officials argued in vain for greater changes. Towards the end, it was recognized that the argument had been lost, and officials simply stopped raising the matter with her.

The compromise was the 1989 Security Service Act, which for the first time placed MI5 on a statutory basis. The three-page bill defined the role of MI5 as 'the protection of national security and, in particular, its protection against threat from espionage, terrorism and sabotage, from the activities of agents of foreign powers and from actions intended to overthrow or undermine parliamentary democracy by political, industrial or violent means. It shall also be the function of the Service to safeguard the economic well-being of the United Kingdom against threats posed by the actions or intentions of persons outside the British Islands.'[3]

The act formalized a previous arrangement under what was called the Maxwell-Fyfe directive, which made the director-general directly responsible to the home secretary with access to the prime minister on demand. To try and deal with the critics who see MI5 as lawless, the act severely restricted their powers, charging the director-general with 'securing that no information is obtained by the Service except so far as is necessary for the proper discharge of its functions or disclosed by it except so far as is necessary for that purpose or for the purpose of preventing or detecting a serious crime; and that the Service does not take any action to further the interests of any political party . . . Information in the possession of the Service is not disclosed for use in determining whether a person should be employed, or continue to be employed, by any person, or in any office or capacity, except in accordance with provisions in that behalf approved by the Secretary of State.'

In an attempt to introduce some form of oversight, the act allowed for the appointment of a commissioner who was given responsibility for controlling the issue of warrants for searching property or the planting of bugs. Such warrants can only be authorized by the home secretary and are issued rarely (around 200 times a year in the past few years). However, the act failed to address the activities of GCHQ which is responsible for most of the bugging carried out by British intelligence. Unlike MI5, which plants single or multiple bugs against specific targets, GCHQ has a vast worldwide sweeping operation which is largely indiscriminate. Its ground stations and satellite systems extract millions of microwave telephone conversations, fax messages and telexes for later analysis. All of this material is collected automatically and brought to the attention of operators if messages or conversations contain key words or phrases. It is possible to refine the system to gather very precise information, but at both ends of the scale there are no warrants or legal process to follow. The government considered drawing GCHQ into the new act but no way could be found legally to define or restrict what the organization does. Instead, a new honour code was issued, which essentially means that GCHQ is not to use any of the information it obtains against British citizens.

The commissioner is required to produce an annual report, which has proved of little value, in part because the reports do little more than give the number of warrants and the barest details of any case investigated. There has been no instance where the commissioner has found evidence of wrongdoing. To the supporters of MI5, this simply demonstrates that MI5 operates within the law, something they have claimed for many years. To the Service's critics, the commissioner was merely an establishment stooge whose report was worth very little.

While the Security Service let it be known that they were happy with the new act, senior officials in MI5 wanted much tougher legislation. They had argued that the commissioner overseeing the working of MI5 should be given broader powers of investigation and that his reports should be made public, provided they did not provide details about sources and methods. Behind this was an underlying concern that public confidence in the working of MI5 was falling away and only a visible, effective and impartial oversight system could begin to counter this. At the same time, there were worries that recruiting, which had remained unaffected by the adverse publicity surrounding the *Spycatcher* affair, would start to fall away. But despite their best arguments, Mrs Thatcher, concerned to maintain as much secrecy as possible, overruled them.

The act also provided for a tribunal of three of five lawyers who would hear complaints from members of the public who believed they had been victims of injustice by the Service. Despite the intense lobbying for some form of oversight, plus repeated allegations by trade unionists and MPs that MI5 routinely breaks the law, the tribunal has had virtually nothing to do since it was established.

The act formalized existing conventions under which the Security Service is essentially apolitical, so information passed to ministers has to be carefully sanitized. There is no spying on members of the Opposition, for example, and no information is handed over that might be of use in a political campaign. Before the act, the custom had grown up that, if something went wrong, it was the director-general who took responsibility and not ministers. This was always a strong argument for having non-governmental supervision as the D–G was charged only with telling ministers 'what they need to know'.

Operations were authorized after a brief was prepared by the MI5 secretariat on the basis of information passed on from the relevant branch in MI5. The brief was then passed to the home office desk officer responsible for the subject area, to the permanent undersecretary, a civil servant, and from there to the home office minister. The brief would outline the purpose of the operation, why the operation cannot be carried out by any other agency, the type of information expected, the kind of operation involved and the risk. Although this was a cumbersome process, it could take as little as half a day.

Across the river, SIS have always provided foreign office ministers with far fuller briefings, in part because the foreign office has always been particularly sensitive to incidents that might have international ramifications. But neither organization ever had to explain itself to any form of visible oversight structure as is now proposed. One of the extraordinary ironies of these changes is that SIS has been playing a key role in helping intelligence organizations in countries like Hungary, formerly part of the communist bloc, to set up new intelligence services with effective oversight.

While these changes were unfolding, Duff began to open lines to the media, a group of people who for years had been regarded as an enemy. A handful of senior journalists were invited to private lunches at Gower Street where they met with the directors and talked about general issues of the day. For these visitors, MI5 was a peculiar place. All the hosts appeared intelligent, they were both interested and interesting, with little of the stuffiness often associated with government civil servants. The conversation was polite but reserved. To the guests, it often appeared as if the hosts knew little about the world outside their own. To the directors, the journalists appeared irreverent, informal and, on the whole, remarkably ill-informed about the kind of work MI5 does.

The point of contact for future meetings was David Bickford, the legal advisor, who proved a good foil for the journalists. He is excellent company, gives very little away and is a good listener for all the journalists who are flattered at having someone in intelligence listen to their views. He moved swiftly to open lines to the national media and soon obtained contacts in major news outlets where he has become adept at dealing with journalists who try to publish something damaging to the Service, by producing a voice of anguish as he explains earnestly that, 'We simply don't do that sort of thing,' or, 'Haven't people read the act? That would be illegal and we do not break the law.'

Bickford has been an effective ambassador for the Service because he genuinely does believe in the rule of law and it is difficult to imagine him agreeing to anything that would involve illegal activities. That said, without visible and effective oversight – and a high court judge is not that – whatever his protestations, the Security Service would continue to be accused of being buggers and burglars.

But these meetings with the media did have significant benefits. For the first time, journalists were able to ask questions about the organization, and the Security Service had a way of drip-feeding positive stories to the media. The result was mostly positive. For example, Patrick Walker, who was appointed Duff's successor in 1988, hosted a lunch in Gower Street for Andreas Whittam-Smith, the editor of the *Independent*, and Sarah Helm, the paper's home affairs correspondent, in the first week of September 1989. The result was an article published in the paper on September 5 headlined 'MI5 may step out of the shadows: Recruitment crisis pushes Security Service towards following CIA example of openness'. The article said that, 'according to highly authoritative sources', the Security Service was considering 'openly advertizing for intelligence officers and regularly using head-hunting firms to seek out high-class recruits; setting up a publicly accessible secure telephone line for use by informants wishing to contact the Service; allowing the director-general to become a publicly known figure to comment on general issues relating to the service, and allowing other MI5 personnel not directly involved in operations – such as lawyers – to be named and contactable by the outside world; establishing more open channels with the press.'

The article went on to say that senior officials in the Security Service had decided that a more open policy was essential, that they needed to move with the times to reflect a changed public attitude to the work of the intelligence community.

This article convincingly got across that the Service was modernizing, that changes were happening and that the nature of the business was moving away from their previous focus on subversion (enemies of the state) to new targets (terrorists and drug barons). In other words, this was exactly the kind of positive public relations the proponents of change had hoped for.

In the classic British way of doing things, these covert relationships allowed MI5 considerable secret influence and placed an onus on favoured journalists both to check their stories and warn the Service of any potential bad publicity. For some journalists who had made a healthy living printing lies about the intelligence world, these changes were very unwelcome. Within a few years, their stories dried up or were discredited, with the result that the intelligence community at last began to be treated in a similar fashion to any other branch of government.

Even so, there remained a number of critics within government generally and the intelligence services in particular who were still nervous of the new openness. There was a concern that once the floodgates of information were opened, it would be impossible to avoid compromising sources and methods, the twin pillars of successful intelligence work. There was the additional worry that in the past all senior members of British intelligence were guaranteed complete anonymity and took no more security precautions against terrorist attack than ordinary members of the public. Until recently, the head of MI5 drove a plain Ford Granada, with no armour plating and an unarmed chauffeur too old and unfit to deter an attacker. By contrast, the head of the FBI always travels with an armed security detail.

Duff had instituted one reorganization of the Service, but by the time Patrick Walker became head of MI5 the world had moved on dramatically with the collapse of the Soviet Union and a complete change in the structure of what was evolving into the Russian intelligence service. As an experienced Whitehall hand, Walker knew that it would not be enough to mouth the usual platitudes about the traditional threats. To keep the service intact and to retain its budget, Walker believed that a new justification for its existence and a new examination of its future roles were necessary, and in 1989 Walker established the Policy Review Group.

'We went back to the basic definitions,' explained one of those involved. 'What is national security? What is economic well-being? We looked at everything and tried to established a coherent rationale for what we do.'[4]

The result was another reorganization, which produced five different priorities: counter-espionage, counter-terrorism, proliferation and technology transfer, protective security of people and buildings, and subversion, which now accounted for 20% less of MI5's budget than five years earlier. Today, the Security divides its resources like this: Irish and other domestic terrorism 44%, international terrorism 26%, subversion 5% and counter-espionage and counter-proliferation 25%. Most active intelligence gathering is carried out by the 340-strong General Intelligence group (GI).[5]

Of all the tasks announced with a fanfare in July 1992, only proliferation is not a serious part of the Security Service's effort. They do pay some attention to the problem but devote few resources to it. The decision was taken to include it as part of the broad task because after the failures in Iraq, proliferation has become a high profile issue which gains the attention of government ministers. Calculating as ever, the Service wanted to make sure there were no chinks in their armour when ministers came to scrutinizing their budget in the annual pay round later that year.

Within that published structure, there is also a greater degree of cooperation with SIS, the organization that is always portrayed as their traditional rivals in British intelligence. In fact, MI5 has established joint sections to cover both the Middle East and the Soviet Union. In addition, there is a shared research and development department so that for each piece of offensive equipment designed by the scientists for MI6, a defensive system is made at the same time for MI5. This kind of sharing is part of a closeness that has evolved in recent years, driven in part by budget constraints and in part by a gradual erosion of the social barriers between the two groups (MI6 equalled Eton and Oxford, MI5 equalled minor public school or even state school and minor or even no university; MI6 were swashbuckling adventurers while MI5 were plodding bureaucrats).

A year after Patrick Walker was appointed head of MI5, Colin McColl, a fifty-six-year-old veteran of service in Bangkok, Laos, Warsaw and Geneva, replaced Christopher Curwen as director-general of SIS. McColl was an insider who had made the grade at the traditional age for the elevation to chief (he is not known as C within SIS). SIS, which is responsible for gathering intelligence abroad, had not been affected by any of the scandals that had plagued MI5 in the 1970s and 1980s, and

McColl inherited a 2,000-strong staff with high morale and a mission that had spent the largest single proportion (37%) of its time and money (an annual budget of £150 million in 1993 money) on targeting the Soviet threat. But when McColl took over his tenth floor office at Century House, with its panoramic view of London from the south bank of the Thames by Westminster Bridge, he faced a rapidly changing world.

One of his first acts was to order a thorough review of SIS work, in part to look to the future and in part to justify his budget into the next decade. Not surprisingly, he, like his counterparts in MI5, was able to produce enough reasons for continued work, but there was still the need for radical surgery. Stations in Africa, the Far East and Central and South America were closed. Although it is still a source of some pride within SIS that it retains stations on every continent, today the buzz word in the organization is 'capacity' not 'presence'. SIS now wants to be able to insert people into any country at short notice rather than retain expensive assets on the ground permanently who might not be used properly.

Today, the organization spends 15% of its resources on the former Soviet Union (compared with 37% at the height of the Cold War), 15% on the Middle East, including some aspects of proliferation, 5% on China and Hong Kong, 4% on Argentina, 10% on counter-terrorism, 10% on proliferation generally, 10% on the former Yugoslavia, 5% on Southern Africa, 2% on Japan, 5% on counter-narcotics and 5% on money laundering. The balance is made up of resources that can be moved at any one time to deal with particular crises.

In theory this system should remain sufficiently flexible so that an organization that matured with an understanding of running long-term penetration agents in the Soviet bloc can now react swiftly to a crisis anywhere in the world. The first test of the new structure occurred in Yugoslavia where civil war broke out in 1991 after the country divided into three separate countries, Bosnia, Croatia and Serbia. In January 1991, SIS was running a few Yugoslav sources, all of them federal officials, who had no knowledge of the new countries that emerged from the break up of their country and could provide no information to their handlers. At the same time, the policy makers wanted information on the different factions that were emerging, particularly Serbia which was considered a major threat to the stability of the region.

Within eighteen months, SIS managed to recruit a number of sources at a high level in the military and political structure of all three protagonists in the former Yugoslavia. These sources fed back to London a steady stream of data which in turn was passed to the British government, to the UN peace negotiators and to the Americans.

British HUMINT, when combined with American SIGINT and ELINT, produced a very detailed intelligence picture which included not just the military plans and capabilities of the different factions but also early warning of political intentions. Even so, the conflict proved intractable and politicians were unable to agree a way forward. This was perhaps the first example of the real limitations of intelligence in the post-Cold War era.

Serbia was a traditional challenge: find and run the sources who can produce accurate and timely intelligence. A larger problem emerged with the identification of the new threats and the decision to tackle such areas as drugs and money laundering. Instead of being able simply to produce information which diguised sources and methods, both MI5 and MI6 had to consider the endgame. In the war against the Soviets, there was a common goal of preventing war, and if that failed ensuring the allies had enough intelligence to win. Now the challenge is not just to gather intelligence but to ensure that that intelligence contributes to an evidential chain that results in the successful prosecution of an arms dealer or a drug smuggler. The questions that have yet to be resolved within the intelligence community include: how much information is supplied? what is said about sources and methods? to whom is the information released and what action is taken upon it? what steps should be taken to ensure that sources and methods are not compromised while, at the same time, a prosecution is successful? Just how these questions will be answered has not been decided but it is already clear that more intelligence agents will be forced to give evidence in court and that, for the first time, the information they gather will be subject to detailed scrutiny by outsiders.

Until McColl's arrival it had been assumed that SIS, which had remained outside the 1989 Security Service Act, would continue to operate without any legal remit. It had been argued internally (not least by Mrs Thatcher) that as SIS operated abroad, there was no need for legal sanctions. But many of those who were now rising stars in SIS came from a background where the arguments for such obsessive secrecy appeared increasingly unreal. In SIS, the compulsory retirement age is fifty five, so the successful spies tend to get promoted to very senior positions in their mid-forties; the people at senior levels in SIS in 1990, therefore, were largely children of the 1960s. This generation had not been so absorbed by the Soviet threat that they were unable to cope with the changes demanded by a post-Cold War era. This group of young Turks lobbied hard for another act to legalize SIS and to allow for more visible oversight of the intelligence services.

During 1990 and 1991, after John Major became prime minister, the nature of another Security Service Act was discussed in Whitehall in an atmosphere where the concept of open government had become a platform of policy. SIS favoured a system which would allow a small group of members of both Houses of Parliament to have complete access to intelligence documents. They would be able to review cases and, with the aid of a professional staff, hear complaints and produce judgements. This view was supported by the Security Service. The appointment of Stella Rimington as director-general in December 1991 was for the first time, made public and she issued a statement to Reuters saying that, 'The Security Service has performed a vital task in the national interest since the early part of this century. Despite the changes which have taken place in the world in recent years, the service continues to have a difficult and essential job to do.'[6]

It was a radical change of fortune for Mrs Rimington, who in the 1970s was so convinced that she had no future in the male-dominated upper echelons of MI5 that she applied to be head of Roedean, the girls' public school. There was no doubting her qualifications as a spymaster: those in the Service talk of her creative mind, good analytical brain and her fine record combating terrorism in Northern Ireland. But, despite being portrayed as an enthusiast for the new era, she had some reservations about the drive towards more openness for the Service. As with many others in MI5, the obsession with sources and methods which had coloured all her work over the previous twenty-two years made her wary of any oversight or publicity. Once she was in place, contacts with journalists continued but the substance of what was discussed diminished on her instructions.

But she also recognized that the Security Service was now fighting its battles over very different ground. She needed to be able to meet the other Whitehall mandarins on equal terms, on occasion taking her case to the public, but always making sure that it was her voice that was heard and not some civil servant acting as intermediary. The role of the Security Service was changing from being a simple information gatherer according to policy set by others, to being an actual policy maker. She believes this is essential if the Service is to retain its influence and credibility. For that reason she decided that she would become more of a public figure than any of her predecessors, in the expectation that this would improve her influence and in the hope it would undermine the demands that the Service become more open at lower levels.

The result of this change of policy was that on July 16, 1993, Mrs Rimington came out officially for the first time at an unprecedented press conference where she also passed out a thirty-six-page booklet explaining the origins and work of the Security Service. For the first time, too, she was allowed to be photographed. The press conference was a major coup for the organization and was front-page news across the country. At a stroke, she had managed to dispel some of the more fanciful myths surrounding the Service, portray herself as a champion of a new openness and set down the markers for the rest of Whitehall that MI5 was ready to fight its corner.[7]

Despite this new openness, in private she accepted the idea of a new Security Service Act which in particular broadened oversight. But she was concerned that oversight should not lead to the leaking of operational information. This was not an attempt to disguise wrongdoing, but a concern for sources and methods. (Her prejudices about security were confirmed on March 7, 1993, when *The Sunday Times* published a front-page story detailing how easy it was to obtain the plans for Mrs Rimington's house, the details of her credit card purchases which showed where she shopped and at what time each week, as well as how poorly defended her London home was. Mrs Rimington was outraged by the article, which she considered irresponsible. She moved house the day the article appeared, and her security has increased dramatically. Exactly the same thing had happened to Sir Colin McColl two years earlier when the *Sunday Express* published a photograph of his house in the Cotswolds, where he and his family had lived for many years. He, too, was forced to move immediately.)

Stella Rimington also worried that the mystique of the intelligence community would suffer and that members of the Service, who currently live a life of comfortable anonymity, would be exposed to the public gaze. Experience in the United States, which has the most open society in the world, does not support this view. Those members of the intelligence community who work in operations, gathering intelligence in the field, remain well protected, despite a very intrusive oversight system. It is rare for an agent to be exposed and most work their entire careers under cover. There is no reason to suppose that a more open system in Britain would work any differently.

To many of the intelligence community's British critics, oversight is seen as a panacea. But, while oversight does provide some windows into the workings of intelligence, it does not cure all ills, and it is also dependent on how seriously the overseers take their work. Initially, the prospect of being on the oversight committee was seen by Congressmen as a prestigious post and every member of the House and Senate would faithfully turn up to the different hearings. But a generation has passed since oversight was first introduced, and complacency has set in.

In 1992, the American intelligence community met more than 4,000 times with members and staff of Congress and provided over 50,000 documents.[8] This massive volume of information and time is a measure of the cost of an oversight system. At the same time, the interest of law makers in the substance of intelligence appears to have declined. This is how Bob Gates describes the current situation:

We had a single budget hearing for fiscal year 1993 in the Senate Intelligence Committee last spring. The heads of all the intelligence agencies were present. Of the fifteen members of the committee, the chairman and a handful of members, perhaps three or four, showed up. A half hour or so into the hearing, it was recessed for a vote, and when the hearing resumed, the chairman and only two or three members returned. All but the chairman were gone within twenty minutes. The result is that for the single most important hearing of the year, on the budget of the entire intelligence community at a time of great change, only Chairman Boren was present throughout.

By the same token, the next day there was a hearing on covert actions. Twelve out of fifteen Senators attended and stayed throughout; and that was for a covert program that involves but a fraction of one per cent of the intelligence budget and is just one tenth the size of the program two years ago, and where there are virtually no controversial activities under way.

Budget hearings on the House side were often attended only by the chairman and the ranking minority member and a very small number of others technically dropping in for a few minutes at a time. I know that the members can read the record of the hearings, but how many really do? The result is that enormous responsibility then falls to the staff of the committee. They are neither elected nor confirmed by anyone, and yet they acquire enormous influence on the structuring of issues as well as the attitudes and votes of members.[9]

Initially, the new legal process and oversight will bring some disloca-
tion to Service life, not least because those MPs involved will find their
opportunity to peer into the secret world so interesting they will want to
talk about it. Early evidence of this was provided on January 18, 1993,
when six MPs, all members of the Home Affairs Select Committee, set
off from the House of Commons for lunch with Stella Rimington. The
lunch had been agreed to discuss new legislation for the intelligence
community. It was the first time Mrs Rimington had hosted such an
affair. The venue was kept secret by MI5, but a number of MPs passed
on the details to journalists. At the appointed time, two MI5 Ford
Granadas picked the MPs up in Westminster for the twenty minute drive
to Gower Street. In scenes reminiscent of a Charlie Chaplin film, the
MI5 drivers were followed by cars filled with photographers and reporters until they turned into the underground garage beneath MI5 headquarters. The reporters then set about trying to interview a number of
MI5 security men and women who were patrolling the outside of the
building. The occasion was a farce, but in fact, nothing leaked from the
lunch.[10]

But the climate in government was for change. Whatever reservations
anyone in MI5 may have had, the drafting of the new bill which would
cover all branches of intelligence including GCHQ was completed in the
summer of 1992 for debate in parliament that October. However,
Conservative opposition to the Maastricht Treaty on European Union
meant that all legislation was delayed, and the bill will not now become
law until late 1993 or early 1994.

Colin McColl understood the value of developing more open relations
with the media, and began to invite editors to lunch in his office at
Century House. The first lunch took place in the summer of 1992. Over
the next year, McColl entertained every editor of a national newspaper
and most of the senior editors from the BBC and ITV. The single
exception was Kelvin Mackenzie, editor of the *Sun*. His office was
telephoned by McColl's personal assistant and an invitation to lunch
extended. The secretary replied that Mackenzie does not lunch. The SIS
man, slightly taken aback, underlined the invitation by stressing that
McColl was the head of MI6. The secretary conferred briefly with
Mackenzie and simply repeated that Mackenzie did not have lunch
outside the office. This was the first and last time such an invitation was
turned down.

SIS were particularly concerned that, with the role of intelligence under
attack everywhere and a widespread assumption that the intelligence

community could take substantial budget cuts, McColl's organization had no mechanism for getting its arguments for survival across to the public and the politicians. At each of the lunches with senior editors, McColl would go over the reasons why SIS was still needed and why their budgets needed to be supported, even in the difficult economic climate. Unable to give formal interviews, McColl had to resort to extraordinary measures to try to spread his message to a wider audience. In January 1992, Bob Gates was persuaded to give an interview to *The Sunday Times*, the first time ever a serving director of Central Intelligence had spoken to a foreign newspaper. He duly passed on what SIS wanted the British people to hear – that intelligence was needed now more than ever in the uncertain world that had emerged after the Cold War.[11]

McColl was supposed to retire in October 1992 and pass on the reins to one of his deputies in an orderly progression. But the reviews he had been conducting over the past three years had convinced him that firmer, more radical action was necessary if SIS was to survive and prosper. He worried that a 'business as usual' approach would leave in place people who had grown up in the Cold War. For them, the adjustment to new priorities was proving difficult as was the new regime of tight budgets and new commitments. McColl decided on radical surgery. In May 1992, he proposed a palace revolution to ministers which was agreed in July. In what became known as the Christmas Massacre, the fortunate and the victims were told of their fate a month before the changes took effect in January 1993. All the old directors were given early retirement and a new generation brought in. At a stroke, men in their forties were suddenly in power at SIS, with one of them certain to take over when McColl finally retired in 1994.

Today, SIS has the youngest senior management of any intelligence organization in the world. In theory that should make SIS more capable of dealing with a changed environment and more flexible to cope with the challenges of the future. But it remains to be seen if the young Turks will institute the necessary reforms.

Another reason why MI5 and MI6 had to be brought into the open was because both organizations were planning to move to new, highly visible headquarters in London. For the first time since its founding in the Second World War, MI5 would be located in one building at Thames House, an ugly and featureless gray stone building near the Ministry of Defence in Whitehall.

Until the move, the Security Service occupied nine buildings in central London with different branches scattered illogically around the city. It was a bizarre and extraordinarily inefficient method of operating, with some officials spending much of their day shuttling from one building to the next (one director had to visit three buildings to see all his staff). For example, B and K directorates, responsible for personnel and the secretariat respectively, were in Curzon Street off Piccadilly, while G Branch, responsible for counter-terrorism, was in Gower Street. The move to Thames House would consolidate the operation in one building, with only a few outstations for particularly sensitive meetings and operations remaining. The idea for a move was first proposed in the late 1970s but the cost of around £250 million was considered too expensive, even though there would have been considerable operating savings over the longer term. There was also some internal opposition to a move. The obsessive secrecy that is almost a cult inside the Security Service led some to argue that a visible and known headquarters would help the organization lose its prized anonymity as well as allowing people to poke fun at those working there. There might even be demonstrations outside or graffiti scrawled on the walls. These arguments, addressed and dismissed by every other government department including the Ministry of Defence and the Northern Ireland Office, were more a reflection of the insular attitude of many of those working in MI5 than real security concerns. After all, the CIA has been in the telephone book and its headquarters well signposted outside Washington DC for many years. Even their secret training ground at Camp Peary near Williamsburg is signed and easily visible from the road.

The second problem for the Service was to find a suitable building, within walking distance of Whitehall and near shops and other facilities. Finally Thames House, an old Ministry of Energy building, became available and ministers were persuaded to put up the money. Until her elevation to director-general, Stella Rimington was in charge of what became the largest office refurbishment in Europe, running a team of nine people to ensure total site security. The move has been an opportunity to upgrade the computer systems used by MI5, and Rimington has told friends there is enough wiring in the building to run 'from Trafalgar Square to Red Square'. In December 1993, the building was handed over by Mowlem, the main contractors, to MI5 for the final batch of secure systems to be installed in time for complete occupation at the end of 1994.

In 1994, SIS will move from Century House in Westminster Bridge Road. Their old headquarters, a twenty-storey skyscraper constructed in the 1950s and now falling apart, is universally hated by all who work there. With a move anticipated for years, little money has been spent on maintenance with the result that doors don't shut, paint is peeling and the central heating works intermittently. The building is known within SIS as Gloom Hall.

From such miserable surroundings, SIS is moving to the most magnificent spying HQ in the world. Designed by controversial post-modern architect Terry Farrell, the building is on the south side of the Thames over Vauxhall Bridge. Known as Vauxhall Cross, it rises in four tiers from the riverside, presenting a sheer wall to the traffic artery behind. From the river side, the building is clad in honey-coloured concrete panels with cascades of sea-green floors in the lower depths, easily visible from the river and the northern bank of the Thames. Several large atria – the big open conservatories to be found in the middle of most new office blocks – offer staff the chance to overlook each other. But Farrell, more than most contemporary architects, likes to design little nooks and crannies into his buildings as well as big standard office floors. He eventually incorporated 12,000 square metres of glass and aluminium to cover the six perimeter cores and the atria inside the building. The first stage of the development included a sports hall, computer rooms, library, restaurant, covered parking and archive stores.

The fifth floor even has a line of yew trees facing the river which were grown in Italy and acclimatized in Scotland before being shipped to London. Four tons of earth were used to plant them in containers with water, feeding and drainage systems built in. At ground level, plane trees, box hedges, wisteria and lavender have been planted with a gazebo, fountains and a kiosk designed to humanize the view from the river.

The more complex and secure offices were fitted out by SIS in consultation with the government's Property Services Agency. Air-conditioning vents and sprinkler systems were removed and replaced with secure ducts. Walls were made more resistant to bomb damage and some windows and verandahs have been sealed. The total cost of the move will be around £230 million, a cost that has infuriated some Foreign Office officials who have to carry the SIS budget on their books. In the 1993 public expenditure round, where the government sought large cuts from every department, the spending on what some Foreign Office civil servants see as an exceptionally lavish headquarters so annoyed them that the cost of the building was leaked to MPs and journalists. It was pointed out that the £45 million set aside for fitting out the building in 1993–4 was almost as much as Britain planned to spend on overseas emergency aid and refugee relief aid in the same period.[12]

The leaks infuriated SIS who embarked on their own burst of counter-leaking, pointing out what good value for money the building represents and how wise an investment in the nation's future security it is. This silly row has had the effect of forcing both SIS and the Foreign Office to focus on the ancient convention of burying the SIS budget within the budgets of the Foreign Office and the Ministry of Defence (the Security Service budget is hidden by the Home Office and the Department of Environment). To everyone's relief, that practice will now stop and, beginning in 1994, the budgets for all the intelligence services will be published.

Today, the 1,800 SIS employees basically work on two floors inside the building, a transformation from Gloom Hall, which was a rabbit warren with departments split between floors and a great deal of difficulty communicating between departments. Even with the obvious security restrictions of 'need to know', Vauxhall Cross allows for open plan offices and a culture change that reflects the new management style.

MI6 indirectly has Michael Heseltine to thank for its new riverside premises. The site, behind which is one of the bleakest and most depressing traffic interchanges in London, had been derelict for twenty years when it was earmarked in the 1970s for the notorious 'green giant' office tower, halted by public outrage. In 1982 Heseltine, then Environment Secretary for the first time, held an architectural competition for buildings on the site. Farrell was in the top three but was rejected by the developer, which promptly went bankrupt. In 1987 another developer, Regalian, bought the site and signed up Farrell to build a complex of riverside apartments and shops. Farrell revamped his earlier designs. Then came the housing slump and Regalian asked Farrell to make it offices instead. He went back to the drawing board. Then, in February 1989, the Government offered to buy the whole lot from Regalian for £130 million, before a brick had been laid, and Farrell submitted yet another design.

SIS retain a small outstation in south London which is used by some of their clandestine operators. They have also held on to the Fort, their training establishment near Portsmouth on the south coast of England. In addition, they share a research and development facility in London with the Security Service. There, government scientists develop all the tools of clandestine warfare. By bringing both Services under one roof, the government ensures that for every new scientific breakthrough there is also a counter so that both MI5 and MI6 can, in theory, remain on the cutting edge of espionage and counter-espionage techniques.

In the rivalry that exists between the Security Service and SIS, there is some satisfaction within MI6 that they have such an elegant and visionary office building while MI5 are confined to drab and unimaginative new headquarters. To some both inside and outside the intelligence world, the new buildings are an accurate reflection of the men and women who work in them.

The new relations with the media, legislation, more public headquarters and a new generation of senior officials should do a great deal to help reestablish the intelligence community as both credible and trustworthy. But there remains a strong residual distrust between the public and the politicians on the one hand and the intelligence community on the other that will take more than just shadowy deals with the media and well-meaning legislation to overcome. Two recent illustrations demonstrate how wide the gulf remains.

In April 1993, Alan Clark, the former Tory minister of trade and minister of state at the Ministry of Defence published his memoirs. This autobiography, one of the frankest of political memoirs, detailed a meeting Clark had with Robert Armstrong, the secretary of the cabinet, to discuss his recent appointment as a junior minister at the Department of Employment. Armstrong produced two files, one red, the other orange, and pointed out that Clark had had contact with the right-wing National Front (which Clark denied). He added that matters of 'personal conduct' (numerous affairs) might leave him open to blackmail.

'I thought about it for a little while,' Clark wrote. 'They *must* have been bugging my phone. There was no other explanation. And for ages.'[13]

That a senior government minister with top secret clearance should seriously believe that the Security Service has the time or the authority to listen to his telephone calls almost beggars belief. But the apparent revelation caused a sensation and produced an exchange between the home secretary and Stella Rimington when the head of MI5 dismissed the allegations. In fact, Clark had been subjected to the normal vetting process and as a noted philanderer and gossip it had not been difficult for the vetters to gather details about his private life, a standard procedure in such cases. Normally private philandering is of little concern to MI5 but in Clark's case there was one incident where he had had an affair with a mother and her daughter. This was considered potential blackmail material and so became part of his file.

Of more substance were the two conversations between members of the royal family that were recorded and then released to the press. The first, revealed in August 1992, was a conversation between James Gilbey and the Princess of Wales where he referred to her by the nickname Squidgy. This tape gave the clear impression that the two were lovers. Cyril Reenan, a retired bank manager, claimed to have recorded the conversation on his ham radio before passing it on to a tabloid newspaper.

The second tape recorded a conversation between Prince Charles and Camilla Parker-Bowles, a friend of the royal family. It was clear from that tape that Charles and the woman were lovers. Both tapes had allegedly been recorded around the end of 1989 or the beginning of 1990, at a time when Charles and Diana were supposed to be a happily married couple.

A third series of allegations were made by James Whitaker, the royal correspondent of the *Daily Mirror*, in his book *Diana v Charles* which was published in May 1993. He claimed to have tapes of other conversations between Charles and Diana and that 'hundreds of hours of transcripts' were available.

'The reality is that conversations of the Prince of Wales, the Duke of York and their separated wives – as well as other key royals – have been closely monitored for some years,' Whitaker wrote. 'MI5, which is split up into small cells called IGUs (intelligence gathering units), has a specific group that concentrates on monitoring the royal family. Its existence was confirmed by former MI6 officer James Rusbridger in 1993, and other sources suggest that it is made up of six men who mount a round-the-clock surveillance of calls passing through all royal switchboards.'[14]

The Whitaker tape turned out to have been faked by a well-known British hoaxer. But it should have been clear that Whitaker appeared to have little knowledge of his subject. First, no one believes that James Rusbridger, who has claimed knowledge of British intelligence for many years to gullible journalists, has ever been a member of MI6 or any other part of British intelligence. That being so, he would have no access to any inside knowledge about the current, or even recent past workings of the intelligence community. Second, to carry out round-the-clock surveillance on the royal family would require far more than six men. In fact, it would require more resources than MI5 have available for all that kind of surveillance.

There is no routine surveillance of the royal family. There is no special unit that has been set up for that purpose and none could be established without a warrant from the home secretary. It would be a brave home secretary indeed who authorized such a warrant and it would be a foolhardy politician who believed that such a matter could remain secret for long.

Of more serious concern was the source of the two other tapes, both of which appeared genuine. There was widespread speculation in the press that both tapes originated with the Security Service or with GCHQ, with some newspapers speculating that their leaking was part of a complicated plot to undermine the monarchy which was considered too liberal for the conservative diehards in the intelligence services. The Prime Minister questioned both Patrick Walker and Stella Rimington about the matter and was satisfied that MI5 was not involved.

However, the Queen requested that MI5 conduct an investigation to discover the source of the leaks which had embarrassed the Palace and undermined the monarchy. The investigation revealed that the first tape, allegedly recorded by the bank manager, was genuine in that it was indeed Diana speaking to James Gilbey. But it had been edited using very sophisticated equipment and then rebroadcast a number of times, clearly in the expectation that someone, somewhere, would eventually pick up the recording.

When the story surfaced, different versions of the same recording were circulating among news organizations. MI5 believed that whoever had done the original recording used the bank manager as cover and then distributed other versions of the same conversation in the hope that the minor differences would not be noticed.

The second tape of the conversation between Charles and Camilla Parker-Bowles was also genuine, although that, too, had been heavily edited. The Diana-Gilbey conversation had taken place with Diana using a mobile phone. While one end of such a conversation can be easily intercepted, recording both sides is more difficult. The Charles-Camilla call had also been taken over a mobile phone, and MI5 decided that it was likely the same person had intercepted the different calls.

This conclusion, which was hardly startling, led them no closer to the identity of the person who had carried out the tap and the editing. The idea that an amateur would have had the equipment, which is not available in Britain, to carry out the bugging was considered unlikely. Also, the investigation could find no hard evidence that any individual had received money for the recordings. If the motive was not financial, then it would have to be political, and MI5 turned towards GCHQ for their answers.

The Thatcher government had banned all trade union activity at GCHQ, and the recordings had been made shortly after that affair, which had provoked great bitterness inside the communications centre. The equipment in GCHQ is perfectly capable of routinely picking up mobile telephone conversations, editing and rebroadcasting them. Indeed, all mobile telephone calls in the UK are routinely plucked out of the air by GCHQ with some numbers specifically being targeted for monitoring at the request of the police or intelligence services. The MI5 investigation was inconclusive. Suspicion fell on a disgruntled GCHQ employee but there was not enough evidence for a prosecution.

As a result of the inquiry, the royal family have been advised that in future they should not use mobile telephones for sensitive calls.

The 'Squidgygate' and 'Camillagate' tapes were interesting in part because of their dramatic content and in part because of the assumption, which was widely accepted, that the whole affair was part of some dark plot, probably organized by the 'buggers and burglars' at MI5. The allegations infuriated MI5, who were powerless to deny even the most fanciful conspiracy theories as they still have no public voice. To the reformers inside the intelligence services, that is the most powerful argument for the changes that have taken place in the past three years.

CHAPTER EIGHT

SAME OLD STUFF

The nondescript obituary in *Red Star*, the Russian army newspaper, might have gone unnoticed by most readers, had it not been placed next to the popular chess puzzle on page four of the July 1992 issue. It was a different story in the West – the five short paragraphs sent a shiver down the collective spine of Western intelligence. The obituary paid glowing tribute to the work of Mikhail Yevhenyevich Orlov, 32, a major in the KGB who had died suddenly. He had enjoyed 'a short but brilliant life which was totally dedicated to the struggle of removing the threat of nuclear war hanging over mankind. Over a long period, he performed special missions and made a major contribution to ensure the state security of the Soviet Union.'

The Communist Party newspaper, *Pravda*, followed this up with a fulsome obituary which identified Orlov as Souther, an American defector, and claimed that he had access to 'the most valuable documents [and had] disclosed the plans for the use of the US Navy in a nuclear war against the Soviet Union and other socialist countries'.

'Souther did everything to help the forces of peace,' *Pravda* said. 'He occupies a place in that line of KGB intelligence agents to which such outstanding soldiers of the "invisible front" as Kim Philby and George Blake belonged.'

This was followed by the appearance at an extraordinary press conference of Vladimir Kryuchkov, the head of the KGB, who came to add his voice to the chorus. He confirmed the identity of the dead man, who had a 'very sensitive personality'. He claimed to have met him on several occasions and considered his suicide 'a real tragedy . . . and a personal loss'.[1]

Not since the death of Kim Philby, an acknowledged master spy, in

May 1988 had such a fulsome tribute appeared to a Russian agent. What worried Western intelligence about this identification of Orlov as Glenn Michael Souther, an American sailor who had defected to the Soviet Union in 1986, was that he had been dismissed previously as a low-grade agent. His only previous appearance since his defection had been on Soviet television where he claimed to have evidence that America had specifically targeted the French embassy in Tripoli during the 1986 bombing raid. That allegation was untrue and a weak attempt to sow divisions between the French and Americans.

The obituary and his stated rank in the KGB established Souther as a much more significant figure, perhaps even an 'illegal', who had been planted in America as a child, with a much wider brief to betray the West. Immediately the news came over the wires, the damage assessment teams in the FBI, the CIA and the US Navy dusted off their files to begin again the exhaustive examination of Souther's past that had earlier been abandoned after it had revealed little of significance.

Would the investigation reveal the Russian James Bond everyone at first feared, or a sad, lonely man and a largely unsuccessful spy who committed suicide in a Moscow flat?

The middle-class parents of Glenn Michael Souther proudly paid for an advertisement announcing his birth in the *Times* of Hammond, Indiana, a Chicago suburb, on January 30, 1957. According to the school records of Munster, Indiana, Souther enrolled in kindergarten in 1962 and remained in the school system until 1974. Aside from two years in the athletics team, he had an unremarkable school career. But, like many students of his age, he did fall in love with a fellow student, who shared his interest in God, Jimi Hendrix and the pop group Chicago.

Amy Rodenburg, a graduate of the Guildhall School of Music in London, remembers Souther as her 'first love'.

'You don't forget the first person you ever love. He was a very ordinary, sweet boy. I was fourteen, he was fifteen. The only thing that could be said against him was that he was very headstrong,' she said. 'I suppose you could say we were both Jesus freaks. We met in a coffee shop, and would go to meetings together and pray. He always seemed totally sincere in his beliefs.'

Souther left Amy and Munster High School behind when his family moved to Maine on the east coast in 1975. He graduated from Greely High School the same year, and immediately joined the navy. Official navy records show that after basic training at a base near Chicago, he attended a photography course in Florida and then, from July 1976 to

April 1979, was assigned to the *USS Nimitz*, an aircraft carrier based at the headquarters of the US Atlantic Fleet in Norfolk, Virginia. After returning to photography school for three months Souther was transferred to Gaeta, Italy, where he served with the Sixth Fleet until 1982.

He was then transferred back to the naval air base at Patuxent River, Maryland, where, friends say, he was involved in interpreting satellite photographs. In December 1982, Souther left the navy with the rank of petty officer first class, and enrolled as a Russian language student at Old Dominion University in Norfolk, Virginia. He proved an able student, winning a prize and getting a degree in 1986. Until his defection later that year, he was a member of the Norfolk Naval Reserve Unit, where he had access to satellite photographs, which he is believed to have passed on to the KGB.

Precisely when Souther became a spy is not known, but two theories exist. The first is that he was recruited in Italy. While there his Italian wife denounced him as a spy, but naval investigators thought she was drunk at the time. She could provide no evidence, and Souther's friends said she was simply being spiteful. The investigation was dropped.

Friends and teachers who knew Souther at university have another theory. John Fahey, Souther's Russian language teacher, said he was a 'wild kind of guy' who seemed to have an uncontrollable urge to make obscene remarks to women. At restaurants, Souther used to crawl around on all fours barking like a dog and biting the legs of female diners and waitresses. On April 2, 1984, Souther's strange behaviour landed him in court after he attacked a woman student, wrestled her to the ground and bit her on the neck. He was convicted of sexual battery, which was reduced to disorderly conduct, and fined $100.

The conviction was sufficient to stop Souther being accepted as a naval officer, or as an investigator with the immigration service. These rejections soured Souther, who may have turned against America and then sold out to Russia. What is certain is that by the middle of 1986, Souther had raised the suspicions of the FBI. Investigators had interviewed him once, but could find no hard evidence. Clearly spooked, he bought a one-way ticket to Rome and disappeared, reappearing two years later at a press conference in Moscow to denounce the United States and claim he was being persecuted by the FBI.

Once in Moscow, Souther was given a flat, the rank of KGB major, and a job which presumably took advantage of his skills at photo-interpretation. But a traitor is rarely fully trusted by his new masters, and Souther was never given work with a high security classification. As he

116

admitted during his 1988 press conference: 'There's a lot of work here, but I haven't found my niche exactly.'

Exactly how much influence Souther had, whether he was a serious spy or just an enthusiastic amateur, will not be known until the archives in Moscow and Washington are accessible. Some in the CIA and other Western agencies insist he was a bit player whose role was blown out of all proportion by the KGB. Others say he did do serious damage to Western interests by leaking details of America's nuclear war plans.[2]

It is only in his death that he has become significant. A pawn to the KGB in life, it appears that in death he served a higher purpose. The obituary had one immediate effect, which was to embarrass Western intelligence. Raising the spectre of a new and devastating coup caused consternation in the United States, and the Russians rightly calculated that the Americans would have to waste manpower checking Souther's record again. But the most important reason for raising Souther to star status was for consumption by an internal Russian audience. In the new liberal atmosphere in Moscow, the KGB had come under attack as a backward and repressive organization. The Souther obituary attempted to counter this image by portraying the KGB as the master of an intelligence coup. Also, the phrasing of the obituary emphasized that the spy had been working for world peace over many years – in Russian doublespeak, a clear guide that the KGB had the same goal.

It was significant, too, that Vladimir Kryuchkov, then newly in charge of the KGB, was personally on hand to explain the importance of the Soviet master spy. He was advancing himself as the architect of the new, acceptable face of the KGB, and the whole charade clearly had his personal approval. To Western analysts, the fact and phrasing of the obituary suggested that the KGB had been forced on the defensive by its Russian critics. In fact, the Souther affair was the opening salvo in what has become a new phase in the war between Russian and Western intelligence.

This round is not fought with the crude weapons of the Cold War, which included obvious forgeries and the spreading of lies such as the American bomb that only killed black people, as well as other, more believable, attacks. For example, on September 16, 1980, a number of black radio stations and newspapers in America received copies of a document titled Presidential Review Memorandum NSC 46, which was supposed to be a study of the relationship between the black movement in the US and black Africa which had been requested by President Carter's national security advisor, Zbigniew Brzezinski, two years earlier. The memorandum called for American support for South Africa and recommended action against 'coordinated activity of the black nationalist movement in Africa and the black movement in the United States'. It also suggested that American intelligence agencies monitor and collect sensitive information on the activities of black representatives at the UN who opposed US policy towards South Africa.

The document caused a furore in America and forced the White House to issue a series of denials and to conduct a detailed analysis of the document. It turned out that a number of NSC studies had been declassified under the Freedom of Information Act during the Carter presidency and one of these, prepared during the Nixon years, had been used as a model for the forgery.[3]

This was part of a concerted campaign by Service A (Sluzhba Aktivnykh Meropriyatiyi) or the Active Measures Department of the First Chief Directorate which has been officially disbanded by the SVR.

A year after he was appointed head of the SVR, Yevgeni Primakov stated categorically: 'I have been in this job for one year already. I cannot recall a single case of such propaganda. It gives nothing and often it is counterproductive.'[4]

However, Western intelligence believes that Service A has been renamed the Measures of Assistance Department, and is carrying out the same type of work, notably through its public relations department. To try and control the new propaganda efforts, there are now twice-yearly meetings with the Russians to discuss disinformation.

Where the forgeries and lies were usually very obvious (even if widely believed in the developing world), the new war is no longer an ideological struggle between communism and capitalism or between West and East but is for the hearts and minds of the politicians and public on what remains of the political divide between Russia on the one hand and Europe and America on the other. This campaign is designed to bolster waning support for the intelligence effort in all the countries, to try and guarantee the funding and staff necessary to continue into the next century.

Six months after the publication of the Glenn Michael Souther obituary, Pravda reported the capture and sentencing to death of 'one of the most important spies' of recent years, identified only as Donald F.

'He might have been the fellow next to you on the subway or in the line for the cinema, as ordinary a Russian as you might find in the Soviet capital, but "Donald" was a spy for the United States – and had been so for nearly thirty years,' the paper said. 'Having access to many state secrets, Donald sold everything of interest to the US intelligence service.'[5]

According to *Pravda*, Donald F, the pseudonym allegedly given to him by his CIA handlers, passed over political and military information, plans for chemical and biological warfare, diplomatic codes and nuclear war plans. Donald was recruited while serving with the Soviet mission at the UN and he continued spying for the CIA after transfers to India, Burma and Moscow. According to the article, his handlers would keep in touch with Donald through personal ads in the local papers. When he was transferred to Burma, the CIA placed an ad which read: 'Moody – Donald F. I was pleased to learn how lucky you are. See you soon. Everything is fine. John F.' Another ad read: 'Moody. Donald F. Please write as you promised. Uncle Charles and Sister Clara are OK.'

Donald F was in fact Lieutenant General Dmitri Fedorovich Polyakov, who had the CIA codename Top Hat. He had indeed worked in the posts set out in the *Pravda* article but had been arrested in the mid-1980s and probably executed at that time. The exposure of his role at the beginning of 1990 was a graphic illustration of just how complex the propaganda war had become. At the time, the KGB were under attack at home for general incompetence and for being the architects of repression at home since the revolution. Their rivals, the GRU, were considered to be less venal, and dedicated to the relatively simple role of gathering intelligence. Top Hat was a spy in the heart of the military and for a time had worked for the GRU. By exposing Polyakov, the KGB hoped to blacken the reputation of the GRU while bolstering their own image at home as the successful controllers of the counter-espionage mission.

The article also lavished praise on KGB Colonel Aleksandr Dukhanin who uncovered Top Hat. At the time the article was published, he was being criticized for bungling a corruption investigation involving Yegor Ligachev, a conservative Politburo member and critic of Gorbachev. The article also emphasized the KGB role of exposing corruption at home. Also, the fact that Top Hat had supposedly been uncovered 'spying as usual' at a time when relations between the US and Russia were supposed to be improving, clearly demonstrated that the KGB was needed abroad as well.[6]

These not-so-subtle power plays have been matched in Russia, Britain and America by a major effort to rewrite the espionage history of the Cold War in the most favourable possible light with extraordinarily detailed revelations about the triumphs and failures of the KGB, SIS and the CIA. The CIA and SIS authorized a detailed history of the case of Oleg Penkovsky, who gave vital secrets to the West during the Cuban missile crisis.[7] Oleg Gordievsky co-authored two books with Christopher Andrew which portrayed his former employers in the KGB as a bunch of bungling incompetents who lied, cheated and drank, gathering intelligence from magazines which was then disguised as high quality material from top grade agents.[8]

But in this new propaganda war, it is the SVR that is winning. They have skilfully managed to exploit the new climate of openness by allowing access to some of their archive material. A series of books have begun to be published in the West that consistently undermine the reputation of the CIA, SIS and other Western intelligence services. For example, *The Red Web*, one of the earliest books of the genre, claims that a post-World War II attempt to penetrate Eastern Europe by SIS was not betrayed by Kim Philby, as had previously been suggested, but by skilful counter-espionage by the KGB.[9]

In June 1992, Crown Books of New York acquired the world rights to publish books based on the archives of the former KGB. The intention is to produce at least five books focusing on the Cuban missile crisis, the Berlin crisis, Soviet intelligence operations in the United States and Soviet penetration of British and American intelligence organizations. The first volume, *Deadly Illusions*, which was published in 1993, dealt with the life of Alexander Orlov, who had been thought to be one of the highest ranking KGB defectors. The book claims that Orlov remained a dedicated communist until his death and that the CIA were duped.[10]

While the CIA and SIS deny many of the allegations made in books like *Deadly Illusions*, the KGB argues that they have opened their files, so the Western agencies should do the same. As the Russian side of the publishing venture is being run by Oleg Tsarev, a former KGB colonel with long experience in Service A and of working undercover in England and other Western countries, it is understandable that there is some scepticism about how 'open' the KGB are being. None of the information released to date is damaging to the KGB, and all of it has bolstered their image as a strong defender of Soviet, now Russian, national security.

Western academics do not have access to the KGB files. Instead, they are examined by Tsarev in consultation with a small SVR committee. Decisions are then taken on what is to be released to the American and British academics who co-author the work. This first attempt at writing the revised intelligence history of the Cold War may be just another effort by a revamped SVR active measures unit to continue the old fight, or it may be serious history. Until the CIA and SIS relax some of their archaic secrecy rules, the public will never know, and the Russian organizations will continue to reap the benefits.

CHAPTER NINE

WITH FRIENDS LIKE THESE

The plain brown envelope that arrived at the CIA's headquarters at Langley in the middle of April 1993 looked innocent enough, but inside was an espionage bonanza. Page after page of top secret material gave details of planned weapons purchases, new satellite systems, America's position in forthcoming trade negotiations and intelligence on senior officials.[1]

When the documents were first examined, it was assumed they were a hoax by some member of the public, wishing to cause friction in French-American relations. But the twenty-one-page dossier was extraordinarily detailed and provided insights into French intelligence requirements for a two-year period, 1989–1991. It listed 49 companies and 24 financial institutions, setting out details of particular projects and the priority assigned to them. For example, the listing under the Boeing Co. read:

(1) Commercial airliner sales tactics. Production capacity. Technical problems with existing aircraft. Development of future 757 and 767 models. Orbital aircraft research. Cost, production and use of new composites, resins and alloys. Litigation with Airbus, particularly through the General Agreement on Tariffs and Trade in Geneva. Strategic Defense Initiative research. Equipment for special forces. Offsets for Saudi companies in Saudi government contracts. Priorities with European partners. Ground to air missile and communications research.

(2) V-22 Osprey technology and marketing plans. Electronics in E-6A aircraft.

(3) Space station series one contracts.[2]

121

Further analysis of the document, which was in French and stamped 'Défense Confidentiale', by the CIA and other US government agencies revealed that it was apparently issued by the Department of Commerce, Science and Technology which frequently acts as an overt intelligence gathering arm for the DGSE, the French secret service. It was clear to senior administration officials that the French were up to their old tricks and spying on one of their most important allies. Peter Tarnoff, the assistant secretary of state, was charged with confronting the French about the affair and in a heated exchange with officials from the French embassy the document was forcefully disavowed.

'They just lied, lied, lied and lied,' said a Treasury official.[3]

The result of the confrontation was a series of advisories issued to American defence companies and government departments, warning them that the French were after their secrets. The State Department's Overseas Security Advisory Council, a group that coordinates with corporate security officers, began a series of precautionary briefings with companies around the country, while the CIA provided their own warnings to top company officials and government offices.

Hughes was told by the CIA that one item in which the memo showed an interest was the HS 601 communications satellite made by the company which recently lost a competition with French firms to provide $258m worth of communications spacecraft to Arab countries.[4] It is precisely that kind of benefit that has spurred the French to become one of the most aggressive nations in the field of economic espionage.

Hughes' chairman, Michael Armstrong, alerted the heads of Boeing, McDonnell Douglas, General Dynamics and Lockheed. For each of them, the news was confirmation of something their own security people had warned them about with increasing frequency: if you are going abroad, don't take anything you would prefer not to lose and if you have to take it, make sure it stays with you at all times.[5]

But it was not just American companies which were being targeted by the French. Britain was included, and the Americans sent a copy of the relevant text to London for analysis. It referred to all the main British defence companies and read:

British Aerospace (BAE)
Priority: 1
Needs: Industrial restructuring
    Business strategies
    Connections with American corporations

Military aeronautics
Corporate activities in the EFA project
Target countries: Asia – Middle East
Placement of offset projects or exchanges (oil trade and bargaining – raw materials)
Proposals for joint production or local cooperation or joint ventures.

Subject: BAE
Priority: 1
Needs: Activities linked to uses of satellites
Probes
HOTOL
Reusable capsules.

Priority: 1
Needs: Technology
Research and development in the area of steels and alloys (aluminum-lithium AL-LI)

Subject: British Aerospace
Priority: 2
Needs: development of Tornado (version Wild Weasel) – electronic warfare.
Priority: 2
Needs: Air to Air missiles
ASRAAM (Advanced Short Range Air to Air Missile) development
Carrier aircraft electromagnetic missile compatibility study
Marketing of AMRAAM (Advanced Medium Range Air to Air Missile) developed in the USA – licence transfer problems.

Priority: 2
Needs: GB connections with the Franco-Italian project (family anti-aircraft missile system) in the NFR90 (Nato Frigate 90) framework.

Priority 2:
Needs: Marketing of Rapier systems. Sale of surplus to Army.

Subject: BNSC
Priority: 2
Needs: Space Programme

Subject: Ferranti
Priority: 2
Needs: Corporate Business Activity in airborne radar.

Subject: Marconi
Priority: 2
Needs: Marketing of ground radars

Subject: Westland
Priority: 1
Needs: Helicopters
    Target countries: Middle East – Asia: business activities
    Marketing of Blackhawk (Sikorsky)
    Involvement with TONAL corporation

Subject: Vickers
Priority: 1
Needs: Marine
    Marketing and forecasting studies in Asia/Spain
    Continuation of SM project in Canada
    Technology of Retentive Casing

Subject: Ministry of Defence/DESO
Priority: 1
Needs: Weaponry
    MoD/Industries deployment
    General activities in Asia and the Middle East
    DESO activities and remote post locations.

Subject: Transportation Department (CAA)
Priority: 1
Needs: Commercial Aeronautics
    Negotiations with Boeing

The revelation of the document's existence followed a Defense Intelligence Agency draft report prepared on April 3 which examined the implications of dual use technology efforts. 'Diversions and espionage aimed at acquiring controlled technology can be expected to continue and increase.' Activities 'include government orchestrated programs for broad technology collection such as French intelligence services targeting US business representatives.'[6]

Without exception, counter-espionage chiefs in Europe and America will cite France as the most conspicuous example of a country engaged in economic spying. There are good reasons for this, as France's efforts in the field have resulted in some notable mistakes which have soured relations between France and America.

In 1987, the FBI discovered that the French secret service had planted their own agents inside three American computer companies, IBM, Texas Instruments and Corning, at their subsidiaries outside the US. The attempted penetrations were part of a worldwide attempt to gather industrial secrets and technical know-how from friend and foe. According to Pierre Marion, the former head of DGSE, a special unit was set up in 1981 at the organization's headquarters in Paris, known as La Piscine, or the Swimming Pool.[7]

Marion was perfectly open. 'I would try to get documents and intercept communications. All in the service of French companies,' he said. Marion said that while the military and political secrets of France's allies were off limits, 'in the economic competition, the technological competition, we are competitors and not allies.'

Allegations that the DGSE planted bugs in the headrests of the first-class seats on board Air France flights are untrue but there is ample evidence that the French routinely copy documents carried by foreign businessmen in France, listen to their telephone conversations and make great efforts to find out sensitive pricing information on bids and contracts.

In the IBM case, the CIA discovered the plot and shared the intelligence with the FBI. As a result, a number of employees at the American companies were fired. Immediately after the case, the State Department confronted the French with the evidence. 'While they didn't admit anything, they said if they had been doing something, they promised not to do it again,' said an intelligence source.[8]

There remained some doubt that the French would keep their word, and persistent reports from American companies claimed that the French were targeting US business executives, but the American government lacked hard evidence for a further confrontation.

In January 1991, while the United States and France were preparing to launch the ground offensive against Iraq in the Gulf, a van stopped outside the private house of a senior executive working for Texas Instruments in Houston, Texas. Two men jumped out and began to burrow through the man's trash, pulling out pieces of paper and placing them into bags which they then loaded into the back of a van. A suspicious off-duty policeman noted the number of the vehicle and ran it through the police computer which traced it to the French consulate. The FBI were called in and confronted Bernard Guillet, the French consul-general, with their evidence. He denied any wrongdoing and claimed that his men were collecting grass cuttings to fill a hole in the consulate garden.[9]

This pattern of economic espionage was reaffirmed in 1992 when President Mitterrand authorized a 9.7% increase in the budget for the DGSE. A special fund for covert activities under the control of the prime minister was also increased by 4% and the government has enlarged by a half the number of case officers to run spies, up by 1,000 to 3,000.[10]

At the same time, the DGSE was reorganized to improve the quality of its analysis and its HUMINT. For many years, the agency has had a reputation as a refuge for second-rate military officers who failed consistently to predict big changes in the world. Now, the organization has more graduates and recruits are drawn from the French civil service, which has a high reputation.

'The French have seen their market share in almost every area decline in recent years,' commented one intelligence source. 'They know that the cheapest and best way to keep their companies in the game is to steal information from the competition.'[11]

The French first learned the real value of economic espionage when they recruited a Soviet spy, codenamed Farewell, in 1980. He proved to be one of the best agents ever run by Western intelligence, providing a unique insight into the priority Soviet intelligence gives to economic espionage, a priority which has remained unchanged with the end of the Cold War. It was the message that Farewell brought with him that helped convince the French that economic espionage against friends and enemies alike was in the national interest. To understand just why the French are prepared to risk the enmity of their allies, it is worth looking at Farewell's contribution to the Cold War and the impact he continues to have on the debate about the role of intelligence in the future.

CHAPTER TEN

THE ENEMY WITHIN

Farewell was a senior officer in Directorate T, one of three subdivisions of the KGB's First Chief Directorate, which was specifically charged with gathering technical and scientific information abroad. At the time of his recruitment, Farewell was supervising the evaluation of material gathered by Department T from all over the world and so was uniquely qualified both to copy that information and give French intelligence some idea of the extent of the KGB's activities.[1]

Farewell first came to the attention of French intelligence when he was posted to Paris ten years earlier. He was marked down as a potential recruit at that time but nothing was done and he returned to Moscow from where he contacted a French businessman and asked for a meeting. During his posting to Paris, he had been tracked and evaluated by the Direction de la Surveillance du Territoire (DST) which is responsible for counter-espionage. Uniquely for such a case, Farewell continued to be run by the DST after he became active, rather than by the DGSE which is responsible for gathering intelligence abroad.

Farewell proved to be a goldmine of information. He told the French that the scientific and technical network was centred around the Military Industrial Committee, VPK, of the Soviet Presidium which until then the West had believed was a purely bureaucratic body designed to produce arms production quotas and avoid duplication of research and development. In fact, Farewell pointed out, the VPK had a parallel function, which was to decide on the priorities of the Soviet military industrial programme, and how those could best be met. They would then tell the different intelligence organs what information was required from abroad to help meet those targets.

Farewell told the French there were six government departments responsible for carrying out the orders of the VPK including the KGB's Department T; military intelligence, the GRU; the Soviet Academy of Sciences; the State Committee for Science and Technology (GKNT); the Ministry of Foreign Trade; and the State Committee for External Economic Relations (GKES).

In 1979, according to Farewell, VPK recorded that 58,516 documents and 5,824 industrial samples had been obtained from abroad. As a result, 164 new research and development projects were initiated in the Soviet Union, while work on 1,262 existing projects could be accelerated. The following year, the haul of documents was down, but even so, 200 new research and development programmes were launched and work reduced on 1,458 others. Farewell maintained that over a four-year period 30,000 samples were obtained from the West along with 400,000 documents. In 1980 61.5% of the information came from the United States, 10.5% from West Germany, 8% from France, 7.5% from Britain and 3% from Japan.[2]

Given the Soviet intelligence system's propensity for exaggeration and boosting newspaper clippings to 'information from a major source', many of these documents would no doubt have been of little value. But all Western countries had noticed for many years the similarity in products manufactured in the military and civilian sectors in the Soviet Union to those available in the West. Directorate T stole the plans for the Harrier jump jet; the American Airborne Warning and Control aircraft (AWAC) became the Russian Mainstay aircraft; the BI-B bomber became the Blackjack bomber. In addition, the designs for the MK-48 torpedo and numerous air and ground radars were copied and are now in the Russian inventory. These coups had real value. For example, the Soviets stole documents relating to the fire control radar for the F-18 fighter which saved the Soviets $55m in development costs, 1,000 man-years of scientific research and enabled them to install identical radars in their own MiG-29 Fulcrum and Su-27 Flanker aircraft.[3]

This kind of spying is estimated to have saved the Soviets billions of dollars. For every advance the Soviets made, Nato had to invest in new projects to try and maintain the qualitative edge. Thus, economic espionage helped spur the arms race.

With Farewell's exposure in 1982, an important contributor to the West's knowledge about Russian economic espionage was removed. The Western intelligence community continued to work on the assumption that Directorate T and the VPK remained active. That in part accounted for a new offensive against the techno-bandits by restricting the flow of equipment and knowledge to the communist bloc through the coordinating committee of Nato members (with the addition of Japan), or CoCom as it was called. At best this was a porous controlling mechanism, as countries were always forced to set economic expediency against future security interests, and frequently the demand for jobs at home outweighed the compelling arguments for security abroad.

Britain should have been uniquely well placed to cope with the Soviet Union's emphasis on economic espionage. In 1971, 105 Soviet spies had been uncovered as a result of the defection of Oleg Lyalin, a member of the Soviet trade mission in London. All were either expelled or declared persona non grata, and a large part of the Soviet spy network in Britain was destroyed at a stroke.

About eight KGB officers and five GRU men survived the purge and formed the nucleus of a new espionage network in Britain. But around 1975, Oleg Gordievsky was recruited by MI6, and for ten years he passed over a stunning amount of detail about Soviet activities in Nato countries. When he defected in 1985, he was deputy head of the KGB station in London, and brought with him the names of all KGB spies working in the country. Immediately after his defection, 37 KGB and GRU agents were expelled. Once again the Soviet network was wiped out.

Over the next few weeks, Department K of the Security Service, which is responsible for counter-espionage in Britain, reported an influx of known Russian agents into the UK. All were members of the new order of spies: in their early or mid-30s, with a technical or scientific background and comfortable with the English language and British society. As usual, they arrived as journalists, press attachés and trade counsellors.

They were followed around the country by an MI5 team of watchers, known as Statics and Mobiles, as they toured factories, exhibitions and trade shows making contacts, picking up information and attempting to get samples from gullible manufacturers. All too often the men found what they wanted. This was in the middle of the Gorbachev revolution when the Soviets had become friends of the West. In fact, British intelligence believed – as did the Americans – that during the Gorbachev years, the efforts to steal Western scientific secrets had increased rather than declined.

The observation of the new Soviet spy network was completed and enough evidence gathered to convince foreign minister, Sir Geoffrey Howe, by December 1988. After he had examined the dossier supplied by MI5, Howe confronted the Soviets with the evidence and demanded that they stop their espionage on British soil. Nothing happened. In May

1989, eleven Soviet spies from the KGB and GRU were expelled from Britain, and a few days later four Czechs were added to the list.

It took the Soviets and then the Russians two years to build up a new network which is a shadow of its former self. Today there are eighteen KGB officers working in Britain and ten men from the GRU. Until the end of the 1980s, these spies would have divided their work between political reporting, subversion, military spying and economic espionage. Now, subversion is no longer part of their brief, and economic espionage receives the highest priority.[4]

As one senior British intelligence official put it, to maintain his revolution, Gorbachev had three problems: the economy, the military and an aggressive foreign policy. 'If he is going to reform the economy and industry, then he has to get the latest technology from the West. Then the military are only going to agree to force reductions if they are confident their weapons are a match for those in the West. At the same time, if you have a fairly adventurous foreign policy, then you want to know how other countries are going to react to what you are doing. All that means a very active intelligence gathering effort.'[5]

That statement in May 1989 remains an accurate reflection of the American and British view of Russian intelligence gathering today, except that Russia no longer has an aggressive foreign policy. Since the fall of Gorbachev, Russia has suffered hyperinflation and the pressures to produce economic intelligence have increased as the economy has become destabilized. At the same time, as the former KGB searches for new roles that allow it to maintain its influence and status in Russian society, economic espionage represents the perfect vehicle.

In the United States, both the CIA and the FBI have defined economic espionage as an important problem confronting the US into the next century. 'Some governments in Asia, Europe, the Middle East and, to a lesser degree, Latin America, as well as some former communist countries – nearly twenty governments overall – are involved in intelligence activities that are detrimental to our economic interests at some level,' said Bob Gates.[6]

Today the CIA estimates that the countries most involved in economic espionage against America include France, China, Brazil, Russia, India, Israel, South Africa, South Korea and a further ten developing nations.[7] A 1992 survey of 246 companies by the American Society for Industrial Security found that proprietary information theft has risen 260% since 1985 and that foreign involvement is found in 30% of the cases, a four-fold increase.[8]

These countries all try to steal the secrets of any country or industry that may allow them to gain the commercial edge, either by taking advantage of knowledge gained through expensive research and development, or by winning lucrative contracts or gathering details on other nations' negotiating positions in trade talks. In one typical case of economic espionage uncovered in 1992, a South Korean company paid an employee of General Electric $1m a year for trade secrets about producing synthetic diamonds.[9]

'Direct theft of American private secrets by foreign government intelligence services is not yet a massive undertaking,' said David Boren, the former chairman of the Senate Intelligence Committee. 'But as we go into the next century, and as international relations become much more a matter of economic competition than military competition, it's going to really increase.'[10]

Government agencies in all the developed countries have taken steps to meet this new challenge. For example, the FBI has established the Development of Espionage and Counter-Intelligence Awareness Program, designed to alert defence contractors and other US companies doing business abroad of the risks they might encounter. In the last three months of 1992 and the first six months of 1993, the number of industrial espionage cases investigated by the FBI rose from ten to 500 an indication not so much of the increase in such cases but of the resources the Bureau now devotes to the problem.[11]

It has become common practice for governments to issue advice to businessmen visiting countries which might target them for intelligence information. Frequently this is done through a briefing which is sometimes accompanied by documents which the executive is supposed to read, learn and then leave behind when he travels abroad. A good example of such advice was prepared by the British Security Service, MI5, for businessmen travelling to China. The four-page document, entitled 'Security Advice for Visitors to China', was issued in 1990 and is still considered current. It is worth quoting at length as it gives a clear flavour of the risks that British intelligence believes are posed.

Aims of the Chinese Intelligence Service

The motive behind the Chinese Intelligence Service cultivation of Westerners is primarily to make 'friends': once a 'friendship' is formed the Chinese will use the relationship to obtain information which is not legally or commercially available to China and to promote China's interest. The information required may not be classified: it can range from comment and analysis of Western political and economic trends, to Western security and defence matters, commercial practices, negotiating positions and industrial developments. Information on Western scientific and technological progress is a high priority requirement of the Chinese Intelligence Service.

A second objective of a 'friendship' can be for 'talent spotting': that is to meet other Westerners through the original contact who may have more political influence or better access to information of interest.

Characteristics of a Chinese Intelligence Approach.

The Chinese Intelligence Service approach to Western visitors differs from the more familiar techniques and methods of intelligence services of other communist countries, for example the Soviet KGB. A Western visitor is more likely to be the subject of a long term, low key cultivation, aimed at making 'friends'. This technique leaves those visitors with an appreciation of China and a love of Chinese culture particularly vulnerable.

Cultivation of a visitor or contact of interest is likely to develop slowly: the Chinese are very patient. An initial business transaction may be followed up by friendly social contact, such as an invitation to a meal or tickets to a cultural or sporting event. The target of the cultivation may be invited to return to China, ostensibly to discuss further business ventures or to speak at learned institutions; businessmen may be offered advantageous commercial opportunities; students may be offered exceptional research facilities. In reality, the return visit will be for the Chinese Intelligence Service to assess the potential of the target.

The aim of these tactics is to create a debt of obligation on the part of the target, who will eventually find it difficult to refuse inevitable requests for favours in return. The target or 'friend' may be asked fairly directly for scientific and technological information. The line often taken is that China, not being nearly so advanced or wealthy as the West, cannot possibly hope to achieve the same developments. China can present no military threat, therefore perhaps the 'friends' could lend, for example, an item of equipment, or send a technical instructor. Businessmen who hope such assistance may lead to an eventual sale are vulnerable to this technique.

The target may be persuaded to disclose unclassified but authoritative views or hearsay on, for example, the political situation in his country. The Chinese Intelligence Service may develop this relationship to obtain, in the long run, classified political information.

In these instances, the Chinese Intelligence Service will seek to persuade the target that a fair exchange of information is an ideal situation. But the Chinese principle of fair exchange is to obtain as much as possible in return for as little as they can get away with. There have been examples of the Chinese seeking to exploit the theme of the USSR as the common enemy in order to learn about defence matters normally denied them.

Thus a relationship built first on a business and then on a social footing can gradually develop into a tacit agent recruitment, making the businessman a controlled source of information for the Chinese Intelligence Service.

Techniques of Chinese Intelligence Service Operations Against Visitors

The Chinese have extensive resources at their disposal. They can and do place listening devices in hotels, guest houses and restaurants. They can search luggage and hotel rooms, scrutinize mail, and mount surveillance operations against visitors. Although this type of attack is more likely to be used against targets of particular interest, its possible use against others cannot be ruled out.

Visitors to China should be aware that all private and business papers are at risk if left in offices or hotel rooms (even if locked in a briefcase), and they should assume that most hotel, domestic, bar and restaurant staff are subject to the influence and control of the Chinese Intelligence Service.

Until recently the Chinese were not known to use sexual compromise and blackmail as a way to obtain cooperation. Recent evidence suggests, however, that, given appropriate political approval, sexual (including homosexual) compromise may be used. The Chinese will also exploit existing intimate relationships between Chinese citizens and foreigners. Although they are unlikely to try to contrive such a relationship, they are always on the alert for such contacts.

Compromising Offences

Visitors should observe local laws and rules of behaviour scrupulously. Ignorance is no excuse when they should come into conflict with the law. There should be no involvement in black market or illegal currency deals. Requests to carry personal correspondence out of China must be refused. Military areas should be avoided and cameras should not be used there. The local Chinese may also be sensitive to the use of cameras in poor or backward areas.

To Sum Up

Understanding how the Chinese Intelligence Service operates is the best protection a visitor can have. Remember that status, occupation and background afford no immunity from special attention. Be especially alert for flattery and over-generous hospitality. Be careful about personal behaviour and be alert to compromising situations. If arrested and charged with infringing local regulations, or caught in an embarrassing situation, always insist on being allowed immediately to contact either the British embassy in Beijing or the British consulate-general in Shanghai.

A visitor should remember that it is always in his own interest to tell the British authorities abroad or the police at home if he has been in trouble or if he suspects that the Chinese Intelligence Service is unusually interested in him. Anything the visitor says will be treated as strictly confidential and advice will be given on how to avoid any further difficulties. There are many cases on record where people have been compromised and left to think that their troubles were over, only to find themselves some years later subject to a threatening approach.

The degree to which intelligence should be used to assist governments or companies has provoked fierce debate within the intelligence community. There are those who argue that all intelligence gathered by a government should be used to assist that nation in any way possible. In other words, the CIA works for the US government and is funded by the taxpayers. If the Agency gathers information on a bid being placed by a French computer company for a contract in the Philippines which an American company is also bidding for, then that information should be shared with the US company. After all, the argument runs, what is good for the company is eventually going to be good for Uncle Sam in ensuring continued market share and export earnings.

Within the intelligence community, the issue of economic espionage has been treated differently depending on the country and the degree of involvement a government has in a nation's industrial base. In the former

Soviet Union, the needs of the nation were the same as the needs of industry, and there was no distinction between the government and the different branches of the economic system. So, if the KGB gathered intelligence on a planned defence buy in Malaysia with some details of the bids being offered by the US and Britain, there was no hesitation about passing on those details to the Soviet Union's defence manufacturers. In other countries such as France, where the state has a significant share of the industrial base, the government is seen as an extension of the company. Any intelligence gathered by a government intelligence agency that might be of benefit to a government-owned company will be shared.

Economic intelligence has to be divided initially into strategic or tactical intelligence: for example, a foreign government is planning to devalue its currency or change its stance at trade talks. If this information could be gathered in advance, then it would be of national or strategic importance, and routinely would be shared by the intelligence agency with the relevant government department. All countries try and gather such strategic intelligence and all intelligence agencies routinely share such information. It is when the information becomes tactical that the problems arise and decisions have to be taken about passing on details of a particular contract or opportunity to individual companies or even to individuals.

The problem of sharing comes either when the nationalized industry is in competition with private industry within a single country or where there are virtually no state owned industries. In Britain, state-owned industries were almost entirely service industries such as water, gas and electricity and little effort was made to gather intelligence that would have been of use to them, not least because they rarely competed internationally. However, intelligence was routinely gathered and shared about negotiating positions in trade or arms control talks as well as the posture of different countries towards Britain or towards alliance or countries with which Britain was friendly. American intelligence operates in almost exactly the same way. For example, the sixth floor of the Commerce Building in Washington DC houses a CIA cell of around fifty people which spends all its time looking at America's competitiveness in the world. Established in the late 1980s under President Reagan, the cell acts as the liaison group between Commerce, the CIA, NSA and other agencies which gather economic intelligence around the world. The cell is supposed to help the Commerce Department formulate policy and it does so by supplying detailed analyses of current issues.

In November 1990, the cell prepared a briefing for Commerce Secretary Robert Mosbacher on sixteen emerging technologies in America, Japan and Europe, in an attempt to assess American competitiveness into the next century. With comparisons measured by three criteria – static, losing and gaining – the CIA estimated that American industry was even with the Japanese in nine areas and losing ground in seven. The situation with the Europeans was even worse, with a static relationship in three areas and losing ground in the remainder.

'What was striking was that the areas where we were doing well against the Japanese, we were losing against the Europeans,' said one Commerce Department official present at the briefing. 'The problem was that we were not losing in the way we thought we were. In microprocessors and high definition television, for example, we were really doing fine.'[12]

Such interpretation of intelligence – supposedly one of the strengths of the intelligence community – is frequently flawed by such misjudgements. In part this is because there is a lack of communication between the user and the provider. In this instance, Commerce wanted certain information, while the CIA believed it should have the information it was being given.

In 1989, Bob Gates ordered a review of the CIA's policy towards economic espionage. The task force reported that, if the current spying effort was broadened and the product shared with American industry, it would be a violation of US anti-trust laws. At the same time, it was argued that given the multi-national nature of today's corporations, with shareholders from all over the world and offices in many countries, it is virtually impossible to decide which is a national company and which is not. Even if that can be decided, to be fair the information would have to be shared with every national company to avoid anti-discrimination lawsuits from all those companies which did not benefit from the information. To satisfy those criteria, the CIA would be required to develop a new infrastructure to analyze America's industrial base (itself a violation of the Agency's charter). Bob Gates expressed his reservations about getting more involved in economic espionage like this:

There are a number of reasons for us not to do it, some practical and some philosophical. One of the practical reasons is that I think it gets us into a welter of legal problems here at home in terms of what happens to the information we gather, who does it go to, how do we avoid advantaging one business over another. I think that we would have to quadruple the size of our legal staff to begin dealing with a problem like that. And I'm not sure how the rest of government would react, either, in terms of how we help people use it. I think from a practical standpoint it's a bottomless well. I think that it is difficult to identify what industries you might target without, what is Industry A going to say if he learns that the government to which it pays taxes is devoting resources to helping Industry B and not Industry A?

From a broader standpoint, I don't think that it is the proper use of our resources. I think that it is legitimate for us to be on the lookout for other governments that are not playing by the rules, and to bring that to the attention of our policy makers. I think that it is legitimate for us to track technological developments that have national security implications. I think that it is more than legitimate for us to keep an eye on foreign intelligence services that are trying to spy on our industry. Finally, I think it's a lot to ask our case officers. I had a case officer tell me many years ago: 'I'm prepared to put my life on the line for my country, but not for one or another company.'[13]

Despite these reservations, the election of President Clinton in January 1993 gave new impetus to the argument for a greater sharing of economic intelligence. President Clinton appointed Admiral James Woolsey as DCI, with a remit to look again at the reforms implemented by Bob Gates. During his confirmation hearings, Woolsey made his reservations clear about the ability of the community to do more in the field of economic intelligence.

First of all, our economy is, of course, more closely involved with the rest of the world than it has been at any time in the past, and economic issues are extremely important ones. The CIA has collected, and the intelligence community has collected, economic intelligence of one kind or another since its inception. But there's economic intelligence and then there's economic intelligence. I think first of all it is important and useful for the intelligence community to be in a position to assist not only the United States government but American companies in counter-intelligence, in the sense of helping them understand the intelligence collection threat that they are under from foreign governments and foreign intelligence services, because not everyone around the world plays the game the way we do. Some of our friends and allies are involved in economic intelligence operations against our corporations.

Second, there are important economic intelligence issues in the field of monitoring sanctions.

Third, there are many trends in the world, not only agricultural production, and raw materials and natural resources production and levels, but also new technological developments that might be strategically important, perhaps because they are dual use – military and nonmilitary electronics of various types – that the US government should, I believe, know about and understand.

The very difficult question on this often comes at the point at which the question is asked whether the US government under any circumstances should share any types of economic intelligence, however it is collected, with private citizens or corporations. That is a subject and an area and an undertaking that is fraught with complexities, legal difficulties, foreign policy difficulties and the rest.[14]

One of Woolsey's first acts on taking office was to order a reexamination of the issues surrounding the sharing of economic intelligence. That study, which is not yet concluded, is unlikely to produce any new recommendations that will allow the CIA to share its information with American companies. The 'level playing field' in international trade which President Clinton promised the American public during his election campaign will remain elusive. For the Russians, French, Japanese and sixteen other nations which target American corporations, intelligence will continue to be a vital weapon in the international economic war for which America currently has no effective defence.

To date, the intelligence community has responded in a typically structured way to the problems posed by economic espionage. It is certainly true that information gathered from sensitive sources should remain secret. It is also the case that in democracies it is impossible to disseminate information that may be of assistance to one company without making it available to all. But this is an overly restrictive interpretation. A vast amount of commercially useful information collected by embassies all over the world is drawn primarily from open sources. There is a lesson here in the way the Japanese work. Their Ministry of International Trade and Industry (MITI) and the Japan External Trade Organization use Japanese diplomats, trade organizations and intelligence services to assemble vast amounts of information, nearly all of it open-source, for translation and distribution to any Japanese company that wants it. This material has proved a priceless resource for a country that has grown rich by appropriating the ideas and inventions of others and exploiting them.

This kind of approach has been impossible to reproduce in countries like America and Britain, because intelligence is equated with secrecy, and a secret is only to be revealed to those in government with a need to know. But today it is generally accepted within the intelligence community that a great deal of so-called secret information can be declassified. The volumes of information collected by the CIA and other agencies from open sources such as foreign newspapers and magazines or scientific conferences should never have been classified in the first place.

This valuable national resources could easily be drawn together under a National Information Management Agency, who would decide what could be released and then make it available in a timely fashion to anyone who wished to access the database. This would remove the more general legal objection that prevents an intelligence agency distributing information by selecting a particular company. It also addresses the problem of compromising sources and methods as the intelligence would be sifted before distribution.

The single objection would be that foreign companies and governments would be able to make use of the database and this would be unwelcome. But countries like Japan and China already have very efficient methods for trawling all the open-source material, so they would be getting little they do not get already. No doubt countries like France which steal what they want would continue to do so, and would be unaffected by the change.

Much of the duplication in the analytical capability of different intelligence agencies would be eliminated as each would contribute their people to the new Agency which would not only process material but could produce detailed economic analyses at the request of users for which they would no doubt charge a large fee.

With a single imaginative move, a national asset would be created, expensive duplication among intelligence agencies eliminated, timely intelligence be made available and countries such as the US would begin to play on the kind of level playing field the policy makers and intelligence community talk about but do little to achieve.

THE CHALLENGES:
TERRORISM

CHAPTER ELEVEN

SUPPING WITH THE DEVIL

Before dawn on September 5, 1972, eight terrorists from the Popular Front for the Liberation of Palestine scaled the six-foot high wire fence surrounding the specially constructed village housing the athletes competing in the Munich Olympic Games. Dressed in tracksuits, the men crept through the darkness towards the building housing the Israeli contingent. They burst through the door and found the team gathering in the main room for breakfast. Two of the competitors – wrestling coach Moshe Weinberger and weightlifter Yossef Romano – tried to intervene and were shot dead with two bursts from an AK-47 Kalashnikov automatic rifle.

As was typical in those days, there had been no warning of the attack. The West German and Israeli governments had no effective contingency plans to deal with the crisis. The terrorists demanded the release of 234 prisoners held in Israel and members of the Red Army Faction in jail in Germany. The Germans were prepared to free their prisoners but the Israelis had already adopted a policy of no negotiation with terrorists and refused the demands. Mossad chief Zvi Zamir immediately flew to Munich to try and persuade the West Germans to stand firm, and to allow an Israeli *sayeret* counter-terrorist squad to plan the assault.

The Germans compromised. They refused to release the terrorists from jail and tried to rescue the hostages themselves. The terrorists were flown by helicopter from Munich to Fürstenfeldbruck military airfield, ostensibly to board a Boeing 727 to Cairo. As the terrorists left the helicopters, snipers on the roof of the airport terminal opened fire on the terrorists, killing two and wounding others. But the assault was a half-hearted effort with two of the snipers losing their nerve and failing to fire. Also, the inexperienced German police had miscalculated the number of snipers required and their effectiveness. (Today, no serious counter-terrorist team would rely on snipers alone to kill a number of terrorists simultaneously.)

The remaining terrorists had time to reboard the helicopters and, when the Germans followed up the sniper attack with a direct assault using soldiers and armoured cars, the Palestinians killed five of the bound and gagged hostages in one helicopter and blew it up. As the firefight continued, the second helicopter with another four Israeli hostages on board also exploded. Although five of the terrorists were killed and three arrested, nine Israelis died.[1]

The massacre of the eleven Israeli athletes at the Munich Olympics acted as a catalyst for the world's intelligence community in their efforts to combat terrorism. The attack illustrated the abject failure of the community to act proactively. The military had a relatively simple solution to their part of the problem. The French, the Germans, the British and the Americans all eventually established special counter-terrorist units dedicated exclusively to the rescue of hostages or the elimination of terrorists.

For the intelligence community, countering the terrorist threat was not so easy. More terrorist organizations were springing up every week. Attacks were carried out for a wide variety of reasons, using different methods and often across international borders. With the exception of the efforts of military intelligence to counter the threat of the Warsaw Pact, little attempt had been made by the industrialized nations to share intelligence. On the contrary, after the Second World War, every effort had been made to contain intelligence information within a national border, the natural distrust of one intelligence service for another ensuring that as little as possible was shared to avoid compromising sources and methods.

Now the terrorists were exploiting these precise weaknesses, using all the advantages of the late twentieth century – excellent land, sea and air communications – to their political and military advantage, while their opponents squabbled among themselves. When the terrorism threat first appeared at the end of the 1960s, it was the Israelis who raised the alarm. They warned that a number of Palestinians, frustrated by years of indifference by the international community, were trying to raise the people, cash and arms to move the struggle away from the conference table and into the streets. Until this time, the intelligence world had focused its attention on the Cold War, with the occasional diversion into insurgency warfare in countries like Yemen and Malaysia, or the overthrow of inconvenient dictators in countries like Iraq and Oman.

From the onset of what appeared to be an international revolution, far broader than the narrow Middle East problems about which the Israelis had been warning, the intelligence community were besieged by their political masters with demands for information. To many it seemed that no modern democracy was to be spared this new scourge, with bombs exploding on the high streets of European capitals, and prominent politicians and businessmen targeted for assassination and kidnap all over the world. The intelligence community had no answers to offer. There were no sources, technical or human, to produce the information on which the analysts could base any recommendations.

The Germans did deals with the Palestinians, the French (as usual) offered money in exchange for peace, while the Americans tried a little of both. This led to some extraordinary compromise deals, the most interesting of which concerned the man who organized the massacre at Munich, Abu Hassan Salameh. Known as the Red Prince, Salameh was in charge of operations for the Black September terrorist group. He was responsible for the planning and logistics of the operation from his base in East Germany.

Salameh made an unlikely terrorist. He was the wealthy son of a Palestinian merchant, Sheik Hassan Salameh, who had been at the forefront of local resistance to the formation of an Israeli state in 1948 until he was blown up by an Israeli car bomb during the Arab-Israeli war of that year, a fate that was later to befall his son. Young Abu Hassan had assumed his father's mantle even though he had very little in common with poor firebrands like Yasser Arafat, who were at the heart of the growing Palestinian terrorist movement. Educated in Cairo, at Bir Zeit University on the West Bank, and in West Germany where he studied engineering, Salameh developed a Western style that was criticized by his traditional colleagues in the PLO. He enjoyed designer clothes, fast cars and attractive women, and took up karate to help his muscle tone. He was handsome, with sensual good looks, and he enjoyed living the playboy lifestyle with a villa in Geneva and regular trips to the South of France.

He was a dangerous, ruthless and well educated man but he was also a pragmatist like Arafat. When the initial work of Black September had done its job of attracting world attention to the Palestinian cause, Salameh left to head up Force 17, Arafat's personal bodyguard. He also became point man for Arafat's delicate relationship with the Americans. For his part, Arafat wanted to convince the Americans at an early stage in their relationship that he was a realist who did not want to see the destruction of Israel, whatever he might say publicly. At the same time, the Americans were desperate for information about the PLO, its leaders, its methods and its objectives.

In 1969 Bob Ames, then the CIA's man in Beirut, had opened links with Fatah, the wing of the PLO he felt had both staying power and some degree of moderation. He told Salameh he was acting on behalf of President Nixon and his national security advisor Henry Kissinger who were anxious to establish a dialogue with the Palestinian movement. Naturally, Salameh and Arafat were enthusiastic about the arrangement, which gave them access and credibility.

Salameh was now in charge of around 6,000 PLO fighters in Lebanon and clearly had a tough grip in a lawless land. His skills as a diplomat and a leader so impressed the Agency that they made him, via a CIA intermediary in Rome, a cash offer of $3 million to work for them. Salameh, comfortable with the role of intermediary but outraged at the idea of betraying his people, turned them down and refused to take Ames' calls for several months. Then the CIA discovered the other side to Salameh, learning that he had been behind the hijacking of a Sabena aircraft to Lod airport in Israel. Then there was the massacre at Munich and clearly further contact became very difficult.

When the dust from Munich had settled and Salameh had taken up his new position with Force 17, he approached Ames again in mid-1973 and said that Arafat would be willing to join in peace talks on the basis that Israel had a right to exist and that Jordan would become the home for a Palestinian state. Ames contacted Richard Helms, then US ambassador in Iran and later director of the CIA, who relayed the message to Kissinger when he travelled with the Shah to Washington in late July. At this stage, Kissinger was not prepared to countenance negotiation with the PLO or the betrayal of Jordan, a strong ally of the US, so he rebuffed Arafat.

But in October that year, the Yom Kippur War between the Arabs and Israel broke out. After early gains by Egypt it became clear that Israel had turned the tide and was heading for victory. On the fourth day of the war, Salameh again contacted Ames to say that both Egypt and Syria would be prepared to discuss peace and so would the Palestinians. Once the war was over and a ceasefire in place, Kissinger looked again at the Arafat offer and found it more attractive. There might be a way of reducing the influence of the PLO in the region and cutting the Soviets out of their role in the Palestinian movement if the PLO could be coopted into some form of talks. On November 3, 1973, General Vernon Walters, then a deputy director of the CIA, was sent on a secret mission to meet with Salameh who attended as Arafat's personal representative in Rabat, Morocco. It is inconceivable that the CIA did not know of Salameh's involvement with international terrorism at the time of the meeting. The meeting produced little of political value but the PLO were anxious to convince the Americans that they were reasonable people.

'Walter's meeting achieved its immediate purpose: to gain time and to prevent radical assaults on the early peace process,' Kissinger later wrote. 'After it, attacks on Americans – at least by Arafat's faction of the PLO – ceased.'[2]

On the personal instructions of Yasser Arafat, Salameh was responsible for enforcing the agreement. To do so, he developed a relationship with Bob Ames, station chief in Beirut, which at the end of 1973 produced exactly the kind of result the Agency had hoped for. Salameh warned the CIA that there was a plot to shoot down Kissinger's plane when it arrived in Beirut as part of his Middle East shuttle after the Arab-Israeli war, when he was trying to broker acceptable territorial boundaries. The aircraft was diverted and Salameh provided armed men from Force 17 to look after Kissinger during his stay in Lebanon.[3]

Because of this new relationship, Salameh, one of the world's most notorious terrorists, was able to visit the US with considerable freedom. In 1974, when Arafat made his famous speech at the United Nations, Salameh came in the PLO's official party to New York and met with CIA officials in a room at the Waldorf Astoria Hotel. At that meeting, Ames introduced Salameh to his successor as CIA chief in Beirut to ensure there was no break in what had developed into a mutually beneficial relationship. Both Arafat and Salameh were buoyed up by the apparent covert support of the US and the Americans were grateful for a productive intelligence connection into the heart of the Palestinian terrorist network. Their faith appeared to be justified when Salameh promised that rather than just keeping Fatah from attacking American targets, he would try and ensure other PLO groups kept away as well.

Two years later, in the middle of the Lebanese civil war, it was Salameh who helped the Americans to evacuate 250 US citizens from the country. Two American convoys, one from the city to the sea and the American Sixth Fleet and the other by road through the Shouf Mountains to Syria, were protected by the heavily armed fighters of Force 17. The protection merited a personal letter of thanks to Arafat which, with Kissinger's usual caution, omitted to mention either Arafat's name or the PLO. Salameh received his own vote of thanks when he married

Georgina Rizak, a former Miss Lebanon and Miss Universe. The Agency invited the couple on an all-expenses-paid honeymoon to the States, where they went first to Hawaii and then – realizing a lifetime's ambition for Salameh – to Disney World in Florida.

Salameh also made two trips to the CIA headquarters at Langley, where he charmed his hosts and provided a detailed analysis of the Palestinian movement and the character of Yasser Arafat. He also told them that Arafat was not beholden to the Soviet Union or anyone else and, while they might take money from the Arabs and send some men for training in Moscow, a Palestinian state would be neither communist nor a dictatorship.[4]

This delicate courtship between the Agency and the PLO led Arafat to believe that he had greater access to the American political process than he really had. He believed that by showing good will and providing proof of his moderate policies, he might both engage in peace talks and persuade the Americans to support his ideas for a Palestinian homeland. When Jimmy Carter entered the White House in 1977 and made clear that peace in the Middle East was a priority, Arafat thought that his time had come. But his and Salameh's operations were not taking place in a vacuum. The Israelis had been following Salameh's contacts with the CIA almost from the beginning.

In late 1973, for example, a Palestinian called the US embassy in Beirut, warning that he had information about threats to American citizens. To establish his bona fides, he told the American diplomat to listen to a specific message on Radio Damascus which was broadcast at the exact time he had described. Bob Ames got in touch with Salameh, who denied all knowledge of the contact. Concerned that Arafat may have been trying to open a back channel to the Americans, Salameh tracked down the Palestinian in question who confessed to being a spy for Mossad, and was executed.[5]

In July that year an Israeli hit squad had tried to assassinate Salameh in Lillehammer in Norway. They tracked their target to a restaurant and gunned him down, to discover the next day that they had shot the wrong man. Their victim was Ahmed Bouchiki, a Moroccan waiter who had married a local girl. In what was an unusual example of Mossad incompetence, the whole hit squad was arrested by the Norwegian police. After one of the team was placed in solitary confinement, it was discovered that he suffered from claustrophobia. He spelled out details of the whole operation in exchange for a bigger room with a window. It was then that the world learned that the Israelis had decided to track down and kill all those who had been involved in the Munich massacre. From then on, Salameh took extraordinary precautions to protect himself from assassination.

But marriage to Georgina Rizak appears to have dulled Salameh's well-honed instincts for survival. A reconnaissance unit from Mossad discovered in late 1978 that, when he was in Beirut, Salameh broke the cardinal rule of any security risk: he drove to work every day in the same Chevrolet station wagon from his flat along the Rue Verdun to the Fatah headquarters. In January 1979, Mossad occupied an apartment with a clear view of this route, parked a Volkswagen packed with explosives on the Rue Verdun and blew it up as Salameh's car drew alongside. He and his two bodyguards were killed in the explosion and, at a stroke, Western intelligence lost its single most important conduit to Middle East terrorists.

For ten years, Salameh had provided security for Americans living and working in the Middle East. He had saved Henry Kissinger from assassination, alerted American ambassadors in Beirut to plots against them, and helped evacuate 250 US citizens from Lebanon. He had also passed on valuable intelligence about the workings of the PLO and the views of Yasser Arafat. The Americans and their allies had received what all intelligence agencies want: real time intelligence from a top source, who not only had access to operational information but could provide details about the thinking and the relationships in the leadership of the PLO.

His relationship with Salameh helped advance the career of Robert Ames, one of the Agency's most talented operators. He became the CIA's national intelligence officer for the Middle East, then personal advisor on the Middle East to Secretary of State George Shultz. As Shultz records in his memoirs, Ames retained excellent contacts with the PLO leadership but, with Bill Casey as DCI, there were occasions when the two men operated back channels to Arafat in defiance of explicit orders from the Secretary of State. Even so, Shultz considered Ames valuable enough to keep on as a close advisor.[6]

There is no doubt that Ames' decisions to sup with the devil, at a time when Arafat was encouraging terrorist attacks on Western targets, was an act of classic political expediency. For the CIA it was a trade-off between no intelligence at all and good intelligence, which might save the lives of Americans and perhaps of American allies. Above all, it was a bargain which worked. It gave the US access and insight into the PLO. It was this, of course, that infuriated the Isarelis. Without the Salameh conduit, it is doubtful if the impression could have been sustained through the

Nixon, Carter and Reagan years that Arafat was really a sheep in wolf's clothing, a moderate who was ready to do business. The kind of deals Arafat wanted (a Palestinian homeland in exchange for recognizing Israel's right to exist) were anathema to successive Israeli governments. It is clear, therefore, that Salameh was not murdered simply out of revenge for Munich. With his death, Americans became a terrorist target once again and, while Ames retained good contacts in the PLO, the supply of reliable operational intelligence was substantially reduced.

Ironically, it was Ames himself who was to fall victim to a new form of terrorism four years after Salameh's assassination. After Ayatollah Khomeini took power in Iran in 1979, there was an immediate growth of terrorism, spread by Islamic fanatics in Tehran who wanted to gain influence in the Middle East and the world. Their most active groups were based in Lebanon. It was Hizbollah who organized the car bomb at the American embassy in Beirut on April 18, 1983. Ames had just begun to chair a meeting in an office above the portico of the embassy when the bomb went off, killing Ames, CIA station chief Kenneth Haas, and all but two of the Agency's officers in Beirut. It was a devastating blow, and a tragic illustration of how valuable real human intelligence is to prevent that kind of attack. The Americans had no warning of the bombing, in part perhaps because the PLO had been virtually destroyed in Lebanon following the Israeli invasion the year before. At the same time, despite their best efforts, the CIA had no reliable sources inside the new Iranian-sponsored terrorist network and had to rely instead on technical intelligence.

In this instance, the National Security Agency had intercepted and decoded cables from the Iranian foreign ministry to the Iranian embassy in Damascus, which suggested that a major attack was imminent. They also discovered that $25,000 had been transferred to the Iranian embassy in Damascus to pay for it. But the intercepts gave no indication of the time, place and method of the attack, so the general warning in a hostile environment like Beirut was ignored.[7]

After the bombing, there was some doubt among American intelligence officials about whether Iran had operated alone or with Syrian complicity. The NSA intercepted a telephone call from the Syrian foreign ministry to the Iranian embassy in Damascus, when the Syrian official complained that the attack had taken place without their knowledge. This did not solve the problem. Some argued that the Syrians knew the call would be monitored, which was why it had been made. Others argued it was genuine. At this distance, it matters little where responsibility lay; both Iran and Syria have been guilty of enough terrorist acts to satisfy the most sceptical of analysts. What does matter is that the incident demonstrated just how difficult it is both to predict attacks and to place responsibility for them without human source intelligence.

In 1969, there were 179 terrorist incidents. Five years later they were running at 425 a year, a rate of well over one a day. By the end of the decade, the incident rate had steadied to around 350, reflecting changing tactics of the terrorists and the counter-terrorists.[8] While each nation dealt with the problem in different ways – the Germans introduced draconian laws, the Italians floundered, the French bribed and black-mailed abroad and cracked down at home, the British began with repression but evolved a more sophisticated approach – the American intelligence community tried a little bit of everything.

From the outset, there was disagreement within the community about the nature and extent of the problem. Some saw the Soviet hand behind every bomb and gun while others argued that terrorism was a more complex problem. All agreed that there was an acute shortage of intelligence and that more had to be done to gather information on which to base more accurate and swift analysis. Above all, the policy makers wanted to be able either to prevent the attacks or catch the attackers. To do that it was clear that precise and timely intelligence was vital.

This demand coincided with a revolution in communications and the capabilities of technical intelligence, both in the form of intercepts and satellite and other imagery. To those who had access to the stunning technical developments that had occurred with the refinement of satellite technology, and the recent advances in microcircuitry, the capability of technical intelligence appeared to be limitless. The scientists were promising faster decryption, more secure encryption, and imagery that would soon allow analysts to practise lip reading.

These systems were just coming into vogue when Jimmy Carter was elected president in 1974 and Admiral Stansfield Turner was made DCI. In Turner's autobiography, he recounts the capabilities of some of these systems.

There are two technologies behind most new technical intelligence capabilities: the computer, with its vast increase in computational power, and microprocessors, which make it possible to put computers into very small packages . . . Until there were high speed, high capacity computers, it took far too long for us to sort out much of the extremely detailed intelligence data that we were beginning to collect. Today's sensors can detect a huge variety of signals, even when they are very weak or are obscured by other signals. For example, a concealed microphone can hear a wide range of sounds, but only with the help of a computer can we separate the background noises on one set of frequencies from conversations on another . . . In photography we can lift from millions of black and white dots that compose a photograph only the ones we are interested in.

The second development, microprocessing, by enabling us to put the vast computational power of computers on to microchip, allows us to reduce the size and weight of cameras and listening antennae to the point where they can be placed into a satellite or a high flying aircraft . . . or to build a microphone and sorting system that is so small that it can be concealed in clothing, furniture, or other sensitive locations . . .

Today [the development of technological spying] all but eclipses traditional, human methods of collecting intelligence.[9]

Turner found the apparent certitude of machines seductive, when set against the unreliability of the people from the Operations Branch. In 1976, when George Bush had been DCI, a study had been produced which recommended cutting 1,350 jobs in Operations Branch. Although nothing was done at the time, Turner determined to take action. On August 7, 1977, he announced the axing of 820 positions, a body blow to the division and one from which it has not recovered. There was no argument that the CIA was overstaffed, or that too many people had been kept on after they had outlived their usefulness. What later events were to demonstrate was that Turner had misunderstood the nature of modern intelligence, gambling that technology would produce the answers.

The fact that it did not and could not was clearly demonstrated when the Shah of Iran fell in 1979, despite months of claims by the American intelligence community that the opposition to the Shah would be stifled. This momentous miscalculation was compounded when Iranian revolutionaries seized the American embassy in Tehran on November 4, 1979.

The next day, on the instructions of Zbigniew Brzezinski, the National Security Advisor, preparations for a rescue mission began. The plan centred around the use of a new unit called Delta Force, which was then completing initial training under the command of Colonel Charlie Beckwith at their headquarters in Fort Bragg, North Carolina. Delta was a dedicated hostage rescue outfit, whose members trained for months to evacuate people from hostile environments where they were being held against their will. Once the operation became a possibility, Delta moved from Bragg to the CIA's Camp Peary, a compound on the outskirts of Williamsburg, Virginia. There the Agency constructed a model of the Tehran embassy compound so that the Delta team could practise and refine the rescue mission.

The first and most important requirement was the collation of detailed intelligence from inside Iran, which could help pinpoint possible routes in and out of the country. It was vital for the Pentagon to know just where inside the embassy compound and in the foreign ministry the hostages were being held. Very shortly after planning began, the nature of the intelligence gaps became apparent. The CIA had broken one of the first rules of deployment in a 'friendly' foreign country the size of Iran. They had neglected to build any kind of independent 'stay behind' network that could be activated in an emergency.

'The CIA didn't have a single on-the-ground operative in Iran, so far as I could tell,' said Commander Richard Marcinko, a navy **SEAL** who was intimately involved in the rescue mission. 'We were able to obtain fragments of information through foreign embassies, and there was still a large contingent of foreign nationals in Iran – Turks, Germans, French, Irish, Canadians – but there was no organized network, and nobody supplying the "hot" information a team of special operators needs to mount a rescue operation.'[10]

Beckwith himself was even more critical: 'Without "stay behind assets", intelligence agents, information gathering was slow and tedious. That's where America was in November 1979 – without anyone in Tehran working for it. The Central Intelligence Agency was working to locate someone in the area, but that process would take some time. Hell, it takes five to seven years just to train and emplace an agent. He or she has to be spotted, recruited, trained, assessed and introduced to the country. Then he or she can become productive only after they've lived their cover for a reasonable period of time.

'The Carter administration had made a serious mistake. When Admiral Stansfield Turner went into the CIA, a lot of the old whores – guys with lots of street sense and experience – left the Agency. They had been replaced with younger, less experienced people or, worse, not replaced at all. Why this happened, I don't know. But I do know that in Iran on November 12, 1979 there were no American agents on the ground. Nothing could be verified. Delta was proceeding thus far without accurate and timely intelligence.'[11]

The Pentagon's solution was to send Dick Meadows, a former highly decorated special forces soldier, into Iran disguised as an Irish businessman. He would be accompanied by three other special forces volunteers, all of whom would be given false identities. They were tasked with obtaining accurate intelligence about the location of the hostages as well as preparing the ground for the mission. Meadows proved to be an inspired choice. A legend within the special forces community, he had taken part in the abortive rescue mission on the Son Tay on November 21, 1970 when a special forces team flew by helicopter to a camp twenty-four miles from Hanoi, which was supposed to hold sixty-one American prisoners of war. It was a brilliant and daring mission which failed at the last because, by the time the rescue team arrived, the prisoners had all been moved. This was another graphic illustration of the need for good intelligence.

Meadows was provided with a false identity as a Portuguese businessman, and he spent months making sure his 'legend' would withstand close examination by Iranian interrogators. Just days before he was due to leave, Portugal announced an economic boycott of Iran and the identity had to be abandoned. In its place, Meadows, given the codename Esquire, was supplied with a new identity as Brian McCarthy, with no time to prepare a proper legend or even a believable Irish accent.[12]

By mid-December a plan had been worked out. The rescue team would fly in helicopters to a desert site outside Tehran (Desert One), refuel and then fly on to a further staging post where they would lay up for a day before making a move on the embassy. While the assault was under way, a team of Rangers would secure a nearby airfield, from where the hostages and Delta would be evacuated. It was decided to use RH-53-D Sea Stallion helicopters which, although normally used against floating mines, could carry the necessary number of people and had the required range. Beckwith estimated that he needed seventy of his men to do the job and, if all the Delta Force were to be evacuated along with the hostages, then he would need a minimum of six helicopters. The group eventually flew in with eight choppers, allowing what appeared to be a reasonable margin of error.[13]

Aside from Meadows and his team, the Agency had found two people with experience of Iran to go into the country. They had also recruited a number of Iranian nationals to gather intelligence. The DIA, drawing on satellites and pictures taken by SR-71 Blackbird reconnaissance aircraft, produced detailed graphics of the embassy and its grounds. By comparing each set of pictures, the intelligence staff were able to build up a detailed idea of the daily routine inside the compound. Aerial photography of the ground south of Tehran had revealed a desert strip alongside a one-lane unpaved road some 265 miles south of the city and 500 miles from the sea. The CIA organized a light plane to fly in to plant homing beacons and to take soil samples at the site to make sure the sand was dense enough to take the enormous weight of fully-laden C-130 transports. The CIA team reported traffic on the road while they were on the ground, and intelligence reports suggested that the route was used fairly regularly by smugglers as well as by ordinary Iranians. But the risk of discovery was considered acceptable and the mission planning went on.

Meadows and his team hired vehicles and a warehouse to store them, so that Delta would have a way of getting to the embassy compound after their overnight staging post in the hills just outside the city. In addition, he gathered exactly the kind of detailed intelligence from on-the-ground observation that the team needed to complete their planning. What they did not know was where the hostages were being held in which of the fourteen buildings inside the compound.

The day before the operation was due to begin, a Pakistani cook, who had continued to work at the embassy after it was seized, was given permission to leave the country. By an extraordinary coincidence, one of the undercover CIA agents left Tehran on the same flight and found himself in the next seat to the Pakistani. The two began talking. When the CIA agent realized the nature of the almost real-time intelligence that the cook possessed, he arranged for the CIA to debrief him. The cook explained that the hostages, with the exception of three people in the foreign ministry building, were all held in the chancellery. This information made Delta's task much easier. They no longer had to seize and search every building, and could focus on one.

The next day, January 24, the Delta C-130s took off from Cairo, staged for four hours at Masirah Island off Oman, then flew on to Desert One. The aircraft followed a complicated zig-zag route into Iran on a course plotted by the National Security Agency and the CIA. It was designed to allow them to fly through the large holes that had been detected in the country's radar cover. All the aircraft arrived at Desert One undetected. At 22.00, under cover of the desert darkness, the first aircraft approached the landing site, activating the homing beacons planted by the CIA team a month earlier. As the plane began its approach, its forward looking infra red system picked up traffic on the road running alongside the strip and it circled until the road was clear before coming in to land.

First off the aircraft were the Rangers with their two motorcycles and a jeep. The motorcycles had two headlights specially rigged to make them look like trucks. Bandits were known to operate in the area, and they would be more likely to stop if confronted by a heavy vehicle. Before a perimeter guard had been established, a large Mercedes bus full of passengers appeared and only stopped after the Rangers had fired several warning shots.

While the problem with the bus was being sorted out, another vehicle appeared, this time a fully laden petrol tanker driven by smugglers. It too refused to stop. One of the Rangers fired a LAW anti-tank rocket, causing a massive explosion which lit up the night sky for miles around. Immediately, another smaller van appeared, halted by the blazing truck, picked up the driver and his mate and sped off before the Rangers could get their motorcycles started. The smugglers had made good their escape and presumably would not be too keen to talk about the incident.

Even with such unforeseen difficulties, nothing had happened yet seriously to jeopardize the mission. Further reassurance was provided by Dick Meadows who radioed, 'All the groceries are on the shelf', the signal that the holding sites outside Tehran were ready.

All now depended on the helicopters which were on their way from the aircraft carrier *Nimitz*, in the Gulf of Oman. Two helicopters suffered mechanical failure, and the remainder arrived at Desert One over an hour late, after running into a sandstorm. The rescue team were down to their minimum number of helicopters. Beckwith judged that the risk was too great to continue with the mission without any built in redundancy in case of further accidents. He recommended cancellation of the operation and President Carter agreed.

To reduce the risk of engine failure, the C-130s were all sitting next to each other on the ground with their engines running. The helicopters, meanwhile, were obliged to move about the landing site in order to refuel. The result was a maelstrom of heat, noise and dust where men were simply opaque shapes in the darkness, orders couldn't be heard and visibility was so poor that distinguishing officers from men was impossible.

No plans had been made for evacuation. It was decided that the helicopters would fly out on their own, after they had completed refuelling. The C-130s would take the assault force and the rest of the ground crew back to Masirah. Orders flew to and fro amid the noise and dust and eventually the men started climbing back into the aircraft. Just then, the rotor blades of one of the helicopters struck the fuselage of one of the C-130s, causing the Sea Stallion to cartwheel into the ground and explode, igniting the C-130 moments later. Three of the crew from the helicopter died and all five of the crew in the C-130 were lost. The remaining members of Delta, the ground crew and the crews from the other helicopters, piled on board the remaining C-130s and flew back to Masirah.

The helicopter crews left behind a rich haul for the Iranians who turned up at Desert One two days later. Instead of destroying the aircraft and their contents, using pre-positioned explosive charges, the pilots had simply deserted the helicopters, leaving their engines running. Inside were secret communications equipment, code books and operational plans for the mission, including the location of the warehouse where Dick Meadows had stored the civilian vehicles.

Meadows received the message that the mission was cancelled in his hideout overlooking Tehran. He had expected to be evacuated with the rescue team and had made no contingency plans. He had to hole up in the Sheraton Hotel for two days, while the Iranians launched a full scale hunt for the American spies they presumed had been working inside Iran to prepare the way for the Delta team. He eventually flew out on a commercial flight along with two other members of his team. The fourth member was left behind, and had to walk the six hundred miles to the Turkish border.

The day after the black farce at Desert One, the President authorized planning to begin on a second rescue mission, this time using a massive force of 2,000 men to secure the hostages and bring them out. But the hostages had now been dispersed around Tehran. It proved impossible to find them or to assure the rescue team that they would still be in place by the time Delta arrived. At one stage, the CIA actually produced photographs of two buildings where the hostages were being held. This intelligence might have been sufficiently reliable to launch the mission but it proved to be wrong. Because the intelligence was not good enough, the operation was never authorized. It was not until Ronald Reagan was sworn in as president in January 1980 that the hostages were released.

Although the Desert One disaster was a military failure, valuable lessons for future operations were learned. One of the most important was the price to be paid if good intelligence is not available. As with the PLO, there was no shortage of technical intelligence. Indeed, the DIA managed to produce some extraordinary information by analysing all the photographs supplied by satellites and other overhead systems. The NSA was able to produce transcripts of most of the conversations between the students holding the hostages and government officials. While valuable, however, this did little to help in the specifics of the planning beyond giving some indication of numbers and routines.

It was extraordinary, after the fall of the Shah, that the CIA had no assets available in Iran who could deliver the required on-the-ground information. As the Holloway Commission which later investigated Desert One made clear, this was a serious intelligence failing. Dick Meadows and his team did an outstanding job under the circumstances and the CIA also managed to produce some valuable intelligence by the time the rescue actually began. But this was an ad hoc response to a failure, rather than a planned reaction to a circumstance that should have been foreseen.

The lessons learned from Desert One were not lost on the military, who immediately moved to establish their own organization. With their love of acronyms, the military had called Meadows' unit the Forward Operating Group or FOG. After Desert One, this became the Intelligence Support Activity (ISA), headquartered at Fort Belvoir. The Pentagon believed, rightly, that the CIA's own HUMINT capability had been so emasculated by the Turner cuts that they would be unable to give reliable intelligence to their men in the field. The military argued that this was a critical capability at a time when terrorism was on the rise and low intensity conflict (LIC) was an increasing preoccupation.

ISA was given an initial budget of $2 million which rose to $6 million in 1983, peaking at around $10 million in 1986, with a complement of about 300 staff. Among the uniformed branch, ISA was considered a vital asset and a way for the Pentagon to control its own intelligence gathering. General Shy Meyer, when he was chief of staff (army), backed the establishment of ISA. He was supported by General Richard Stilwell, when he was appointed deputy undersecretary of defense for policy which included intelligence responsibilities for the Secretary of Defense. Stilwell had such a jaundiced view of the existing HUMINT capabilities that he wanted the military to establish a whole new agency under the codename Monarch Eagle to gather HUMINT. Understandably, the CIA opposed this land grab, and the continued existence of ISA was a middle-ground compromise.

155

Both Meyer and Stilwell had a special forces background and were understandably sympathetic. In 1982, Frank Carlucci, the Deputy Defense Secretary, argued the alternative view and suggested that ISA be disbanded. 'We seem to have created our own CIA, but like Topsy, uncoordinated and uncontrolled . . . we have created an organization that is unaccountable.'[14]

What provoked Carlucci's outrage was the revelation that year that ISA not only existed but had been operating all over the world, apparently without official mandate. News of the organization first surfaced when Lieutenant-General James 'Bo' Gritz was giving testimony to a Congressional committee about his plans to rescue American prisoners of war who were still being held in Laos, a forgotten legacy of the Vietnam War. (Gritz had mounted an unofficial rescue mission which failed, perhaps because no prisoners were found to be still in captivity.) He mentioned that he had received intelligence and support from 'the Activity', an organization that Congress had never heard of before. The Deputy Assistant Secretary of Defense for East Asia and the Pacific, Richard Armitage, had never heard of them either, and told Carlucci, who began an investigation.

Armitage discovered that ISA had been roaming around the world, and in the process had acquired a wide range of exotic equipment, including a hot air balloon and a Rolls Royce, purchased from the Drug Enforcement Administration. Armitage viewed the group as a bunch of cowboys. There was evidence that they had bugged a room used by a Soviet official on the West Coast, an Arab airline office in West Germany and the conference room of a Central American head of state. It was unclear just what value these operations had had or exactly where they fitted into the intelligence requirements of the United States.

But this was the start of the Reagan years when a more freewheeling approach to the problems and requirements of intelligence was encouraged. Clearly, ISA had to be brought under control, but there were enough supporters of the need for increased HUMINT to ensure the survival of the organization. For administrative purposes, they were brought under the control of the DIA at Arlington Hall Station, near the Pentagon, where they are directly responsible to the secretary of the army and administered by the assistant chief of staff of army intelligence.

A week after Reagan's inauguration, the hostages that had been held by the Iranians for 444 days were home and the President was promising 'swift and effective retribution' for acts of terrorism. The problem with such a grand statement was that America actually did not have the capabilities to deliver on the rhetoric. The new administration had inherited a demoralized intelligence community and a depressed military that had been operating with a reduced sense of mission for some years. Everywhere the 'idealists' surrounding Reagan looked, communism appeared to be on the march, and nowhere was it more threatening to American interests than in the area of terrorism.

To the holdovers from the Carter administration such as Ambassador Anthony Quainton, the head of the State Department's Office for Combating Terrorism, there was nothing too alarming about the situation. Certainly attacks were mounting, and Americans were a main target, but only ten had been killed in 1980, which hardly placed terrorism at the top of the league of international priorities. But terrorism was a symbol of bigger issues, as Alexander Haig made clear in his first press conference as Secretary of State.

'International terrorism will take the place of human rights in our concern because it is the ultimate abuse of human rights.' He went on to accuse the Soviet Union of 'training, funding and equipping' international terrorists. For Haig, the counter-terrorist cause was a particularly personal one. While Supreme Allied Commander in Europe at Nato, his car had been attacked in Germany by terrorists who had planted a landmine along one of his routes to work. The bomb, which exploded on June 25, 1979, went off a fraction of a second too late and missed Haig's Mercedes, destroying instead the car full of security men which was following him. After the attack, Haig asked Admiral Stansfield Turner at the CIA to find out who was responsible. A few days later he got the answer that a splinter group of Belgian nihilists had done the attack.

'This seemed unlikely to me, since I was not aware that I had ever done anything to offend a Belgian nihilist, so I turned to the West German intelligence service for a second opinion.'[15]

The Germans told him that he had more probably been attacked by one of the local terrorist groups trained by the KGB or one of its Eastern European allies. This answer fitted perfectly with Haig's preconceived ideas.

The Western intellectual fashion at the time, widely reflected in the news media, was to consider such people as idealists who had been driven over the edge of some precipice of conscience by the injustices of capitalistic society. It was also an article of faith that the various terrorist organizations were independent, self-sufficient groups that had no connection to one another or to any foreign power. In fact, they were all to some extent part of a general, if loose, conspiracy of the lunatic Left.

I always maintained, sometimes in the face of ridicule, that the Soviet secret service played a key role in the international terrorist movement . . . As the new government of the old USSR opens the archives of the KGB, it will become evident that they were often financed, trained, and armed by the communist intelligence services, which used them to carry out operations against Western interests and individuals, especially Americans and Israelis. Nearly all terrorist organizations had some connection with the Palestine Liberation Organization.[16]

Both Reagan and Haig were influenced in their prejudices by a book published in 1981 called *The Terror Network*. Claire Sterling, its author, was a journalist with extensive contacts in some parts of Western intelligence and she managed to make a strong case that international terrorism was a single interconnected phenomenon with groups sharing information, equipment, training and targets. It was a prodigious piece of research helped in part by elements of the intelligence community who wished to portray the Soviets as the guilty controlling party. Haig had seen early proofs of the book and was convinced of its veracity.

To the serious professionals inside the intelligence community, the idea that the Soviets had control of the whole terrorist apparatus was ridiculous. There was ample evidence that the Eastern Europeans had provided some training and equipment, as well as sanctuary for some terrorists, but there was no real evidence of Soviet guilt. After Haig's outburst, the State Department supplied him with a copy of a report on international terrorism prepared by the Intelligence and Research Department, which essentially rebutted his allegation of an international conspiracy. Unsatisfied, Haig asked the CIA to prepare a National Intelligence Estimate on the subject.[17]

As was common in those days, the whole project became bogged down in a wrangle over definitions. In preparing the NIE, the CIA only included groups who could be judged by their intentions indiscriminately to target innocent civilians. This excluded all terrorist organizations such as the IRA or the PLO who had clear political goals and who used terrorism as a tool to attack specific targets which sometimes included innocent civilians.

Not surprisingly, the CIA's first draft uncovered little evidence of

Soviet support, not least because most of the acts which Haig and others considered acts of terrorism were not even examined. The head of the DIA, Lt. Gen. Eugene Tighe, wrote to Bill Casey complaining that the CIA estimate was hopelessly narrow. He submitted his own estimate, which went to the other extreme to embrace every single movement, large and small, which had ever used violence of any kind. The State Department then argued that the whole exercise was counterproductive and should be scrapped. Casey ignored this and brought in Lincoln Gordon, a former ambassador and university president, who was outside the Agency's bureaucracy and therefore likely to be more impartial. He widened the analysis net by defining terrorist groups by their acts. Organizations that used bombing and assassination to achieve political goals were terrorists, he considered. This middle ground produced a more comprehensive NIE which still failed to satisfy the Haig/Reagan concept of a Soviet conspiracy.

The study concluded that the Soviets had helped set up a number of training camps for Palestinians in Czechoslovakia, which had been run by Czech, Soviet and East German specialists. The graduates of these camps had then set up their own camps all over the Middle East which had welcomed terrorists from all over the world. But there was no credible evidence of Soviet operational control of the recruits or the graduates and ample evidence that the Soviets had little to do with terrorist training after 1970. The study concluded that Soviet support for terrorism was essentially 'opportunistic'.

The disagreements that had marred the production of the NIE were to continue through the Reagan years. To some, terrorism was an ideological problem that could only be solved when the Cold War was won, and the Soviets eliminated as a threat. To others, terrorism was now established as a fact of political life, which would very probably be around for the foreseeable future. As there were disagreements about the cause, so there were arguments about the solutions. Some wanted the quick fix of massive retribution against the perpetrators or the sponsors, while others argued for a more cautious approach. Throughout the Reagan/Bush years, these two forces would battle each other with varying degrees of success. But for most of the time there was a constant struggle simply to keep the tide at bay, to reduce the terrorist problem to levels where it could be managed effectively.

CHAPTER TWELVE

THE BAGHDAD BOMBERS

The foundations for the Western world's current capability against terrorism were laid in the 1970s and 1980s but came to fruition following the invasion of Kuwait by Iraq in August 1990. When Saddam Hussein despatched his forces to conquer Kuwait, the Israelis warned that nine Arab and Palestinian groups, including the Abu Nidal Organization and the Palestine Liberation Front, would support Iraq in the event of conflict. They also warned that Iraqi intelligence was attempting to orchestrate a series of terrorist attacks around the world.

In October 1990, Ahmed Mohammed Riyadh, a member of the Libyan-based Islamic Unity Movement, surrendered to police in Cyprus, saying that he was part of a terrorist cell which had been planning to blow up the French embassy in the city of Nicosia. At the time, the French government appeared to be vacillating in its support for the allied coalition and, in particular, for military action to expel Saddam Hussein's forces from Kuwait.[1]

Ahmed told his interrogators from the British SIS that Baghdad expected a well placed and well timed bomb attack might prove to be the deciding factor in keeping the French out of the war. If the French crumbled, then Saddam hoped that the whole alliance would collapse. The exposure of that cell led to a massive intelligence operation in the Mediterranean.

For months the British, American, German and French intelligence services had reported that Iraqi Airways, the country's national airline, had been used to distribute weapons and explosives to terrorist cells in the Middle East and Europe. Once the trade embargo imposed by the United Nations took effect, these movements stopped but the intelligence community were aware that the weapons and people were already in place to carry out attacks.

160

The centre of Iraqi intelligence operations was their embassy in Athens. For years Greece had been a centre for Arab terrorism, with organizations using the country as a transit point for cash, weapons and people. Countries such as Libya, Syria and Iraq, which had sponsored terrorist organizations, also used Athens as their base of operations, so the city has become to counter-terrorism what Vienna used to be to the Cold War: a centre of intrigue where spy spies on spy and terrorist meets with terrorist to exchange information and gossip.

From August, the size of the Iraqi embassy in Athens had doubled and a number of diplomats had been observed shuttling between Athens and Cyprus where there had been meetings with a number of different terrorists. The FBI sent a crisis management team to Cyprus to deal with the threat, and they also took over a whole floor of the US embassy in Athens to coordinate the intelligence. In addition, the GCHQ listening post on Cyprus is believed to have intercepted Iraqi diplomatic communications, which spelled out in some detail the nature of the worldwide terrorist campaign the Iraqis were planning. These operations were under the control of the Da'Irat al Mukhabarat al-Amah, or GID, Iraq's main intelligence organization, controlled by Sabba'a al Tikriti, Saddam Hussein's half brother.

A series of warnings were issued by intelligence agencies to alert embassies and businesses that were considered vulnerable. In Britain, even the BBC was warned by the Security Service that it might be a target, and precautions that would normally have only been instituted in case of full-scale war were brought into force. In the United States, airports, government buildings and military facilities were given increased security as were the individuals who might be considered likely terrorist targets. In France, the gendarmerie and the French Territorial National Guard conducted Operation Vigipirate, which increased protection for potential victims.

Iraqi nationals in more than thirty different countries were arrested, expelled or placed on a watch list. In Britain, eight Iraqi diplomats and sixty-seven other Iraqi nationals were expelled after information was supplied to the government by MI5. The diplomats were believed to be members of Iraqi intelligence while the citizens were considered potentially dangerous, although there was no hard intelligence to support their terrorist links. In fact, Iraqi terrorism was not high on MI5's list of priorities. There had been few terrorist attacks in Britain by people from Middle East countries since the 1970s, and the MI5 list was neither complete nor accurate.

A further ninety-one Iraqis and Palestinians were detained in January. These people had been arrested after MI5 supplied a list to the police which turned out to be hopelessly inaccurate and based on out-of-date or wrong information. The list was drawn in part from the names of people who had taken part in pro-Iraqi demonstrations, but it failed to take account of the fact that a large number had been forced to take part by the Iraqi embassy. Thirty-two others, allegedly members of the Iraqi armed forces, turned out to be students who were described as soldiers because their visas had been organized by the Iraqi military attaché. Others, described as supporters, were in fact dissidents seeking sanctuary in Britain. The arrests were widely and rightly criticized, while MI5 defended the list, pointing out that no terrorist attacks took place in Britain and so they must be doing something right.[2]

Kenneth Baker, the home secretary, later announced an investigation into the circumstances surrounding the arrests, to be carried out by Sir Philip Woodfield, a former permanent undersecretary at the Northern Ireland Office. His report was severely critical of MI5, pointing out that the Service had failed to keep its information up to date and its vetting of the people on the list had been inadequate.

All the measures to counter any potential threat were undertaken with maximum publicity, to act as a deterrent. Up to a point, the game favoured the defence. A terrorist act usually takes from three to six months to organize. It requires the selection of a target, the gathering of detailed intelligence, the placing of terrorists with false identities, arms, cash and safe houses, and the formulation of an attack plan that allows for the escape of the terrorists after the act. There is no evidence that Saddam had set the terrorist train in motion before the invasion of Kuwait, so the GID had to try and organize these attacks from a standing start in a very hostile environment.

The fact that the Coalition included such countries as Saudi Arabia and Syria allowed the Western countries to apply pressure on traditional sponsors of terrorism to curtail their usual activities. Among the Coalition countries, Syria had long been considered a major sponsor through its support for groups like the Popular Struggle Front, the Popular Front for the Liberation of Palestine (General Command) and the Abu Nidal Organization.[3] Other countries, such as Kuwait and Saudi Arabia, had been paying off terrorist groups for years in exchange for freedom from attack on their territory. This blood money had been one of the main reasons why so many Middle East terrorist groups had survived for so many years. But after the invasion, those traditional planks of terrorist support were withdrawn. The Arab members of the Coalition made it clear that if any terrorist attacks took place no further cash would be forthcoming. For once the threat worked.

The single exception was Yasser Arafat's Palestine Liberation Organization. In a classic political miscalculation, Arafat believed that he could broker a peace deal between Saddam and the Arab countries, including Kuwait. He publicly came out in support of Saddam's invasion, thinking this would give him a voice in Saddam's counsels, while bolstering his position with the militants in the Arab world. In classic Arafat style, he also thought that he would be able to parlay this extreme position into a middle ground where he would bring all the different factions to the table. It was a serious miscalculation which infuriated the conservatives (Saudi Arabia and Kuwait) and the militants (Syria), and left his position as leader of the Palestinian movement seriously weakened.

But Arafat himself was not prepared to go so far as to order any of his followers to carry out terrorism in his name. He realized that would have fatally compromised his image as a moderate in the US and Europe.

Libya and Iran, who are major sponsors of international terrorism, were not part of the Coalition. Iran, which had just completed a lengthy and costly war with Iraq, was unwilling to do anything that would help the cause of Saddam Hussein, even in the name of Islamic solidarity, and so remained on the sidelines. The United States encouraged Egypt and Syria to pressure Libya either to expel terrorists operating from their territory or to restrain those they could control. The carrot offered was warmer relations with Western governments and the Arab world after the war. The stick was complete isolation from their neighbours and possible military retaliation if they failed to comply. By November, Gadaffi had expelled 145 members of the Palestine Liberation Front, led by Abu Abbas who had been openly supportive of Saddam Hussein. Abbas was forced to relocate in Baghdad. Gadaffi also shut down four terrorist training camps in his country.[4]

So Saddam was deprived of the cooperative services of all the major state sponsors of terrorism. He had to rely on his own resources, which were vulnerable because they depended largely on his diplomatic network and other national organizations, such as Iraqi Airways. At the end of January, Saddam dispatched a number of terrorists across the border into Saudi Arabia, with orders to try and attack strategic targets such as command headquarters or senior officers in the Coalition. These were unrealistic missions, as Saddam had very poor intelligence about the disposition of the allied forces, and no idea at all about the location of particular individuals. At least six of these terrorists were captured and executed by the Saudi authorities.[5]

When sanctions and preemptive strikes resulted in more than a hundred Iraqi diplomats worldwide being sent home, Saddam had little left but rhetoric to encourage the faithful to launch a jihad against the United States and its Coalition partners.

'The main thrust of the military battle may be Iraq, but the theatre of our operations includes every struggler and holy fighter whose hand can reach out to harm aggressors throughout the whole world,' said Saddam.[6]

This call to arms was answered largely by enthusiastic amateurs, who had little of the patience or training of the professional terrorist, and made an easier target for the intelligence community. A number of attacks were prevented by such intelligence. For example, on January 20, 1991, the State Department issued a travel advisory warning that the US government had intelligence about a planned attack against American, British and Australian installations in Bangkok. The target list included hotels and restaurants where Europeans stayed and ate as well as businesses owned by Coalition partners. This information was obtained from an Iraqi defector who had surrendered to US authorities two weeks earlier.[7] Within a week, Thai security officials, acting on information supplied by the CIA, arrested two Iraqis, Muhammad Ali and Mahmood Muhammed, and a Jordanian, Radi Shammari. The three were linked to supplies of weapons and explosives which were being stockpiled in Bangkok. The trio were deported to Malaysia where officials in Kuala Lumpur refused them entry. On their return to Thailand they were placed in custody.[8] Two Iraqi diplomats, Muzir Razoki, the commercial attaché, and Saleem Nahiur al Jaddouri, were thought to be members of Iraqi intelligence and ordered to leave the country.

Even with the expulsions and the counter-terrorist successes, the intelligence community continued to warn governments that more attacks were certain. These warnings were generated in part because of the flood of information coming in from agents and communications intercepts. Undoubtedly there was a mass of activity, but at the same time the intelligence analysts, sitting at the centre of a worldwide information gathering web, were reacting to the smallest indicators, events which under normal circumstances would have been ignored. The clearest statement of the threat came in an unusual and alarming statement on January 11 from Malcolm Rifkind, then the British transport secretary.

For some time, Iraq has threatened to mount terrorist attacks. Since the beginning of the Gulf crisis we have taken this into account in our counter-terrorist planning. The threat will certainly increase in the event of hostilities in the Gulf.

In the past, civil aviation has attracted terrorist attacks. Terrorist groups have the capability to operate from countries outside the Middle East, including Europe. Governments, including the United Kingdom, have required airports and airlines to take additional security measures to protect their operations. Throughout the world, aviation security is at an unprecedentedly high level. Governments, again including the UK, also have in place contingency plans to bring additional security measures into immediate operation should there be hostilities in the Gulf.

Inevitably, security measures will cause some inconvenience to travellers. People who are considering travelling can help by co-operating with airport, airline and other security staff. They should minimize the amount of luggage they take with them and should not leave it unattended. They should avoid carrying, so far as possible, all but the smallest personal electrical items. They should be particularly careful not to accept gifts from people they do not know well, nor should they offer to carry articles or packages for other people. At airports, they should be prepared to declare any electrical items which they have packed and they should answer carefully and clearly any questions asked them about their baggage. In the UK, it is now a criminal offence to give false answers to such questions. They should never check in bags for anyone else or carry anything on to an aircraft for anyone else.

Despite the intensified security measures, the risk, although it cannot be quantified, will increase substantially in the event of hostilities. No government can guarantee security. Members of the public should be aware of this when deciding whether to travel by air.

Despite such efforts, a number of attacks did take place, with the Rand organization, a California-based think tank, listing 63 in their Chronology of International Terrorism from January 15 to February 1, 1991. But these were all low-level attacks ranging from the firebombing of a PanAm office in Turin by members of the PFLP, to a Molotov cocktail attack on an army reserve centre in Eugene, Oregon by anti-war protesters. There were no 'spectaculars', no attacks that could begin to shake the resolve of the Coalition.

The Gulf War was a model of how effective international cooperation can be. There was unparalleled sharing of information between countries with normally good relations such as Britain and America. But there was also extraordinary cooperation between countries like Syria – until the war seen by the US State Department as a major sponsor of international terrorism – and less central countries like the Philippines and Australia. The policy succeeded. There was not a single major operation by any terrorist organization anywhere in the world, and several attacks were prevented by good advance intelligence. Saddam Hussein promised a terrorist war and failed to deliver.

Between mid-January and the end of February 1991, more than 200 terrorist incidents were recorded by the State Department. About one fifth of the attacks were by indigenous terrorist groups which claimed the attacks were related to the Gulf crisis. Dev Sol in Turkey, 17 November in Greece, the Tupac Amaru Revolutionary Movement in Peru and the Manuel Rodriguez Patriotic Front in Chile were responsible for forty of the incidents and were clearly using the Gulf crisis as a convenient excuse for carrying on business as usual.[9]

But there were other major attacks that went wrong, not because of good preemptive intelligence, but because the terrorists were inept, and rushed into action without adequate preparation. On January 19, for example, a massive bomb exploded prematurely as two terrorists tried to place it in the Thomas Jefferson Library in Manila, killing one of them and wounding the other. It transpired that the men failed to connect the wires from the explosives to the detonator in the right sequence. In the days following the explosion, an Iraqi diplomat, Sabah Saddiq Saad, was ordered to leave the country. Two students, Hisham and Husham Abdul-Sattar, sons of the Iraqi ambassador to Somalia who had previously served in Manila, were arrested when police raided their house and found belongings of the two terrorists along with some bomb-making equipment. Husham Abdul-Sattar was a leader of the National Union of Iraqi Students and Youth, Philippine Branch, and had been active in organizing anti-US demonstrations. He had also received some terrorist training in North Korea.

Another went wrong when a bomb with twenty-four sticks of dynamite was planted outside the US ambassador's house in Jakarta and failed to go off because of a dead battery.

After the war was over, there was a comprehensive after-action analysis by the intelligence community to examine the lessons learned. Five reasons were cited for the successful foiling of what would have been the largest ever coordinated international terrorist campaign. First, from the beginning of December, once war looked certain, Britain, America and other nations began expelling Iraqi diplomats and known intelligence agents. Second, Iraq had constantly used Iraqi Airways as a method of infiltrating people into foreign countries and for shuttling cash, arms and explosives around the world. This avenue was blocked when UN sanctions came into effect. Third, there was an unprecedented exchange of intelligence between all the countries involved in the campaign against Saddam. Even countries not directly involved, such as Thailand, cooperated in the international effort. Fourth, nations implemented stringent security precautions, which were a mixture of the public (tightened security at public buildings, airports and railway stations) and the secret (there was a massive campaign to inspect air and sea cargo as well as all international mail).

The final and perhaps most significant contribution to the successful counter-terrorist campaign did not emerge until after the war.

'We assumed from the outset that Iraqi terrorists had to execute orders, and therefore would begin attacks as soon as hostilities began,' explained a senior State Department official. 'As it turned out, however, individual cells did not possess explosives. Rather, they were housed in embassies and other holding places. [Explosives were regularly transported by Iraqi diplomatic bag.] The cells were asked to size up targets, but were not given the go-ahead to execute an attack at their discretion. Instead, the terrorists required official approval and then needed access to the explosives. Official approval never came, however, because our first strikes broke the communication links between the Iraqi foreign ministry and its embassies and intelligence agencies.'[10]

Yasser Arafat's support for Saddam Hussein had infuriated the two Arab states most directly affected by Saddam's invasion: Kuwait itself and neighbouring Saudi Arabia. After years of financing the PLO and providing Arafat with much needed political support, the two countries saw the Palestinian's action as a terrible betrayal. So, when Abu Nidal's representative came calling in Riyadh and Kuwait City soon after the Gulf War ended, he found a receptive audience. Nidal had two messages: first, if you want to get your revenge against Arafat then I'm your man; second, my people have not attacked you in the past because you have been generous with your support.[11]

The enmity between Arafat and Nidal is legendary even in the snake pit of Middle East politics. Both have tried to kill the other several times and the PLO claims that Nidal, the nom de guerre of Sabri al-Banna, organized the assassination of Abu Iyad, Arafat's second-in-command in Tunis in January 1991.

For many years Nidal has been based in Tripoli and has now established a training camp in southern Sudan where some of his four hundred men now operate. Uniquely among Middle East terrorist leaders, Nidal operates an extraordinarily tight cell structure which has been very difficult to penetrate. He has also demonstrated a ruthlessness which makes him stand out from other Palestinian terrorists. For nearly twenty years he has left a trail of destruction around the world. His organization was responsible for the attack on El Al at Rome and Vienna airports in 1985, when eighteen people were killed and forty injured. He also ordered the attempted assassination of Shlomo Argov, the Israeli ambassador to Lebanon, which provoked the Israeli invasion of that country in 1982.

In June 1991, Nidal was allowed to open an office in Jeddah, following a visit by Prince Saud al-Faisal, the Saudi foreign minister, to Damascus the previous March, where he met with a number of terrorist organizations, including the ANO.[12] From the summer of 1991, Nidal's group received up to $20m in cash from the Saudis and Kuwaitis. Ordinarily, this huge cash inflow might not have been noted but Nidal suddenly became so flush that he in turn began to spread the cash around the Middle East, giving handouts to Hamas, the Palestinian terrorist organization on the West Bank, and to Hizbollah in Lebanon. It was then that both the CIA and SIS began looking into the source of the money.

When it was learned just who was behind the funding, there was outrage in both Langley and London and a determination to cut off the cash without delay. It was decided that senior officials in London and Washington would be given the information and advised that the two countries on whose behalf Britain and America had gone to war only a few months earlier were now financing the world's most dangerous terrorist. But even the habitually cynical intelligence officers were taken aback when their information received a frosty reception in both capitals, and by the decision to do nothing. The explanation for such inaction was simple: both countries were actively pursuing billions of dollars in defence deals and in contracts to help rebuild Kuwait after the war. Neither the Americans nor the British wanted a confrontation which might put at risk such big business, which would then go to a rival like France. Better to do nothing.

On Friday November 1, at an angry meeting between an SIS official and a member of the cabinet office, it was pointed out that if the British government did nothing, the information was sure to end up on the front page of a newspaper like *The Sunday Times*. By complete coincidence, two days later the story did indeed appear on the front page of *The Sunday Times* to the consternation of both the SIS officer and the cabinet office. Citing American intelligence sources, the story spelled out the bare details of the funding. That same day, in a series of angry telephone calls, SIS denied any involvement in the story. But, for the intelligence community, the job had been done. With the story aired publicly, the Americans and the British had no choice but to confront the Saudis and Kuwaitis. Not surprisingly, the allegations were denied, but the funds dried up soon afterwards.

The experiences of the Gulf War and its immediate aftermath demonstrated that international cooperation can make a real difference in the fight against terrorism. For many of the professionals involved over the past thirty years, this has seemed blindingly obvious, but the ideal has always crumbled in the face of entrenched views and political realities. In the Gulf crisis there was a single common enemy which united all nations, including many which traditionally sponsor terrorism.

In theory, this success should have provided the foundation on which a new counter-terrorist initiative could have been built. But within weeks of the ceasefire it was back to business as usual with even those strong allies in the Coalition resorting to the normal double dealing and payoffs that are the international currency of terrorism. The Saudis and Kuwaitis began bribing Abu Nidal, while the Syrians resumed their sponsorship of international terror, and the Iraqis began to rebuild their intelligence network which runs terrorism around the world.

During the Gulf War, even Iran kept its terrorists in Hizbollah on a tight rein despite considerable pressure to authorize strikes against the Coalition. But it is now clear that the Iranians were simply biding their time and laying their plans for a new type of terrorist war which caught Western intelligence by surprise.

CHAPTER THIRTEEN

THE IBRAHIM LINCOLN BRIGADE

The American people have largely been spared the horrors of modern terrorism. There have been occasional incidents abroad when innocent civilians were caught in the crossfire, such as the December 1983 bombing of Harrods department store in London when Kenneth Salvesan, a twenty-eight-year-old American tourist, was killed by the IRA. The bombing of the Marine barracks in Beirut in October that same year killed 241 men and wounded 100 others. But these were the exceptions, that might have discouraged Americans from travelling abroad. At home, however, they were safe, secure in the knowledge they had the best defences in the world against even the most professional terrorist.

America has always been considered uniquely vulnerable to terrorist attack. Communications inside the US borders are designed for ease of passage and so diverse are the road, rail and air links that they are virtually impossible to police effectively. For the terrorist, who above all wants to escape the scene of the crime to attack again, such conditions are perfect. But America escaped the terrorist scourge of the 1970s and 1980s that hit every other developed country. There were some outrages by Puerto Rican groups, and a few isolated incidents by such organizations as the Jewish Defense League and the Symbionese Liberation Army, but these were largely ineffective and badly organized. No Middle East terrorist group chose to attack the United States at home, despite the focus of their rhetoric on America as the principal supporter of Israel, the hated enemy. Instead, these groups confined their activities to attacks on Americans abroad.

There were several reasons for this. First, America was an alien nation to most of the terrorists. Few had travelled there and, to most of them, the very sophistication which made it vulnerable also made it daunting.

The primary rule for nearly all terrorists is to attack and survive. America was the one country where escape in the face of the vast array of technology ranged against the terrorist seemed almost impossible. Far easier, then, to hit America far away from its own shores.

Second, the American intelligence community was designed to assemble information about terrorists in foreign countries, to collate indicators of planned actions and act preemptively. In recent years, this strategy has become more effective, as cooperation between governments and agencies has grown. Many of the groups that emerged in the late 1960s and flourished in the 1970s have been destroyed or seriously weakened. Baader Meinhof, Action Directe and the Cellules Combatantes Communistes have all been destroyed. The Japanese Red Army has disintegrated, and the rump of Italy's Red Brigade is largely ineffective. What remains from twenty years ago are the Middle Eastern terrorist groups. Enough effort has been expended by Western intelligence agencies to understand the funding, training, support and methods of these groups that good intelligence is gathered on a regular basis.

Those targets have become part of the intelligence routine. Whole funding and bureaucratic infrastructures have grown up around combating these groups and, in the post-Cold War reorganization of intelligence, one of the principal justifications for retaining numbers and money was the terrorist threat. But as the community moved to shift its priorities, so terrorism itself was evolving in ways that the community seems ill-prepared to combat.

The most graphic illustration of this change occured on February 26, 1993 when a massive car bomb exploded at the World Trade Center in New York.

The operation began on February 23 when Mohammed Salameh, a twenty-five-year-old illegal Palestinian immigrant who had lived an apparently blameless existence since arriving in America in 1988, went to the Rockview Branch of the Ryder car rental agency in Jersey City outside New York. He was driven to the agency in a red GM sedan by Nidal Ayyad, a twenty-five-year-old Kuwaiti chemical engineer who lived in Maplewood, New Jersey. The sedan had been rented on February 15 by Ayyad, who listed Salameh as an additional driver on the rental form. Salameh hired a Ford Econoline E-350 van with Alabama plates for a week and left a $400 security deposit.[1]

The van was driven to the Space Station Storage facility in Jersey City where Salameh had rented a unit the previous November under the name Kamal Ibraham. Over the previous three months, several thousand pounds of urea and nitric acid had been shipped in drums to the unit, and Ayyad had been charged with combining them to produce a chemical which, if triggered by a small explosive, could produce a massive blast.

On February 25, Salameh, accompanied by some other Arabs, arrived with the van at Space Station Storage and spent several hours loading the chemicals into the vehicle. It was then driven to level B-2 of the World Trade Center, directly under the Vista International Hotel, and parked. The vehicle was left with the timer ticking and set to explode at 12.15 pm on February 26, around lunchtime, when the maximum number of people would be in and around the building.

The 1,200 pound bomb detonated on schedule, blasting up through the floor of the Vista Hotel and down through the lower levels of the parking lot. The massive floor joists which supported the huge World Trade Center structure were fractured and thrown aside by the force of the explosion. Ceilings and floors collapsed like a concertina, piling floor upon floor in the cavernous hole that had appeared at the bottom of the building. The rubble crushed water pipes and put out of action the building's fire-fighting system, while burning walls and exploding gas tanks produced clouds of billowing black smoke that filled halls and stairways trapping many of the 50,000 people in the building. Six people died and more than 1,000 were injured in the blast. It was the worst terrorist attack on US soil in memory.

'Until [the] blast, many Americans regarded terrorism as something that happened elsewhere: a problem endemic to the already violent Middle East and revolution-prone countries of Latin America that occasionally spilled over on to the streets of Paris, London and Madrid,' said Bruce Hoffman, a terrorism expert with the Rand Institute in Santa Monica. 'The bombing shattered not only that complacency, but America's sense of security. Though frequently the target of terrorists abroad, the attack demonstrates that Americans can no longer believe themselves immune to such violence within their own borders.'[2]

This view was underlined when four alleged members of the Abu Nidal Organization were arrested in St Louis and charged with discussing blowing up the Israeli embassy in Washington, conspiring to murder Jews and acting as a conduit for money from other ANO cells around the world to members in America. According to the indictment, the group received their instructions following a trip to Mexico City in April 1987. This was the first time members of the ANO had been found operating in the United States and marks what American intelligence believes is the start of a sustained effort by the group to attack targets in the US.[3]

172

In the immediate aftermath of the World Trade Center explosion, there were nineteen calls from different organizations claiming responsibility. Three claimed the bombing on behalf of one of the factions involved in the crisis in Bosnia, and at first investigators thought this the most likely explanation, not least because none of their intelligence antennae around the world had picked up any sign of activity among the usual suspects. Balkan terrorists had been behind America's previous worst outrage, in December 1975, when Croatian nationalists planted a bomb in a left-luggage locker at La Guardia Airport which killed eleven and injured seventy-five. A year later, Croats hijacked a TWA aircraft and at the same time planted a bomb in New York's Grand Central Station which killed a policeman who tried to defuse it.

But then the forensic experts combing through the rubble around the site of the explosion found part of a vehicle that they thought could have carried the bomb. Most of the other cars in the garage had been crushed by the debris or destroyed by the blast, but it was clear that the recovered parts – part of a wheel, an axle, a hub cap – had been literally blown to pieces. Further examination revealed the vehicle identification number stencilled into the metal and the FBI swiftly traced it to the Rockview branch of the Ryder truck rental agency.

When the FBI arrived at the agency they were astonished to learn that, within two hours of the blast, Mohammed Salameh had returned to the office to ask for his $400 security deposit back. He claimed that the vehicle had been stolen the night before but the clerk insisted that the money could not be refunded until Salameh filed a police report. Salameh left promising to return with the necessary documents. The FBI ran his name through their computer and discovered that he was already on file.

In 1990, Salameh had joined a small group of Arabs demonstrating on behalf of El-Sayyid Nosair, an Islamic militant who had been charged with the murder in 1991 of Meir Kahane, the Arab-hating founder of the Jewish Defense League. Although Nosair had been acquitted of the murder he had been found guilty of lesser charges, including possessing a gun. He was sent to the Attica state prison in New York State. Salameh had visited Nosair in jail.

With hindsight, the FBI should have recognized that a terrorist cell was developing in the United States. When Nosair's apartment was searched, ammunition for an AK-47 automatic rifle was found along with a hit list of prominent politicians and other public figures. Even then, the attack on Kahane was treated as an aberration, not as the beginning of what may prove to be a long campaign.

Once the database had coughed up Salameh's name, it was possible to run the cross references that began to produce a pattern of names and some common links. For example, Salameh's New York State driver's licence listed his home as 57 Prospect Park, Brooklyn, the same address as Ibrahim Elgabrowny, Nosair's cousin who had helped with his defence.

While the FBI tracked Salameh and tried to establish a motive for the attack, the *New York Times* received a typewritten letter that gave the first clue to the identity and motives of the terrorists. The letter, which was posted the day of the attack, read:

The following letter from the LIBERATION ARMY regarding the operation conducted against the W.T.C.

We, the fifth battalion in the LIBERATION ARMY, declare our responsibility for the explosion on the mentioned building. *This action was done in response for the American political, economical, and military support to Israel the state of terrorism and to the rest of the dictator countries in the region.*

Our Demands Are:

1. Stop all military, economical, and political aids to Israel.
2. All diplomatic relations with Israel must stop.
3. Not to interfere with any of the Middle East countries interior affairs.

If our demands are not met, all of our functional groups in the army will continue to execute our missions against military and civilian targets in and out the United States. This also will include some potential Nuclear targets. For your own information, our army has more than a hundred and fifty suicidal soldiers ready to go ahead. The terrorism that Israel practices (which is supported by America) must be faced with a similar one. The dictatorship and terrorism (also supported by America) that some countries are practicing against their own people must also be faced with terrorism.

The American people must know, that their civilians who got killed are not better than those who are getting killed by the American weapons and support.

The American people are responsible for the actions of their government and they must question all of the crimes that their government is committing against other people. Or they – Americans – will be the targets of our operations that could diminish them.

We invite all of the people from all countries and all of the revolutionaries in the world to participate in this action with us to accomplish our just goals.

'. . . If then anyone transgresses the prohibition against you transgress ye likewise against him . . .'

LIBERATION ARMY
FIFTH BATTALION

Abu Bakr Al-Makee

The letter was typical of many similar demands made over the past twenty years: poor spelling and punctuation, rambling rhetoric, incoherent and unrealistic demands. However, the FBI had never heard of the Fifth Battalion of the Liberation Army. There was no reason to suppose this claim of responsibility was any different from the eighteen others received around the time of the attack. (The FBI later found a copy of the letter on computer disk at Ayyad's apartment.)

While the analysis of the document was under way, the FBI continued their stakeout of the Ryder rental outlet in Jersey City. Six days after the explosion, *Newsday*, a New York newspaper, reported that the FBI had traced the vehicle which contained the bomb to the Ryder agency. Thinking their undercover operation was exposed, the police and FBI decided to arrest Salameh when he next turned up at the dealership. Later that day, he arrived once again to ask for his deposit back. FBI agents promptly arrested him.

Forensic examination of Salameh's clothes provided clear evidence that he had handled explosives. When he was detained, Salameh was carrying Nidal Ayyad's business card and when they searched his apartment in Jersey City, the FBI found a timing device along with other evidence that Ayyad had been the bomb maker for the cell.

A further five search warrants widened the net, drawing in Ibrahim Elgabrowny, Nosair's cousin, who was charged with resisting arrest and possessing forged passports. Bilal Alkaisi, a twenty-six-year-old Jordanian was charged with aiding and abetting the bombing. Two other suspects, Mahmud Abouhalima, a thirty-three-year-old Egyptian cab driver, and Ramzi Ahmed Yousef, a twenty-five-year-old resident of New Jersey, fled the country soon after the bombing. Investigators later discovered that Yousef had arrived in America on Pakistan International Airlines flight 703 from Karachi to New York on September 1, 1992. He was carrying an Iraqi passport without a valid entry visa and claimed political asylum. The INS is unable to process all those claiming asylum and so, as Yousef would have guessed, he was released pending a formal hearing. He promptly vanished into the vast New York immigrant community.

Travelling on the same flight with Yousef was Mohammad Ajaj, a twenty-seven-year-old Palestinian, travelling under the name of Khurram Khan on a forged Swedish passport. The forgery was so poor that it was detected by immigration. When Ajaj's luggage was searched, customs officers found a library of terrorist manuals including directions on how to make bombs, plant mines, use poisons and fight with knives. He also had videos of suicide car bombings. He was taken into custody and later sentenced to six months in jail for travelling on a false passport. Even though the World Trade Center bombing took place while he was still in jail, he was later charged with complicity.[4]

On March 12, Abouhalima was arrested in Egypt by men from the Mukhabarat, the country's security service. Without the restraint of Western concerns about habeus corpus or human rights, Abouhalima was ruthlessly interrogated by his captors. He was repeatedly beaten and burning cigarettes were applied to his groin to make him confess to his involvement. After a week in prison, he was extradited to the United States for trial.[5]

Meanwhile, the other strands of the investigation were coming together. The New York police had traced the storage unit where the explosives had been hidden, and the composition of those explosives matched the traces that had been found on Salameh's clothes. Eyewitnesses reported that several men had loaded containers into an Econoline van the night before the explosion. A check of the calls made from a nearby public telephone revealed a number of calls that day to the office phone of Nidal Ayyad.

The common thread joining the individuals was Sheik Omar Abdel-Rahman, a blind Egyptian cleric who had illegally entered the US in May 1990, despite being on an anti-terrorist watch list. Rahman had been tried and acquitted on three terrorist charges in Egypt, including the assassination of President Anwar Sadat. He preached a particularly fierce brand of Islamic fundamentalism which called for a return to the simpler, purer days when Islam was untarnished by corrupting Western influences. Like another spiritual leader, Ayatollah Khomeini, Rahman had found a wide and loyal following in his own country.[6]

With his own government after him and hundreds of his followers under arrest, Rahman applied for a tourist visa to the US in May 1990 at the American embassy in Khartoum. Allegedly his name was checked against a list held in the State Department's automated visa lookout system, which failed to find any reference, so he was given his visa. He moved to New York, began preaching and, like Khomeini during his Paris exile, recording cassettes and videos for distribution to the faithful back home.

Realizing its mistake, the State Department revoked his visa, and Rahman was forced to leave the country. But his exile was only temporary. A few weeks later, he slipped past an unwitting immigration official at Kennedy airport. Once back in the country, perhaps realizing how extraordinarily incompetent the Immigration and Naturalization Service is, Rahman applied for a green card. His faith was justified. In April 1991, he was given permanent residence in the US, despite having had a previous visa revoked, reentering the country illegally and living in New York as an illegal immigrant.

Soon after the attack, the FBI discovered that Salameh and Ayyad held a joint bank account at the Jersey City branch of the National Westminister Bank into which funds had been transferred from abroad over a period of months, the most recent being a draft for $2,420.87 from Germany, wired nine days before the bombing. The FBI traced several sums, never totalling more than $10,000 at a time, amounting to just under $100,000 which had been sent to the suspects from overseas. Information from Israeli and Egyptian intelligence led the American investigators to believe that Sheik Rahman was receiving money from Iran via one of his two wives resident in Cairo and that the other funds might also have originated in Tehran.[7]

This in turn led investigators to suggest that the bombing had been orchestrated or even ordered by Tehran, as part of a new international onslaught. This was a line firmly pushed by the Israeli government in briefings both to journalists and to other intelligence agencies. Others, such as the author Yosseff Bodansky, staff director for the House Republican Task Force on Terrorism and Unconventional Warfare, argued that the World Trade Center attack was part of a new jihad or holy war against America sponsored by the Iranian government.[8] There is no serious evidence available to back up this assertion. However, there is ample information to suggest that the Trade Center bombing was part of a new phenomenon, an outgrowth of the Islamic fundamentalism of the 1970s and 1980s which does pose a definite threat to democracies worldwide.

In June 1993, the FBI arrested what was alleged to be another terrorist ring also operating out of New York. This time, the terrorists were apparently planning to bomb the United Nations headquarters and two tunnels carrying commuter traffic under the Hudson River, as well as assassinating the UN secretary general and two prominent local politicians. This plot, had it succeeded, would have been a devastating blow both to New York City and to America. But all was not as the FBI wanted it to seem.

The whole operation was in fact a classic sting, set up with the help of an informant, known to the FBI as 'the Colonel', who was in fact a former Egyptian military officer resident in New York. He had become close to Sheik Rahman. Disapproving of that attack, the Egyptian, forty-three-year-old Emad Salem, approached the FBI offering his services for a new identity and $250,000 in payment. The FBI, stung after their failure to detect the World Trade Center attack, viewed Salem as the perfect opportunity for them to infiltrate the gang, and see if any other attacks were being planned.[9]

In May, 1993, Salem had approached Siddig Ibrahim Siddig Ali, a thirty-two-year-old New York cab driver, and offered his services as both a bomb maker and a man with access to timing devices. Immediately after the World Trade Center blast, the FBI had launched a major undercover operation to discover any common links between the arrested men. Some of the terrorists arrested for that attack were linked with Said Nosair, who was involved with the assassination of radical rabbi Meir Kahane and is now in jail. The FBI immediately began to target other individuals who had been active in Nosair's defence or who had visited him in jail. Siddig had raised money for Nosair's defence and had visited him a number of times in jail. What is not clear from the evidence so far is just how far the FBI's informant encouraged the group to carry out the planned attacks and how much they thought up the plot themselves.

To Siddig, Salem must have appeared as the answer to a prayer, but exactly who suggested what to whom remains a mystery. In a series of meetings that month, the two men hatched their extraordinary plot, a plot that probably would have led to the deaths of thousands of innocent people. Security guards who got in their way would have been killed, and they hoped they would get access to the UN car park with the aid of false number plates supplied by two Sudanese associated with Sudan's UN mission. According to one FBI wiretap, Siddig claimed the World Trade Center bombing was a message that, 'We can get you anytime'.

But as the operation expanded to draw in at least eight other conspirators, every conversation was being monitored by the FBI, and every meeting photographed by hidden video cameras. The FBI had planned to wait until just before the attacks before pouncing, but then they learned that two of the men were planning to leave the country, the first heading home to Sudan the next weekend. They decided to move in just as the team mixed the fuel, oil and fertilizer to make a 400lb bomb in a specially rented safe house in Jersey City.

'As we entered the bomb factory, the five subjects were actually mixing the witch's brew,' said James Fox, the New York FBI director. 'We entered so fast some of the subjects said they didn't realize strangers were in the bomb factory until they had the handcuffs being put on them.'

There is considerable doubt whether either the World Trade Center group or the second cell to be arrested were the kind of professional terrorists that would pose a serious threat to American society. The World Trade Center bombers were caught because one of the team insisted on returning to the car rental agency to ask for his deposit back after the truck had blown up. Other members of the cell talked openly to each other on the telephone, providing the FBI with a clear electronic trail.

This latest team seem to have been equally inept. One is a Puerto Rican stock clerk, another a kindly figure who buys ice cream for the local children, while a third owns a petrol station in a New York suburb. Siddig Ibrahim Siddig Ali is a former translator for Sheik Rahman, the blind cleric also linked to the World Trade Center bombing. Sheik Rahman was eventually indicted as a criminal conspirator in a massive plan not only to bomb the UN and the World Trade Center but also to assassinate President Mubarak and American military leaders.[10]

Despite giving codenames to the targets – the UN headquarters was 'the Big House', the office building 'the Center', hand grenades were called 'balls' – because they were worried about electronic surveillance, one of the accused talked to the FBI informant on the telephone and explained how difficult it had been to obtain some explosives. After the first arrests early on Thursday morning, one of the cell went to the house of another member and stuck a note on the windscreen which read: 'We have an extreme emergency. The FBI came by early this morning. They raided the apartment and the gym. Please contact me at the house immediately.'

The current wave of terrorism carried out by Muslim fundamentalists

179

is causing considerable concern in the intelligence community, in part because so little is known about who is involved and who is supplying the arms and training. There appears to be no terrorist army or single hand controlling the groups. But there is some common ground: many of the participants fought with the mujahedeen against the Soviets in Afghanistan; also, Iran is involved in supplying cash, training and arms in the same way as the Soviet Union used to in the 1970s and early 1980s.

'The Iranians do not appear to select the targets,' commented one intelligence source. 'Rather they hand out the equipment and the knowledge and let each group get on with it. Sometimes the cash disappears, sometimes nothing happens but sometimes the terrorists do attack. The difficulty for us is covering all the people and learning which is which.'

Some training is provided at terrorist camps set up in the past two years in Sudan which, like Iran, has a Muslim fundamentalist government. Iran has become closely allied to Sudan, and despite the poor state of the Iranian economy the government in Tehran has underwritten a £300m Sudanese arms deal with China. Some intelligence reports say that in Sudan there are twelve training camps, others talk of as many as twenty-five. What is certain is that dozens, perhaps hundreds, of terrorists have been trained by Iranian specialists in these camps and have now fanned out across the world.

The roots of this new terrorism lie not in Tehran but in the ten-year war in Afghanistan which began after the Soviets invaded the country in 1979. Following the invasion, the American government embarked on what was to become one of the largest covert efforts ever to fund, arm and train a guerrilla army. Over ten years, the US spent a total of £3 billion in secret aid, which was running at around £600m a year just before the Soviets withdrew in 1989. That money was spent largely on supplying the guerrillas who were trained and housed by the Pakistan government. Other Arab countries, particularly Saudi Arabia, also contributed to the underwriting of the guerrilla effort.[11]

To many Muslims, the fight against the Soviets became a jihad or holy war, and for young Muslims all over the world the fight was both a call to arms and an inspiration. In New York recruiting of volunteers was organized from the Alkifah Refugee Center on Atlantic Avenue in Brooklyn above the Fu King food shop. From this seedy address, several young Muslims were sent to join the holy war. Among them was Sayyid Nosair, who was later involved in the shooting of Meir Kahane, the founder of the Jewish Defense League. Another was Mahmud Abouhalima, who the FBI believe became the ringleader of the group who bombed the World Trade Center.[12]

At the time the covert operation was under way, there was little concern in Washington about who actually received the money or the guns. The only concern was that they should be used to kill Soviet soldiers to help make Moscow pay dearly for the invasion. If the guerrilla groups had been united both in their support for the United States and their hatred of the Soviets then the task would have been much simpler. In fact, there were seven major guerrilla groups that ranged from the Jabahai-yi-Nijat Melli (National Liberation Front) which was conservative and pro-monarchy, to the Hizb-i-Islami (Islamic Party) led by Gulbuddin Hekmatyar, which was revolutionary, fundamentalist and, as well as being anti-Soviet, virulently anti-American. The war gave people like Hekmatyar, a smart political pragmatist, temporary common cause with the US. So he accepted all the guns, cash and training the US had to offer.

There were few in the intelligence community who were prepared to try and stop this supply of arms, particularly because the most militant often fought the best, and so were most deserving of support. The focus was on short-term gains, even though Hekmatyar had close links with Iran, a country with which the US had no formal relations. Another beneficiary of both American and Saudi support was the Itchad-i-Islam-Baray Azadi Afghanistan (Islamic Alliance to Liberate Afghanistan). It was supported also by Saudi Arabia and the Muslim Brotherhood, a shadowy underground movement active all over the Middle East, dedicated to the overthrow of many Arab governments, including that in Saudi Arabia.

While the war was going on, the guerrillas were fully occupied. Thousands were killed, many thousands more wounded and, rather than diminishing, the campaign drew an ever larger number of recruits from all over the Middle East and Europe, as well as from the US. Altogether around 25,000 men arrived in Pakistan from abroad to join in the fight. Hardly a country was unrepresented, and, for many young Muslims, a period in the jihad became a badge of honour, similar to making the pilgrimage to Mecca as their forefathers had done for centuries.

'Each mujahid [Islamic fighter] was a flower and a jewel who had a right to come and fight the jihad,' said Lieutenant-General Hameed Gul, a former head of Interservices Intelligence, Pakistan's secret police, which was responsible for orchestrating the guerrilla war. 'They were educated people, many from American universities, who had discovered the hollowness of the West and the pristine glory of Islam while living in America. Some tore up their passports when they arrived. The ISI never had any record of them. They stayed for a time and then left.'[13]

When the war ended in 1989, the temporary and fragile alliances between the guerrilla groups and their sponsors fragmented as each leader sought to consolidate his power base within Afghanistan. The millions of dollars that had been siphoned off from the US-led covert operations by the guerrilla bands and their Pakistani supporters were reinvested into the drugs business and into arms trafficking. For some guerrilla leaders, the war had given access to undreamed of power and the control of thousands of well trained and highly experienced guerrilla fighters, men who were used to fighting for a cause, used to living underground for months or even years at a time, and who were used to showing initiative in the field. In other words, these men were trained for battle, whether it be terrorism or conventional warfare.

During the Afghan War, much of the northern part of Pakistan had become the separate fiefdom of the guerrilla leaders. The central government held no writ, drugs were the principal currency and guns the only tool of law enforcement. In such an environment, to a guerrilla leader like Gulbuddin Hekmatyar, who had always had a closer allegiance with Islam than with the American government and felt a greater affinity to Tehran than Washington, the end of the war provided new opportunities to spread his brand of revolution.

In 1989, soon after the Russians abandoned Afghanistan, the government in Tehran underwent dramatic changes, with the death of Ayatollah Khomeini, the spiritual founder of modern Iran. After Khomeini took power in 1979, a new kind of fanatical terrorism was unleashed on the world. The Iranian government sponsored a wide range of terrorist acts including the bombing of the Marine barracks in Beirut. Iranian-sponsored Hizbollah was responsible for the kidnapping of Western hostages in Lebanon and for a number of attempted acts of terrorism during the Gulf War. But the predicted spread of Iran-style revolution through the Arab world never happened, in part because the Shia, who support Khomeini's brand of Islam, proved too diffuse and disorganized to take the step beyond terrorism to guerrilla warfare or even popular revolution. It took ten years for Iran to understand that terrorism was not working, and that they would have to change direction if the revolution was to run its planned course.

The death of Khomeini was greeted with considerable relief among other Arab governments and in the Western countries that had been on the receiving end of Iran's terrorist exports. Learned articles were written in journals and newspapers about how the new president of Iran, the former speaker, Ali Akbar Hashemi Rafsanjani, was a new influence for moderation in the country. It was assumed that terrorism would decline as Iran curbed its territorial ambitions. Nothing of the kind occurred.

On November 23, Spanish customs intercepted a ship which had arrived from Sidon in Lebanon carrying a cargo of preserved fruit. Instead of fruit, the customs officers seized 1,000 pounds of Semtex high explosives, electric detonators and hand grenades, which had been shipped by Hizbollah terrorists. The shipment was intended for distribution to a number of terrorist cells which had been established in European countries. Eight Lebanese Shiites were arrested in Valencia and Madrid, and the Spanish police believe they captured the major components of the terrorist cell in their country.[14]

The following month, American intelligence received information from the PLO that Iranian-sponsored terrorists were planning to blow up a civilian aircraft in Western Europe. An advisory was issued, warning of a potential terrorist attack. Nothing happened, however, in part because the supplies for the attacks had already been intercepted. But the fact that Hizbollah was prepared to invest a large cell, considerable sums of money and significant quantities of explosives to seed their operations in Europe was a major development. With that seizure, it became clear that Hizbollah was moving away from its previous focus on the Middle East, with occasional forays to Europe and elsewhere. Now they are planning a major campaign outside their normal turf. What concerns the intelligence agencies is that so far they have only intercepted one shipment of weapons and explosives. There is every indication that the Hizbollah network has spread to Europe, Latin America and Asia and what is not known is just how much equipment has already reached these cells.

In 1990, British and American intelligence detected the first signs that Iran's sponsorship of terrorism had shifted from the simple backing of groups which came from the right branch of the Islamic faith. Iran began to reach out not just to the Shia but to individuals and groups all over the world who shared a common faith.[15]

Starting in the summer of 1990, before Saddam Hussein's invasion of Kuwait, Iran began pumping millions of dollars into organizations such as Hamas, which fights for Palestinian rights in Israel, to opponents of Saddam Hussein, and even to the Abu Nidal Organization. Given the timing of this cash disbursement, intelligence analysts believed that it was part of a longer term strategy to increase the influence of Iran around the

183

world in the aftermath of the Iran-Iraq War. Iran clearly saw terrorism as a way of combating the growing power of Saddam Hussein in the region. Emasculated by the eight-year war with Iraq which ended in a ceasefire in 1988, Iran was left with little political influence and a severely damaged economy, which had limited leverage outside its borders. Terrorism was a cheap way of increasing its influence on the world stage, and it is clear that Rafsanjani and his colleagues had learned the lesson of the Khomeini years – that limited support to the Shia is largely counter-productive.

They were helped in their objective by the crumbling of traditional Middle East alliances caused by the Gulf War when Syria and Iraq were forced to change their longstanding support for terrorist groups (Iraq because it was cut off from the rest of the world and Syria because President Assad wanted to use the war as an opportunity to get closer to the US and was prepared to pay the price of reducing ties to groups such as the PFLP-GC and Abu Nidal). At the same time, the ending of the Afghan war freed thousands of volunteer guerrillas to return as heroes to their families. The scattering men made homes in the States, Egypt, Saudi Arabia and other Middle East countries as well as in Europe and the Far East, taking jobs as taxi drivers, car salesmen or ordinary entrepreneurs. It was among this group that Iran found its most willing recruits.

But, where Western intelligence had been used to finding ordered structure and an understandable hierarchy, there was little coherence and no evidence of a central control dictating attacks, providing a clear strategy or even common tactics for all the recruits to follow. There were some examples of traditional alliances such as the support Iran provides for the Palestinian Islamic Jihad, which has been responsible for some of the worst attacks in Israeli-occupied territory since the start of the Palestinian uprising in 1987. According to the founder of Jihad, Fathi Shikaki, Iran began supporting the organization at its inception.

'Iran gives us money and supports us,' he said, speaking in his modern office in Damascus, supplied to him courtesy of the Syrian government. 'Then we supply the money and arms to the occupied territories and support the families of our people. Just about all of it goes there because that's where most of our organization is.'[16]

But such support for the large and established groups is more the exception than the rule. It is a diffuse set up, composed of individuals or small cells who operate largely independently. They absorb the £30m a year Israeli intelligence estimates Iran spends on Islamic terrorist movements worldwide.[17] To some in the intelligence community, this new terrorist alliance is known as the Ibrahim Lincoln Brigade after the Lincoln Brigade that fought the fascists in the Spanish Civil War. That brigade drew together individuals such as Ernest Hemingway, Langston Hughes and Paul Robeson who had nothing in common but a hatred of fascism. The new brigade has only a common faith in Islam to unite them.

Not surprisingly, the headquarters of this 'organization', or loose alliance of likeminded individuals, is Peshawar, the northern Pakistani town on the border with Afghanistan that was the heart of the covert operations against the Soviets. Exactly who works for whom and where the chains of command lie have proved virtually impossible for any intelligence organization to decipher. Some facts have been established. For example, Sheik Rahman is known to have strong links to Peshawar and has travelled there frequently, meeting regularly with Gulbuddin Hekmatyar, the militant leader who in turn is closely allied with Iran. A few days before the World Trade Center bombing, Rahman's organization sent out faxes from Peshawar warning Western investors to pull out of Egypt before they were bombed out.

In fact, it is to Egypt and Algeria that most Western intelligence agencies are looking for illustrations of techniques and tactics which the Islamic fundamentalists are planning to use as their power base develops around the world.

In Egypt, the outlawed Islamic Group is pledged to replace the government of President Hosni Mubarak with an Islamic state, using violence if necessary. To achieve this, they have established a network of underground cells throughout the country which began with general acts of terrorism. As they have become more powerful, these cells have started to levy taxes, intimidate government officials and take whatever other steps they feel are necessary to loosen the control of central government over the people. By mid-1992 attacks had left more than 150 people dead, with the violence steadily increasing and the police and intelligence community struggling to cope.[18]

What has particularly damaged Egypt, however, are three attacks on tourists which killed a Briton, a Swede and a Turk and in 1992 brought about a 53% decline in tourism compared with the previous year.

To combat this new wave of terrorism, the Egyptian government has carried out massive arrests, and even made it a criminal offence to have received military training with Afghans.

In April 1993, James Woolsey, the director of Central Intelligence, made a secret visit to Cairo as part of a familiarization tour of the Middle

East. While there he met with President Hosni Mubarak who warned him that Iran was supporting the terrorists carrying out attacks in Egypt. He also passed on hard intelligence about the location of training camps in Sudan, which Mubarak claimed were established with Iranian money and trainers. Those camps, Mubarak said, were being used as a base for attacks on Egypt and could be used to carry out attacks elsewhere in the world.[19]

Mubarak is convinced that Iran has clear expansionist ambitions, and is using terrorism as a specific political tool to further its aims. At every opportunity, he has warned American, British and French officials of the dangers posed by Iran, but there appears to have been little sympathy for his concerns. This is partly because Western intelligence does not have the information to confirm his allegations, and partly because there is considerable caution among Western analysts about falling into the same trap that bedevilled counter-terrorism in the 1970s: seeing a grand conspiracy when in fact there was simply a large number of like-minded people operating independently.

Mubarak reinforced his arguments with Woolsey by pointing out that Egypt had been warning the CIA and the FBI for months about the presence of Muslim fanatics in America. Since early 1992 the Egyptians had been claiming that a large network containing several separate cells had been established in the US with the aim of carrying out terrorist attacks. This information had been greeted with scepticism in Washington where it was felt that the Egyptians were trying to draw America into what was essentially a local struggle against dissidents.

In the aftermath of the World Trade Center bombing, the Egyptians argued that if their warnings had been heeded, the outrage could have been prevented. This is overstating the case. The warnings were always too general to be of much use, and there was no evidence to suggest that an attack was imminent.

Algeria, once a peaceful example of post-colonial rule, is now in the middle of a bloody civil war as a result of a bloodless coup in January 1992. The takeover by the military, which installed a civilian puppet as president, was organized to thwart a probable election victory by Muslim fundamentalists from the Islamic Salvation Front, FIS. This was the Arab world's first serious attempt at parliamentary democracy and, in the end, it was more than the military could stomach. The result has been a period of bloodletting the like of which the country has not seen since the war of independence ended French colonial rule in the country.

Charlie Allen, the current head of Warning at the CIA, has the job of predicting the world's trouble spots. It was he who raised the warning flags about Saddam's forthcoming invasion of Kuwait, and it was he who sent up warning flags about Algeria in the summer of 1992. Allen, a big, tough and straight-talking career CIA man, has spent most of his recent time at the Agency in counter-terrorism. He helped craft some of the CIA's more innovative policies and made a lot of enemies in the process. This time, his concerns were not just Algeria but the whole of North Africa. If Algeria went, he argued, then it would not be long before Egypt, Tunisia, Morocco and even Libya – Gadaffi could not last forever – would follow. There is already an Islamic government in Sudan and with Algeria controlled by fundamentalists the moderate regimes would be in a pincer between two hard-line governments. The result would be Muslim fundamentalists orchestrating violence, and perhaps taking power in all of North Africa. It was a frightening prospect, and one which justified the warnings that Allen began to distribute around the Agency, the NSC and the State Department.[20]

The purpose of such warnings is to give the intelligence and diplomatic community an opportunity to agree a plan of action. It gives them time to preempt a result which the intelligence community feels would not be in the national interest. In this case, with turmoil in the former Soviet Union and concern with brokering a new Middle East peace deal on the front burner, Algeria was moved firmly to the back burner. Nothing was done to try and control a worsening situation.

After nearly two years of struggle, the Muslim fundamentalists have moved the fight from a minor terrorist campaign to full-scale insurgency. Six hundred people, half of them from the security forces, were killed in the first year of the war, and the deaths are rising daily. Today there may be as many as 15,000 Muslims under arms who can count on the covert support of thousands more from among Algeria's 26 million population. Their tactics have changed from lightning hit-and-run attacks to more sophisticated battles which sometimes last for days. This is a classic insurgency campaign which the government are losing. Unless something is done, the eventual defeat of the government appears inevitable.[21]

At the heart of the fundamentalist army are 1,000 veterans of the Afghan War. They provide the experienced core of the fighting units, training volunteers, planting the bombs and leading the battles. The Algerian government claims that Pakistan has allowed some fundamentalists to flee the country and hide in Peshawar from where they foment revolution. It alleges also that the Islamic Salvation Front is behind the publication of two fundamentalist magazines in Pakistan which urge followers to wage jihad against Algeria. These magazines are similar in tone and substance to magazines produced in the 1980s to exhort Muslims around the world to join the jihad against the Soviets in Afghanistan.[22]

Both the Pakistanis and the Egyptians blame the CIA for this legacy of terror. But in Washington there is little sympathy for such complaints. The US has responded to the attacks by threatening to place Pakistan on its list of state sponsors of terrorism along with traditional enemies like Iraq and Libya. The threat provoked the Pakistan government in May 1993 to sack Lieutenant General Javed Nasir, the head of ISI, who was suspected by the CIA of running secret training camps for Muslim fundamentalists with the help of retired ISI officers and veterans of the Afghan campaign.[23]

This kind of response reflects considerable frustration in Western democracies with the whole concept of Islamic fundamentalism or Muslim terrorism or both. There has been an attempt to treat the problem as a terrorist issue in the same way as the conspiracists saw Moscow-backed terrorism in the 1970s. But such a policy requires a degree of coordination and sophistication that has been lacking so far in the spread of fundamentalism around the world. The attack on the World Trade Center was an amateurish affair. From the moment the first two terrorists arrived in New York from Pakistan in late 1992, it was clear these were enthusiastic amateurs rather than the seasoned professionals a high profile target like the World Trade Center might have warranted.

While their ineptitude gave the FBI the lucky breaks it needed to wrap up what might otherwise have been a very difficult case, it suggests that either Tehran is recruiting second-rate terrorist talent or that they are spreading their net so wide that they are drawing in a large number of unprofessional operators. At present, the balance of opinion in the intelligence community is towards the latter conclusion. There is ample evidence that Tehran, like Moscow thirty years earlier, is exploiting the existing situation where there are large numbers of experienced fighters living in virtually every country in the Middle East, Europe and the Americas. These fighters, with some modest financial encouragement, might be expected to carry out acts of violence in the name of some specified but probably incoherent goal. This in turn will provoke resentment against Muslims and allow the Iranian government to act as a focus for exploited and disenfranchised Muslims everywhere. It is cheap seed corn that could reap huge crops in future years.

The Israelis have made much of the Iranian link to the militant fundamentalists and in a skilful use of propaganda have managed to equate Islam with fundamentalism in a way that has distorted the debate to create yet another stereotype. Within the intelligence community, there is a growing view that the fundamentalist problem is manageable, provided Western nations adopt a more intelligent set of policies to meet the threat. In the summer of 1993, British intelligence prepared a classified paper for the foreign office titled 'Islamic Fundamentalism in the Middle East'. This paper set out the causes of the fundamentalist phenomenon and the nature of the threat it poses. Away from the shrill headlines in the media, it is a cool assessment that places the problem in a less alarmist context.

Reasons for the proliferation of fundamentalist political groupings vary from country to country. There is contagion. Leaders meet in Europe, South Asia, Khartoum or Tehran. Some have an international following.

The coincidental rise of fundamentalism across North Africa and the Levant has certain common factors. But the main causes are internal. It breeds on failure to resolve economic and social problems, corruption in government and the bankruptcy of political ideologies – Communism, Nasserism, Baathism, etc. It is prevalent in overcrowded cities plagued by poverty and unemployment.

The Iranians are peddling mischief throughout the region. Private Saudi and Gulf money donated for Islamic causes is a common factor in much of the region.

The absence in Islam of a clear divide between the spiritual and the secular and between state and religion enhances Islam's potential as a focus of opposition, offering a ready-made ideology emphasizing social justice. Fundamentalist groups can offer effective welfare services to the poor which the state cannot match. Endemic problems (limited resources, economic growth rates unable to keep pace with demographic pressures) will continue to provide a fertile breeding ground for fundamentalism.

Fundamentalism is not necessarily synonymous with political radicalism or anti-Western policies. The fundamentalist groups advocating violence and revolution are in a minority. Nevertheless, there is a strong anti-Western streak in all main political fundamentalist movements in the region. Western, particularly American, culture and materialism are seen as a threat to Islamic values.

The fundamentalists' wider objectives are more or less incompatible with Western liberal principles – they are opposed to political pluralism, religious tolerance and women's rights. They will continue to oppose an Arab/Israeli settlement. They are prepared to use the ballot box to gain power. But there is every doubt that these 'parties of God' would subject their political authority, once achieved, to further democratic process.

Fundamentalism does not present a coherent and monolithic threat to Western interests in the way that Communism once did. It is not supported by a superpower. Its appeal in Western countries is confined to Muslim minorities and the threat of subversion is, in the UK at least, minimal. Dealings with extremist fundamentalist regimes would be highly unpredictable but not necessarily unmanageable. Some countries which are vulnerable to fundamentalism would have out of economic necessity to maintain working relations with Europe (e.g. Algeria which depends totally on exporting oil and gas to Europe).

The problem for the West is how to deal with the threats of terrorism, migration, proliferation and a cut in oil supplies which fundamentalist governments could contribute to in the future. The answer is not to equate Islam with fundamentalism, as the Israelis suggest. On the contrary, the fundamentalists remain a very small minority who have Islam as a common religion. The solution is to try and address the basic underlying problems, such as corruption and social injustice, that allow fundamentalism to gain currency in the Middle East and elsewhere.

CHAPTER FOURTEEN

THE AMATEURS GROW UP

In theory, running intelligence operations in Northern Ireland should be a simple matter, with MI5 controlling operations and either their agents or the army or police carrying them out. In fact, both the problems and the solutions are much more complicated. Since the current campaign began in 1969, a bewildering bureaucracy has grown up around all security operations in the province with the result that they are frequently cumbersome and time-consuming. In the beginning it was much simpler, as both the SAS (specially drafted in to deal with the crisis) and MI5 were given a relatively free hand. As a result, the SAS roamed freely over the border into the Republic and carried out a range of unmonitored actions against the IRA, which included kidnapping suspected terrorists south of the border and a number of unauthorized assassinations.

When the current campaign began, the responsibility for gathering intelligence in Northern Ireland fell to the Royal Ulster Constabulary with MI5 and the army making some contribution. But, the RUC had almost no experience in agent handling, so MI5 sent in a team to teach the RUC and to recruit assets. In effect, MI5 handled intelligence in the North while SIS had control in the South, as it was 'abroad'. The IRA, although dormant, had what remained of their old cells in both the North and South. In part, too, this was a legacy of World War II when the Nazis attempted a number of operations from Ireland which fell to MI6 to intercept. In theory the army should have had an intelligence structure in the North but in fact the province had been a backwater for years and only lip service had been paid to the requirement.

Once the killings began, there was a frantic rush to improve the information-gathering techniques of all branches of the security forces.

Little attempt was made to coordinate the effort, with the result that every branch of the security forces had its own intelligence empire. For a brief period at the beginning of the 1970s, SIS was brought in to the North to try and reduce IRA activity. This was a typical bureaucratic solution to a complex problem which demanded more than simply extra resources. Prior to the imposition of direct rule in 1972, MI5 acted in a purely advisory role to the RUC SB who focused on both the Provisional and Official IRA with some success. After direct rule, the Security Service took a more prominent role in intelligence gathering, concentrating on the gathering of technical intelligence and political analysis. There was also some effort to recruit sources inside the Protestant terrorists. It is only within the last five years that MI5 had directly recruited agents inside PIRA and this has always been done with the knowledge of the RUC. The division of labour is that the RUC tends to handle agents which have operational value i.e. they can pass on information relating to specific acts of terrorism, while MI5 takes a closer interest in political and technical intelligence, bomb-making techniques or the voting in the Army Council.

In an attempt to boost their own intelligence-gathering capability, the army invented the Military Reconnaissance Force (MRF), based on the successful use by Frank Kitson of 'pseudo-gangs' during the recently completed Mau-Mau War in Kenya. The idea was to recruit members of terrorist gangs and persuade them to work for the British, turning the terrorist tactics back on themselves. At the time (1970–1972) Frank Kitson was the commander of British forces in Northern Ireland and believed that he could use his experience in urban counter-insurgency against the IRA. To some extent he was right. The MRF did produce some good intelligence but they were always loosely controlled and their actions were more suited to the bush than the streets of Belfast. Rather than reporting the intelligence they gathered, they tended simply to take the law into their own hands and deal with the terrorists as they saw fit.

On June 22, 1972, four Catholics standing on the corner of Glen Road in Andersonstown were hit by a burst of machine-gun fire from a passing car. The gunman used a Thompson submachine gun with the circular magazine so popular in 30s gangster movies. The IRA, not the British army, used Thompsons and it would have been logical to assume that this was just another piece of terrorist violence gone wrong. But on this occasion the police were near enough to give chase to the car. They arrested the driver and his passenger, who turned out to be a British army captain and a sergeant, who later admitted to membership of the MRF.[1]

Four months later, the IRA opened fire on a van belonging to the Four Square Laundry, killing the male driver. A female passenger escaped, but the Provisionals let it be known that the laundry was in fact a front for the MRF, which had infiltrated the Catholic community very effectively. The delivery van did indeed collect and deliver laundry but it was also a mobile reconnaissance unit with photographic and other surveillance equipment hidden in the back. At the laundry, shirts, suits and dresses were compared with the collection addresses and matched with army files for the known occupants. At the same time, the clothes were examined for traces of explosives or powder residues. This allowed the army to detect IRA men and women hiding in safe houses and gather valuable intelligence on the movement of terrorists.

The MRF also ran a massage parlour in the city and employed women to go door-to-door in the Catholic areas selling lingerie and to host lingerie parties where local women tried on the products and the spies could pick up the local gossip.

The MRF was a good idea but it was betrayed by the very people it recruited. It was an IRA man, who had apparently become a double agent for the British but was in fact a triple agent, who gave away the Four Square Laundry and so compromised all MRF operations. It was clear that the idea of employing double agents on any large scale was not going to work, and using British soldiers to infiltrate the IRA was also risky. As the IRA became more security conscious and learned from their mistakes, so the British had to adapt their intelligence operations.

When the war first began, there was a general assumption in the Ministry of Defence, and in the intelligence community, that it would be over in a short time. The IRA had few modern weapons, no money, were small in number and seemed to owe more allegiance to their pre-war heritage than to the current organization. But this was a serious miscalculation. The IRA was able to draw on a large reservoir of disaffection within the Catholic community and their ranks swiftly swelled from the dozens to the hundreds. They proved a tough and very professional adversary, with the enemy and with any of their own people who stepped out of line. It became clear that, whatever government ministers might say, the war would continue for a long time with no prospect of a victory for either side. It was clear that a different kind of intelligence was needed – not simply information about a particular attack (always a priority) but details about personalities and intentions so that the policy makers could look beyond the next day or the next week towards the next year or even the next decade. To meet that requirement, intelligence had to get inside the organization in ways that had not been achieved before.

In 1974, the army set up the 14th Intelligence and Security Group, comprising volunteers from different army units whose primary task was to carry out long term surveillance of terrorist suspects. The unit was originally given the cover name of 4 Field Survey Troop, Royal Engineers and was based at Casteldillon. It was also known as Northern Ireland Training and Tactics Team or NITAT. Its tasks were largely separate from the regular army's intelligence corps (known as the Green Slime after the colour of their beret), which largely managed both analysis and tasking as well as liaison within the army and with the RUC's Special Branch, which was responsible for gathering their intelligence. 14th Int were trained by the SAS, not at their Hereford headquarters, but at another, secret camp at Pontrilas about ten miles to the south-west. This camp lies just outside the village of the same name and is spread over about 100 acres, surrounded by a wire fence topped with razor wire. The security is something of a farce, however, as a village road runs straight through the middle of the camp, and attempts by the SAS to get the road closed have failed following objections from local farmers. The whole area is covered by security cameras and any delay while moving along the road or around the perimeter will immediately bring an armed patrol to the scene.

Inside the camp are buildings, bunkers, firing ranges and an extremely difficult obstacle course. It is here that 14th Int recruits get shown the ropes and it is here too that other covert operators from the police and other branches of the security forces come to be trained. But even before the first 14th Int men could get started, the situation in Northern Ireland spiralled into crisis, with 3,206 terrorist attacks in 1974. The kill ratio between the IRA and the security forces was running at a ratio of around fifty to one in the terrorists' favour. A ceasefire the following year cut the attacks in half, but when the ceasefire ended in November there was an immediate increase in attacks which returned to their former levels. On January 5, 1976, six armed men flagged down a bus near the South Armagh village of Whitecross and the eleven Protestant passengers were lined up by the side of the road and machine-gunned. Ten died and the eleventh was seriously injured in an atrocity the IRA claimed was a retaliation for similar attacks by Protestant terrorists. The killings caused outrage in Ireland and Britain and there were fears that sectarian violence was going to reach new levels. The government had few options to choose from.

There were already 15,000 troops on the ground and the RUC was stretched so thin there was little more it could do. The patchy intelligence being gathered by both MI5 and the RUC Special Branch was patchy and clearly inadequate to meet the threat. Yet the public and the politicians were calling for something to be done. Prime Minister Harold Wilson settled on the idea of sending the SAS to Northern Ireland. He had little knowledge of the regiment but had been told of their fearsome reputation. His advisors felt their deployment would calm some of his critics while perhaps making some difference on the ground. The day after the Whitecross massacre, Wilson ordered the SAS to Northern Ireland – specifically to South Armagh – and their deployment was announced the following day when Wilson appeared on television to explain his decision.

'We have a very special situation in Armagh. It is not merely that it is along the border and that people are doing these dreadful atrocities and then hopping back. But we were in danger of seeing a kind of gun-law regime develop on both sides. And we felt it right to put in the SAS, who are highly trained, skilled and courageous.' He added that 'some of the descriptions of the SAS were a bit like science fiction.' Merlyn Rees, the then Northern Ireland Secretary, put the decision in context. It was, he said, 'more presentational and mystique-making than anything else'.[2]

For the twelve men from the regiment who left that day for Northern Ireland, the experience was not to prove rewarding. Some individual SAS officers had been seconded to Northern Ireland to help coordinate intelligence activity and to act as liaisons between the regular army and the RUC and MI5. Those individuals had found a fractured intelligence operation with each organization carefully controlling its own fiefdom. And, in the paranoid atmosphere of a security situation spiralling out of control, there was little willingness to share intelligence fully, even on techniques for gathering intelligence. With the arrival of a full SAS unit, and the promise of more to come (more than sixty were in South Armagh within a few weeks), all the old turf priorities bubbled to the surface. The SAS, the interlopers, were considered as a threat by all the already entrenched groups. The army didn't understand their skills and used them on regular foot patrols. The RUC saw the SAS's arrival as criticism of their own performance and resented their presence, while MI5 instantly distrusted the mavericks from the military.[3]

Fresh from a freewheeling war in Oman, the SAS carved out an independent method of operating, which caused some concern in the more formalized structure of the regular security forces. Acting (often prematurely) on GB intelligence, they launched raids across the border and kidnapped IRA men, they booby-trapped guns and explosives and loosely interpreted the phrase 'shot while resisting arrest'.

While the SAS were trying to establish their role, 14th Int were getting into their stride. In some ways, the work of the two organizations was complementary. The task of 14th Int was to carry out covert surveillance of suspected terrorists or their targets, and to pass on their intelligence to the police and the army. But there remained a cowboy element to the intelligence operations, a feeling that the 'Paddy Factor' somehow made the IRA a less serious opposition than the intelligence gatherers had been used to. This patronizing miscalculation led to some serious mistakes.

On the night of May 14, 1977 Captain Robert Nairac, a member of 14th Int, went for a drink at the Three Steps Inn at Drumintree in County Armagh. Nairac, a twenty-nine-year-old Grenadier Guardsman, Oxford boxing blue and keen falconer, saw himself as a proficient practitioner of 'the Great Game'. He believed he had perfected an Irish accent and could actually pass as an Irishman. He enjoyed the thrill and the challenge of going out undercover to mix with the Catholics in the communities around his base at Bessbrook Mill. However, the IRA were well aware that Nairac was a British officer; he was tolerated on the principle of 'the devil you know . . .'

That night he had left the army base promising to call in at 11.30. He had no back up, and the only method of contacting base was through a panic button hidden in his car. He was dressed in jeans and an anorak, and carried a 9mm Browning automatic in a shoulder holster. After a night of drinking and singing, Nairac left to drive back to base, when the car was surrounded by nine members of the local IRA cell. He was knocked unconscious, bundled into the back of a car and driven south into the Irish Republic.

He was driven to the nearby Ravensdale Forest and brutally tortured to make him reveal the identity of other undercover operators working in the North. Nairac tried to pass himself off as a Belfast civilian and only one of the gang was at all familiar with the city so the bluff worked for a time. The terrorists could not decide whether he was a spy and moved away to discuss the matter, leaving Nairac under the control of one guard. He managed to overpower his captor, seizing his pistol. As the gang rushed him, he pulled the trigger but the gun misfired. With extraordinary bad luck the gun misfired again. Nairac ran off and was recaptured after a short chase. A senior IRA figure was summoned from Dundalk and he was sentenced to death. Knowing he was about to die, Nairac, a firm Catholic, asked to see a priest to receive absolution. In a macabre and humiliating final act, one of the terrorists dressed up as a priest and heard his confession. Nairac died without revealing any information.

While undoubtedly a brave man, Nairac also broke most of the rules about intelligence gathering in a hostile environment. He had no effective back up; he was operating in enemy territory with no 'legend', and a cover that would have been laughable if it hadn't cost him his life. Back at base, other shortcomings were exposed by his disappearance and death. Although he was supposed to call in at 11.30, the alarm was not raised until 6.00 am by which time any chance of rescue had long gone. There had been no proper chain of command which had authorized Nairac's mission. He had decided, on his own initiative, that his forays to the local pubs was a good idea. There is no evidence that these adventures had produced intelligence of any value. Despite this, Nairac was awarded a George Medal for heroism, after the men who had kidnapped, tortured and murdered him had been jailed.

In March the following year there was an incident between two SAS men working undercover in Londonderry that confirmed that even the most basic systems for gathering intelligence were not in place. The men were hidden in the hedgerow overlooking a house outside the village of Maghera, which the IRA were supposed to be using as a base. Through their night vision glasses, they saw two men coming towards them who appeared to belong to the Ulster Defence Regiment. Both carried rifles and were wearing camouflage jackets, with the word 'Ireland' stitched on their shoulders. As they drew opposite, one of the SAS men stood up and shouted a greeting. One of the IRA men, whose rifle was pointing at the hedgerow, immediately opened fire, fatally wounding one soldier and badly injuring the second.

Without effective liaison between different branches of the security forces there can be no security for operations. If the SAS had known they were in an area that had been placed off limits for other units then there would have been no case of mistaken identity and the terrorists would have been captured.

As a result of the Nairac incident and the SAS ambush, a new intelligence coordination system was put in place, designed to eliminate duplication and ensure that information was passed along the chain of command in a timely fashion. The province was divided into three regions (Belfast, South and North), headed by a Tasking and Coordination Group (TCG). The TCG has a free-flowing structure which involves the RUC Special Branch, the SAS, MI5, 14th Int and other undercover units depending on the type of operation involved. Each unit appoints someone to the TCG which is staffed by GB officers with a Regional Military Intelligence officer on secondment. Depending on the operation, other liaison officers from the SAS or MI5 can be brought in as required.[4]

In theory this should have eliminated much of the squabbling, but in practice, for every coordinating group that was established a new layer of bureaucracy emerged which was needed to bridge the gaps between the army, the police and MI5. A number of very good relationships have been built up over the years between those sent to serve in Northern Ireland and the locals, but they are the exception rather than the rule. The Northern Ireland police and Special Branch make a life's work out of combating terrorism on their own ground. Every bomb that goes off and every killing that takes place is a personal affront and a blot on their record. It is personal business and it matters. They view any outsiders who come to the Province as transients, with no serious commitment to the problem or the solutions. For their part, both the army and MI5 officers talk of the difficulties they have with their police counterparts, of the incomprehensible nature of their deep-rooted prejudices and their unwillingness to share information. There is some truth to all these biases which have resulted in repeated attempts to bridge the divide or to eliminate sources of friction.

One solution was to give the RUC prime responsibility for counter-terrorist operations in Northern Ireland in 1976. This gave the RUC the opportunity they wanted, not only to run their own sources but to act on the information they supplied. Attempts were made to eliminate the army's right to recruit and handle its own sources, but this was strongly resisted by the military which argued that their sources were much better than the RUC Special Branch's, and that it was the army and not the police who really produced good intelligence. But the army continued to treat agent-running in a haphazard fashion with sources being handed from one controller to another as each unit ended its four-month tour of duty. This not only created paranoia among the sources, who had no sense of security or even concern as they were bundled from one controller to the next, but it was also lax security and cost the lives of a number of agents.

Having lost the battle of agent-running, the RUC then moved to establish its own covert surveillance section to rival 14th Int. It was given the codename E4A and began operations in 1977. Initially, the unit worked mostly in the urban areas but then expanded so that it covered the whole province and could seriously rival the capabilities of 14th Int. At the same time, the RUC wanted to have a cutting-edge unit that could act on E4A intelligence rather than having to call on the SAS or other army units. The result was the Special Support Unit (SSU) of undercover men trained by the SAS at Pontrilas, who were openly critical of what they considered the poor discipline of the RUC men.

In March 1979, with a raid on three houses around Belfast, the RUC discovered just how sophisticated the enemy had become. In one attic they found sophisticated monitoring equipment which was hooked into the army's communications networks and was able to tap into ordinary telephone lines, including the private line of the General Officer Commanding British forces in the province. The police uncovered hundreds of pages of transcripts of highly classified conversations which showed that the terrorists had been operating with almost full knowledge of military and police plans. Clearly, this was an organization which had moved far beyond the Paddy Factor. No longer could any of the players in the intelligence arena rely on the mistakes the opposition might make. Instead they had to try and outthink them. As the number of organizations continued to grow so did the frustration of some of the men combating the terrorists. This led to costly mistakes.

It was clear to the army that they, too, had to reorganize to meet the greater sophistication of the IRA. In the past, individual units had been responsible for handling sources, with each battalion running a research unit to collate all the intelligence from these sources. Under a reorganization implemented in 1980, the research units were combined into the Field Research Unit (FRU) which ran all sources on a province-wide basis from their headquarters in Lisburn. This arrangement gave the army better control over its own agents and produced a comprehensive over-arching structure with FRU and 14th Int gathering the intelligence and the SAS or the SSU acting upon it.

Then, on November 11, 1982, Eugene Toman, Sean Burns and Gervaise McKerr were shot dead in their car just outside Lurgan. The RUC claimed the men had been shot after their car failed to stop at a road block. In fact, the men had been under surveillance and the RUC believed they were members of the IRA. They drove into an ambush and the police fired 108 bullets into the car from rifles, a Sterling sub-machine gun and a pistol.

On November 24, two male teenagers were shot dead as they climbed into a hayshed outside Lurgan. Although the youths had no known connection with a terrorist organization, they were going into a barn that was under surveillance both by the SSU and MI5. A month later, two other unarmed men were shot by police.

These killings gave a clear impression that the government had sanctioned a 'shoot to kill' policy, and that suspected terrorists were being methodically murdered by the police. The killings were investigated in a desultory fashion by the RUC and a number of policemen were tried and acquitted. Two years after the shootings, John Stalker, the deputy chief constable of Manchester, was called in to hold an independent inquiry. For the next two years he carried out a thorough investigation, despite a bitter campaign waged by officers and men in the RUC to stop the outsider finding anything out. Stalker became convinced that, while there was no shoot to kill policy, some policemen had indeed been operating a shoot to kill policy and he recommended that a number should be arrested. However, no criminal charges were brought, because the Director of Public Prosecutions ruled that any trial would not be in the national interest.

As a result of the Stalker investigation, the SSU was reformed and while the TCGs use the police in the vast majority of incidents, once again the SAS took primary responsibility for responding to specific terrorist threats learned from intelligence gathering.

Meanwhile, in Europe the IRA had begun to wage an effective campaign aimed primarily at British troops based in Germany as part of Britain's contribution to Nato. Barracks in Germany were bombed in 1978 and 1979 and Colonel Mark Coe was shot and killed while parking his car at the Bielefeld army base. These were body blows to the British army in Germany which had long prided itself on its close integration with the local community. They were trained to deal with a massive conventional assault across the East German border by Warsaw Pact forces, not with a few terrorists planting bombs in their midst.

Colonel W. C. Deller, the head of the German section of the Intelligence and Security Group responsible for intelligence gathering against terrorist targets, suggested 'penetrating the Irish community as a means of obtaining some forewarning of a PIRA attack. His suggestion anticipated sources run in Northern Ireland travelling to the Federal Republic of Germany in the labour stream and reporting back on their return. This raised many difficulties and was not pursued in that form.'[5]

Instead, the operation, now codenamed Ward, specifically began to target members of the Irish community in Germany. This was not only begun without the approval of the German authorities, but it ran alongside another intelligence-gathering effort by SIS, codenamed Scream.

Two other players, the Security Service and the army's British Services Security Organization (BSSO) also had an interest in counter-terrorist operations in Germany and were furious when they heard about Ward, which they considered of questionable value and in breach of Anglo-German accords on intelligence operations on each other's territory. A control group was established to bring Ward under control and to see if it could be merged with Scream. This was eventually found to be impractical. Instead the two operations ran in parallel. Ward produced no intelligence of value and appears to have recruited only sixteen low level agents who knew little if anything about IRA activities on the continent.

Some time after 1984, the IRA managed to obtain copies of three documents stamped Secret which provided detailed accounts both of Scream and Ward and the internal bureaucratic infighting they had provoked. This was a major coup for the IRA, which waited some time before publishing the documents in 1989 to the embarrassment of all concerned. When the IRA resumed their bombing campaign in Europe in March 1987, they were able to avoid the rudimentary networks established by Ward and Scream, and chose as their first bombing target the army base at Rheindalen, the headquarters of the BSSO.

Both Ward and Scream clearly demonstrated that there needed to be better coordination between intelligence organizations on the continent, and the result was that MI5 were given control. By June 1990, MI5 was able to claim that, because of an aggressive effort to infiltrate agents into the Irish community in Germany, Belgium and Holland, the IRA cells on the continent had been thoroughly compromised and their attacks had stopped.[6]

This clear success gave the Security Service the leverage they needed to push once again for an expansion of their sphere of operations and in the spring of 1991, the Security Service was given overall responsibility for agent-running and analysis worldwide against the IRA.[7]

This was a major achievement for the MI5 bureaucrats concerned about budget and status in a future uncertain world. It also made sound strategic sense. With one controlling hand, intelligence operations became simpler, the handling of sources more secure and the intelligence product could be disseminated promptly to those with a need to know. The single exception was Northern Ireland, where the RUC Special Branch retains overall responsibility for agent running, intelligence, analysis and operations.

As the empire grew, so did the importance of counter-terrorist work within the Security Service. After the appointment of Tony Duff as director general of MI5 by Margaret Thatcher in 1985, the priorities of the organization changed. Counter-terrorism and counter-espionage became the main focus. To underline the importance of the former, Duff appointed Stella Rimington to head the G directorate which handled counter-terrorism. She was the first woman to be made one of four directors (the deputy director-general, the director of counter-espionage and the legal advisor) and was designated by Duff as a potential future director-general. Rimington had considerable experience of the counter-terrorist war in Northern Ireland and Duff's successor as d-g, Patrick Walker, had also specialized in counter-terrorism.

Even with these changes, there are still clear difficulties in combating the IRA effectively in Northern Ireland. These are partly technical – the terrorists have a good understanding of British capabilities to intercept communications and conversations – and partly moral, in that the security forces are severely constrained as to how much latitude they are allowed to give an agent working inside the IRA. The dilemma for the security forces occurs when an informer gathers information on a planned terrorist act and passes that information on, but action to prevent the attack would clearly implicate the informer. By doing nothing, the security forces become accessories to the crime. By taking action they compromise their source. The IRA understand this problem and have exploited it by making sure that those with access to good intelligence have participated in acts of terrorism.

It is in the nature of intelligence gathering that some compromises with the strict letter of the law have to be made. But for those not involved in the work, this is not understood, as was illustrated by the case of Brian Nelson. A former member of the Black Watch, Nelson had left the army in the mid-1970s and had been recruited as an informer for the army when he went to live in the Protestant community in the province. He joined the Protestant terrorist organization the Ulster Defence Association and began to pass information back to his army handlers in the FRU. In 1985 he went to live in Germany and then in 1987 was asked by one of his former army handlers to a meeting at an hotel near Heathrow airport. There he met a representative from MI5 and his former handler, and it was decided that he would return to Northern Ireland and rejoin the UDA to act once again as an informant.[8]

Nelson was promoted to be head of the UDA's intelligence section, a unique position which gave him access to virtually all the terrorists' plans to attack Catholic targets. For the army, Nelson became a prize asset, the perfect agent in place with extraordinary access to first-grade intelligence. His identity was jealously guarded. Within the FRU, there was considerable distrust of the predominantly Protestant RUC. Nelson had told his handlers that the UDA had excellent sources inside the RUC and received regular intelligence on the IRA from them. So the army was careful about the information that was passed on, and always made sure to disguise the source. Under the security arrangements that existed then, the army were required to share everything with the RUC, as they were the primary civil power. By not doing so, the army were in clear breach of the rules, and may even have been breaking the law.

For three years, the army claimed that Nelson was a goldmine of hard intelligence, providing information that saved the lives of some 217 people targeted by the Protestant terrorists, including Gerry Adams, the leader of the political wing of the IRA.

The Nelson case unraveled after UDA men claimed they had been targeting IRA men on the basis of information supplied by sources inside the RUC. An inquiry was set up in 1989 under John Stevens, then the deputy chief constable of Cambridgeshire and now the chief constable of Northumbria. Stevens' investigations turned the spotlight on Nelson. Fearing exposure of their prize asset, the army began an extensive campaign of disinformation, hiding files, denying the existence of an agent and attempting to undermine the inquiry through leaks to the press.

When Nelson was eventually confronted by the Stevens team, he admitted his role. The police discovered that the Army had passed on only around 25 per cent of the intelligence Nelson had produced. The Inquiry team say that, at best, Nelson may have prevented the death of one or perhaps two IRA supporters. According to one member of the team, 'We found no evidence or hard information to support either the claim that he proved to be a gold mine of intelligence or that he saved the lives of at least 217 people.'[9]

To the army's horror and disgust, he was charged with two counts of murder, conspiracy to murder four others and several other lesser charges. He pleaded guilty and was sentenced to ten years. During his trial the former colonel in charge of the FRU appeared as a character witness for Nelson, and gave an impassioned plea for leniency. The fact that the colonel was allowed to appear and to talk about Nelson's role in such detail, indicated that the army at the highest levels thought the prosecution was an outrage.

For their part, the police inquiry team felt that the army disregarded all the rules for agent running in their obsession with an asset who was, in the inquiry's view, cleverly playing on the army's inexperience in the field. In early 1991, the Province Executive Committee, comprised of MI5's director and coordinator of intelligence, the commander land forces, the deputy chief constable and the head of SB, was set up to oversee all security matters. New rules were drawn up for the handling of agents with the RUC SB in overall control, the army still handling some agents and MI5 handling assets outside the province or some in Northern Ireland with particular political or technical knowledge. But, whatever the bureaucratic structure, the scars of the Nelson case still run deep within the Army and the police.

Different intelligence-gathering units in Northern Ireland have been forced to rely increasingly on their own resources, trying to find ever smarter methods of inserting undercover operators into IRA territory. For example, Crossmaglen, a town in the heart of South Armagh where the IRA has considerable influence, has always been a hard target for British intelligence. Several known IRA terrorists live in the town, operations are planned there and the IRA can count on the support of the majority of the local people. Recruiting any agent in the town has proved almost impossible, and establishing observation posts on the outskirts is difficult as they are almost always spotted. However, there is a large oak tree on the crossroads leading out of town which in summer is a massive, leafy landmark dominating the countryside. The SAS proposed inserting a two-man unit into the tree so that they could keep the town under observation, note the movement of any known terrorists in and out of town and record the people and vehicle registrations driving to and from the area. The idea seemed feasible, the suggestion passed up the chain of command and was approved.

Intelligence operations in the Armagh area of Northern Ireland are frequently planned in an anonymous red-brick building in the heart of Gough Barracks in Armagh City. It is here that the Task Coordination Group plans covert operations including surveillance, ambushes and meetings with sources in one of the most dangerous areas in Northern Ireland. From the outside there are no distinguishing features to the building, no high technology aerials, no surveillance cameras, not even any sense of size or importance. Only two white metal plates screwed into the wall with the letter S and the number 50 painted in black give it some identification. A single brown door opens on to a short corridor with a second brown door at the end with a security camera mounted above it. Although the outside door is supposed to be kept shut, the camera works on ambient light and only functions when the door is propped open.

A bell by the side of the second door rings a buzzer inside the building where a security guard can check the television monitor before letting the visitor in. Directly opposite the front door is a small kitchen with a sink and a draining rack, which is usually filled with drying mugs. On the left is a small operations room, a lavatory and shower. To the right is the heart of the building and, as if to emphasize its importance, the floor-covering changes from rubber matting to brown carpet tiles. To the left, desks are laid out for four people and to the right are another two desks. Both the desks and the walls are dark, institutional brown giving the room a depressing, gloomy feeling.

One of the right-hand desks is a blue metal rectangular box with a telephone handset with no dialling ring or buttons. This is the Goliath secure telephone, which army intelligence believes guarantees a conversation will remain secure for around twelve hours. Other desks have a green telephone, which is a Brinton and secure for all conversations.

The room is dominated by a map of Northern Ireland on the wall to the right which measures about 15 feet by 8 feet high. The map is in 1:50000 scale with relief shown in colour so the hills match the brown walls. The map is a graphic illustration of just how long the war against the IRA has been continuing. It is covered with a plastic skin and contains many little red boxes drawn in chinagraph with a number in each. These are the Out of Bounds areas (OOB) which are either the subject of a current covert operation or contain a suspicious incident or object. Orange strip tape to mark the positions of patrols hangs from various points and old strips dangle from the bottom of the map which sags away from the wall and is pitted with the tears and bulges of age.

The furniture is completed by metal-framed chairs, a colour television in the far left corner and a pinboard on the far wall which usually contains recent information about sightings of known or suspected terrorists complete with photographs. There is also a calendar supplied by a local racing stables, as one of the detectives is a member of a local syndicate.

This is the waiting area where those involved in an intelligence operation gather before a formal briefing or to dissect an operation after it is completed.

'The welcome is usually friendly, straight to the point and quickly turns into abusive banter shared only by people who know what they are doing is different, important and to be taken seriously,' said one army intelligence officer. 'The abuse usually features a mistake or a foul-up in a past operation.

'The whole atmosphere is relaxed people, tired furniture, sad decoration, all overcome by enthusiastic upbeat people who interact with their type. Alcohol is not usually present but every desk contains a supply. A success or weekend evenings may involve a glass of spirit. Beer is a waste of space for the Special Branch. Spirits are more effective – more alcohol, whilst taking up little room in your stomach and bladder.'

In the far wall is another door which leads to a corridor with offices running off it. First on the left is the sergeants' office which is cramped by a desk and metal filing cabinets. Once again the wall is dominated by a map of the province. A cork board is covered with an aerial photograph of the nearby town of Crossmaglen. The only sign of informality is the ageing dart board hanging from the wall.

Next door is the superintendent's office which is smaller and narrower but more attractive, with cream walls and a comfortable swivelling arm-chair behind the desk. Horizontal Venetian blinds give the room a light and airy feeling. A cabinet stands to the left of the desk, the top half with two glass doors and a shelf with manuals, maps and reference books stacked neatly inside. Below are two wooden doors with a lock which conceal the drinks cabinet. No maps, photographs or papers appear on the walls which are instead lined with mementos handed over by units or agencies which have served with the TCG. The favourite memento is the regimental plaque. The two exceptional items are a pencil drawing of three SAS soldiers in full assault gear and a limited edition print of the painting of Operation Nimrod, the SAS assault on the Iranian embassy in May 1980.

The next room along is where the formal operational briefings take place and this is different in tone and content from the others. A Georgian-style sash window dominates the left-hand wall which has a rarely drawn roller blind hanging above it. Green and beige metal filing cabinets line the walls, containing the reports of past operations filed by year and the coded task number (each operation is given a unique codename and task number which are randomly generated by computer). The wall opposite the window is dominated by the familiar, tatty map of the province underneath which are eight orange and black chairs for the men being briefed. Those chairs face a wooden desk, used by the briefer.

The briefing for the oak tree insertion took place in this room, and the two men were dispatched under cover of darkness to climb the tree. For the next three weeks the same two men squatted high up in the tree recording the passage of people and cars and photographing those of interest. They would come down from the tree for four hours after midnight and climb back up before dawn. The only occasion they came close to discovery was when some boys from the town came out to the tree, sat underneath it and began drinking Coke. As one boy finished his can he tilted it up to get the last drop and looked straight into the eyes of the anxious SAS man peering down from above. Clearly the boy failed to register what his eyes saw and the men remained undiscovered.

There are currently at least fourteen different agencies responsible for different aspects of intelligence gathering in the police, the army and MI5. This structure has remained largely intact and has even grown in recent years, despite some efforts at reform. As intelligence gathering in Northern Ireland has evolved, without the overall control of a single central authority, a complex number of organizations and procedures have been developed for authorizing any covert operation (see Appendix III). Once these procedures are understood, it clearly lays the lie that Britain operates any kind of shoot to kill policy in the province or indeed that there is any significant amount of freelance counter-terrorist activity carried out by any agency. The organization is too rigid and far too many people have to be involved in every decision for illegal acts either to be authorized or to remain secret for very long.

Clearly, the larger the number of organizations, the greater the opportunity for confusion and error and the more likely it is that the terrorists will successfully reach their targets. Officially, the public face of counter terrorism in Northern Ireland is a story of united effort by every agency against a common threat. The reality is very different. The RUC like the Army to work low level sources as they believe that is the limit of their competence. The Army believe they can handle major sources effectively and, more importantly, are convinced they understand better how to act on the intelligence in a timely fashion rather than accepting what they see as the more plodding approach of the police. It is difficult to find anyone who either likes or trusts MI5 although their competence in the field is generally not questioned. These differences in perceptions and methods of operating mean that the IRA has been able to exploit divisions that are both unnecessary and unacceptable. Radical reform that gives intelligence gathering, including agent running and political and operational analysis, to a single agency is long overdue. There is no military or intelligence justification for the maintenance of the existing system. There is no reason why entrenched bureaucratic interests should be allowed to resist changes that every organization recognises are needed if the IRA is to be fought effectively.

CHAPTER FIFTEEN

ATTACKING HOME BASE

England has always been a priority target for the IRA. Bombs planted in Belfast or Londonderry may hit the headlines in the Irish papers but they rarely make more than a few paragraphs in the national press in Britain. But even a relatively small bomb planted in any English town or city is guaranteed to receive massive coverage in the press and on television. To that extent the IRA are right when they argue that to the English, Northern Ireland is a foreign country. But the mistake the IRA continue to make is to confuse headlines with diminishing political resolve. There has never been an occasion when an IRA attack on the mainland has produced a discussion at cabinet level about British withdrawal from the province. On the contrary, no British politician could afford to be seen to surrender to the terrorists and expect to survive politically. While the IRA's mainland campaign may be militarily futile, however, it plays well to their home audience and causes the British government to react, ceding the initiative to the terrorists which is itself a victory for them.

Their current campaign in Britain began in August 1988 when a bomb exploded at the Inglis army barracks in Mill Hill, north of London, killing one soldier and injuring nine others. This attack has been followed by dozens more across England, with the IRA constantly varying their methods and the type of targets chosen to keep the security forces guessing. The last attack before 1988 was four years earlier, when the IRA planted a bomb at the Conservative Party conference in Brighton. The bomb was meant for Margaret Thatcher, but it narrowly missed her, killing five other people. Since then, increased security has made operating in England very difficult for the IRA whose previous mainland campaign ended in December 1975 after four terrorists were arrested at the end of the Balcombe Street siege.

Since that campaign and the Brighton bombing, the IRA have restructured into a number of cells, divided according to tactical requirements such as reconnaissance, logistics and operations. Each cell has a controller and only the controller knows the identity of the cell members. The controllers of the cells do not know each other and report back to the Army Council in Dublin. It is an effective security system which means that any penetration managed by British intelligence will tend to be of limited value as no source knows everything and only a handful know the targets or the dates for attacks.

While the IRA had been reforming, the structure of the counter-terrorist effort in England remained largely the same as it was at the beginning of the century. Special Branch was formed on St Patrick's Day in 1883 to counter Fenian bomb attacks, which included an attempt to blow up Nelson's Column in Trafalgar Square. Originally known as the Political Branch, its name was changed to the Irish Special Branch. Five years later it became simply the Special Branch. With about 500 men, the SB is responsible for criminal law enforcement and the operations of the Provisional IRA in Britain.

The Security Service, until the changes approved in 1992, was responsible for combating Protestant terrorism in Britain, the IRA abroad and in the Irish Republic. The RUC is responsible for PIRA in Northern Ireland. In England, SO13, the counter-terrorist squad, is run by the Metropolitan Police at New Scotland Yard. It has a quick reaction squad on permanent standby to go to an incident anywhere in the country, but its deployment is left to the discretion of the fifty-one regional constabularies who jealously guard their own turf and are reluctant to invite in outsiders from London. In theory, the police already have a group to coordinate the response to terrorism, a committee run by the Association of Chief Police Officers. But cooperation remains fragmentary, with information and turf still defended on the basis of historical counter-terrorist structures rather than current needs. The IRA, who study the counter-terrorist threat very closely, have an excellent understanding of British capabilities, and it is striking how the mainland campaign, begun in 1988, was specifically designed to exploit the weaknesses of the existing structures. They used between two and four different cells based in the south east and the Midlands to strike at different targets in different areas on an apparently random basis. This campaign is the most effective the IRA have ever run and it has been helped by a series of errors by the counter-terrorist forces.

Just before midnight on December 22, 1988, Lionel Barrett, an eighteen-year-old petty thief, spotted a green Renault parked behind a block of flats in Clapham in south London. He broke the rear quarter-light of the car and put his hand inside. To his horror, from underneath a blanket on the back seat rose a figure who produced a pistol and fired a shot into Barrett's stomach. The gunman then leapt out of the car, ran into the block of flats and, a few minutes later, drove off with an accomplice.

Members of SO13 were quickly on the scene and the police and Special Branch began a search of the ground floor flat the men had left. They discovered 100lb of Semtex plastic explosives, detonators, machine guns and rifles and electronic timers with three-day, six-day and 48-day delay mechanisms. Police also found parts used in the manufacture of home-made mortars along with handwritten notes scrawled in a school exercise book showing how much explosive was needed for each mortar round to fire a certain distance. The men were in the middle of assembling a number of booby trap bombs for planting in parked cars, which police matched against maps which had army bases marked on them. On its own, this was an impressive haul, the largest ever found in England. From other documents in the house, police named the two IRA men as Patrick Sheehy, a twenty-eight-year-old unemployed labourer from County Limerick in the Irish Republic, and Jim Errington, also known as I. P. Flynn.

Two weeks after the discovery of the safe house in Clapham, a new resident in the apartment decided to replace the living room carpet. When he lifted up a corner, he was surprised to find a passport which belonged to Sheehy. The flat was searched again and nothing else found. A month later the tenant called again after unscrewing a central heating duct on the living-room wall. Behind the iron grille he discovered a book and a pile of papers. Police returned for the third time and found a copy of *Who's Who*, a list of fifty politicians and public figures drawn from it, plans of how to make mortars and a stolen American passport. After this discovery, a number of prominent people were given armed guards and others were given advice on security precautions.[1]

The fact that such basic steps as looking under a carpet or unscrewing a central heating duct were not taken by the police during the first search was extraordinary. Four days after publication of this failure, senior officials from all the counter-terrorist agencies gathered at New Scotland Yard for their weekly meeting. Instead of focusing on correcting the procedures that failed, the discussion quickly degenerated into a partisan bout of name-calling with each member blaming his neighbour for the leak. The police and Special Branch were convinced (wrongly) that MI5 were the source of the leak as part of their campaign to undermine SB. Stella Rimington, present in her capacity as head of counter-terrorism, angrily defended her position but returned to Gower Street also convinced that the leak had come from her people. This childish response to what was a serious intelligence failure graphically demonstrates that whatever may be said publicly about the growing cooperation between different units, it doesn't take much to reintroduce the traditional paranoia and incompetence.

Worse was to follow. After a tourist in Wales stumbled on an IRA arms cache in November 1989, police successfully staked out the site for forty-two days in an operation codenamed Pebble. As a result they arrested two Irishmen who were later tried and jailed. Those arrests led the police to an IRA safe house in Luton where a second hit list was found. The police decided to launch a massive undercover operation – the largest ever seen in England – involving thousands of police officers who would guard potential IRA targets twenty-four hours a day. Around 200 people were selected for protection, including cabinet ministers, prominent businessmen, senior civil servants and serving and retired military officers. For some, the operation was an uncomfortable experience: one civil servant had armed police living in his dining room for months, while another had men hiding in his garden shed.

The operation was codenamed Octavian. To keep it secret, the media were fully briefed about the scheme and asked not to report on it. Everyone agreed.

On the night of September 15, four months after Octavian began, two IRA terrorists crept up the drive leading to the house of Sir Charles Tidbury, the sixty-five-year-old chairman of the William and Mary Tercentenary Trust, in Wickham, Hampshire. The men, who wore balaclavas and army fatigues, were armed. While one kept watch, the other began to inspect the cars parked in front of the house. Constable Gary Leigh, one of three policemen on guard in the house, was watching the front of the building through a window that was slightly ajar. He heard the crunch of a footstep on gravel and then made out a figure stooping to inspect one of the cars. A policeman went to wake up Sir Charles who was sound asleep upstairs, his two hearing aids on the bedside table.

Sergeant Marcus Lancaster, the policeman in charge, ordered his men to cock their Heckler and Koch MP5 semi-automatic rifles. To cock the weapon it is necessary to pull the bolt back and let it fly forward, an action which produces a distinctive sound. The noise was enough to alert the two IRA men who immediately fled down the drive where a third man was waiting in a Ford Sierra. The policeman in the house watched them drive off. He mistakenly identified the car as a Renault, which allowed it to slip by the reinforcements, which were on their way from nearby Portsmouth.

The police then set up Operation Trojan to try and find the vehicle and arrest the men. During the following seventeen days, the car was spotted twice but evaded capture. Finally, on October 2, the car was observed in Wiltshire and followed. There were hurried consultations between Wiltshire police and Special Branch in London, who wanted the car with two men inside followed to see if it would lead to the other cell members. This is classic counter-terrorist practice and is routine for both the Special Branch and MI5. However, the Wiltshire police refused to cooperate, insisting that they make the arrests immediately. The London force had no choice but to accept. The men were followed to Stonehenge where they were arrested. However, while on remand in Brixton, Pearse McCauley and Nessan Quinlivan escaped after a gun was smuggled into jail hidden in the sole of a running shoe which had been posted to the men from the Irish Republic. A third man arrested in connection with the Tidbury attack was later acquitted after a trial at the Old Bailey.[2]

It emerged later that Staffordshire Special Branch were running a prison guard at Brixton jail as an agent. He made friends with McCauley and Quinlivan, who asked him to smuggle a gun into the jail. He contacted his control for advice; Staffordshire SB contacted London, who dismissed the warning by a provincial force and did nothing.

Despite the Tidbury setback and the fact that the IRA must have guessed that the police were keeping a number of potential targets under full surveillance, Octavian continued for several more months. At the same time the police, who had no real intelligence about the IRA in England and were desperate for a lead, had been analyzing the pattern of attacks. They thought they detected a tendency to attack armed forces recruiting offices. It was decided that these would be staked out in a new operation, codenamed Neon, which began in July 1991. However, there were not enough police to go round so the burden was spread across the country, with different offices being watched on different days in the hope that sometime, somewhere one of the armed teams would strike it lucky.

Once again, the media were taken into police confidence and once again there was no publicity. Then, at the end of October 1991, it was learned that Octavian had been abandoned. When Scotland Yard were contacted about this change of strategy and asked for permission to publish details about Octavian, the police replied that they wanted the ban on publicity to continue indefinitely. This was an abuse of the delicate relationship between the press and the police, and on October 31, Scotland Yard held a further briefing where they gave the press permission to write about both Neon and Octavian.

Although the police claimed that 'valuable intelligence' had been produced by both operations, this was untrue. Together they represented the biggest single expenditure of taxpayers' money in a counter-terrorist operation. The net result was that 40lbs of Semtex were seized in the Luton flat, and three arrests were made with no convictions resulting. The police had been forced to launch Octavian and Neon because they had no useful intelligence on the IRA in England.

Meanwhile, the IRA continued their attacks in England with bombs at Victoria and Paddington stations. To rub salt in the wound, the terrorists launched three mortar rounds at 10 Downing Street on February 7, 1991 at the height of the Gulf War, when security against terrorist attacks was supposed to be exceptionally tight.

Three months later, police believed they had discovered an IRA safe house in north London. They set up surveillance from building on the other side of the street. But the surveillance team had not counted on the leaves growing on the trees in the spring and soon they found their view of the house obscured. Seeking a fresh vantage point, they approached another resident and asked if they could use his house. In the pub that evening the resident warned the suspects that they were under observation. The police were forced to move in prematurely, arresting two but allowing the rest of the cell to slip through the net.[3]

The campaign escalated. A number of attacks appeared to focus on the City of London, and it was clear that, whatever the protestations, the IRA were winning the campaign. The police simply were not able to cope with the threat.

After several years of tough infighting in Whitehall, the Home Office commissioned Ian Burns, an undersecretary at the department, to examine the way terrorism is fought in England. His report was delivered to the then home secretary, Kenneth Clarke, at the beginning of 1992, with the recommendation that the Security Service take control of all counter-terrorist operations in England, Scotland and Wales. This was a significant victory for MI5 and finally consolidated twenty-five years of ambition. First they had isolated SIS from Northern Ireland, then they had curtailed the activities of SIS and the army in Europe, and now they had control of operations in Britain.

There was some intense last-minute lobbying by Special Branch to try and undermine the Burns report. In meetings with senior civil servants and ministers, the Branch argued that MI5 had no experience of running operations in Britain, and that Burns, a desk-bound academic, had misunderstood the problems of running an effective counter-terrorist operation. It was not MI5 which should be taking control but the Branch. Freed of the constraints and restrictions of the petty bureaucrats at MI5, the SB argued, they would really be able to deliver the goods.

The arguments fell on deaf ears, and the decision to award control to MI5 was announced by the Home Secretary in April 1992. Resentment within SB boiled over in a vicious campaign to undermine MI5. A series of embarrassing leaks began to appear in newspapers which portrayed the Security Service as a bunch of bungling amateurs. For example, in September 1992, it was revealed in *The Sunday Times* that Special Branch had uncovered a Russian spy working for GEC-Marconi, which has major contracts with the Ministry of Defence.

It emerged that the man had passed details of the WE177 nuclear bomb and blueprints of the Rapier anti-aircraft missile system to the Russians. More embarrassingly, it turned out that the man had first come to the attention of MI5 in 1976, while he was working for EMI, which later merged with Thorn. British intelligence were told by a defector only that there was a spy working for a British defence company with a particular surname. As the name was a common one, it took MI5 months to narrow the search which eventually pointed to EMI. The Security Service believed that the man had passed on details of the trigger mechanism for the nuclear bomb, but there was not enough evidence to stand up in court.

The man had his security clearance withdrawn and shortly afterwards left EMI and joined GEC-Marconi. The Security Service lost track of him and, when his employers applied for another security clearance, he passed the vetting process with flying colours. He stayed with GEC-Marconi, working his way up the ladder to become a manager, while passing dozens of classified files to his employers in the KGB. One senior security official described the man as 'probably the most proficient KGB spy since Geoffrey Prime'.[4]

Whatever he did to Britain's national security, the fact that he was able to pass through all the security checks to get a top secret clearance was an outrage. Positive vetting is carried out by a staff of twenty MI5 officers, many of whom are ex-policemen. The process, which takes between six weeks and three months, used to be a casual affair which relied on friends putting in a good word for the person being vetted. Today it is a much more thorough operation but even so, because the process is so structured and the people doing the work tend not to be the most imaginative, some individuals slip through the net. The Marconi case indicated a high degree of incompetence within MI5 which the Special Branch were anxious to exploit. They also leaked a number of other stories related to apparent MI5 bumbling.

These leaks caused fury in MI5. Several attempts were made to plug the leaks. One such effort involved Special Branch tapping the phones of SO13 officers at New Scotland Yard, but, as the source was within their own ranks, this achieved nothing. The Security Service responded by appointing new people in SB and clearing out what one intelligence source dismissed as 'the Luddites'. Six months on, the Security Service claim that relations are better between the different branches, and that the task of combating the terrorists is being tackled with more concentrated effort. It will take time for MI5 to prove just how effective they can be. They have launched an aggressive penetration effort on the IRA and its supporters, but it takes at least two years for an agent to become effective. Meanwhile the IRA are bolstered by each success and encouraged to continue their campaign in England.

There is some evidence that even the current reforms have not gone far enough. On April 24, 1993, the IRA planted a massive 1,000lb bomb in the City of London which exploded killing a photographer, injuring forty people and causing around £1 billion in damage. The warning call to the police came at 9.20 am using a recognized code word. The police bomb squad based at Cannon Row police station was immediately alerted. Under normal circumstances they would have been on the scene within five or ten minutes and there would have been an opportunity to defuse the bomb. The very large devices used by PIRA in England are made out of a mixture of fertilizer and fuel oil, and their size makes it difficult to booby trap and almost impossible to conceal the detonators and timers. So, unlike smaller devices made from Semtex high explosive, which can be very complex and booby trapped, time is critical in being able to defuse the large bombs.

On this occasion, the policeman on duty for the bomb squad was out of the office in north London, examining some World War II hand grenades. The duty officer was at home with the flu and his superior was

215

at home near Heathrow, west of London. Getting from there to the site of the bomb took at least twenty minutes longer than it would have done from the office. He arrived too late even to attempt to defuse the device, which exploded at 10.25 am. This allowed the IRA to score a major victory, and unless action is taken to ensure that such a situation will not be repeated, it could happen again.

According to a survey of the twenty worst atrocities committed by the IRA since the Harrods bombing in 1983, 35 people have been killed, 544 injured, two attempts have been made to murder incumbent prime ministers, and damage to property adds up to over £2 billion.[5]

In addition, around £350 million has been spent in making military bases and government buildings more secure. By any judgement, the IRA's most recent campaign has been a significant military success. They have been able to strike at will, using weapons of their choice, at targets they have been able to attack whatever precautions the security forces may take. The police argue that their record since the campaign began in 1988 is not all bad: 25 people have been charged with terrorist-related offences and eight convictions have been secured. The police have made 24 separate finds leading to the recovery of more than 15 tonnes of home-made explosives, more than 40 guns and over 3,000 rounds of ammunition. But these figures provide yet another gloss on what has been a dismal performance. Only a handful of arrests have come through good intelligence, the balance through luck, or mistakes by the terrorists. The overwhelming weight of explosives recovered come from bombs which either failed to explode or which were discovered by accident and defused.

The early indications are that consolidating the counter-terrorist effort under MI5 has done some good, both on the mainland and in Northern Ireland. In the House of Commons on November 1, 1993, Prime Minister John Major defended the record of the security services. In 1993, he said, some 50 people had been charged with murder or attempted murder in the province and 3,600kg of explosives, 164 guns and 42 rockets had been recovered.

Alone among her European allies, Britain has been unable to cope with modern terrorism. Of those groups that emerged at the same time as the recent manifestation of the IRA, all are now either destroyed or seriously weakened. Baader Meinhof in Germany, Red Brigade in Italy, Action Directe in France, and CCC in Belgium failed because they were matched against a superior counter-terrorist force. For every country with a terrorist problem, the early years were tough, and it looked as if the terrorists might succeed in destabilizing traditional democratic societies. But each country learned from its mistakes – except Britain. The single factor that sets the British apart is not the professionalism of the IRA (they have been at it longer than any other group in Europe and should be good at what they do) but the incompetence of the counter-terrorist forces. Of course there are exceptions, and there have been some successes. But overall, whatever senior police officers or intelligence officials may tell the politicians, the record is one of failure.

Since 1989, senior officials in the Home Office have tried to convince those involved with counter-terrorism to accept the idea of a single intelligence-gathering and response force to counter national crime, modelled along the lines of the FBI. This idea is strongly supported by Sir Hugh Annesley, the chief constable of the RUC, and arguably the man with the most experience of the successes and failures of British counter-terrorist policy. In a controversial and important speech to the Police Foundation on July 21, 1992, Sir Hugh argued the case for a restructuring of the counter-terrorist effort.

'It has constantly been argued that policing is essentially a local service and, as most crime is local, we need local police forces. I believe this argument is flawed.

'Most crime is indeed local, but most major crime – kidnapping, drug trafficking, money laundering, robbery and even the better class of burglary – is not. It is national and international.

'However, as I cannot foresee a national police force in the immediate future, I do suggest, that in two elements of policing, we now need to establish national operational units whose remit is outside the jurisdiction of local chief constables and police authorities.

'The first of these is a National Crime Squad . . . which has responsibility for the gathering, analysis, evaluation and operational exploitation of criminal intelligence. Is this not the way in which we ought to be tackling the ruthless and sophisticated criminals whose activities involve such large sums of money that they threaten to undermine legitimate businesses? In the United States, with its large population and land mass, and in particular with its varying jurisdictions, the benefits of investigating defined serious crimes by a central squad, the FBI, have long been recognized.

'I [also] propose the early formation of a National Anti-Terrorist Unit which would have four major divisions: the cultivation of informants; the gathering, analysis and assessment of intelligence; an operational capacity to respond to such intelligence; and a training, legal and support services wing.'

This 'would provide a cohesive and common approach to all terrorist activity. It would provide a single police and intelligence focal point for liaison with the RUC, the Garda and the police forces and intelligence services of Europe and North America.'

Given the extremely parochial nature of British counter-terrorism, with every participant anxious to preserve their fiefdom, it is hardly surprising that Annesley's proposals were resisted by every government department, without exception. The few senior civil servants who support the creation of a British FBI recognize that there is insufficient political will to drive such a proposal through. At the same time, MI5 do not want the change as their remit would be reduced at the very time they are beginning to consolidate their position as the lead agency in intelligence gathering against the terrorist target. Without the counter-terrorist portfolio, the rationale for maintaining an MI5 separate from MI6 would be much more difficult to justify.

The chief constables do not want it, as they see their individual power being eroded, and the police themselves are fearful of any move that might imply criticism of their performance. In any event, the police are deeply conservative and resist change almost by reflex. The fact that successive governments have tolerated this in the face of the most sustained terrorist campaign the IRA have ever launched in England is an indication of their weakness. It has done nothing but bolster the IRA economically, militarily and politically.

In the face of continued government inertia, perhaps the best hope for the future lies not in England but in Northern Ireland. For several years, British intelligence has been receiving patchy reports of a growing rift in the upper ranks of the IRA, between the politicians such as Gerry Adams and the hard-line militarists on the Army Council, such as Gerry Kelly. For some time, Adams has recognized that the military campaign, whether in Northern Ireland or on the mainland, is unlikely to cause the British to pull out of the province. The creeping political withdrawal by Westminster from the North combined with an improving relationship between Belfast and Dublin has led to the political marginalizing of Sinn Fein, the IRA's political wing. Stuck with around 10% of the vote in the North and diminishing support in the South, Adams recognized that it would be hard, if not impossible, to move the political agenda very much. As a realist, he understood that the longer the military campaign continued, the greater the danger that the IRA would become less relevant. What he had been telling his close advisors was that some form of accommodation was essential if Sinn Fein and the IRA were to remain a credible political force.

His opponents argued just the opposite, claiming that the mainland campaign had given the organization a new lease of life. Recruiting remained solid; there was a good intake of new, committed, young people; the 1993 local elections showed a small rise in Sinn Fein support; and for the first time they were able to strike almost at will on the mainland and cause devastating damage.

What one source described as 'hard, solid intelligence' led the British to believe that the rift in the high command was so serious that it could perhaps be exploited. Sir Patrick Mayhew, the Northern Ireland Secretary, stated in the House of Commons on November 29 that the contacts between the IRA and the British government had been initiated by the Provisionals in a verbal communication with an intermediary on February 22, 1993. The message which was from Martin McGuinness, the vice-president of Sinn Fein, read in part: 'The conflict is over but we need your advice on how to bring it to a close.'[6]

Mayhew's statement took senior intelligence officials and North Ireland Office civil servants by surprise as it ran directly counter to all the available information about IRA intentions at the time. It also did not accord with information that had been made available to the author in the Spring of 1993, at the very time Mayhew claimed the IRA had made the initial approach to the British.

In fact, the British and the IRA had a long-standing method of communication with the IRA which began in the early 1970s. The chain began with Michael Oatley, a British intelligence officer codenamed Mountain Climber, who met face to face with McGuinness and passed messages through a trusted intermediary from 1975 until his retirement to work for Kroll Associates. The meetings were sporadic with frequent discussions in 1975 which led to an IRA cease-fire, a long gap and then further discussions during the Maze hunger strikes in 1980 and 1981. He had a final meeting with McGuinness in October 1990 prior to his retirement in January 1991. This meeting was not part of the government discussions with the IRA but an effort to establish a new line of communication with a different British intelligence agent with the intermediary continuing to be a priest from West Belfast.[7]

It was this link along with other separate contacts which was activated in the autumn of 1992. 'The intention was that all the contacts could be totally deniable,' said one British official involved. 'There were no face to face meetings and everything was contained so that it could be totally deniable.'[8]

Mayhew was later to describe the meetings, which he wrongly claimed began in 1993, as 'contacts' rather than 'negotiations'. This semantic interpretation was designed to distance ministers from what had actually been going on in the midst of one of the IRA's most effective terrorist campaigns in England. As an opening bid Adams proposed an amnesty for all prisoners, a commitment by the British to withdraw some troops at the same time as a cease-fire, an agreement to withdraw all forces in due course, a united Ireland, and he wanted his men to be allowed to keep their weapons.

In 1974 and 1975, the British had held prolonged discussions with the IRA, resulting in a cease-fire which the IRA interpreted as the beginning of a process that would lead to their victory. The cease-fire failed to hold, and the resulting violence proved difficult to bring under control. This time the British were determined not to make the same mistake. The government countered that all weapons would have to be handed over and that an amnesty would be politically unacceptable although early parole for some terrorists might be possible. Until there was a lasting peace in the province, the army would remain, and there was no question of any withdrawal from the province until a cease-fire had been proved to work. However, the British would consider a change in patrolling patterns which would mean a complete withdrawal from Londonderry and a partial withdrawal from large parts of Belfast, contingent upon their being no terrorist acts committed in their absence, and law and order imposed either by community police or the RUC. There would be no unification without a popular vote and the British government calculated that Catholics would not be in the majority in the North until 2045.

There was some optimism that there was enough common ground for Adams to deliver the Christmas cease-fire in 1992. It never happened, because he was finally unable to deliver the hard-liners who wanted the military struggle to continue. Adams believed that if he had called a cease-fire – irrespective of the concessions the British then made – many of his followers would have continued fighting. His credibility would be undermined and his leadership of the movement challenged. It was an unacceptable political risk.

In the spring of 1993, once again using intermediaries, the discussions resumed. Again a cease-fire was the goal, but this time the British planned a major new initiative that might force Adams to cut a deal.

Mayhew prepared the new initiative to try and kick-start the stalled peace process. Officials proposed, and he accepted, that the new initiative would not act as a blueprint but as a basis for future discussions by all parties, including the Irish government. The plan included a new Northern Ireland Assembly with representatives from all political parties elected by proportional representation. A majority of 75% would be required for all legislation, to ensure that the Protestant majority had to forge alliances with the Catholic minority. There would be a series of bilateral Dublin-Belfast agreements to establish joint policies on such issues as tourism, water, fishing and power.[9]

Then came the unexpected resurgence of Sinn Fein in the local council elections in May 1993, attributed in part to the success of the IRA's terrorist campaign in England which delayed the new initiative and strengthened the hand of the militants in the IRA. They held out for withdrawal by the British army and a cease-fire which allowed the terrorists to keep their weapons, two conditions unacceptable to the British. Towards the end of 1993, British intelligence concluded that Adams had lost control of the Army Council to the hard-liners. A series of votes went 4–3 and 5–2 against him, bad news for those who hoped that some form of political accommodation might have been possible.

The negotiations might have remained secret and even revived if details of the talks had not been revealed in the press. Ironically, the Northern Ireland Office believed details of the talks would be published in *The Sunday Times* on November 14, 1993 and had prepared a statement which would dismiss the expected story as 'fantasy'. This lie was never delivered as *The Sunday Times* had never planned to run the story which appeared instead in the *Observer* on November 28.

The well-sourced story which quoted directly from government documents left the government no choice but to provide some details of what had gone on. A full account would have been immensely damaging to the government and would have led to the certain resignation of Mayhew at a time when Prime Minister John Major's government was already in very low standing around the country. Ministers decided to place the initiative for the talks squarely with the IRA and published a series of documents which began with the McGuinness communication. This was an effective offer of surrender, something which no intelligent observer of the IRA would consider credible. It did not accord with what British intelligence knew about McGuinness, who is admired as a smart political operator, and it did not accord with known intelligence about Army Council thinking at the time.

The ploy worked. Mayhew survived relatively unscathed but the IRA were furious at what they saw as an attempt by the British to make propaganda out of what had been a genuine effort to make peace. McGuinness released his own version of events which in turn put his own biased gloss on events. The damage done to what might have been a fruitful relationship has been considerable and such is the mistrust on both sides, that even if Adams reached some kind of political accommodation on the basis on agreements reached between London and Dublin in December 1993, there is no doubt the hard-liners will continue the struggle. That means that IRA terrorism will continue to confront Britain for the foreseeable future.

Those hard-liners have been encouraged by their successes in England and so they should be. They have run a very effective campaign against a divided and frequently incompetent counter-terrorist force. Putting the Security Service in overall charge of counter-terrorist operations in England is a useful first step to improving what has become a lamentable situation. Further reform to cut through the entrenched prejudices of individuals, police forces and different agencies involved in the counter-terrorism effort is needed. The answer – accepted by every experienced policemen, soldier or intelligence officer I have ever met – is to establish a single national agency to handle the whole counter-terrorist effort. A British FBI would cut through the current bureaucratic morass and finally stop the IRA exploiting the many historical weaknesses in the current counter-terrorist structure. The logic of the argument is inescapable. What is now required is a political leader with sufficient political courage to make it happen.

CHAPTER SIXTEEN

GADAFFI AT BAY

The bombing of PanAm 103 over Lockerbie in Scotland in December 1988 finally gave the international community the incontrovertible evidence it needed to link Libya with a major act of international terrorism. The forensic evidence, supported by a defector from Libyan intelligence, blamed two members of Libyan intelligence. Abdel Basset Ali-Al-Megrahi, a thirty-nine-year old Tripoli resident, and Lamen Khalifa Fhimah, aged thirty-five, from Suk Giuma in Libya, were identified in indictments filed simultaneously in Britain and America as officers and operatives of the Jamahirya Security Organization (JSO), the 'intelligence service through which Libya conducted acts of terrorism against other nations'.[1]

Gadaffi was ordered to hand over the men for trial, which he refused to do. The international community, in a new post-Cold War spirit of cooperation, imposed sanctions against Libya in April 1992. For months afterwards, the Libyans used every intermediary and every excuse to try and avoid handing the suspects over. Middlemen approached governments in Egypt, Britain, the US, France, Germany and elsewhere offering deals, but for once there was a united front against the wily Gadaffi.

As part of his search for a compromise, and to try and convince Britain and the United States that he had changed his ways, Gadaffi let it be known that he had abandoned his support for terrorist activities. At the beginning of 1992, the British government passed on a message saying they would need a gesture of good faith to prove there was substance behind the rhetoric. Specifically, they wanted details of Libyan support for the IRA.

Since Gadaffi had come to power in 1969 through a popular revolution he had made it his business to support other revolutionaries around the world. His approach to this task was both generous and ignorant. He paid little attention to the politics of those he supported, and only appeared interested in the supplicants' credentials as revolutionaries. In his terms this seemed to mean a commitment to the violent overthrow of existing governments. The IRA, as sworn fighters against the colonial oppression of the British government (as they described it), were natural beneficiaries of Gadaffi's largesse. The first contacts began in 1972 when Brian Keenan, an experienced and pragmatic Republican leader, travelled to Tripoli and met with the Libyan leader. The result of that meeting was a promise of cash and arms.[2]

The IRA tend to be very insular, with an absolute conviction in their cause which frequently seems incomprehensible to an outsider. Gadaffi was not particularly interested in the detail of the IRA's campaign, only in the fact that they appeared to oppose the British colonialists. So from the beginning, this was not a relationship built on solid foundations. Both sides found their worst fears justified when the first arms shipment was picked up from Tripoli in March 1973. Five tons of weapons were then ferried on board the vessel *Claudia* towards Ireland, under observation from Royal Air Force reconnaissance planes and Royal Navy ships from the moment it entered international waters. Finally, the Irish navy intercepted the *Claudia* off Muggles Bay, near Waterford. All the arms were seized by the Irish navy, but David O'Connell, a senior IRA terrorist who had been shepherding the weapons from Tripoli to Ireland, escaped in a rubber dinghy with a black briefcase loaded with cash, the first payment from Gadaffi to the IRA.

For both sides, the interception of the shipment was a great disappointment. At the time, the IRA had not developed other sources of weapons in the Middle East or America and were desperately short of equipment. Gadaffi had expected his arms to be put to immediate use against the British, and had to accept that his dreams of fomenting a Libyan-style revolution in Ireland would have to be postponed. It was clear to both sides that the operation had been penetrated from the beginning, and each suspected the other for the leaks. In fact, it was the IRA who bore the responsibility. In those days they had a less sophisticated understanding of security. They dispatched to Libya two of their top people, who had been openly scouting the international arms markets for a suitable ship to carry the weapons. It was hardly surprising that British intelligence got wind of the plan.

The following year, Gadaffi heard about a strike organized in Northern Ireland by the Protestant Ulster Workers' Council which had caused serious disruption in the province. It reminded him of the bloodless coup that had brought him to power and he invited a delegation from the Protestant Ulster Defence Association to Tripoli to discuss establishing closer relations. When news of this reached the IRA, they immediately sent their own team to argue their case. For Gadaffi, who saw just one revolution against the British, the arcane arguments of Protestants and Catholics about the historic relevance of their mutual enmity were too confusing. He severed all contact with both sides for the next ten years.

On April 17, 1984, policewoman Yvonne Fletcher was gunned down in St James Square, London, after police had been alerted by a security guard who saw Libyan diplomats carrying rifles, only partly hidden by blankets, into the People's Bureau. The shots that killed her came from a sub-machine gun fired by a diplomat from inside the Bureau. It was a shocking and brutal killing, which provoked outrage in the British government and the media. All Libyan diplomats in London were expelled and diplomatic relations cut off amid fierce condemnation of the Gadaffi regime in the House of Commons. This seems to have provoked Gadaffi, who decided to exact punishment on the British for being so rude.

Gadaffi sent a message to the Provisional IRA via the Libyan embassy in Dublin offering them cash and arms. After their previous experience, there was some hesitation in the Army Council about accepting the offer. Then a massive arms shipment of 157 tons of guns and explosives from America was seized on board the vessel *Marita Ann* just before she unloaded her cargo in the Irish Republic. Once again, British intelligence had penetrated the operation and the IRA determined that next time they would operate with total security.

Gabriel Cleary, a senior member of the IRA's Dublin headquarters staff and their director of engineering, was put in charge of liaison with the Libyans. Part of Cleary's job was to obtain weapons and to ensure that his terrorists received the right training. Both problems were solved by Gadaffi. In Tripoli, Cleary met with Colonel Nasser Al Ashour, a senior officer in Libyan intelligence, and was offered as much equipment as he wanted. Although it is not known exactly what the two men agreed, it appeared from later analysis of the equipment supplied that Cleary came with a shopping list, which included modern Semtex explosives, detonators, rifles, machine guns, pistols and surface-to-air missiles. Al Ashour took him to a warehouse on the docks at Tripoli and pointed out a vast pile of equipment carefully stored in packing cases marked 'Libyan armed forces' and offered him the lot. Cleary obtained everything he needed, plus some surplus ammunition or unsuitable weapons which the Libyans were clearly anxious to offload.

Over the next two years nearly 120 tons of arms and explosives were delivered to the IRA from Libya, in four different shipments using two different boats. None of these shipments was detected by British intelligence, a tribute to the IRA's improved security. Nor were they detected by American intelligence, which at the time was devoting a considerable amount of effort against Libya, considered the most important state sponsor of international terrorism. The shipments were discovered by accident in October, 1986 when French customs intercepted a 237-ton merchant ship, the Panamanian registered *Eksund*. The French suspected the vessel of smuggling drugs, and boarded her off the port of Roscoff in north-west France just before she set a course for the Irish Republic. On board were 110 tons of weapons including 20 SAM-7 surface-to-air missiles, 1,000 AK-47 assault rifles, 10 Soviet 12.7mm Kalashnikov machine guns with ammunition and anti-aircraft mounts, 1,000 82mm mortar rounds, 120 RPG-7 portable rocket launchers, 3,000 rounds of ammunition for an American-made 106mm M40 recoilless rifle, up to 100 tons of ammunition and 2 tons of Semtex explosives with detonators and fuses. The 110 tons of weapons had a total value of around $5m.

The Security Service were taken totally by surprise by this haul. Although the three IRA men on the *Eksund* refused to talk, the skipper, Adrian Hopkins, who had simply been hired to ferry the weapons, had no such qualms. He revealed that there had been four previous shipments including one earlier that month on another vessel, the *Villa*, which had a cargo of 105 tons of weapons. Never before had the IRA received equipment on this scale and of such modern specification, and the fact that such quantities had slipped through was a disaster for the security forces.

All the weapons had been unloaded in the Irish Republic, then split up, to be hidden in arms dumps at a number of locations. In the ten days immediately following the capture of the *Eksund*, Irish police launched the biggest search for arms ever seen in the country. More than 50,000 houses were searched, 7,573 under warrant and 42,559 without. Also, 164 cruisers on the River Shannon and 775 caravans were searched without a warrant. The total haul from this massive operation was hardly significant: 22 rifles, 15 revolvers, 13 shotguns, 4,312 cartridges, 2,277 bullets, 43 detonators, 2 timing devices, 1 cwt of suspected explosive mix, 7 gas cylinders of the type used in mortars and 25 cylinder bombs. None of the equipment supplied by the Libyans was recovered.

Later analysis by MI5 suggested that the IRA now had enough weapons and explosives to sustain a stepped-up campaign well into the next century without resupply. Gone were the days when the same rifle had to be used again and again. There was now no need to manufacture the bulky and dangerous fertilizer mix to make the huge bombs that had been a trademark of the organization. Instead, they had several tons of Semtex, a potent high explosive which is pliable, virtually undetectable, can be moulded to fit any shape and is much safer than anything they used in the past.

As if all this bad news was not enough, MI5 also learned that Gadaffi had been providing cash and training to IRA terrorists. Over the next few years a gradual picture began to emerge of the close links between the IRA and Libya. Intelligence was still thin – there were no precise details of exactly what equipment they had received from Gadaffi. There was also no precise knowledge of who had been trained or how much money had been handed over, just a general sense that the relationship was close and was continuing.

Because of the *Eksund*'s cargo of SAM-7s, it was assumed that the previous arms shipments had contained some of the missiles, so all British aircraft flying in Northern Ireland were fitted with electronic and other decoy systems designed to confuse the SAM's heat-seeking guidance system. These precautions appear to have worked and no SAMs have yet been fired at any British aircraft.

Alerted to the nature of the new IRA-Libya relationship, both MI5 and MI6 launched an intensive campaign to make sure that no further arms shipments slipped through. In part because the security precautions were good enough, in part because the IRA decided that more shipments were not worth the risk, no more have been made. Diplomatic approaches through the Spanish, Algerians and Egyptians were made over several months to Gadaffi requesting that he stop all assistance to the IRA, and he claimed that he had done so. The British continued to insist that Gadaffi would have to do more than simply make promises about future action; he would have to make a statement that he had broken with the past, and also supply serious intelligence about his relationship with the IRA.

The involvement of Libya in the downing of PanAm 103 helped to isolate Gadaffi further, and make him more amenable to international pressure to demonstrate his new moderate attitude. In May 1992, in an interview with *The Sunday Times*, Gadaffi said that he would not hand over any information about the IRA. 'If I give them such a history of our connections, then they could use this information to accuse me of specific crimes. It could create another problem such as the Lockerbie accusations,' he said.[3]

The day that interview was published, Vladimir Petrovsky, a special envoy of Boutros Boutros Ghali, the UN secretary general, arrived in Tripoli. During a three-hour meeting with Gadaffi, he was told that all the British questions would be answered in full. MI5 and MI6 prepared a list of nineteen questions for submission to the Libyans. Preparation of the list was a difficult task as, if it were too detailed, it would give away intelligence known to the British; if too vague, it would not tease out the right answers. If the questions were loosely formulated and were then passed to the IRA, as the British expected they would be, the terrorists might gain some understanding of just where the gaps in British knowledge about their operations lay. So the list focused on people, money, training and arms. The British wanted to know just who had been trained in Libyan terror camps, how much money had been passed on and what arms had been shipped. They requested details of when the relationship began and its duration. For their part, the Libyans promised to provide written answers to questions and to support them with documentary evidence.

On June 9, 1992, Edward Chaplin, the British chargé d'affaires in Geneva, met in the office of Antoine Blanca, the UN's director-general in Europe, with Abdul-Atti al-Obeidi, Libya's ambassador to Tunisia. Chaplin, who had simply expected to be handed a pile of documents, instead found himself handwriting answers to the nineteen questions which al-Obeidi dictated in Arabic and then waited while they were laboriously translated into English, despite Chaplin's fluency in Arabic. As soon as the Libyan and the British official had shaken hands, the UN official left the room, his job as intermediary completed. The meeting lasted two and a half hours with two 'refreshment breaks', and according to Chaplin's report to the Foreign Office, the atmosphere was 'friendly and conciliatory'.[4]

The Libyan official said that relations with the IRA began in 1973 at the urging of the Soviet government, which wanted to see Gadaffi encourage terrorism abroad as part of their own expansionist ambitions, which involved the destabilization of Western democracies. That phase had ended in 1976 when Gadaffi had invited a group of Protestants to Tripoli, and succeeded in alienating all parties.

The relationship resumed after the killing of PC Yvonne Fletcher in 1984. Over the next three years the Libyans admitted they had shipped more than 100 tons of arms to the IRA. These included at least ten tons of Semtex, hundreds of rifles and pistols, thousands of rounds of ammunition, detonators and timing devices. The Libyans claimed that, contrary to what the British believed, no SAMs had been supplied. No more weapons were shipped after the discovery of the *Eksund* and the relationship tailed off in 1988 although there were still some contacts up to 1990.

Libya admitted training twenty IRA terrorists over the whole period of their relationship. The men had gone to Tripoli, some for weeks and some for months, to be trained in the use of arms and explosives as well as specific techniques such as counter-penetration operations and assassinations. This group of trained terrorists now forms the core elite of the IRA, and has been responsible for many of the organization's most successful operations, beginning with the assassination of Lord Louis Mountbatten in 1979.

The Libyans also admitted to handing over at least $12m in cash from 1984 to 1988. This figure, the equivalent of the total budget for the IRA for two years, was far higher than any British estimate and showed that Gadaffi had been easily the most important source of income for the terrorists during the 1980s. The money had been handed over in German marks, French francs, American dollars and British pounds to IRA men in Libya. In addition, IRA terrorists on training missions had been given generous expense allowances.

In wrapping up the meeting, the Libyans complained to Chaplin about the presence of Libyan opposition groups in London. They are terrorists like the IRA are terrorists, the Libyans complained, adding: 'We are telling you this so that you can control the activities of the IRA, and not so that you can put Libyans on trial.'

Immediately after the meeting, the Libyans, clearly concerned that the extent of their betrayal of their former allies would leak, tried some damage limitation. Acknowledging the fact of the meeting and its subject, the Libyans said they had handed over nothing new. 'The people on the list were mostly either dead or no longer involved in operations,' said one official. 'Also, we told the British that we couldn't say what happened to any of the weapons or explosives once they left Libyan territorial waters.'

Later analysis by British intelligence convinced the British that the Libyans were not providing a full account. In particular, some of the men and women who the British knew from their own sources had been trained in Libya did not appear on the list. There was also some concern that the relationship may not have ended in 1990. For example, during July 1992 a visitor was taken around what the Libyans claimed was a former terrorist training camp in the desert south of Tripoli used by the PLO. But all the signs were in English, the recreation room had snooker tables and, among a pile of half burned papers, there was what appeared to be a medical file with the name Gavin O'Reilly.

Later that summer, at the insistence of the British, there was a further meeting in Geneva when the Libyans filled in some of the gaps. While the information signified a considerable intelligence coup and filled in some historic gaps, there remains some doubt whether the whole nature of the Libyan-IRA relationship has been revealed. What is clear is that Gadaffi has decided to sever his links with the organization while he tries to repair his image abroad in the wake of the attack on PanAm 103.

At the same time, Gadaffi has moderated his involvement with other international terrorist organizations. One of his chief acolytes is Sabri al Banna, also known as Abu Nidal, who has been resident in Tripoli since 1987 when he was expelled from Syria. Since the imposition of sanctions, Nidal remains based in Libya but is firmly muzzled and has been prevented from travelling (apart from some visits to Sudan). A number of his followers have left Libya for Lebanon, which is now the main headquarters of the organization.

For the intelligence community, Gadaffi's moves to cut down his involvement with terrorism are welcome. But, as always with Gadaffi, this is a consequence of political expediency and not because there is any evidence that he has decided terrorism as a tool is redundant.

CHAPTER SEVENTEEN

MEETING THE CHALLENGE

When terrorism first exploded on the world stage in the early 1970s, the intelligence community struggled to cope with this new threat. At first it was treated as a criminal matter by the countries in which the individual acts occurred. Then, as the various groups that formed the Palestine Liberation Organization began to internationalize their conflict, so the intelligence community began to look at multi-national solutions to the problem. The result was greater sharing of intelligence by agencies who had previously refused to cooperate. This sharing remained a patchy business because of residual distrust, and because different methods of collection and analysis produced a different product which made a common response difficult.

The terrorists have always understood the benefit of a multi-national approach. Action Directe, which launched attacks in France, had a strong logistics base in neighbouring Belgium, while the IRA have relied for many years on the safe havens they have established in the Irish Republic. This understanding of the porous nature of international borders and the disunity that exists among governments and intelligence agencies has always been one of the strengths of the terrorist movement. The terrorist, after all, is able to choose the time, place and weapon for every attack, while the security forces either depend on getting intelligence in advance or attempt to catch the terrorists later. As terrorism became a focus for most Western governments so the emphasis evolved towards proactive tactics.

Many of the famous names of the 1960s and 1970s have now vanished, destroyed by a combination of good police work and the toll that time takes on political will.

Thirty years on, some of the relationships that have developed within the intelligence community as a result of the common anti-terrorist cause have been very good. The British and American struggle against Middle East terrorists and against the IRA is perhaps the best example of strong links being made stronger. Since the end of the Second World War, the British have maintained an almost symbiotic relationship with American intelligence. Today SIS and GCHQ share everything with their American colleagues and the days of distrust bred by the Philby, Burgess and Maclean defections and the suspicions of the paranoid James Jesus Angleton have long gone. The British maintain a strong intelligence presence from both the Security Service and SIS at their embassy in Washington. Their task is entirely liaison, to pass on information that may be useful to the Agency or to the FBI.

Neither the British nor the Americans trust the French, who have a long history of cutting deals with terrorists either by paying to secure the release of hostages or by trading light jail sentences or expulsions in exchange for reduced attacks on French soil. The Israelis are distrusted for different reasons. For years they have played their own game, on the premise that as long as it is good for Israel then it is acceptable. This has led to information being shared which is either wrong or distorted.

Various models have been devised for tracking terrorist activity. It is generally agreed that in the past terrorist acts fell into three categories: attacks by domestic groups within their own country; attacks by groups in a foreign country; and attacks outside the country on a country's nationals, properties, or interests.[1]

Within those parameters, terrorism is generally seen as causal. In other words, groups such as the PLO have a cause to fight for (whether one agrees with it or not). Also, governments have tended to see the operations of each group as part of a bigger policy issue. So the PLO is part of the Arab-Israeli dispute while ETA would vanish if only the Basques in Spain could be given what they want.

Having established the parameters, most governments have understood that to combat terrorism effectively there has to be a coherent long-term strategy designed to attack the causes of the violence and to undermine the particular organization's political base. In Northern Ireland, for example, the British government have adopted a strategy that requires the gradual erosion of the IRA's political base, by attacking all the points that they stress in their political rhetoric. When the current generation of the IRA emerged in the early 1970s, the Catholic minority in Northern Ireland suffered discrimination in housing, voting, jobs and law enforcement. Over the years, the British government have chipped away at these grievances so that today there is no discrimination in housing, Catholics have the same voting rights as Protestants and prejudice has been attacked in the work place and in the police force. This in turn has given the Catholics an investment in their own community and reduced the bonds between the religious group and the terrorists.

After twenty-five years of war with the IRA, the organization's influence in Northern Ireland has been reduced to a fraction of what it once was. Funerals of IRA men shot by the security forces are attended by a few hundred hard-core supporters rather than the several thousand who used to turn up. The votes that Sinn Fein can count on in elections have reduced from a peak of 102,000 votes in the 1983 general election to a trough of 78,000 votes in 1992. For the first time for many years, the IRA have no elected MP, and no prospect of getting one following the defeat of Sinn Fein and IRA leader Gerry Adams in the 1992 election.[2]

None of these advances suggests that the IRA is nearing defeat. On the contrary, the IRA is now better trained and armed than ever before and it will continue to pose a serious threat to the British people for the foreseeable future. It will never be defeated militarily, given that it has enough equipment and trained personnel to keep operating at current levels almost indefinitely. What matters is that a war which was claiming a life a day in the early 1970s has now been contained to a level where the violence can be tolerated. The damage that the IRA can cause is strictly limited, the successes of the campaign in England notwithstanding.

But the British model does have two lessons for the rest of the world. First, terrorism is a long-term problem that requires a long-term solution. In the early days of the recent struggle against the IRA, the British looked for a series of quick fixes that ranged from illegal acts against the terrorists to attempts at a negotiated settlement. Neither would work as long as the terrorists could count on significant support among the population they claimed to defend. A wiser strategy was then adopted to isolate the terrorists from the political process and from their supporters by eliminating many of the legitimate reasons for discontent among their followers. That policy has gradually eroded support for the IRA; it is now very probably at a level where it is unlikely to fall much further.

The sad part of the British story is that while the government has vacillated, the terrorists have learned their lessons well. And what the IRA have learned through hard experience, newer organizations, such as the Muslim fundamentalists in Egypt, have discovered by observation.

233

They have seen terrorist successes and failures of the last twenty years and have a much better understanding of what is needed to achieve political and military success.

When modern terrorism first appeared in the 1970s, the intelligence community viewed it as a series of isolated events unconnected by a common hand. Then, because so many of the terrorists supported armed revolution, voiced support for communism and appeared to receive a sympathetic audience in Moscow, some analysts saw a Soviet-led international conspiracy to destabilize the world's democracies through terrorism. Books such as Claire Sterling's *The Terror Network*[3] supported this thesis with the help of sympathetic conspiracists in the CIA.

There were many who disagreed with this view, and the end of the Cold War appears to have vindicated the sceptics. Ample evidence has emerged that terrorists were trained in East Germany, Russia and Bulgaria. There is also evidence of arms and cash being supplied by the Eastern bloc. But there was never the orchestrated international terrorist campaign that some feared. Instead, the Soviets and their allies were happy to give support to the revolutionaries in the hope that they would head off to their own countries to fight their own wars. At worst this would be a distraction for the Western powers in the Cold War and at best it might actually result in some changes of government. But the Soviets never dictated the nature, timing and place of attacks, nor provided any kind of central control.

By the mid-1980s, the intelligence community had a fairly clear understanding of the links between terrorist groups and the kind of assistance they were receiving from some communist countries. That led to very specific methods of cooperating to counter the terrorist threat. There was shared intelligence on methods and equipment as well as planned attacks. Systems were drawn up to track the movement of cash around the world so that planned operations could be stopped and the establishment of new cells prevented. By and large these efforts worked well and the incidence of terrorism steadily declined.

With the end of the Cold War, the sharing of intelligence on terrorism has actually improved. There is now working level cooperation between intelligence organizations in the former Warsaw Pact countries and their former enemies among the Nato nations. More importantly perhaps, countries which were traditional safe havens for some terrorists are shutting their doors. Abu Nidal can no longer travel to Sofia in Bulgaria to run SAS, his arms dealing company. Ahmed Jibril will not be able to go to East Germany for open heart surgery. Information on contacts, connections, arms supplies and false papers was made available to the CIA and SIS from the files of Eastern bloc intelligence agencies.

The peace accord signed between Israel and the PLO on September 13, 1993 will have little effect on Middle East terrorism in the short term. Those groups under the direct control of Yasser Arafat will certainly reduce their terrorist activity, and attacks against Israel will also fall. But for rejectionist groups such as George Habash's PFLP, the peace agreement is no cause for celebration. On the contrary, any hope they had for winning a military victory against Israel evaporated with the signing of the agreement in Washington. Arafat is seen as a traitor to their cause and he, along with his immediate entourage, is now as much of a target as the Israeli leadership.

The Camp David accords took eighteen months to translate into a formal treaty and it was five years before the accords began to be implemented. It is reasonable to expect that the negotiations this time will last even longer, giving the terrorists who oppose the deal plenty of opportunities to strike. In theory, as the Arab nations work out how to live with the State of Israel, they should reduce their support for terrorism. In the long term that will no doubt happen. But countries like Syria and Saudi Arabia have always used their support for Palestinian groups as part of a larger political game where terrorism can bring influence. It will be a long time before that kind of support stops.

Even where state sponsorship is reduced, terrorists have proved sufficiently adaptable either to find new sponsors or to thrive on their own. Since 1987, Abu Nidal, the leader of the most feared terrorist group in the world, has relied on Colonel Gadaffi for support. But economic sanctions against Libya in retaliation for Gadaffi's involvement in the bombing of PanAm 103 have taken their toll. Nidal is now muzzled. But in the spring of 1993, Karim abd al Banna, Nidal's nephew and the Abu Nidal Organization's representative in Baghdad, formed a separate group drawing on ANO followers in Iraq and Lebanon. Saddam Hussein is providing some support for the new group but it may be that Nidal himself ordered the change as a way of circumventing Libyan restrictions.

The future of terrorism is uncertain; but what is known is that the new terrorists do not fit the cozy patterns established over the past twenty years. After the World Trade Center bombing, evidence emerged of Iran's complicity in the attack. This, combined with other intelligence of Iran's involvement in terrorist attacks around the world, has led some to conclude that Iran's guiding hand is controlling the current resurgence in terrorism. This is the same argument advanced by the conspiracists during the 1970s and 1980s, who saw a Soviet hand behind bombs in Berlin, London and Buenos Aires. Such analysis is convenient because it fits existing patterns and the causal method of analyzing the terrorist threat. But what the Iranians have done is to tap into a worldwide network of potential terrorists to supply with cash and, on occasion, limited training, and set them free to do what they want.

'The Iranians have nurtured an alumni association,' said one US intelligence official. 'All those people who went to the jihad in Afghanistan are back and looking for work. They communicate by fax with others in the association and have nothing much in common except for a shared experience. There is no hierarchy in this, just a flat chart with perhaps 15,000 people ready to carry out terrorism in the name of Islam.'[4]

What makes Islamic terrorism so difficult to understand and to combat is the sheer scale of the problem. Even the conspiracists of the 1970s and 1980s did not argue that the IRA had similar operating patterns or a shared political faith with Baader Meinhof and the PFLP. Even those who saw a central guiding hand in terrorism back then understood that each nation's problems were unique, and a national response with international cooperation would do a great deal to combat the threat. Islamic terrorism is different in that a common faith binds every participant from Peshawar to New York to Khartoum. Islam spreads all over the world, with seventy-five countries practising the faith, the largest centres being in Indonesia, Pakistan, Bangladesh, India and the former republics of the Soviet Union. One fifth of the world's population, spread across 11,000 miles from western Africa to southeast Asia, follow the teachings of Mohammed.[5]

After suffering a crisis of identity in the face of spreading Western democratic and financial ideas, Muslims in many countries are rejecting Western ways and returning to their own heritage. Of itself, there is nothing threatening to other countries in the tenets of Islam, an all-embracing system of faith bringing together religion, government, family life and business where actions and a moral code are based on rules written in the tenth century. These rules, with their apparently old-fashioned ideas, do not need to disturb existing Muslim governments or Western democracies, but they frequently cause concern because of the violence and fanaticism that accompany the call for a rejection of Western influence and a return to traditions.

For the intelligence community, the spread of Islamic fundamentalism, and particularly the growing incidence of Islamic-related terrorism, poses a unique challenge. While the World Trade Center bombers may have little in common with terrorists in Saudi Arabia, they do share the same faith, and they all read the Koran. Without a logical structure to this phenomenon, it has been impossible to develop a coherent and effective response.

'We insist on seeing the threat in terms of Islam against the West but there is no reason that it should be so,' said one senior Western intelligence official. 'Much of what the terrorists do in the name of Islam is actually secular. Iran is helping terrorists not because it wants an Islamic world but because it wants influence and power, so what Tehran is doing today is no different from what Moscow was doing twenty years ago, and we should see the problem in those terms.'[6]

Bob Gates, the former DCI, describes the problem posed by Islamic fundamentalism as 'one of the most significant challenges facing the world in the immediate future.'[7] He, too, believes that neither governments nor the intelligence community have a real understanding of the problem. The intelligence community is not producing the information that would allow policy makers to understand the issues and so decision making is based on reactions to events.

'Islamic fundamentalism is an indigenous country problem but Iran is aiding and abetting the opposition and making a country's ability to cope with the problem much more difficult. Governments in the region have to be more imaginative in dealing with the problem rather than just arresting those involved. At the same time, we need to speak more positively about Islam and detach secular problems that exist in different countries from Islam itself. We also have a weapon to persuade the faithful that perhaps the people supporting them are not necessarily working in their best interests and that perhaps there is more common ground between Christianity and Islam than people think.'

This concept of combating the spread of ideas with other ideas has gained currency within the intelligence community in recent months, but so far there has been no serious coordinated effort to devise a common policy, nor a common approach to address the issues. The intelligence community remains focused on combating individual groups and the problems posed by insurgency movements in different countries. For example, one head of Western intelligence sees Islamic fundamentalism as an issue for the West to confront, as a threat to the Christian values which most Western nations claim to support. With such a stark view, there is little room for the kind of nuanced compromises suggested by Bob Gates.

For the politicians, who now understand that terrorism will be with us for many years, there is still an 'us and them' attitude. There has been no serious attempt to seek any common ground with Muslims around the world, no effort to bridge the gaps that currently exist between Western democracies and Islamic theocracies. Where democracy threatens to bring with it a return to traditional Islamic values, the West will stand by as military hardliners seize power and civil war results, as in Algeria.

In Egypt, where President Hosni Mubarak's government is under attack by fundamentalists, there has been no sustained effort to address the problems that give the opposition such political currency. Like the Shah in Iran, Mubarak is seen as a tool of the Americans, and the president of a country in economic chaos, with a huge gulf between rich and poor. His opponents in the forty-five Islamic organizations that make up the Gama'a el-Islamiya, or Islamic Group, call for a holy war to overthrow Mubarak and establish an Iran-like regime in Egypt. Should that happen, it would be the end of the Middle East peace process. There would be a considerable reduction in Western influence in the region, which would provide Iran with a powerful springboard for further influence in North Africa and the rest of the Middle East.

Despite such a prospect – and many in Western intelligence believe such an outcome is now likely in the medium term – there has been no effort to undermine the influence of the fundamentalists. America, despite the muscle provided by $2.6 billion in annual aid, has not been driving Mubarak to introduce social and economic reforms. Instead, Mubarak has responded in the same way the Shah responded to Khomeini, by arresting thousands in the hope that this will discourage others. Increasingly, Egyptian security forces are assuming the role of ruthless oppressor, and are becoming hated in the same way that Savak, the Shah's secret police, were before the Iranian revolution. Civil liberties are being curtailed – even fax messages and telephone calls abroad are now restricted – and the opposition are able to cite the oppressive nature of the current regime as one of their legitimate arguments for change. The result of the Egyptian government's policies so far has been not to cut the violence but to swell the ranks of the opposition.

But the intelligence community, like every other government department, is resource driven. Every agency in recent years has faced cutbacks and priorities have had to be decided. Despite all the rhetoric, and even after the World Trade Center bombing, terrorism is a lower priority than it was ten years ago.

In September 1992, one of the State Department's most experienced counter-terrorist officials, who had been involved at a senior level since the late 1970s, wrote a comprehensive policy paper for James Baker, Secretary of State. The paper was designed to examine the history of the international counter-terrorist effort, the current and future threat, and to consider solutions. As an insider's analysis it provides a real insight into where America's policy needs reform.

Since 1972, after the massacre of the Israeli athletes at the Munich Olympics, the task of coordinating American policy had fallen to the State Department's Office of the Coordinator for Counter-terrorism, known by the acronym S/CT. Initially it was a part-time operation but then, as the terrorist threat grew, it was formalized with the head of the office being awarded the title of ambassador at large. Its current mission statement says: 'The Office of the Coordinator for Counter-terrorism has primary responsibility within the US government for developing, coordinating, and implementing American counter-terrorism policy. The office plays this role as chairman of the Policy Coordinating Committee on Terrorism (to develop and coordinate policy) and as Chairman of the Department of State's task force (to coordinate responses to international terrorist incidents). The office coordinates all US government efforts to improve counter-terrorism cooperation with foreign governments, including the policy and planning of the Department's Anti terrorism Training Assistance Program. The office also coordinates all other US counter-terrorism assistance programs and the inter-agency research and development program for counter-terrorism.'

In theory S/CT should act as a first and last stop collator of intelligence, analysis and response from all the different agencies including the CIA, the DIA, the NSA, the Pentagon and State itself. In practice, after some bumpy starts, that is indeed how it works, and over recent years the relationship between the agencies has worked remarkably well.

The paper was written against a background of unprecedented decline in acts of terrorism worldwide. According to the State Department report on terrorism for 1992, incidents fell 35% compared with the previous year, to 361 from 561. Fewer US casualties occurred than in any year since the United States began reporting statistics in 1968. The incident rate was at the lowest level since 1975.[8]

However, the State Department warned of 'ominous signs' that inter national terrorism is escalating and cited the bombing of the World Trade Center, the killing of two CIA employees in a Washington suburb and several airplane hijackings as evidence. The most incidents in 1992 occurred in Latin America, and the worst attack was the March 17 truck bomb planted by Islamic Jihad which destroyed the Israeli embassy in Buenos Aires, Argentina, killing 29 people and wounding 242.

Six countries remained on the list of state sponsors of terrorism, which makes them subject to US trade restrictions: Iran, Iraq, Cuba, Libya, North Korea and Syria. Sudan was added to that list in August 1993. While the administration and the media suggested this was in response to evidence linking the World Trade Center bombers to two Sudanese diplomats at the UN mission, the evidence in fact went back much further. During the final year of the Bush administration, evidence was produced by the CIA that Pakistan and Sudan were sponsoring terrorist organizations. Representations were made to both countries. Then acting Secretary of State Larry Eagleburger decided to hand the problem on to the Clinton administration. During the first six months of 1993, discussions continued and the Pakistan government took steps to reduce its involvement with terrorist groups. Sudan, however, continued to deny any involvement, despite the mounting evidence of training camps and the supply of cash, arms and false papers to the terrorists operating in Egypt. Finally the decision was taken to place them on the list of countries sponsoring terrorism.

Laurence Pope, the State Department's acting coordinator for counter-terrorism, warned that the terrorism problem would get worse. 'Terrorism is now back in the headlines, and we see ominous signs that the problem will escalate, compounded by the resurgence of regional and ethnic conflicts around the world. These incidents remind us of our vulnerability to violent attacks.'

What makes the Baker report particularly interesting is that it was written eight months before publication of the 1992 State Department report, before the World Trade Center bombing, and at a time when it appeared terrorism was diminishing as a problem. What follows is an extract from the complete report.

The world has come to recognize that terrorism is indeed a transnational problem, not just a domestic problem for some countries, and that all countries have a responsibility to their citizens to cooperate in opposing states, sub-national groups and individuals engaged in or supporting terrorist activities. Many states have developed counter-terrorism policies, although the amount of resources committed generally reflects the degree to which a country's citizens are perceived to be at risk. For most countries, the risk is primarily domestic. For the United States, however, which is physically separated from most centers of terrorist activity by miles of ocean, which has the largest population overseas of any country, and whose citizens are preferred targets of many overseas groups, the risk is primarily foreign.

US counter-terrorism has been, on balance, a rare success story of multi-agency policy-making and implementation. First of all, the emphasis has been placed on inter-agency coordination and cooperation. Secondly, the policy is one of conflict management, not conflict resolution. It is designed to emphasize keeping international terrorism within manageable proportions rather than seeking to eradicate it once and for all. Thirdly, counter-terrorism policy has evoked a laudable degree of international cooperation – particularly in airline and airport security – probably more than we thought possible a decade ago. Enhanced international cooperation in many areas of the world has made the environment in which terrorists and terrorist organizations must work far more hostile than it was just a few years ago.

International cooperation has also reduced the ability of states to support terrorist activities, even those that publicly support the political goals of specific terrorist organizations. The four states currently most active in supporting international terrorist activities – Iran, Iraq, Syria and Libya – have all curtailed their support in recent years. International pressure on them to do so has been a major factor (though not the sole factor) in each case.

Although few are still willing to claim that there was a world wide terrorist network manipulated by the Soviet Union, the Cold War did indeed reinforce the perception among US policy makers of the universality of the terrorist threat. The only major non-communist oriented or affiliated terrorist groups that received major US policy attention were Palestinian and Islamic fundamentalist groups in the Middle East that not only threatened lives and property, but also appeared to be a threat to US interests in protecting Israel and in maintaining the free flow of oil at reasonable market prices. (Ethnic terrorism between Sinhalese and Tamils in Sri Lanka and Hindus and Sikhs in India, and right-wing death squads in Central America, on the other hand, evoked relatively little policy interest in Washington.) With the Cold War over, the cohesiveness of terrorist groups has begun to decline, and with it, the global, strategic threat posed by local acts of violence. Moreover, many terrorist groups that once sought legitimacy as 'national liberation

241

movements' have lost not only much legitimacy but Soviet support as well.

The end of the Cold War has also encouraged a fragmentation of multiethnic states and a decline in regional cooperation, as ethnic and national rivalries revive in the absence of a global adversary. Thus, whereas terrorist acts by traditional small groups might be on the decline in some areas, terrorist acts associated with ethnic strife, low-intensity conflict and narcotics are on the rise elsewhere, as in Latin America, former Soviet Central Asia and Yugoslavia, and are continuing unabated in Afghanistan and Sri Lanka. Many of these acts currently fall outside the purview of counter-terrorism policy, but they are likely to emerge over time as a greater threat to regional stability than many traditionally defined acts of political terrorism. At the present time, formal US government policy coordination is currently inadequate to respond effectively to conflict situations concurrently involving terrorism, narcotics and low intensity conflict.

For example, a form of terrorism that has been growing in recent years is the phenomenon of narco-terrorism – a symbiotic relationship between drug traffickers and political terrorist groups, and more recently political terrorism by drug traffickers themselves, to avoid prosecution. The blurring of the lines between 'pure' political terrorism and violence associated with drug trafficking has led to difficulties in carrying out policies to counter both. In Colombia, for example, narco-terrorism continues unabated. In Peru, there is the added complication of narco-terrorism being ratcheted up into a full scale insurgency by the principal terrorist group, Sendero Luminoso. A lack of policy coordination among agencies fighting the drug war, combating terrorism and implementing counter-insurgency policies has contributed to the lack of effective US policies in both these countries.

The policy implications of increasingly overlapping terrorist, narcotics and low intensity conflict activities in the post-Cold War era are enormous. Over the last twenty years, the United States has publicly justified its counter-terrorism policies on the grounds that political terrorism is a priori unacceptable and must be opposed – in other words, that its very immorality was sufficient justification to oppose it. In fact, however, beyond the responsibility to protect American lives from terrorist acts, the original policy was predicated to a great degree on the implicit assumption that international terrorism was an integral part of the strategic Soviet threat and/or it threatened US political interests in the security of Israel. The Soviet threat is no longer a viable justification and, at least for the moment, the terrorist threat to Israeli security is greatly diminished.

The question arises, therefore, of how far can moral revulsion alone drive a major counter-terrorism policy in the absence of a broader political or strategic threat or where Americans are not directly targeted. The experience in Yugoslavia indicated that there is little domestic support for the US playing the role of the world's counter-terrorism policeman when American lives are not targeted or broader political, economic or strategic interests at stake.

Operationally, this would imply that, without a strong strategic or political interest at stake, US resources to combat global terrorism will begin to decline. One could argue strongly, therefore, for a redefinition of the threat that would more accurately portray immediate and longer-term US interests and concerns in order to avoid the loss of credibility by opposing terrorism only when it is carried out by opponents of broader US political interests. Without that credibility, international cooperation will be difficult to sustain, and without cooperation, counter-terrorism policy cannot succeed.

Specifically, the major policy consideration concerns the relevance of an existing policy that is too narrowly defined to include most acts of political violence – i.e. those carried out in a border context of low intensity conflict and/or the narcotics industry. Operationally, the current narrowly defined parameters risk increasing loss of effectiveness in countries where the problem is multidimensional – terrorism, low intensity conflict and narcotics. All three policy issues should be linked more closely and policy be both substantively and organizationally more closely coordinated and integrated.

The official recommended a complete overhaul of the counter-terrorism, narcotics and low-intensity conflict operations within the State Department. Instead of dividing the responsibilities, they would all be absorbed into one office under the control of an ambassador-at-large. The State Department's Bureau of International Narcotics Matters would be expanded to include terrorism and low-intensity conflict with a deputy assistant secretary for all three areas. This would eliminate much duplication of effort within the State Department by providing a single source for all policy, which would cut through the turf battles which hinder the work of all bureaucracies. At the same time it would give the State Department a similar counter-terrorist structure to the National Security Council and the Bureau for Special Operations and Low Intensity Conflict at the Pentagon.

The logic of these recommendations was clear, but there was little appetite within the bureaucracy for such a radical restructuring. The compromise meant some consolidation, but each of the deputy assistant secretaries would retain operational control over their own areas, meaning that, without a single controlling hand, all the old duplication and inefficiencies would remain.

At the same time as this reorganization was in process, 80% of the experienced experts in the counter-terrorism office were reassigned or retired by the end of 1993. At the National Security Council, the top counter-terrorism official was given multiple responsibilities, including the United Nations and drug policy, and, despite the warnings sounded by its own analysis of the future, the Pentagon is also expected to downgrade the counter-terrorist shop.[9]

These changes could be seen as much needed reforms to enable the counter-terrorist structure to meet future challenges. Sadly, the reforms are not being seen that way either by the policy makers or the people implementing the changes. Policy makers see the changes as a way of downgrading the task to reflect the declining number of international terrorist incidents, a shortsighted way of addressing a cyclical problem. If the State Department, as the creator of American foreign policy, is unable to grasp the nettle of reform to address the new threats into the next century, it is difficult to see how other, less visible, agencies such as the CIA and the Pentagon can reform either.

It would be a tragedy if the great successes against terrorism during the 1970s and 1980s which were won at such high cost were wiped out because of a shortsighted approach to the current problem. Terrorism is not going to go away whatever today's statistics may suggest. On the contrary, the battles won over the past twenty years are just part of an ongoing war where old groups will fade away and new groups with different beliefs will step up to take their place. If the downgrading of the counter-terrorist effort continues, the world will be unprepared for the next phase of the war and, once again, there will be a scramble to catch up with the terrorists who will be dictating the terms of the conflict.

THE CHALLENGES: PROLIFERATION

CHAPTER EIGHTEEN

CRYING WOLF

The Esteghlal Hotel in Tehran has been doing booming business in the past couple of years as Iran tries to establish itself as the most powerful military power in the Middle East. It is here that the international arms dealers from the gray and black market gather to peddle their wares. Russians, Americans, British as well as dealers from South Africa and Brazil have all trekked through in recent months. Iran is the place to be these days. It is the one country that is spending money on arms as if the Cold War never ended. Its pattern of purchasing has set alarm bells ringing in Tel Aviv, Moscow, London and Washington.

During the eight-year war with Iraq, Iran was forced to become increasingly self-sufficient in arms production, after years of relying on Western suppliers during the Shah's rule. The Shah's intention had always been self-sufficiency, and he signed joint ventures with a number of British and American companies which led to large transfers of modern technology. By the time of the revolution, the country could make its own artillery, large caliber weapons, rockets, small arms, ammunition and spare parts for US M-47 and M-48 tanks, and British Chieftains. Iran Aircraft Industries established in 1970 a joint venture with Northrop to manufacture spares for F-5 fighters, while Iran Helicopters Industries, in a joint venture with Bell, assembled that company's helicopters.

Once the Iran-Iraq War began, those cooperation agreements were cancelled. Western nations such as Britain and America, while apparently neutral in the conflict, were concerned that Iran should not be the victor. The result was a practical tilt in favour of Saddam Hussein's regime which involved the transfer not only of intelligence but of sensitive military and nuclear equipment.

245

Immediately the war ended in July 1988, both countries started to rebuild their armed forces. This was a much tougher task for Iran, as the Tehran regime had had to establish a covert network throughout the war with countries such as South Africa, Israel and China. But the Iran-Iraq conflict was essentially a fairly static affair fought with tactics more reminiscent of the trench warfare of the First World War than the fast manoeuvre operations in vogue at the end of the twentieth century. What Iran now wanted was to establish its armed forces as preeminent in the Arab world with enough conventional and unconventional firepower to intimidate some countries and perhaps conquer others. This required a substantial investment in ground- and air-launched missiles, main battle tanks, ships and a wide range of more ordinary equipment.

The dealers have been attracted to Tehran by the promise of a share in an estimated $50 billion in the period from 1992 to 1997. In 1991, Iran spent $19 billion on weapons and in 1992 a further $14.5 billion.[1] This in a country with an estimated foreign debt of $30 billion, with 15 million out of 58 million unemployed and where 800 factories closed in the first four months of 1993.[2]

Within that first year, Czechoslovakia, Romania, East Germany, Bulgaria and Poland all agreed to set up factories in Iran to produce armoured vehicles, anti-tank weapons and other systems. Even the collapse of the former Soviet Union and the change of these countries to democracies did nothing to alter the agreements, as each nation was desperate for the foreign currency.

The Chinese government, which has a long history of proliferation in every conventional and unconventional weapon, did good business with Iran and Iraq during the Iran-Iraq War. The peace provided them with new opportunities. The Chinese are very good at copying other countries' equipment and recycling it. With Iran, they reverse-engineered much of the equipment for the American F-5 and sold it back to Tehran. At the same time, they agreed to sell the F-6 fighter, a Chinese version of the Soviet MiG-19, for assembly in Iran.

By far the most important deal was the defence and economic agreement signed with the Soviet Union in May 1989 which was designed to make Iran self-sufficient in tanks, fighters and ballistic missiles by the end of the century. In 1991, as part of the $10 billion arms-for-oil deal signed in 1989, Moscow transferred arms worth $1 billion to Iran, including part of a delivery of 160 MiG-29 fighters, SU-24 fighter bombers, SA-5 surface-to-air missiles and artillery pieces. After the disintegration of the

Soviet Union, this contract was simply transferred to Russia where the majority of the military-industrial complex is located.

But other former members of the Soviet Union also need to sell arms wherever they can to bolster their weak economies, and the Ukraine, one of the few republics with access to large amounts of high technology modern weapons, was the first to cut a deal. In May 1993, Iran took delivery of eight supersonic Starburst sea-skimming cruise missiles which will give Iran control of the strategically important Straits of Hormuz. The missiles had originally been offered to the US for target practice, but after that deal had been turned down Ukraine turned to Tehran.[3]

The most significant of the missile contracts was one worth $300m signed with North Korea for 150 Nodong 1 ballistic missiles with a range of around 600 miles, which was signed in March 1992. The missiles are of uncertain accuracy as they had not entered service at the time the deal was struck. The North Koreans were following a common practice of developing a prototype, then selling a weapon abroad to pay for full scale development and production. In this way, North Korea has managed to develop a sophisticated defence industry with other countries paying the bills for research and development as well as production.[4]

With ground based offensive missiles and air power secure, the Iranian government then moved to improve the quality of its navy. A deal was signed for the delivery of three Russian Kilo-class diesel submarines for $600m, the first of which was delivered at the end of 1992. Although Israel also has three submarines, the purchase by Iran will alter the strategic equation in the Middle East. The Iranians have made no secret of the fact that they want the submarines to patrol the Straits of Hormuz, through which much of the oil from the Gulf states and Iraq is shipped. During the Iran-Iraq War and during the Gulf War keeping the Straits open became a task for Western navies; one which would have been much more difficult if submarines rather than surface ships had been deployed by either Iran or Iraq. Alerted by the CIA to the purchase of the submarines, the State Department made a formal protest to the Russians in the fall of 1992, but were told that, as the deal had been agreed, there was nothing to be done. At the same time, the Russians pointed out that Western countries were committed to supplying over $20 billion in arms to Saudi Arabia and Kuwait; they could see no reason why one contract for conventional weapons should be treated differently from another.

To complete the naval refurbishment, in 1992 the Iranians agreed a secret deal with China for the purchase of a new fleet of 70-ton fast patrol boats armed with Styx anti-ship missiles. When American intelligence discovered the deal in early 1992, the Chinese were confronted with the evidence but, as is their usual practice, denied any knowledge of any arms sales to Iran.[5]

The arms build-up in Iran caused great concern throughout the Western intelligence community. Memories of the failures with Iraq were fresh in everybody's mind and the parallels between the two countries too obvious to be missed. The pattern of purchases went far beyond what the country could need for its own defence. The purchase of such items as ballistic missiles and submarines suggested an emphasis on the offensive.

A report prepared by the DIA in August 1991 suggested that Iran's military expansion would allow the country to dominate the region. This stark picture was affirmed by a CIA NIE prepared a year later.[6] Currently, a middle ground between British and American intelligence suggests that, by 1997, Iran intends to have trebled the size of significant parts of its armed forces. For example, the number of main battle tanks will increase from 500 to 2,400; combat aircraft from 185 to 577; submarines from zero to three; surface to air missiles from 100 to 120 and surface to surface missiles from 40 to 460. These totals will put Iran well ahead of its Gulf neighbours like Saudi Arabia and Kuwait, leave it better equipped than its old enemy Iraq and a match for countries such as Israel and Syria, long considered to have the best equipped armed forces in the Middle East.[7]

The Israelis began issuing warnings to Western governments about Iran's military build-up immediately after the end of the war with Iraq. But the information got lost in the clutter surrounding the Gulf War, with the allies focusing all their efforts on defeating Saddam Hussein. Soon after that war was won, the focus of the intelligence community switched once again to Iran. There were two reasons for this. First, there was ample credible evidence about the military build-up in the country and no one wanted to see another potential Gulf War appear without plenty of warning. Second, all the intelligence agencies were scrambling to redefine their roles as the communist world fell apart. Proliferation was something they all saw as a potential threat to which they could reallocate resources. Iran was to prove an early test both of their ability and of the international community to act on the information.

In October 1991, the Israelis provided intelligence to the Americans that a North Korean freighter, the *Mupo*, was on its way to Syria with a cargo of eight Scud missile launchers. The Israelis had hoped the Americans would try to force the North Koreans to cancel the shipment. But the US policy makers failed to act. So the Israelis let it be known that if the vessel proceeded to the Syrian port of Tartus, they were prepared to intercept it. The North Koreans backed down. Five months later, in April 1992, another North Korean cargo ship, the *Dae Hung Ho*, left North Korea loaded with Scud-C missiles for Syria and Iran. The ship planned to dock at the Iranian port of Bandar Abbas, where the cargo would be split, with some of the equipment being shipped overland to Syria. Once again it was Mossad who tipped off the Americans about the freighter and pinpointed its destination.[8]

This time the Bush administration proved a little more robust. The North Koreans were told that unless the ship turned back there would be tough action. When this failed to influence the North Koreans, the Pentagon began a series of briefings to explain that plans had been drawn up to board the ship on the high seas. It was hoped that this judicious leak would have the same effect as a similar warning from the Israelis the previous year. As a number of commentators pointed out, any attempt to board the ships would probably be illegal as none of the countries involved had broken the law.

Marine General Joseph Hoar, the commander of the US Central Command, was ordered to keep the vessel under surveillance. At the very least, US aircraft would be able to photograph the ship unloading at Bandar Abbas, which would allow the CIA to develop a detailed picture of the cargo. In the event, neither American resolve nor international law were put to the test. For ten days CENTCOM sent aircraft to search an area of 800,000 square miles and for ten days they failed to locate the vessel. As the ship rounded the tip of India, the navy sent a P-3 Orion reconnaissance aircraft and a cruiser to find the freighter. Although the P-3 picked it up briefly, it had to return to base to refuel. By the time another aircraft got on station, the freighter had vanished. The cruiser which was supposed to shadow the freighter prior to boarding never found it at all. As it approached the narrow Straits of Hormuz, where a single vessel can be easily spotted, the navy failed to put enough ships and aircraft into the area to detect the vessel which had docked at Bandar Abbas and unloaded its cargo before American intelligence even knew it was there.[9]

The fact that the ship was able to slip through such a tightly drawn net is a graphic illustration of the limitations of current intelligence capabilities. The lesson to be drawn from that experience is not so much that intelligence has its limits (everyone in the community knows that) but that it is critical to intercept weapons and technology before they are exported. If the information on the missiles had been picked up before the shipment left North Korea, there would have been an opportunity to get the export stopped. As it was, once it was on the high seas, even if the ship could have been found, all the options available were politically and militarily difficult.

In tandem with the conventional arms build-up, the government of President Rafsanjani is thought to be trying to develop a nuclear weapon. A NIE prepared by the CIA at the end of 1992 concluded that Iran was pursuing an aggressive nuclear programme and would probably have a nuclear device by the end of the century, after building a strong team of nuclear scientists both at home and abroad, some of whom were educated in the US.

This hardline view was reflected by Bob Gates in testimony before the House Armed Services Committee in March 1992, while the NIE was being prepared, when he suggested that, even without major technical assistance from other countries, Iran could have a nuclear weapon by the year 2000.

In March 1992, Paul Munstermann, vice-president of the German Federal Intelligence Service (BND), claimed that Iran had received two or three nuclear warheads and medium range delivery systems that were missing in Kazakhstan. The Iranians denied the charge but then General Victor Samoilov, the man responsible for disarmament issues on the Russian general staff, admitted that three nuclear warheads were missing from their inventory. These reports caused some concern in other Western countries but are now believed to be incorrect. It is true that the Russian nuclear inventory is short of some nuclear warheads, but there is no evidence that any of them have been exported. It is assumed that over the years there have simply been some accounting errors – errors which have also occurred in the US nuclear stockpile. The BND report was wrong.[10]

Iran first developed a civil nuclear programme in the late 1950s with the help of the US and the International Atomic Energy Authority. It ratified the Nuclear Non-Proliferation Treaty in 1970 and signed an IAEA Safeguards agreement in 1972, before developing one of the most extensive civilian nuclear power programmes in the developing world. This all halted after the fall of the Shah in 1979 but contacts with nuclear suppliers resumed in the mid-1980s. Instead of dealing with her traditional nuclear suppliers in France, Germany and the US, Iran had talks with Argentina, Pakistan, India, South Africa and China, all countries which had either already developed a nuclear weapon or were trying to do so.

Iran's nuclear plans were not an intelligence priority before the Gulf War. With the discovery of the scale and sophistication of Saddam's nuclear programme, the intelligence community began to focus more aggressively on Iran's growing nuclear capability. What the community learned in Iraq was that it is possible to build a massive nuclear programme in almost complete secrecy. At the time, Iraq was a signatory to the NPT and subject to regular inspections by IAEA officials. Saddam's solution was to build separate plants away from the civilian operations which were never revealed to the inspectors and were kept secure from satellites and other detection systems. Although opinion was divided in the intelligence community as to exactly when Saddam would develop a nuclear device (one DIA report suggested nine months, the CIA believed at least two years, while SIS were more conservative at five years) there was complete agreement that Saddam was working to make a nuclear device.

With that as background, the intelligence community took all Iran's protestations of innocence very sceptically while tending to interpret the available evidence in the least favourable way. Western intelligence has identified six places in Iran which are involved with nuclear research: Muallem Kaliyah, north of Tehran; Isfahan, south of the capital; Karj, where there is an electro-magnetic facility for enriching uranium; Busheir; Mashad, a holy city; and Tehran itself.[11]

In 1991, the CIA discovered that Iran was negotiating with Argentina and China for equipment that could be used in the manufacturing process towards producing a bomb. China was planning to supply a 20-megawatt reactor that would have included a supply of enriched fuel and would have allowed Iran to do work related to the nuclear fuel cycle. J Stapleton Roy, the US ambassador to China, expressed American concern about the sale during a visit to a Chinese nuclear facility near Beijing in March 1992. As always on such occasions, the Chinese listened but made no commitment. However, they remain anxious to continue the Most Favoured Nation trading status with the US and were sufficiently impressed by the American arguments to announce that the deal would not proceed 'for technical reasons'.[12]

In some respects, the proposed Argentinian sale was more worrying. The equipment in the deal would have allowed Iran to convert natural uranium into precursor forms of highly enriched uranium used in nuclear weapons. The US government in concert with its European allies launched

251

an intensive lobbying campaign to persuade the Argentinians to scrap the deal. Eventually, Argentina was persuaded, not by the moral arguments but by a contract between the state owned company Investigaciones Aplicadas and General Atomics of San Diego which was supposed to make up the revenue shortfall from the Iran deal.[13]

Since the end of the Gulf War, Israel has been lobbying for the isolation of Iran which it now considers the premier threat to its own security in the Middle East. The analysis of Israeli intelligence predicts an apocalyptic future if Iran's militarization is not curbed. They believe that Iran intends to dominate the Middle East and, by becoming the focus of the lobby that rejects the current round of Middle East peace talks, the Tehran regime will carry the anti-Israeli torch whatever happens to the Palestinians. It is the Israelis who argue that Iran is currently building several factories with chemical warfare capability, including two plants to manufacture nerve agents close to Tehran. At the same time, the Iranians began drawing up plans to manufacture biological weapons in 1990 and have begun importing components for the plants from Western countries.[14]

This appeared to be supported by Bob Gates in testimony to Congress in March 1992. 'Although extensive and improving, Iran's chemical weapons program remains relatively crude,' Gates said. 'Nevertheless, we expect Iran to develop chemical warheads for its Scud missiles within a few years. We also suspect that Iran is working towards a biological warfare capability.'[15]

Although there is less certainty about these programmes in other intelligence agencies, it would be logical for Iran to be taking this route. Chemical and biological weapons are a cheap alternative to nuclear weapons, are easier to conceal and appear to be the weapon of choice for developing nations. Iran used chemically armed bombs during its war with Iraq and also possesses chemical mines.

Behind Tehran's arms buying is a determination to make Iran a power at a time when Saddam Hussein's military strength has been eroded by the Gulf War. Bob Gates said Iran spent about $2 billion in cash on arms in 1991 and is spending even more this year. 'They are looking for superpower status in the region,' said one intelligence source. 'They are trying to rebuild what they lost in the war with Iraq and we believe that within five years they will have exceeded their pre-war capability.'[16]

According to Martin Indyk, the National Security Council's senior director for Near East and South Asian affairs, Iran could exceed Iraq's pre-1990 military power in five years if preventive measures are not taken. 'Through its active efforts to acquire offensive weapons, Iran is seeking an ability to dominate the Gulf by military means.'[17]

The Western intelligence communities have played their part in trying to track shipments to countries that may eventually pose a threat. But that judgement is a narrow, subjective one when set against the broader standard of arms proliferation generally. Exactly the same pressures exist today in dealing with Iran as existed in Iraq five years ago. Then, every Western country wanted to be a part of Iraq's growing civilian industry. Business bought foreign exchange or oil and created jobs at home which the politicians could use to help in their re-election. When it came to deciding whether a particular set of goods could be used for military or civilian purposes, the bias was naturally towards the civilian sector, even if the warnings from the intelligence community argued the opposite.

The result was wholesale breaches of agreed embargoes by every major country including Britain, France, Germany and the United States who all contributed to Iraq's nuclear and ballistic missile programme by exporting equipment with a clear dual use capability. Much of this has been blamed on the intelligence community, for either failing to stop such breaches or for failing to warn the policy makers of Saddam's intentions in advance of his invasion of Kuwait in August 1990. There is some truth to both these arguments. The intelligence agencies from Israel to America to Britain to Germany all failed to appreciate the full breadth of Saddam's ambitions. It is also quite clear that there were some serious predictive failures, in that no government took action to prevent the invasion because no government believed it was going to happen. In some cases, this was because the intelligence community failed to provide the information on which the policy makers could act. In Britain, for example, the Joint Intelligence Committee completely failed to warn of either Saddam's general intentions or his specific plans with regard to Kuwait. That was not because SIS did not produce intelligence about Iraq's arms build-up. On the contrary, MI6 ran a number of agents who were part of the Iraqi arms procurement network and had a fairly detailed picture of what Iraq was buying and why; but the policy makers did not want to hear the message that Saddam was becoming dangerous as there were too many jobs at stake.

This has been graphically illustrated by the inquiry set up by the British government under Lord Justice Scott to investigate how the policy of restricting the supply of arms to Iraq during the 1980s was implemented. The inquiry is the most exhaustive in the modern history of the British government and has involved hearing testimony from Lady Thatcher,

John Major, other senior politicians and every senior civil servant involved in devising or implementing the policy. In addition, the inquiry
has gathered over 100,000 documents from government departments
which led to 200 requests for further information.

The inquiry has forced both SIS and MI5 to unveil methods of
operating and revealed the clear division that exists in Britain between
the supply of intelligence and the formulation of policy. For much of the
first half of 1993, both agencies had small task forces established whose
sole job was to comb through the archives and the databases to produce
every single document and scrap of intelligence relating to Iraq's arms
programme for examination by Scott. What has been revealed is not that
the intelligence community failed to warn the government about Saddam's plans. They provided warnings. For example, Lieutenant Colonel
Richard Glazebrook, the MoD official responsible for assessing arms
exports to questionable governments, became so concerned that he
wrote a report to ministers in June 1989. 'UK Ltd is helping Iraq, often
unwittingly, but sometimes not, to set up a major indigenous arms
industry.'[18]

Lord Justice Scott has prised open the normally secretive workings of
the British government to reveal a contemptible disregard of the law and
moral principle by civil servants and government ministers alike. Tempted
by the short-term goal of profiting from arms exports, civil servants and
ministers connived to deceive the public and parliament through outright
lies and deception. Within the intelligence community there is complete
confidence that they will be vindicated by the inquiry and some satisfaction that ministers and civil servants will be blamed for ignoring the
numerous warnings that were presented to different departments.

Scott will recommend wholesale changes in the way the British government works, changes that are long overdue. The result will be better
checks to ensure that intelligence cannot be ignored and other balances
to see that civil servants and ministers are not allowed to deceive
parliament and the public again.

In America, too, there had been sufficient warnings from the intelligence community to alert the government to Saddam's plans. These
culminated in a series of warnings delivered by the CIA's National
Intelligence Officer for Warning, Charlie Allen.

The Warning Center, which produces reports for the National Intelligence Council, is designed to send up signals that a country or an
incident could pose a threat to the United States. Within the CIA, the
Warning Center has traditionally been viewed as unnecessarily alarmist.

Those who work in the field argue that this is their job; they are the first line of defence and it is up to others to act on their knowledge or assessments. But the community's reservations are understandable. For example, on October 6, 1973, four hours after the Syrians had launched a massive attack along the Golan Heights at the beginning of the Arab-Israeli war, the Warning Center produced a report that dismissed the invasion as 'light skirmishes which are part of the action/re-action cycle'.[19]

During the Cold War, Western defences against a massed conventional attack by the Warsaw Pact were designed for mobilization within 7–10 days. To maintain that state of readiness over an extended period of time costs billions of dollars as troops and equipment have to be in theatre with the right levels of spares and ammunition as well as training. As the Warsaw Pact crumbled and the Cold War ended, the warning times were looked at again. At a meeting in London in July 1989, the CIA, with the support of the DIA, proposed raising the warning time to 60 days. This was opposed by the British Defence Intelligence Service on the grounds that there was not yet enough information to justify such a change. In September that year, the Americans acted unilaterally and pushed the warning time for US armed forces up to 60 days and the rest of Nato was forced to follow.

In the past two years, there has been a detailed analysis of what we now know about the structure and capability of the Soviet armed forces. Not only has the CIA learned that in most areas there was a serious overesti-mation of capability but in terms of warning for war, the Soviets had about half the capability the West attributed to them. The CIA now believes that the warning time for war in Nato should have been not 7–10 days but 20–30. This was a serious miscalculation which cost every Nato nation hundreds of millions of dollars over thirty years.

In November 1988 the CIA's Warning Center issued its first broad, strategic alert that Saddam Hussein had definite expansionist ambitions and might be thinking of advancing on Kuwait. This information was passed down the chain of command and produced little reaction, not least because the CIA was still in the midst of a major effort to support the Iraqi regime with intelligence to help Saddam win the war with Iran. The US-Iraqi intelligence relationship had been instigated by William Casey in 1982 when he was DCI, as part of an attempt to blunt Iran's expansionist ambitions. At the time, there was concern that a resurgent Iran might be able to conquer Iraq, and thus come to dominate the Gulf oil-producing nations and the rest of the Middle East. To have what was perceived as an unstable regime controlling such a strategically important area was considered unacceptable, so steps were taken to bolster Saddam.

For much of the Iran-Iraq War, the CIA furnished the Iraqis with intelligence concerning Iranian troop dispositions and capabilities, as well as pointing out the gaps in the Iraqi defences that the Iranians might try to exploit.

'We gave Iraq what they wanted to prevent their defeat by the Iranians,' said Howard Teicher, an expert on the Middle East on the NSC at the time. 'We saw key vulnerabilities in their defensive lines, and we knew that Iran could roll all the way into Baghdad. We could see the establishment of a fundamentalist Shiite state in southern Iraq, and it scared us to death. So we told Saddam, "Wake up, there's a sieve in your lines." That's exactly what we said. We gave them strategic advice. We saved them.

'We sent them information through Jordan and Saudi Arabia to establish our bona fides. We gave them overhead and electronic information – a treasure – that disclosed to Saddam the nature of our intelligence capabilities.'[20]

In April 1988, just seven months before Allen's first warning about Saddam's grander ambitions, the Iraqis launched a major offensive to recapture the strategically important Faw peninsula. This was carried out using CIA intelligence. The Agency not only provided detailed maps of the Iranian positions but helped plan the attack, which was surprisingly successful given Iraq's dismal military performance during the war.

It was hardly surprising, then, that Allen's first warning was heard by people who did not want to listen. A series of other warnings followed which gradually escalated the nature of the threat posed by Saddam's forces. By July 1990, the threat level, which is measured in percentages, had risen to 80%, 'which is about as high as it gets before the shooting actually starts'.[21]

Allen submitted the report to Fritz Ermath, head of the National Intelligence Council and Allen's immediate superior. Allen waited a few days and, when there was no reaction, decided to bypass the Agency and take the matter directly to Richard Haas, the official responsible for Iraq at the NSC. For a bureaucracy like the CIA and for an official like Allen who had spent his whole life in the secret world, this was an extraordinary action. On July 26th, he walked into Haas's office.

'He had the paper on his desk which warned of war and I know the DIA had said the same,' Allen recalled. 'He sort of turned the pages over and I asked him if he understood what it meant. He said he did and that was that. But nothing was done.'

Haas recalls the meeting differently.

'Charlie had been saying he was worried about the situation for some time. I invited him over and he showed me the charts but what he was showing me was capabilities not intentions and I already knew that. They had clearly massed a lot of force and they were clearly trying to intimidate the Kuwaitis.

'As a result of the meeting I sent a message to Scowcroft [the National Security Advisor] saying that I can't rule out that it's something more because they have amassed more than they needed for simple intimidation but then we knew that the Iraqis had always been heavy-handed.

'What nobody said, including Charlie, was that their intention was to invade. There was never any doubt about the technical capability to invade but what we wanted was knowledge of intent.'[22]

(The fallout from this exchange was classic Agency. Fritz Ermath found out that Allen had bypassed him to go straight to Haas, and reprimanded Allen in terms so fierce that Allen believed he was going to be fired. He left the meeting and immediately hired a prominent local lawyer, his good friend Jim Woolsey. When Woolsey later took on the job of DCI in the Clinton administration, Charlie Allen felt that at last he had a defender at the top.)

Since the Gulf War, there has been a great deal of self-justification by policy makers and the intelligence community. The facts are that some intelligence agencies got it badly wrong and so did most policy makers. But one of the benefits of the war is that everyone has had an opportunity to understand where mistakes were made and to make sure they are not repeated.

If inadequate intelligence makes a warning ambiguous, the intelligence itself has to be improved. In the past, the Warning Center structure was designed primarily to cope with the threat posed by the Soviet Union, and to produce clear nuclear or strategic warning of an imminent attack. Other issues, such as the invasion of Afghanistan or the impending collapse of democracy in a Latin American country, were considered peripheral. As part of Gates's reforms, the Warning Center mission has been changed to embrace any pressing military or political event. This proposal initially met with considerable internal resistance at the Agency, as regional problems have traditionally been viewed in turf terms. Politi cal clout and power were related to the influence of regions, rather than their product. Now Warning has the authority to cut across turf

257

boundaries and consider developments from a local, regional or strategic view.

Each member of the US intelligence community has been required to designate a special officer who is the point of contact at the Warning Center. Too often in the past, the goal of the men and women under the deputy director for Operations was the gathering of intelligence which was considered as an end in itself. It was the job of those under the deputy director for Intelligence to try and make sense of the information supplied by the DO. There had always been intense rivalry between the two groups, with the DO people despising the desk-bound DI types, and the DI considering many of those in the DO to be little better than cowboys.

The reform of the Warning process meant that the gap between the two directorates had to narrow, if the information gathered by the DO was to be of any real value. In the DI, the analysis had to improve so that it became timely and accurate, cut down to size for easy digestion, with less of the endless footnoting and caveats that baffle policy makers and disguise the true value of the nuggets contained in each policy paper. At the same time, both the collectors and the analysts working for Warning have had to learn to interpret the new signals, so that they ask the right questions and also understand the relevance of the answers they receive. In turn, the chain of command has had to be educated so that they fully comprehend the information they receive and can make correct judgements.

It is the nature of such a vast bureaucracy that there is a tendency to hedge any recommendation with caveats. Buried in every paper is an escape clause, which allows the agency or individual to claim that the real information was there, it was the interpretation that was wrong. In the new world, this risk-averse attitude has had to change so that recommendations are, in theory, much less ambiguous.

The final reforms of the Warning Center were in place by the end of 1992, with all staff expected to be fully trained after two years. Now, every Friday, a new Watch Committee produces Watch Reports for the National Security Council which are supposed to flag potential problems. Risks are rated in language (high or low probability) and in percentages, so that the process has precise implications which must force the policy makers to react. The average report has been cut dramatically, so that they frequently cover only two sides of paper.

To give the Warning Center more clout, it also sends out Special Warning Memoranda for distribution to the DCI and the principals of the National Foreign Intelligence Board, which still produces the National Intelligence Estimates and includes senior officials from all the agencies which make up the US intelligence community. The Special Warning includes dissenting views, and both the DCI and the NFIB principals are expected to comment on the paper. When a final version is produced, the DCI has to decide whether or not to pass it on to the President. If he takes that decision, then it goes out under his own name, which has the effect of putting both the Agency's and the DCI's full weight behind each report.

In theory all this means that the policy makers will be forced to listen when the alarm bells are rung. But however brief the paper and however tight the argument, action still depends on the policy makers taking a decision and there is every indication that little has changed in that regard.

In November 1991, the Warning Center issued a warning that Algeria was likely to be overtaken by civil war. The report was circulated in the NIC and to the NFIB. From there it went to the policy makers, but no action was taken. Today, Algeria is indeed in a state of civil war, and there is every prospect of Muslim fundamentalists gaining control of a country that was once one of North Africa's more stable democracies. Yugoslavia, too, was the subject of repeated warnings by the Agency that the disintegration of the nation would lead to civil war and chaos. President Bush chose to ignore the problem. President Clinton gave it his full attention, then backed away.

For more than three years, the intelligence community have been unanimous in their assessment that Iran is the most serious threat to stability in the Middle East. Alone among Middle East countries, it has a thriving conventional, nuclear and chemical and biological weapons programme. It is investing money in developing all three areas on a scale unmatched in the region. Despite all the warnings, the country has been able to buy or make the equipment it needs, and there is no sign that the resonant rhetoric delivered at the end of the Gulf War has had much effect on Iran's militarization.

Unlike with Iraq, there is little evidence that Western countries have been clamouring to sell equipment, or that their governments have been turning a blind eye to a potential problem in exchange for cash or oil and the certainty of job security for workers at home. Instead, other suppliers such as Russia, China and North Korea have filled the inventory, ignoring international obligations and pressure. And there is still intense competition among all the arms producers to sell weapons to other

259

Middle East countries. The declining arms market and defence cutbacks at home have pushed government and industry to pursue foreign sales with even more enthusiasm than usual. The result is a new arms race in the Middle East which has been given additional impetus by the Gulf War, when countries like Saudi Arabia used some of their inventory and other countries, like Kuwait, understood their vulnerabilities. For example, in September 1992 the Bush administration announced the sale of $9 billion in hardware to Saudi Arabia including 72 F-15 warplanes and related equipment. This was followed three weeks later by a deal which would allow for the sale of $650m in Apache and Black Hawk helicopters and Harpoon missiles on top of the $1.8 billion in annual aid to Israel.[23]

While the major arms producers pour weapons into countries like Israel, Saudi and Kuwait, it is difficult to sustain the argument that other countries, like Russia and China, should not supply arms to Iran.

'It just does not seem to me that there is any real restraint,' said Congressman Lee Hamilton, an Indiana Democrat, pointing out that in 1991 the US sold $63 billion in arms worldwide of which $23.3 billion, more than a third, went to the Middle East.

'If I were the Chinese, the Russians, the French, the British, I would look and see that the United States continues to pump enormous quantities of arms into the region, and I would not see any reason why I should not sell missiles.'[24]

It was the drive to earn exports and to secure a growing market that encouraged trade with Iraq (as well as the quiet backing of the Reagan and Bush administrations). Those business pressures exist in Iran today. In 1992, the US exported goods worth $747m to Iran compared with just $55m five years ago. A number of contracts that could have a dual use capability have been stopped, such as a proposal by BP-America to sell chemical-manufacturing technology for building a $250m acrylic fibre plant to manufacture clothing and blankets in Iran. The Bush administration objected to the licence on the grounds that the same processes produced hydrogen cyanide as a byproduct. But these are only small gestures when set against the overall trade all the developed countries are doing with Iran.[25]

Other countries have fared even better than the US. Germany, for example, currently earns $5 billion a year from trade with Iran. Germany was one of the most important contributors to Iraq's development of its military-industrial complex throughout the 1980s, largely through the sale of sensitive technology. The CIA repeatedly produced hard intelligence about the diversion of equipment sold by Germany for military purposes. After much of this traffic was exposed, the Germans introduced tough new export laws which were supposed to stop this traffic. However, it is the view of both American and British intelligence that these laws are not tough enough and that export laws are being leniently interpreted so that Germany can win more contracts.

Germany has what it describes as a C list of controlled technologies, which is virtually identical to the list of high technology goods banned from export to the Soviet Union and Eastern bloc during the Cold War. During 1992, 80% of the applications for export for goods on this list were approved, including such technologies as sophisticated metals, precision machine tools, advanced electronics, high-speed computers, avionics, navigation equipment, night vision equipment and sensors.[26]

In theory, Germany has a trigger list of 400 individuals and companies thought to be involved in Iran's military build-up. In practice, this list is almost meaningless. As Saddam demonstrated, it is possible both to set up a very sophisticated secret procurement network and to use perfectly innocent front companies for some purchases. In a totalitarian regime, every business and every person can be a front for the government as non-cooperation is not an option. It is the equipment not the purchaser that matters.

It is unrealistic to expect every government to cut its own throat by stopping all trade, or to police its exports properly. Instead, those countries which are seriously concerned about such matters have to gather the hard evidence with which to confront countries which are contributing to proliferation. This is a tough task, as neither satellites nor intercepts will give a complete picture; this can only be provided by human sources at the heart of such an operation. As all Western intelligence agencies discovered in Iraq, recruiting agents in a country run by a regime which has little or no regard for the law is very difficult. Suspicion is enough to cause whole families to be arrested and killed. Under those circumstances it takes a very brave person to become a spy. Recruiting sources in Iran has also proved tough and there are few agents in place who can feed back the kind of intelligence needed to prevent the export of sensitive equipment to Iran.

The alternative is to apply pressure on the country from outside, to make the diversion of civilian technology and the purchase of offensive weapons too expensive to be tolerated. America believes one way to control the situation is to stop Iran from diverting credits and aid to pay for arms. In the 1990s, Iraq used $5 billion in food credits to pay for weapons. 'This is a guns and butter issue,' said one senior State Department official. 'They want credits to buy butter and then they use their oil money to buy guns. We have to do with Iran what we failed to do with Iraq.'[27]

Warren Christopher, the US secretary of state, used a meeting of European Community foreign ministers in June 1993 to argue for the isolation of Iran by cutting off loans, investment, the sale of arms and militarily useful technology. 'Iran must understand that it cannot have normal commercial relations and acquire dual use technologies on the one hand, while trying to develop weapons of mass destruction on the other,' he said.[28]

But the allies rejected a similar US request at the end of 1992, and merely agreed to form a committee to look at the matter further and report back. It seems unlikely that any effective ban will be introduced. Iran's largest trading partners, Japan, France, Germany and Italy, have always objected to any curbs and, despite the warnings issued by their own intelligence services about Tehran's growing military power, they do not wish to do anything that will place valuable exports in jeopardy.

American policy has come full circle, with President Clinton adopting a strategy of dual containment against both Iran and Iraq, something the Reagan administration agreed to during the Iran-Iraq war but then ignored in favour of supporting Iraq. This time around there seems little doubt that, unless there is a change of leadership in both countries, they will remain hostile to Western interests. This was the conclusion of a policy review ordered by President Clinton soon after he moved into the White House. There is nothing too surprising in such a policy but what really matters is how far it can be implemented. To judge by the record so far, efforts at 'dual containment' are likely to have only a marginal impact.[29]

Immediately after the Gulf War, Saddam Hussein began rebuilding his military machine. According to investigators from the House Subcommittee on International Security, International Organizations and Human Rights, much of the infrastructure destroyed during Desert Storm has been restored. Their investigation revealed that despite the imposition of UN sanctions, Saddam has managed to reactivate his underground arms procurement network, relying on front companies in France, Jordan and Germany to buy and ship weapons and raw materials. Saddam has repaired and returned to service most of the 2,500 battle tanks and 250 fixed wing aircraft that survived Desert Storm, and is also manufacturing tanks, artillery and short-range ballistic missiles. The country is poised to revive its nuclear weapons programme as soon as sanctions are lifted.[30]

The fact that Iraq has been able to do so much to rebuild its military capability in the face of the toughest ever sanctions regime imposed by the UN is evidence of just how limited the system is. The billions of dollars spent on Desert Storm and the high loss of life appears to have achieved little except to buy Iraq's enemies some time. It cannot be long before Iran and Iraq will be back where they were when they called a ceasefire in 1988. But this time it will be Iran that is the better equipped, and which has the more advanced nuclear and chemical weapons programmes.

The Coalition that came together to combat Iraqi aggression against Kuwait was unique in modern times. Old enemies and traditional allies united under a common flag and achieved a stunning military victory. But as soon as the dust had settled in the desert, it was back to business as usual for many of the countries involved. Two of the Coalition partners, France and Germany, have resumed shipments of military equipment while others, such as Egypt and Saudi Arabia, have been seeking ways of accommodating both Iran and Iraq in policies of appeasement that do nothing to stem the expansionist ambitions of Tehran and Baghdad.

It may be that Saddam Hussein will fall and a more moderate leader take his place. A more acceptable government may assume power in Tehran, but luck should not determine foreign policy.

The intelligence community is investing the resources to try to produce the early warnings of potential threats from the proliferation of all types of weapons. Those warnings have been sounded about Iran and Iraq, although with very limited effect. Now, the focus is shifting to other parts of the world where new and dangerous patterns are beginning to emerge.

CHAPTER NINETEEN

A FINGER IN THE DAM

In February 1993, SIS picked up some HUMINT from a source in Malaysia that the Libyans had ordered a consignment of eight stainless steel canisters to store a mud-like solution used for lubricating drill bits used in oil exploration. Superficially, this was just another oil industry contract, but to one SIS analyst the consignment seemed suspicious. After consultations with the CIA, it was agreed that the canisters were the type needed for mixing the highly corrosive ingredients for nerve gas. This deduction was supported by earlier intelligence that the Libyans were constructing a new chemical weapons plant at Tarhuna, forty miles southeast of Tripoli.[1]

The British information dovetailed neatly into another piece of intelligence, picked up by the CIA in Libya – an order for sixty tons of ammonium perchlorate, a chemical ingredient for rocket fuel which the Libyans need for their ballistic missile development programme.

Britain and America moved to try to prevent the contracts being filled, but neither supplier was prepared to cancel the deal, claiming that the orders were for civilian goods, and that UN sanctions on the delivery of military equipment, imposed after the downing of PanAm 103, did not apply. But the goods were to be shipped from Russia via the Ukraine, and from Malaysia via Singapore, so there was a second opportunity to apply pressure. The Ukraine government, which has no love for the Russians and is anxious to curry favour with America, stopped the chemical shipment in June. In Singapore, the government refused to move until the UN issued a statement that the goods were in breach of the embargo. British and American officials convinced the UN Sanctions Enforcement Committee to contact the Singapore government with the result that the goods were seized in March.

This was a major triumph in the battle against proliferation. For the first time, one country from the former Soviet Union cooperated to thwart the exports of another. It was also the first time that the UN had been prepared to commit to the idea of 'dual use' exports, an important step when most developing nations rely on the ambiguous use of many raw materials to bypass export restrictions.

The seizures were important, too, because they showed just how far the counter-proliferation business has developed since the Gulf War, when the scale of Saddam's underground arms procurement network showed how hopeless most of the developed nations' enforcement systems were. Of course Libya is a high priority, and has been since 1985 when plans for a chemical weapons plant at Rabta were drawn up by the West German firm Imhausen-Chemis, which was in financial difficulties at the time. Imhausen commissioned the plans from the Salzgitter steel company, which is owned by the German government, telling the company that the work was for a pharmaceutical plant in Hong Kong. The Japan Steel Works did much of the construction at Rabta, employing Thai workers. By 1988 the plant was producing nerve-gas casings, using steel supplied by other West German companies.

Once again, British and American intelligence had been monitoring the projects closely and, by the summer of 1988, were convinced that the Libyans would be able to produce from 22,000 to 84,000 pounds of nerve agents every day, making Rabta the largest chemical weapons plant in the Third World. When confronted with the evidence, the Japanese government claimed that the Rabta complex was a desalination plant, though it is fifty miles from the sea. No action of any kind was taken against the Japanese; and yet in 1991, the Bush administration was prepared to impose sanctions against Japan in order to protect a rare turtle, whose shell the Japanese use to make ornaments.

By the beginning of 1992, Bob Gates was able to spell out the extent of Libya's chemical capability: 'We estimate the production facility at Rabta has produced and stockpiled as many as a hundred tons of chemical agents. The Libyans have cleaned up the Rabta plant, perhaps in preparation for the long-awaited public opening of the facility to demonstrate its supposed civilian pharmaceutical purpose. But they have yet to reconfigure the plant to make it incapable of producing chemical agents. Even if Rabta is closed down, the Libyans have no intention of giving up CW production. There have been a number of reports that Libya is constructing another chemical weapons facility, one they hope will escape international attention.'[2]

Gates's statement was not entirely accurate. The Rabta plant was indeed still occupied but it is now incapable of producing chemical weapons. In the mid-1980s, and on the advice of the Germans, Libya had stockpiled hundreds of tons of chemical precursors that would be required to make the weapons. They assumed that the international community would eventually discover the Rabta complex and then it would be impossible to purchase the raw materials. They were right about that, but hadn't realized just how complex a chemical weapons plant can be to run.

For some months after the plant was exposed, the Libyans attempted to calibrate the sensitive equipment and largely failed. At the same time, there were no engineers or chemists sufficiently qualified to maintain the equipment. The result, according to Western intelligence sources familiar with the plant, is a rusting shell where almost every piece of equipment is ruined and lies as an expensive monument to Gadaffi's military ambitions.

Despite this setback, Gadaffi decided to continue to pursue his quest to develop an effective chemical capability. He was determined to learn from past mistakes and to keep the project completely secret from the prying eyes of Western intelligence. He selected a site outside the small village of Ras Fam Mullaghah, near Tarhuna, about fifty miles south-east of Tripoli. The site was chosen in part because construction work is under way nearby for the Man Made River project, a huge engineering feat designed to bring fresh water to hundreds of square miles of desert. The extra construction crews in the area would therefore not be noticed.

The design of the plant calls for two huge tunnels to be dug in the sandstone hills outside the village. Each tunnel will be 40 feet wide and 450 feet long connected by a series of smaller cross tunnels. One tunnel houses the production facility and the second is a storage area for the chemical weapons; both have been hardened to withstand direct hits from bombs or missiles. The first indication that the new project was under construction came in 1990 when British intelligence learned that a German company, Westfalia-Becorit, had received a multi-million dollar contract to supply tunnel cutting machines to Libya. The machines were officially for the Man Made River project, but according to plans for the project that had been acquired by Western intelligence, there were no requirements for any tunnels of the size that could be bored by the German machines. Britain and America approached the German government and the contract was stopped.

To broaden the deception and reduce his chances of detection, Gadaffi decided to try and produce many of the raw materials (known as precursors) for the chemical plant himself. Libya already has many of the precursors such as phosphorus, sulphur, chlorine and ethylene, either as raw materials or as by-products from other industries, but the country lacked a plant capable of refining these so that they could be used in the new factory. With extraordinary extravagance, Gadaffi announced plans to build a liquid petroleum product plant which ostensibly would produce lubricants and solvents to protect the drill bits in oil wells. This substance, known as drilling mud, is perfectly legal and none of the components are restricted. But the whole project was a sham, a gigantic cover for the chemical weapons project. To produce the kind of refinement necessary to make precursors, the machinery has to be manufactured to a high specification and it was this small flaw in Gadaffi's plans that first alerted the intelligence community to the Tarhuna project.

In the spring of 1991, the Libyans approached two British companies, Yeoman Projects and Melbray Chemicals, both in Teesside, with the offer of a £1m contract each to supply high quality reactors for the LPP factory under construction. Under the new guidelines issued by the British government after the Gulf War, companies are required to let the government know about any such contracts and to ask for an export licence. The application came to the counter-proliferation department at SIS and immediately the alarm bells began to ring. The specification for the stainless steel reactors was far higher than would normally be needed for a simple LPP plant. The request for an export licence was denied and Gadaffi was forced to shop elsewhere. His next stop was Malaysia where Libyan procurement officials arrived in August 1992. From there, it was a short stop to the UN sanctions committee and the order was stopped – for the moment.

The operation to stop that particular part of Gadaffi's chemical weapons programme was successful but others have been less so. Thailand has a number of lucrative contracts with Libya to supply managers and workers for construction projects. The deals are valuable sources of foreign exchange for Thailand. However, W & M Partnership, which supplies cooks and labourers for military projects, has also supplied around fifty project managers, engineers and geologists to control the tunnelling work at Tarhuna. A second Thai company, Supachok, has supplied around 500 labourers for the site.

Beginning in 1992 and continuing into 1993, the US embassy in Bangkok made a number of protests to the Thai government about their involvement in the project but nothing was done. Finally, in May 1993, Prasong Sunsiri, the Thai foreign minister, visited Washington for talks with US Secretary of State Warren Christopher and the subject was raised once again.

In October 1993, the Thai government finally moved against W & M Company, one of those involved in the supply of workers in Libya. The owner of the company was arrested and charged with sending Thais abroad without government permission. The following month Libya retaliated by ordering all Thai workers to leave the country. However, the Thai government's delay in responding to American pressure has allowed much of the weapons plant to be built and what remains can probably be completed by Libyan or other foreign workers – even assuming the Thai workers all actually leave the country.[3]

To the intelligence officers working in counter-proliferation, this is a depressingly realistic view of their ability to stop a nation like Libya developing a capability in defiance of international efforts. In every case, the mosaic of intelligence is exceptionally difficult to pull together and often there are many fragments missing. The country that wants to defy international agreements almost always has the initiative in being able to choose where and when to try and buy raw materials. Agencies are always going to be playing catch-up, buying time until governments change or a particular programme is abandoned.

'Sooner or later, the Libyans are going to find somebody either who is in a country not prepared to back down, or they're going to find somebody in some Godforsaken part of the world that we just don't find out about. And then they'll get the capability they want.'[4]

Present estimates suggest that the Tarhuna plant will be completed in late 1994 or early 1995 to give Libya one of the most advanced chemical weapons facilities in the world. By the time it is completed it will have cost Gadaffi some $500m, a huge sum, but still a fraction of what it would have cost in time and money to develop a nuclear weapon.

Depressing as the reality of the Tarhuna plant may be, it is an illustration of just how far the intelligence communities have come since the end of the Gulf War. Prior to that time, SIS kept an eye on proliferation provided there was a specific task given by the JIC. But it was a low level effort generally involving a single individual aided by experts from the Ministry of Defence. Immediately after the Gulf War, SIS set up a new counter-proliferation unit with a modest staff who are mostly analysts on permanent secondment from the Ministry of Defence.

At the outset, SIS had no real understanding of the nature of the proliferation problem or any framework for dealing with it.

'We sat in a room and said, what do we do now?' explained one of those involved. 'We started off with a list of the countries concerned, the people who have programmes in CW, BW, nuclear or missile work, and altogether there are 25 of these. For a 10-man operational group, charged with targeting and penetrating these programmes, to do it in an organized way against 25 is not really a starter. So we prioritized things and split into two groups, one doing ballistic missiles and nuclear weapons, the other CW and BW.'

SIS eventually decided to target Iran, Iraq, Libya, Syria and Egypt for their CW and BW programmes. Iran, Iraq, Syria, India, Pakistan and North Korea have been targeted for their nuclear and ballistic missile programmes. Once the targets were decided, SIS asked the CIA and other agencies for any information they could share. Then, for each country a profile was developed which reached beyond a simple requirement to understand capability in a particular field. SIS had to discover exactly who were the individuals responsible for each programme, where the work took place and how it was supported with cash and procurement networks. Out of that data came a list of potential targets for recruitment.

Those targets in turn were divided into three basic groups: the scientists who do the research and development, the staff working in the production and management of the weapons plants and, finally, the members of the procurement network itself.

'It became apparent very early on that in places like downtown Damascus, Tehran and Tripoli there wasn't a whole hell of a lot you could do about these people. They are kept under lock and key in the institutes where the work takes place and they don't wander around freely talking to Westerners.'

With the exception of the Iranians, nearly all national procurement operations in the countries concerned operate outside of the intelligence services. Some, like the Libyans, are centrally organized. Others, like the Iranians, are dispersed in different ministries and it is virtually impossible to develop a complete picture of a procurement system.

Once the structure and the individuals have been identified, every avenue by which a person can be approached is explored.

In the counter-proliferation field, Britain and America are currently devoting the most resources. Other countries are helpful in specific areas. Italy, for example, has some sources in Libya and shares intelligence with its allies.

It is rare indeed for a single source to provide critical information. More usually, a number of different sources run by different national intelligence agencies produce enough information for a government to act. When a single, key source is recruited, his information can have a critical effect not just on a project but on international relations.

CHAPTER TWENTY

THE WEAPON OF SPECIAL DESIGNATION

Vladimir Pasechnik was one of the brightest stars at the Leningrad Polytechnical Institute. Born in Stalingrad in 1937, he had trained as a physicist, graduating top of his class, and like many scientists the world over he had visions of using his research skills to explore the science of biophysics. His vision of using science for peace was particularly powerful given that he had been born in a city that suffered some of the worst ravages of World War II. He determined that he at least would never play any part in the kind of destruction that had cost so many of his family their homes.

After graduation, he had become a researcher at the Institute of High Molecular Compounds in Leningrad, specializing in the study of polymers for biological uses under the internationally renowned Professor Georgi Samsonov. Pasechnik saw the opportunities represented by the development of new antibiotics and methods of treatment for illnesses like cancer for which there were no known cures.[1]

In 1974, General Vsevolod Ogarkov, wearing his hat as the deputy director of the Main Board of the Microbiological Industry, approached Professor Samsonov and asked him to recommend a scientist for work on a new programme being developed by the Main Board. Pasechnik, then aged 37, was made an irresistible offer. He was to set up the Institute of Ultra Pure Biochemical Preparations in Leningrad. He would have an unlimited budget to buy equipment in the West and recruit the best staff from all over the Soviet Union.

The laboratory that Pasechnik would build would be part of a nation-wide network to be known as Biopreparat.

The fact that the offer came from the Ministry of Defence was not as bizarre as it would have seemed in America or other Western nations. The military-industrial complex in the Soviet Union was the engine of most scientific research and had both the cash and the people to control and run such operations. Often, the research and development projects did indeed have a civilian application and owed their existence more to the wish of the military to retain maximum influence in all aspects of Soviet life than it did to any simple military requirement.

For Pasechnik, the offer represented a real opportunity to realize many of his most cherished ambitions for the future of the fast developing biological sciences in the struggle against the country's most pressing medical problems. His early research had presented some promising results that he felt could produce a cure to some forms of cancer. Before the offer from General Ogarkov, he thought he would never have the resources to follow up this research. Now, he was being given the opportunity to develop one of the Soviet Union's most advanced laboratories for the study of biotechnology. He accepted the offer.

From 1974 to 1981, Pasechnik scoured the country to build the Institute. By 1981, he employed 400 people with a budget of R5m a year, and enough hard currency to ensure that the Institute had constant access to the latest biotechnological advances in the West. It was only when the Institute began its work that Pasechnik realized that, far from being the heart of a new civilian research operation, it was, in fact, the centre of a vast new network of factories and laboratories that was working on deadly new weapons of war.

'Officially, we were involved in two problems which were talked about publicly,' said Pasechnik. 'One was vaccine development and the other is producing preparations for protecting crops. In fact, we were developing methods of production and equipment for a huge biological warfare programme.'

In the beginning, Pasechnik had little idea of the scale of the operation and his knowledge was kept to his own Institute, which was the first link in a complex chain of research institutes and manufacturing plants spread across the Soviet Union. Operating with a budget of some R200m and tens of millions of dollars a year, the Biopreparat structure became one of the best kept secrets of the Cold War.

Biopreparat was responsible for overseeing two institutes in Moscow itself, two in the Serpukhov region on the edge of the capital (Obolensk and Chekhov), one in Novosibirsk (Koltsovo), one in Leningrad and manufacturing plants at Omutninsk, Stepnogorsk, Berdsk, Kirishi and Yoshkar-Ola. The plants employed a total of 15,000 men and women, and later included on the staff several members of the Soviet Academy of Sciences.

The real purpose of Biopreparat became clear to Pasechnik during a two year period starting in 1981 when the research laboratories began to produce their first results. The work was then focused on genetically engineering new biological weapons that could be suspended as an aerosol. The problem for the Biopreparat scientists was to develop new strains of known diseases that would be far more powerful than anything known to science. Two of these weapons were based on a form of pneumonic plague and of tularaemia. The task of Pasechnik's new Institute was to ensure that these new strains could be delivered by artillery shell, bomb or missile and have a long enough life in the open air to infect a large enough area to make them militarily effective. Finally, the strains had to be resistant to known antibiotics available to Nato armies.

In 1983, with the help of the technological work in the Institute in Leningrad, the All Union Research Institute of Applied Microbiology at Obolensk, sixty miles south of Moscow, developed a new strain of tularaemia agent. The new weapon was a dry powder, a form of superplague, and the tests were sufficiently encouraging for Moscow to give the go-ahead for full scale development and production of the new agent.

In 1985, Biopreparat's new Five Year Plan called for the Institute at Obolensk to develop an even more deadly agent based on a strain of pneumonic plague. Pasechnik's Institute was required to refine the production processes to make it more and more efficient. After two years of the Five Year Plan, the Soviets had sufficient industrial capacity to manufacture 200 kilos a week of the superplague agent. This would be enough to kill up to 500,000 people for each week of production.

There was no doubt that senior Soviet generals in the 15th Directorate of the Ministry of Defence in charge of the Biological Warfare programme understood the value of these new weapons and they were quickly accepted into service. Known as the Weapons of Special Designation, they would be used, not only as a weapon of last resort, but as a tool in support of a conventional conflict to attack troop reserves and to hamper logistic operations at ports and rail centres.

As the superplague had a short life, there was no manufacture of the agent except for testing. Instead, the Biopreparat network was instructed to be ready to begin full scale production at a time designated Day X. Meanwhile, other institutes in Biopreparat were involved in research into other genetically engineered weapons with similar results.

Every part of this programme was in breach of the 1972 Biological and

Toxin Weapons Convention which the Soviet Union had signed. Aside from being in breach of international agreements, the whole of the offensive biological warfare activity of Biopreparat was against the spirit of glasnost and perestroika which had been proclaimed by Mikhail Gorbachev.

For Pasechnik, the Gorbachev changes presented an opportunity for him to try and change the direction of the programme at his Institute. Over a period of months starting in late 1985, he pressured more senior officials in Biopreparat to try and switch some of the research effort away to the civilian purposes for which it had ostensibly been established.

'I was told many times that I should just get on with my work and stay in my place,' said Pasechnik. 'I realized that you can't do anything when there is someone standing behind you holding your hands. You can't do anything unless you make some other decision.'

By 1988, Pasechnik was the general director of three institutes and two manufacturing plants with a total of 2,500 employees. The Institute of Ultra Pure Biochemical Preparations worked on refining the technology associated with biological weapons, while the Technological Bureau at Kirishi worked on developing new equipment both to manufacture and deliver the weapons. The Institute of Vaccines and Sera at Krasnoe Selo near Leningrad was given to Pasechnik to placate his desire to do civil work but at the same time to provide additional cover to the offensive biological warfare research.

Working under the direction of the Ministry of Defence, Pasechnik had a rank equivalent to that of major general. He was responsible not for the manufacture of biological weapons but for the research and development of processes that would make the weapons more effective, both through the preparation of the biological warfare agent itself and the development of simulants that enabled the production plants to perfect their techniques ready for Day X without the risk of making lethal agents. Although every part of the Biopreparat programme was compartmentalized and given the highest security classification, Pasechnik was on the board of directors of the programme and so came to know something of its vast scale. Although he had no idea that his work was a breach of the 1972 Treaty (he did not even know such a treaty existed), he felt that the weapons he was helping to develop were an abuse of his scientific skills, an illustration of what he thought of as the hypocrisy in the Russian high command about the Gorbachev revolution. Above all, he felt passionately that genetically engineered biological weapons were a crime against humanity.

In late 1988, he began to think about defecting. In his long and illustrious scientific career, Pasechnik had never actually been allowed to travel outside the Soviet bloc. Then, in the summer of 1989, Biopreparat began negotiations with a factory in Toulouse, France, which manufactures equipment for chemical laboratories. Pasechnik volunteered to go to Toulouse to finalize the deal and sign the contracts. As a reward for his overall performance, he was given permission to travel and arrived in France at the beginning of October. He had thought carefully about just how he might escape the network of KGB watchers who travelled with his group, and just who he should approach. One morning, he telephoned the British embassy in Paris and in a brief conversation with a surprised diplomat announced himself, his position, and his wish to defect.

The news of his offer reached SIS in London at a critical time. For the previous five years, SIS, the CIA and a number of Nato military intelligence organizations had been trying to piece together the snippets of information they had been able to gather about the Soviet biological warfare programme.

In May 1979, US intelligence received the first reports of an explosion at a secret research facility known as Military Cantonment 19, or the Institute of Microbiology and Virology on the outskirts of Sverdlovsk, 850 miles east of Moscow. A leak of anthrax from the factory had killed up to a hundred people in the factory and in plants and houses downwind. The US believed that up to 22lbs of anthrax spores had been released in to the air to contaminate an area three miles downwind of the factory. The Soviets had tried to contain the damage with a widespread immunization program which had proved largely ineffective.

Throughout the 1980s, the subject of the Sverdlovsk leak had been raised by British and American officials with their Soviet counterparts. Until 1992, the official line was that a handful of people had died in the city after eating contaminated meat bought on the black market.

President Boris Yeltsin finally admitted the truth in June 1992, during an interview with *Komsomolskaya Pravda*, a Russian daily newspaper. The same newspaper had already printed an interview with a General A. Mironyuk, a retired official from the Ural Military District which controlled the Sverdlovsk area. He said he had learned from the KGB that 'someone from the laboratory arrived early in the morning and began to work without turning on safety filters and other protective mechanisms. Only after they were pinned to the wall did the specialists confess. It was then that an entire programme to disinform the public in the country and the world was developed.'[2]

But before that public admission, Western intelligence agencies had relied on snippets of information from sources in the Soviet Union and some satellite imagery which showed plants and testing sites apparently configured for the manufacture of biological weapons. The DIA produced a series of reports in the second half of the 1980s which estimated that the Soviets had up to eight sites for developing and storing biological weapons. SIS largely concurred with that view, and a series of reports were circulated to both the JIC and to ministers, warning that the Soviet biological programme had not slowed down as a result of the Gorbachev reforms.

As frequently happens when intelligence is fragmentary, the politicians refused to hear the message. At the time, all Western governments had been seduced by the reforms that Gorbachev was introducing across the Soviet Union. For the first time, there appeared to be a thaw in the Cold War, and no prime minister or president was prepared to risk a confrontation with the Soviets that might change the delicate balance of international relations. At the same time, there was a sense that Gorbachev was an honourable man who would not allow anything so terrible as biological weapons to be developed while he was president. As a result of these concerns, the intelligence warnings were ignored.

So when the SIS station chief in Paris flashed a message to Century House in London, it caused considerable excitement. At last, there might be an opportunity to produce the proof that would satisfy even the most sceptical politician.

With the potential defector on French soil, protocol required that the French should be consulted and their permission granted for an SIS operation on their soil. But time was short, as Pasechnik was due to return home. He was met in Toulouse and driven to Paris, where he caught the British Airways shuttle to Heathrow travelling on false papers supplied by SIS.

Pasechnik was met by a small group of senior SIS officials, anxious to question their prize and estimate the value of the intelligence he brought with him. The decision to leave his country and his family had placed an almost intolerable strain on the defector. Aside from that understandable trauma, Pasechnik had convinced himself that the work he had been doing was so terrible that he would probably face serious charges and perhaps prison in the West. It is a measure of his courage that, despite his fears, he still stepped off the plane ready to tell all.

The SIS team, unaware of the extent of his fears, were surprised to see Pasechnik burst into tears as he stepped on to English soil. But as soon as he was settled in the SIS safe house outside London, Pasechnik was reassured that he had found a new home and not a prison cell. There was the normal nervousness, about any defector, that Pasechnik might be a plant. But, aside from the wealth of new information he produced, there were other details that appeared to confirm his bona fides: he did not know how to drive, a clear sign that he was a member of the privileged elite; the distress he showed when he recounted the work he was doing was impossible to fake; then there was his love of Mozart sonatas which he would listen to in the evenings after yet another dinner with his guardians. The SIS debriefers were quickly reassured.

'The information was so stunning,' said one of the debriefers. 'A whole ministry exposed, billions of roubles spent, a complete organization shown to be a front and then there was the clear involvement of Gorbachev, this friend of the West. It just went on and on.'

To cope with all the information Pasechnik produced, a special British task force was set up with officials from SIS, the Ministry of Defence and other government departments to bring together in a single unit scientists, intelligence officers and analysts who could put the intelligence into a wider context. It was a painstaking task that required completely reconstructing Pasechnik's life from his education, his work at the Leningrad Institute and then his work with Biopreparat. The task force developed a new understanding of the relationship between the Academy of Sciences, which had previously been considered a purely civilian body, and the Soviet General Staff The sources of funding were traced, the code words entered into the database and cross-referred with other information which until then had appeared irrelevant or incomprehensible.

As is usual in such cases, the intelligence gleaned from Pasechnik was shared with the CIA, and on both sides of the Atlantic the mosaic of Russia's biological weapons programme was gradually filled in. As the picture cleared, so both the CIA and SIS began to brief their respective political masters. For the first time, the politicians were given unambiguous reports, clearly prepared on the basis of information from a highly placed defector. To further underline the seriousness of the problem, Pasechnik was brought out to brief senior officials on both sides of the Atlantic.

The evidence was so compelling that even the politicians who had no wish to confront Gorbachev were left with no choice. In April 1990, the British and American governments presented a joint démarche to the Soviet Union which spelled out in considerable detail just what they now knew. There was no reaction.

Then, in June 1990, President Bush and Prime Minister Margaret Thatcher met separately with Mikhail Gorbachev and both raised the biological weapon issue. Although he must have been briefed by his own officials about the previous démarche, Gorbachev denied all knowledge of any such programme. Thatcher, who believed she had an especially close relationship with the Russian premier, told him that unless the programme was stopped, the West would go public. Gorbachev promised that he would look into the matter.

Two months later, Soviet foreign minister Eduard Shevardnadze sent a formal reply, rebutting the charges. By this time, both the CIA and SIS had added to their preliminary assessment and produced an even more exhaustive briefing for both Bush and Thatcher. Having succeeded in forcing action at the highest levels after so many years of frustration, the intelligence community was determined to press its case until the Soviets confessed.

In December 1990, the Soviets issued an invitation to Washington and London to visit four of the sites that had been named. A joint Anglo-American delegation was dispatched. If the trip was supposed to be reassuring, it had the opposite effect. At the All-Union Research Institute of Applied Microbiology at Obolensk, the British discovered an aerosol-dissemination test chamber which is used only for the testing of biological weapons suspended in an aerosol. The steel room, which was fifty feet square, had posts on the floor to which animals could be tied while vents in the ceiling allowed aerosols containing the deadly poisons to be sprayed into the room. By monitoring the effect on the animals, the scientists could test the effectiveness of different mixes and the dispersal rate.[3]

At another stage in the tour, the team discovered a chamber used to test delivery systems for biological weapons. Another site produced row after row of fermenters used to mass produce hundreds of kilos of biological weapons – a chilling confirmation of everything the visitors had been told by Pasechnik.

The Soviets continued their denials. In September 1991, a month after the attempted coup, the new British prime minister, John Major, met with Gorbachev in the Kremlin. Publicly, the two hour meeting was confined to economic issues, but Major once again confronted him with the evidence of the secret weapons programme. Again Gorbachev denied everything and reduced the normally unflappable Major to wave an angry finger in the face of the Russian leader. 'We've got the goods on you,' he shouted.

As the intelligence community continued adding to the file, the démarches to Moscow continued through the fall of Gorbachev and the rise to power of Boris Yeltsin. At the first summit since his accession to the presidency, Yeltsin met with Bush at Camp David for four hours on February 1, 1992. In advance of the meeting, American diplomats in Moscow had made clear that the biological weapons programme was a major stumbling block between the two allies and a gesture by Yeltsin in this area would be seen as good sign of a new era in US-Russian relations. This time Yeltsin came prepared, and, for the first time, admitted that there had indeed been a secret programme, and that he had ordered it to be shut down.

He told Bush that he had asked for a detailed report of the programme, which was submitted to Yeltsin in March 1992. Here, the military admitted for the first time that they had secretly developed bombs and missiles capable of carrying anthrax, tularaemia and Q Fever biological agents in defiance of international agreements.[4]

To maintain the pressure, President Bush in a report to Congress in March 1992 stated that the former Soviet Union had 'an extensive, ongoing offensive BW programme' that violates the 1972 Biological and Toxin Weapons Convention.[5] In April, Yeltsin signed a formal decree and the programme was officially shut down.

The announcement that such a programme had existed at all caused a flurry of articles to appear in the Russian press, which featured interviews with prominent Russian officials involved in Biopreparat. These interviews appear to be part of an extensive disinformation campaign, designed to minimize the role of Biopreparat and the capacity of Russia to develop biological weapons. It was a campaign filled with the kind of lies and evasions that were routine during the Cold War but which were supposed to have vanished in the new era of democracy in Russia. For example, Medical General Valentin Yevstigneyev gave an interview on December 2, 1992, to *Nezavisimaya Gazeta*. As the former head of the 7th (now 15th) Directorate at the Ministry of Defence which controlled Biopreparat, he was well placed to discuss the programme.

'In general, there were not as many people involved in our problems as it might seem – there were only 12 medical men in the directorate and as many again chemists and another 70 responsible for personnel groups. At the Institute of Military Microbiology there are 400 people of whom 120 are scientific workers. In total 6,500 people worked in the system. Now their number has almost halved,' he said.[6]

The General maintained – in the face of all the physical evidence that had been observed on the tour of the four plants – that the work of the various institutes was essentially for civilian purposes. He also tried to diminish the role of Vladimir Pasechnik, claiming that it was research in Britain that provoked the Russian work.

'In 1989, Vladimir Pasechnik did not return from a foreign business trip. Although his organization did not have direct tasks from the Ministry of Defence, certain work of interest to us was carried out there. In particular, the research theme they were given was the transfer of the gene equivalent of myelin protein into a microorganism. This protein fulfills the role of isolator of a nerve fibre. Serious studies in this area abroad, particularly in Great Britain, troubled us. We feared that if a microorganism was modified in this way it could affect the normal program of myelin synthesis in an organism, which as a final result leads to flaccid paralysis. So we decided to check whether such modification is possible.'

Such disingenuous statements contributed to growing scepticism in both London and Washington that Yeltsin's order to dismantle the Biopreparat project was being carried out. However, there were some hopeful signs that the status of the programme had changed.

The main testing site on Vozrozhdeniye Island was reported to have been shut down, and some of the sites either began to fire staff or to switch to civilian work. But the man put in charge of the dismantling of Biopreparat is General Anatoly Kuntsevich, the architect of the Soviet Union's chemical weapons programme. His appointment was seen as a clear sop to the hardliners in the military, as Kuntsevich himself was a member of the old guard, a past master at controlling secret projects and disguising their true nature from prying Western eyes.

Since the collapse of the Soviet Union, the West had learned that the Soviets had successfully hidden whole areas of their chemical weapons programme from Western intelligence. In the 1980s, there was fairly general consensus in the West that the Russians had stockpiled around 50,000 tons of chemical agents. Some analysts in the Defence Intelligence Staff in Britain's Ministry of Defence believed that the figure might in fact be as much as 300,000 tons, but this was generally considered to be fanciful.[7]

Today, Russian scientists have admitted that they have stored 323,000 tons of chemical weapons including Sarin, Soman and VX.[8] Moreover, a number of scientists who worked in chemical weapons' development have admitted that, far from the programme being cancelled as the Soviets had been claiming since 1987, it had continued as before. According to

Dr Vil Mirzayanov, a research scientist at the State Union Scientific Research Institute for Organic Chemistry and Technology in Moscow, work on developing a new binary chemical weapon was ongoing in 1991 when he left the project.[9]

He claimed that his research institute had started production of industrial batches of binary weapons based on a new chemical agent that was many times more powerful than VX. This was confirmed by Vladimir Uglev, one of Russia's leading scientists who worked on the chemical weapons programme in the closed city of Volsk-17, 100 kilometers from Saratov. He claimed that he had worked on a new binary weapon based on a new phosphorous agent code named Novichok (the Newcomer).

'Of the three new CW agents that I synthesized, one is the basic component of a binary weapon which, according to my information, underwent successful trials on the test range. A certain quantity of binary weapon components is currently held at a secret storage facility somewhere in the Bryansk Oblast.

'Such a weapon would be ideal for the military in all respects – any country, even one which had committed itself not to produce chemical weapons, could calmly produce binary weapon components at civil plants and use them as pesticides or dyes, and still in case of need be always ready for chemical warfare.'[10]

Given this background, the appointment of General Kuntsevich to head the destruction of Russia's biological weapons programme was greeted with a marked lack of enthusiasm in the West.

'Here was this man who had done nothing but lie to us for years and now suddenly we are supposed to accept that he is willingly going to set about destroying his life's work,' said one senior Western intelligence official. 'We could hardly be expected to take Yeltsin's promises at face value.'

The British and American governments determined to demand access to all the biological weapons development, production and storage sites. Under the 1972 convention, the Russians were obliged to file a list of all sites with the United Nations, and a first draft was drawn up in Moscow in spring 1992. This listed only four of the twenty known facilities that were part of the Biopreparat programme. In July, Sir Rodric Braithwaite, Britain's ambassador in Moscow, and James Collins, the deputy chief of mission at the US embassy, met with senior Russian foreign ministry officials. They warned the Russians that if the list went to the UN, it would be publicly denounced by the British and American governments.

Three reports were eventually prepared, each one failing to give a complete picture of the weapons programme. In the end, the idea of submitting a detailed report to the UN appears to have been abandoned. But, in September 1992, Russia agreed to allow full inspection of all its biological warfare facilities by both British and American scientists. As they had failed to admit the existence of many of the sites, the two Western nations found themselves arguing with the Russians about visiting rights to sites they did not accept actually existed.

Since then, verification has proved almost impossible. Aside from the reported closing of the test site on Vozrozhdeniye Island in the Aral Sea, which is in the independent republic of Kazakhstan and outside Moscow's control, there has been no discernible change. To reinforce Western concerns, the CIA brought out a defector from the Biopreparat programme in late 1992. Like Pasechnik, he was a very senior official in the organization, who was able to confirm all the details supplied by the earlier defector. He also confirmed Western suspicions that, while Yeltsin was claiming the programme had stopped, the research and development of new strains of genetically engineered superweapons were continuing apace.

For the policymakers, this new set of revelations posed a difficult challenge. Initial approaches to Gorbachev had been kept secret, in case he was seen to be publicly bending to Western pressure. It was feared this could jeopardize his delicate relations with the military. The same concerns applied to Boris Yeltsin. Too much publicity about the programme and Yeltsin's clear failure to tackle the problem might undermine his position as president of Russia.

It was decided to take the line of least resistance, and do nothing publicly, on the assumption that Yeltsin was genuinely trying to shut the programme down and in the hope that he might prevail. When President Clinton and Yeltsin met in Vancouver in April 1993, biological warfare was on the agenda. Once again, Yeltsin assured an American president that all work had stopped. This time, Yeltsin was so convincing so that even some of the most cynical in the intelligence community were inclined to believe him.

Five months later, another defector from the Biopreparat project came over to British intelligence. He was not of the same calibre as Pasechnik or the defector debriefed by the CIA. He added little to what was already known about the basic programme, but he was able to tell his debriefers just what steps the Russian military had taken to keep the project going.

In every facility that had been opened for inspection to Western intelligence, the Russians had established convincing cover stories that made it appear as if each site had been converted to research or manufacture vaccines. The secret work continued in parts of the sites that were never visited by the American or British officials. At the same time, a new, secret, facility was under construction at Lakhta near St Petersburg. Far from the Biopreparat biological warfare programme being shut down, it had in fact undergone considerable modernization and work was continuing as before, in defiance of Yeltsin's orders.

From an intelligence point of view, the operation against the Soviet and then the Russian biological warfare programme must be considered a significant success. Early disparate material was married with the priceless information produced by Vladimir Pasechnik to produce a dossier that was sufficiently convincing to force two American presidents and two British prime ministers to confront first Mikhail Gorbachev and then Boris Yeltsin.

But the operation has also demonstrated the limitations of intelligence. As was the case with the Libyan chemical weapons programme, however good the intelligence, its usefulness depends entirely on the willingness of politicians to act upon it. In the case of Biopreparat, the concern not to jeopardize Gorbachev's and Yeltsin's relations with the military led to a less confrontational approach than might have been the case with another country such as North Korea. That policy produced a great deal of behind-the-scenes sabre rattling, but little substantial action and no detailed publicity that accused either Yeltsin or Gorbachev for allowing the programme to continue. Now that he is no longer a significant political figure Gorbachev has been blamed while Yeltsin's impotence to act against the military has been covered up.

This issue is not about the Russian military selling a few small arms to rebels in Georgia, or even the passing of sensitive technology to a country like India. The biological warfare programme currently under way in Russia has already produced the most devastating genetically engineered weapons ever seen. Tiny quantities of the Russian super-plague could devastate any major city in the West, killing millions of people while leaving the buildings, factories and raw materials intact. It is the perfect designer weapon.

If this research is allowed to continue in defiance of the political leadership in Moscow, it makes a mockery of Russia's pretensions to be a democracy. It also raises serious questions about the future intentions of the Russian military who have used political capital and scarce resources to continue a programme that remains a key part of their war plan. Yet, with the end of the Cold War, Russia can have no need of a weapon that can be only used for attack and not for defence.

CHAPTER TWENTY-ONE

KILLING THE GOOSE

The lip service that most governments paid to curbing proliferation during the 1980s was transformed by the Gulf War. The invasion helped focus the attention of Western intelligence agencies on the problem, bringing the full weight of the international community to bear. From the invasion of Kuwait in August 1990 to the end of the war with Iraq in February 1991, there were over 1,000 démarches against governments who continued to ship equipment to Iraq in defiance of UN sanctions. That was a promising sign of what could be done if sufficient attention was paid to the problem. After the war, President Bush promised that a 'new world order' would emerge but this clarion call to found a more stable global environment fell largely on deaf ears.

Egypt has declared that it would like to buy Hawk missiles, M-60 tank upgrades and F-16 fighters. Israel wants portable battlefield-navigation systems, upgrades for the F-15 fighter and the M-109 artillery piece and more Patriot missiles. The United Arab Emirates would like Abrams M1A1 tanks and Patriot missiles, and so would Bahrain and Turkey.

By far the biggest buyer will be Saudi Arabia, already in line to receive a $15 billion arms package including F-15 fighters, Apache helicopters, Abrams M1A1 tanks, AWACS radar planes, Patriot missiles, multiple-launch rocket systems, Seahawk helicopters, and Bradley fighting vehicles. This is on top of a $30 billion deal signed with Britain in 1988 for fighter aircraft, missiles, radars, airfields and ships.

The Western combatants, meanwhile, will need to replenish the stocks that were expended in the war. When the procurement decisions are made, those weapons that performed well – lasers, microcomputers, stand-off systems, Stealth technology – will be ordered. The production of these weapons means that large numbers of the most modern weapons will come on the market and be sold to developing countries while manufacturers also seek rich customers who can afford the new systems, thus reducing unit cost and increasing profits. The replacement of old weapons by new in the arsenals of the West and the drive by arms manufacturers to hold down unit costs by finding more customers – this is the dynamic that has propelled the arms race for so long.

Within that cycle, an additional impetus drives the proliferation of conventional arms after the Gulf War. Defence contractors who supplied the allied forces during the Gulf War believe they have a new opportunity to market weapons that have been proved in battle. At a time of shrinking defence budgets and contracts, exports could make up the shortfall for contractors who would otherwise be forced to shut down production lines and lay off workers. These manufacturers will have little interest in arguments about the morality of their business.

And the West won't be the only seller in the post-war arms bazaar. As Eastern-bloc countries reorganize their military forces and seek new sources of foreign exchange, they will try to produce more weapons for export, and will also sell weapons from existing inventories. For example, Czechoslovakia in May 1991 announced plans to export 5,500 weapons, including tanks, artillery systems, and armoured personnel carriers, which have to be removed from the Czech armed forces under the conventional-arms treaty. Rather than destroy these weapons, the Czechs were discussing selling the T72 tanks to Syria and Iran, and they are looking hard for customers for anything else.

According to the DIA, Russian defence exports in 1992 totalled only $2.5 billion compared with an average of $20 billion a year in the mid-1980s. The output of bombers declined from 700 in 1988 to 20 in 1992. Tank production fell from 3,500 in 1988 to 675 in 1992 and the delivery of artillery pieces fell from 2,000 in 1988 to 450 in 1992. Similar reductions were found in helicopters, fighter jets and armoured personnel carriers, all of which had once been mainstays of the Soviet Union's export business.[1]

Russia's efforts to keep its arms industry alive has led to some strange deals. In July 1993, Russia agreed to ship $800m of arms including 22 MiG-29 fighters and six training aircraft to Hungary in part payment of an outstanding trading debt. Similar deals have been struck with Poland and Slovakia.[2] At the same time, Moscow offered Thailand 20 Mi-17 military helicopters to help settle a debt of $65 million for Russian rice purchases. Moscow offered similar deals for palm oil from Malaysia, bananas from the Philippines and mango juice from China.[3]

The real challenge facing the world in the aftermath of the Gulf War and the Cold War was how to break out of the arms cycle that delivers ever more advanced weapons into the hands of developing nations. While the exact terms of George Bush's new world order have never been articulated, the major Western allies have understood the phrase to mean that the US will lead the way in halting the arms race that has dominated so much of international trade since the end of the Second World War. It was Bob Gates who set out the extent of the problem:

The greatest danger to international peace and order is the proliferation of weapons of mass destruction by nearly two dozen nations, forging arsenals of enormous destructive capability, arsenals all too often in the hands of megalomaniacs, unstable military governments, strong men of proven inhumanity, weak or unstable governments, or in the hands of some who are threatened by such.

Currently only China and the CIS have surface-to-surface missiles that can reach US territory directly. We do not expect any other countries to develop the capability to threaten US territory with air- or missile-delivered special weapons for at least another decade. But there is a growing threat to Europe, the Middle East, and Asia. For example, US or multinational forces deployed abroad could face an increased threat of air-delivered nuclear weapons before the end of the decade. In addition, several countries already have missile rockets that could carry nuclear warheads, and in the coming years other countries will acquire such missiles and some may try to arm them with nuclear warheads.

Most of the major countries in the Middle East have chemical weapons development programs, and some already have stockpiles that could threaten civilians or poorly defended military targets. Most countries have not yet equipped their delivery systems to carry weapons of mass destruction, but over the next decade many countries from North Africa to South Asia will do so if international efforts to curtail this fall.

North Korea and possibly other countries may export extended-range missiles and the technology to produce them. Countries with special weapons that succeed in buying these missiles will accelerate the special weapons arms race already under way in the Middle East and South Asia.

The international community is working to prevent or at least minimize the leakage of special weapons materials, and know-how from the Soviet successor states. President Yeltsin and most of the other republic leaders have announced policies to prevent a haemorrhage of technology, especially in the nuclear realm. But life has become so difficult in the successor republics for both industries and individuals formerly associated with Soviet special weapons programs that we fear some may succumb to the temptations proffered by Third World states that want such weapons or the skilled individuals who can design and build them.

Other highly sophisticated but less controlled conventional weapons and military technologies may also be made available by various successor states. Technologies particularly in demand include stealth and counter stealth, thermal imaging, and electronic warfare. Weapons in demand include fuel air explosives, precision-guided munitions, advanced torpedoes, cruise missiles.

Iraq remains a major proliferation threat. Saddam built formidable programs in all four areas of special weapons: nuclear, chemical, biological, and the missiles to deliver them. Desert Storm significantly damaged Iraq's special weapons production programs, and the UN Special Commission has worked diligently to eliminate what remained of them. But we believe Baghdad has been able to preserve significant elements of each of the special weapons programs. And, of course, Iraq's scientists and engineers retain their know-how. So once Iraq is free to begin rebuilding its special weapons capabilities, it will not start from scratch.

Iran is building up its special weapons capabilities as a part of a massive, across-the-board effort to develop its military and defense industries. Iran continues to shop Western markets for nuclear and missile technology and is trying to lure back some of the technical experts the Khomeini regime drove abroad during the 1980s. Increasingly, however, Iran has turned to Asian sources of military and technical aid. Tehran's principal sources of special weapons since the Iran-Iraq war have been North Korea for regular and extended-range SCUD missiles and China for battlefield missiles, cruise missiles, ballistic missile technologies and components, and nuclear technology.

Syria, too, has turned to North Korea. Because Damascus has been unable to get SS-23s from the Soviet Union, it acquired an extended range SCUD missile from Pyongyang. It also appears to be seeking assistance from foreign firms to improve its CW or BW warhead technology.

Libya is also trying to expand its special weapons capabilities, but only with mixed success. We estimate that the production facility at Rabta produced and stockpiled as much as a hundred tons of chemical agents before the Libyans cleaned it up. We believe the Libyans are constructing another chemical weapons facility, one they hope will escape international attention. Persistent international efforts to deny Libya access to nuclear, BW, and delivery system technology have forced Gadaffi to turn to the less advanced technology and less trustworthy sources available in the black and gray markets in the developing world. As a result, Libya is still unable to project its power very far.

Algeria is nearly finished building a nuclear reactor it bought from China. Both the Algerians and the Chinese have assured us the reactor will be used only for peaceful purposes, but the secrecy that attended the arrangement leaves us with lingering suspicions.

India and Pakistan continue their race to develop weapons of mass destruction. Not only do both countries have nuclear weapon ballistic missile programs, they have recently pursued chemical weapons as well. We have no reason to believe that either country maintains assembled nuclear bombs, much less that either has deployed them. But such weapons could be assembled quickly, and both countries have combat aircraft that could be modified to deliver them during a crisis. One hopeful sign is that both have publicly agreed to certain confidence-building measures.

North Korea constitutes one of the world's major proliferation threats. It has produced and sold copies of the Soviet SCUD missile to several Middle Eastern countries. It has sold modified longer-range SCUDs to Iran and Syria. And Pyongyang is developing a much [longer] larger missile, one with a range of at least a thousand kilometers. In addition, Pyongyang has been building an infrastructure that can, without help from abroad, produce weapons-grade fissile material from scratch. It has domestic uranium mines. At Yongybon it has constructed two nuclear reactors whose sole purpose appears to be to make plutonium. One of these reactors has been operating for four years. The second, much larger reactor may start up this year. Nearly completed is another facility at Yongbyon that can reprocess reactor fuel to recover the plutonium. After North Korea accumulates enough plutonium, making a nuclear device would require several additional steps that could take from several months to two years.

China has been an important exporter of ballistic missiles, nuclear reactors, and related technologies. Beijing is developing two solid-fuel missiles, SRBMs – the M-9 and M-11 – which exceed the range and payload limits of the missile technology control regime. In the past, Beijing offered to sell these missiles, claiming that their range and payload parameters did not exceed the MTCR guidelines. More recently, they have indicated that they would honor the MTCR parameters and guidelines if certain US government sanctions were lifted.

Last fall, China announced its intention to ratify the Nuclear Non-Proliferation Treaty. Now that it has done so, it is obligated to require all recipients of its nuclear equipment to adhere to IAEA safeguards. China has long been a supplier of nuclear technologies in the Third World but has not always required recipients to adhere to safeguards. There is certain to be continuing debate in Beijing over the pros and cons of accommodating US and international interests on the sales of military and nuclear equipment and technology.

There is at the same time some good news on the non-proliferation front. Since the Gulf War and revelations about Saddam's programs, many responsible countries have expanded export control laws, increased penalties for violators, and stepped up enforcement regimes. There is strong international support for both the missile technology control regime and for control of both CW and BW precursor materials and equipment. The level of attention to export controls among the civilized countries has never been greater.[4]

The problems outlined by Gates are just the tip of the proliferation iceberg. It has always been easy for the United States to criticize the proliferators who did not play by the rules established by the major Western nations. With the erosion of the barriers between communist and capitalist, there has been a great deal of rhetoric about a new world order but very little of substance actually done by any nation to make a serious difference.

In 1992, the US continued to dominate the international arms market and increased its share from 49% in 1991 to 57%. The value of US exports fell from $14 billion to $13.6 billion, a small reduction when compared with other major arms suppliers. The overall value of arms sales to Third World countries fell by 20% with Russia's exports falling from $5.9 billion to $1.3 billion.[5]

This rapid downturn in the international defence business has meant thousands of defence workers have been laid off and whole industries have had to restructure to adapt to a rapidly changing market. To try and fight off those changes, each manufacturer and each arms exporting nation is trying to maintain a slice of a diminished market by reducing prices and doing barter deals. Since 1990, Britain has sold Chieftain tanks for $5,000, and Leander frigates which cost $30m new in the 1960s have been sold for $120,000, around $7m below expectations.[6]

These prices, which are not unusual, bring exceptionally powerful modern weapons into the affordable range of the most impoverished guerrilla army or ambitious dictator. With such price cutting and competition, it is difficult to see how any attempt to combat the proliferation of conventional weapons will have much impact – particularly when the US, the most vociferous proponent of such controls, has done the least to enforce them.

The rapidly evolving conventional weapons market has been matched by changes in the development of weapons of mass destruction. Twelve developing countries – Burma, China, Egypt, Ethiopia, Iran, Iraq, Israel, Libya, North Korea, Syria, Taiwan and Vietnam – are now believed to have chemical weapons programmes. Nineteen other countries – Afghanistan, Angola, Argentina, Chad, Chile, Cuba, El Salvador, Guatemala, India, Indonesia, Laos, Mozambique, Nicaragua, Pakistan, Peru, the Philippines, South Africa, South Korea and Thailand – have been trying to obtain chemical weapons and may have succeeded. The developing countries have in general had to acquire their chemical weapons capability on their own, usually illegally but frequently with the complicity of Western companies and governments who turn a blind eye because they have found a useful source of export earnings.

As far as nuclear states are concerned, the problem is less serious, in that a number of countries have been persuaded to abandon their nuclear programmes and smaller countries are less likely to start the process as both chemical and biological weapons offer a cheaper alternative. The Nuclear Non-Proliferation Treaty was signed in 1968, came into force in 1970, and was designed to keep the number of states with nuclear weapons stable at five – the US, the Soviet Union, Britain, France, and China. The treaty calls for those who have nuclear weapons not to ship the equipment or transfer the technology necessary for other countries to develop such weapons. To encourage support for the agreement, those countries that have signed the NPT have been helped to develop peaceful nuclear programmes.

One hundred and forty-three countries have ratified the NPT, but some of the most important have not done so. It is only recently that France, China, and South Africa have indicated that they plan to abide by the terms of the NPT and South Africa has in fact abandoned its nuclear programme and destroyed the nuclear weapons in its stockpile. Israel, India, Pakistan, Brazil and Argentina refuse to do so. But just who has or has not signed seems in fact to have made little difference in the spread of nuclear weapons. An early signatory of the NPT, Iraq pursued an aggressive twenty-year programme to obtain nuclear weapons, with much Western help, notably from Germany. India developed a nuclear capability in the early 1970s and has actually tested a nuclear device. Pakistan, after more than fifteen years of trying to develop nuclear weapons, has either succeeded or is on the brink. According to uncon-firmed reports, Pakistan has agreed to share nuclear technology with Libya, North Korea, Taiwan and Brazil.

In the face of such proliferation, the Western nations have been unwilling to address the failure of the NPT. At the fourth five-year review conference of the NPT, in Geneva in August and September of 1990, some progress was made. Suppliers of nuclear materials, such as Germany and Japan, agreed to sell only to states observing internationally determined safeguards. New measures were agreed to improve the in-spection capacity of the International Atomic Energy Agency. Iraq, as a signatory to the NPT, had its nuclear plant regularly inspected by the IAEA. Not inspected, however, were the centrifuge plant for enriching uranium and the factories spread around the country where materials to be used in the manufacture of nuclear weapons were being designed and made.

If countries have been able to ignore the institutions meant to govern the spread of chemical and nuclear weapons, they have often lacked the equipment to deliver the weapons to their target. This has brought about a whole new aspect of the arms race over the past ten years — with developing nations attempting to acquire ballistic missiles. By the end of this decade at least fifteen developing countries will be able to build and deploy ballistic missiles, and eight of those either have or will soon have a nuclear capability. Scud missiles are currently in service in Syria, Egypt, Iran, Libya and Yemen, and Iraq still has a significant number of launchers and missiles.

In April 1987 the US, Canada, France, Britain, Italy, Japan and West Germany agreed to the Missile Technology Control Regime (MTCR), intended to curb exports of missiles able to deliver nuclear weapons and of equipment that might be used to develop such missiles. (Since 1987 Spain, Australia, Belgium, Luxembourg and the Netherlands have agreed to participate.) The participants agreed not to export rocket systems, unmanned air-vehicle systems, or their components. A number of Western intelligence agencies agreed to share information on any countries that appeared to be trying to acquire ballistic-missile technology. Even countries not participating in the MTCR have provided useful intelligence, but such actions are voluntary and rely on the good will of the volunteers.

With some of the structures in place to control the spread of equipment or arms relating to both conventional and unconventional weapons, the focus has shifted to the intelligence community for the information that allows governments to deal with any breaches of agreements. Every intelligence agency now cites proliferation as one of the major targets that have emerged from the end of the Cold War. Where lip service used to be paid to this issue, it is now one of the principal reasons advanced by the intelligence community for its continued existence.

In September 1991, President Bush signed a secret finding authorizing the CIA to develop plans, including covert action, to control proliferation. The CIA established the Non-Proliferation Center at its Langley headquarters with a staff of around 150 drawn not just from the Agency but from other branches of US intelligence.[7]

This is how Jim Woolsey described the current work of the Center:

The Center has a broad nonproliferation mission, covering the worldwide development or acquisition of production technology, designs, components, and complete military systems in the areas of mass destruction and advanced conventional weapons. The NPC's full time staff is drawn not only from the CIA, but also other national agencies, albeit not yet to the extent I envision. This organization is designed to foster what the current atmosphere of reduced budgets mandates – a more corporate, efficient, and focused management of community resources to attack this most important problem.

Although the NPC is still in its infancy, we are beginning to see some pay-offs from utilizing this type of approach. An important element of our nonproliferation effort is scrutinizing our collection philosophy. What worked against our old enemies isn't guaranteed to work against these new problems and adversaries. We are putting special emphasis in two broad areas. First there needs to be more of an effort on human intelligence. Well placed, first hand information can pull together seemingly unrelated technical tidbits to build a convincing, accurate picture. Second we are working to ensure that our collection is usable and accessible to the policy makers who need it to stop proliferation.[8]

Despite such fine rhetoric, it is unclear just how much the intelligence community is able to do to stop proliferation. One of the major areas of concern is the former Soviet Union which is now seen as a potential source for weapons reaching the black market. Although the CIA had spent billions monitoring nuclear developments in the former Soviet Union, this effort had been devoted to obtaining a macro picture: what are the signs to look for before a nuclear attack? What is the chain of command for nuclear release? What are the enabling codes and how are they used and, more importantly, how can they be accessed? With the collapse of the 'Evil Empire', these issues did not become entirely irrelevant, but they were overwhelmed by a series of micro-questions which had never been addressed before: how many tactical nuclear warheads are there? Where are they stored? What is the technical capability in the individual nation states to break the enabling codes and access the weapons? The intelligence community knew very little.

According to Larry Gershwin, the CIA's leading nuclear weapons analyst, 'the ultimate fate of strategic nuclear weapons is questionable' and we should 'look at the possibility that Kiev might try to seize the nuclear weapons on their territory.' The Agency's current assessment is that Ukrainian scientists could easily break the Russian command and control codes that protect the missiles to acquire their own nuclear capability. 'We judge they could do that in something between hours and weeks, depending on how hard it is to do and the expertise they could mount.

'There are nuclear weapons deployed in areas in Russia that are subject to serious civil unrest. So we should be careful not to kid ourselves that Russia itself is just a fine place for housing 30,000 nuclear warheads. There will be years of concern about how safely they do things, the possibility that weapons could somehow find their way out of Russia, not just out of Ukraine and Kazakhstan.'[9]

It is clear that, despite the careful listing of Soviet nuclear capability during the Cold War, there is no accurate count of just how many tactical and strategic nuclear weapons there are. The strategic count, because it can be directly related to missiles, is an easier equation but the tactical weapons inventory is at best a rough guesstimate.

'We have a highly uncertain estimate of the size of their tactical nuclear weapon inventory,' said Gershwin. He places the current uncertainty at 'plus or minus 5,000'.

Even in the high intensity atmosphere surrounding the Gulf War, there were some notable intelligence failures in the proliferation area. So thin was the intelligence community's knowledge about Iraq's status that in July 1991, five months after the end of the war, UN inspectors were still searching for the head of Iraq's nuclear programme. It wasn't until September that the inspectors discovered some documents that led them to Jaffar Dhia Jaffar, the deputy head of the Iraqi Atomic Energy Commission, who was the real mastermind behind the efforts to develop a nuclear weapon.[10]

If the accuracy is so patchy on a target as large as the Soviet Union or so focused as Iraq, it is difficult to imagine just how the intelligence community, fractured as it is, will be able to control the kind of seepage in the different proliferation regimes that has been going on for years. Only people on the ground can provide the accurate information that can reveal intentions. Too many of those involved in the covert world of black market arms or the proliferation of raw materials for the manufacture of weapons of mass destruction understand very well the capabilities of the technologies arrayed against them. The precautions they take can frequently defeat satellites or listening stations, and require the presence of an observer in the room who can make a detailed report.

There has been some success in setting up dummy companies in Europe and the former communist bloc to gather intelligence on the movement of arms and raw materials. Other operations have intercepted nuclear fuel as it was being moved from the former Soviet Union. But these are small beginnings. Few in the intelligence business believe that it will be possible to prevent new countries becoming nuclear states and others developing chemical and biological weapons. It will be possible to slow down the process, but once the inevitable happens, it will be political action that will decide the consequences.

When the targets are easy (Iraq or Libya, for example) action in the form of sanctions or even military strikes can be achieved through the United Nations. With more complex problems, such as China, there is little stomach for a fight. In 1993, President Clinton renewed China's Most Favored Nation status, despite their record breaching just about every international agreement on arms exports. In 1992, for example,

China delivered key missile parts to Pakistan, which already has the capability to make nuclear weapons. China also sold sophisticated missile technology to Iran and is helping Iran with its nuclear programme.

Part of the political reluctance to attack the proliferation problem is that it is always difficult to get international consensus. Even if political agreement can be reached, military solutions are often difficult. During the Gulf War, there was serious concern that strikes on Iraqi chemical stockpiles and manufacturing facilities could release chemicals into the atmosphere, killing thousands of Iraqis or even allied troops. In fact no such casualties occurred, but when the Pentagon drew up plans to attack North Korea's nuclear facility in late 1992, potential fall-out was a serious concern.

However, new research suggests that there may be a different approach to the proliferation problem that could provide both political and military answers to many of the difficult questions. The CIA and some of the high technology research institutes in America are experimenting with the idea of using new materials and systems, known by the generic 'non-lethal defenses'. This is an area of research still shrouded in secrecy but here is a flavour of what might be achieved:

'Non-lethal defenses involve a suite of technologies designed to disrupt, degrade, or destroy a wide set of targets, with minimum physical damage and no intentional casualties. Electromagnetic, acoustic, materials, information and other technologies are being explored for non-lethal applications. Those potential applications would respond to wide-ranging military contingencies. They might, for example, involve disruption of information, communications, command and control, and other systems by advanced computer viruses, electromagnetic disturbances, and deception; disruption of advancing forces by jellifying fuel and inhibiting combustion in the engines of tanks and armored personnel vehicles, crystallizing the tires of military vehicles, and stalling them with antitraction polymers and lubricants; and destroying air forces by embrittling or otherwise weakening airframes, spraying polymer adhesives on runways, and the like. Certain technologies being considered for these and related non-lethal applications are proven and available; others will require long term research and development.'[11]

During the Gulf War, the first of these non-lethal defences was tested against Iraq. During the 1980s, the Pentagon had been experimenting with a system designed to destroy an enemy's electrical power. During the 1980s, in an exercise codenamed Hey Rube, long lines of rope chaff were dropped at sea to block the radar on enemy ships. Unexpectedly strong winds blew the chaff to the coast around San Diego where it hit power lines and caused failures all over the city. By the time of the Gulf War, this accident had been turned into an effective weapon of war known as Kit 2 which used Tomahawk missiles loaded not with explosives but thousands of metal strips. In a series of strikes codenamed Poo Bah's Party, twenty-eight electrical sites were hit by the special missiles. On the first night of the air campaign virtually all of Baghdad's electrical power system fell victim to the Kit 2s. This military goal was achieved without committing any manned aircraft and without any loss of life among the Iraqi civilian population.[12]

For the moment, the intelligence community is limited in what it can achieve to prevent proliferation. Even if the information it gathers improves and is distributed in a timely and convincing way to policy makers, history suggests that more often than not nothing can or will be done. But there are systems that allow a non-lethal response against a country either selling weapons or developing them. To cautious politicians, this may present a real solution that stands some chance of working.

THE CHALLENGES:
DRUGS

CHAPTER TWENTY-TWO

THE SPREADING PLAGUE

The statistics tell their own story. Between 1980 and 1989 the number of adult arrests for illegal drug sale or manufacture in the US increased from about 103,000 to more than 404,000 a year. Arrests for illegal possession increased from about 368,000 to more than 843,000. Meanwhile, between fiscal years 1980 and 1990, federal spending for drug control rose (in constant dollars) from $1.5 billion to $6.7 billion. In 1990 alone, local governments spent some $18 billion on drug control and the federal government spent $10 billion with about 75% of that money being devoted to law enforcement at home.[1]

In Britain, customs officials believe that 130 tons of cocaine were smuggled into European countries in 1991 and the figure is rising dramatically. Cocaine seizures in Britain rose 90% in 1991 to a record of 1,061 kilos, and finds of synthetic drugs such as amphetamines, made in Poland and Czechoslovakia, rose fivefold in the same period. In Germany, first stop for smugglers from the East, cases of drug overdoses are up by about 80%.

Despite the billions of dollars and thousands of people that have been thrown at the drug problem, there has been no victory in the war, except perhaps for the majority of traffickers who have grown exceptionally rich. Numerous agencies, commissions and fact-finding missions have attacked the incoherent international policy to counter the business of illegal drugs. The appointment of drug czars and task forces have made a significant presentational impact but have had little measurable effect on the ground. Now the intelligence community has decided that drugs are a part of its new mission in the post-Cold War world. Typically that means diverting resources that were focused on the former Soviet Union. It also means making better use of both SIGINT and HUMINT to track the traffic and the money that is laundered as a profitable byproduct of the business.

Of course the intelligence community has been engaged in the counter-narcotics business for years, though without much success. The pattern of their involvement has been marked by some successes but also by a great deal of competition between different agencies.

A major feature of the anti-drug war waged in the Reagan-Bush years was a dual emphasis on stopping the growth and smuggling of drugs abroad while combating distribution and use at home. From the outset, this was a poorly directed and diffuse programme with every agency wishing to take a stake in what swiftly became a lucrative business, with large amounts of money available for anyone who expressed an interest in the problem. The mission was divided between the FBI, the DEA, the Defense Department, the State Department, the CIA and the DIA with some contribution from the NRO and the NSA. Each agency competed for the tax dollars and with each other, rather than uniting to fight the common enemy.

This approach was reminiscent of the counter-terrorist effort in the 1970s and early 1980s where the focus was on the capture of the bombers and assassins rather than on trying to eradicate the causes of terrorism or attacking the infrastructure that enabled the terrorists to carry out their attacks.

Today, every agency involved in the drug war claims that the old rivalries have been sublimated to the common fight, that the drug war is better coordinated and that there are signs that the war is being won. Just how much of a fantasy this is can be exposed by citing one detailed example: the traffic in illegal drugs in South East Asia.

At the beginning of 1992, DEA officials announced what was billed as a major new initiative to clamp down on the trafficking in heroin from South East Asia. Codenamed Operation White Lotus, two new under-cover units were established in New York in an attempt to bust high level smuggling operations.[2] At the same time, the traffic in illegal drugs from South East Asia was rising rapidly, according to a recent State Department study.

'The DEA is now finding purity levels of 40% in heroin sold on the streets of the US compared to 3–4% just a few years ago. Such high purity levels allow the drug to be sniffed or smoked rather than injected. This reduces the risk of transmitting diseases or infections, making the drug more attractive to users. The Office of National

Drug Control Policy (ONDCP), the president's primary policy office for drug issues and government wide program oversight, reported that the number of annual heroin users increased 33% between 1990–91.

According to DEA's heroin signature program, which analyses heroin samples to determine the region of origin, approximately 56% of heroin samples seized in the US in 1990 originated in Southeast Asia. The rest came from SW Asia (Pakistan and Afghanistan), Mexico and Columbia. This indicates a changing trend since 1985, when only 14% of samples analyzed originated in Southeast Asia. Since 1984 opium production in Southeast Asia's golden triangle of Thailand, Laos and Burma, has more than tripled from 730 metric tons to more than 2500 metric tons in 1992. Most of this increase is in Burma where production increased from 500 metric tons in 1985 to more than 2300 metric tons in 1991. Burma is by far the world's leading poppy cultivator, producing about 60% of all illicit opium.[3]

A damning indictment of US government intelligence efforts in the drugs war appeared in a secret report prepared by the State Department in March 1993 on the heroin traffic in South East Asia. The contents of this report, which have not been revealed before, produce a picture of political incompetence, poor leadership, intense rivalry between intelligence agencies and confusion about roles and missions. All the old problems that were at the heart of the failed anti-drug effort in the 1970s and early 1980s remain.[4]

The report identifies five regional issues affecting US counter-narcotics efforts:

1. The US regional heroin strategy cannot be effective due to a policy of disengagement from Burma, where about 60% of the world's opium poppy is grown, and the most southeast Asian heroin is produced. The US government policy towards Burma is, for the most part, dictated by the Burmese government's dismal human rights record. While the human rights problem is severe, we believe the growing heroin problem in the US warrants a review of US policy towards Burma. Accordingly, we recommend that the department under the bureau of East Asian and Pacific affairs leader ship re-evaluate its policy on Burma to give greater recognition to the significant increase in heroin production there. This review

should consider some type of counter-narcotics assistance which would be implemented on a trial basis.

2. Original strategy does not include Taiwan, an increasingly important heroin transit country, a safe haven for traffickers and a money laundering center. Accordingly, we recommend inclusion of Taiwan in the regional strategy and development of an action plan to address transit, safe haven, and money laundering issues.

3. Despite efforts to coordinate counter-narcotics intelligence such as establishing a counter-narcotics center under the direction of central intelligence, better narcotics and counter-narcotics intelligence direction of leadership are needed. Insufficient and unclear guidance from Washington has resulted in an unfocused and parochial approach to collecting and analyzing and disseminating narcotics intelligence overseas. The lack of guidance and focus has been filled, in varying degrees, by ambassadors and senior embassy staffs. However, a more institutionalized approach is needed to administer an effective intelligence program. To address these problems, we recommend that the Bureau for Intelligence and Research (INR) in conjunction with the Bureau for International Narcotics Matters (INM) initiate Washington level inter-agency discussions to designate a focal point and manager for counter-narcotics intelligence efforts overseas.

4. The need exists to obtain support for additional multilateral counter-narcotics activities, that have goals and objectives similar to INM's. Since 1990 Burma, Laos, Thailand and the PRC have signed regional border agreements with the United Nations international Drug Control Program (UNDCP) that include activities complementing INM's regional strategy. INM contributed $2.8 million to multilateral organizations in fiscal year 1991, about 2% of its budget. Despite INM requests, the department and the Office of Management and Budget (OMB) have not approved additional funding for multilateral activities. More participation in multilateral activities could increase US influence in the region, especially in those countries with no bilateral program or where US influence is nominal. We recommend that INM continue and strengthen efforts to obtain additional budgetary support for appropriate multilateral activities.

5. Shifting southeast Asian trafficking patterns point to the need to consider a re-allocation of US law enforcement personnel from Thailand, where there are 25 DEA special agents and 3 intelligence

300

analysts, to the increasingly important heroin producing and/or transit countries of Laos, Taiwan and the PRC, where DEA does not maintain a permanent presence. In addition a GAO report released in 12/92 stated that the DEA has not fully staffed its southeast Asian offices with effectively performing intelligence analysts. Currently, there are 3 analysts in Thailand and 1 in Hong Kong. The report noted that 3 of the analysts assigned to southeast Asia have not initiated, directed or reported on comprehensive intelligence projects.

If the structure is inadequate, so is the leadership provided to the agents in the field. In theory, the CIA's Counter-Narcotics Center is responsible for issuing guidance to the intelligence community about roles and missions, but it is clear from the report that not only has this not been happening, but even when ideas come from the CNC they are frequently ignored in the field.

1. Coordinating counter-narcotics intelligence programs overseas has typically been assumed by the chiefs of mission, with little guidance from Washington. Some ambassadors, assisted by senior staff, have done a good job of managing counter-narcotics affairs and fostering inter-agency cooperation and coordination of the posts. The effectiveness of counter-narcotics programs, however, should not be dependent on the management experience or interest level of senior embassy staff.

2. Recognizing the need for more Washington guidance, the Counter-Narcotics Center, under the DCI, has been designated as the lead organization for coordinating counter-narcotics intelligence collection and analysis. However, GAO reported in April 1992 that there is 'no evidence that the center has issued or intends to issue guidance to facilitate the coordination of drug-related intelligence'.

3. We found that the lack of clear guidance from Washington, regarding the specific roles, missions, and responsibilities of US counter-narcotics agencies overseas, prevented effective intelligence sharing and coordination, and resulted in an unfocused, parochial approach to management of intelligence information. Better guidance, with more clearly defined individual agencies that counter-narcotics roles, especially concerning narcotics related intelligence is required. In addition the need exists to provide adequate guidelines for sharing completed intelligence projects.

For example, intelligence agencies are not always willing to share final intelligence products because of the need to protect sources and classified methods, and law enforcement does not readily share information collected from informant debriefings. The problems we found point to the need for designating a lead US intelligence agency overseas to serve as the focal point and manager for overseas counter-narcotics intelligence collection, analysis, and subsequent dissemination. The intelligence community has the necessary equipment and resources to provide various forms of intelligence on traffic and methods, techniques, organizations and networks. The challenges are to focus this process and manage the diverging views and agendas of agencies involved.

4. Confusion exists over which agency has the lead in counter-drug intelligence issues overseas. For example, a 1990 ONDCP report on the organization of federal drug programs stated that 'DEA is the primary drug intelligence gathering agency, collecting information on trafficking organizations both domestically and overseas.' However, we also found the Defense Intelligence Agency director stated that the DIA was the lead agency for gathering intelligence from human sources in several key areas including 'the storage and movement of narcotics from production countries to the US'. The senior DIA official stated it would be helpful to clearly define agency counter-narcotics intelligence responsibilities.

Based on our review of the CIA national humint plan, it does not provide a clear description of agencies' intelligence responsibilities. Additionally, the 1990 ONDCP report states that the drug enforcement administration is designated as the lead agency for foreign drug law enforcement intelligence, but also designates the CIA as the lead agency for the national foreign intelligence as it relates to drugs.

Having exposed the failure to define the role and the lack of leadership in the intelligence community, the report criticizes the way intelligence is disseminated back to Washington.

We also found the need for more institutionalized and coordinated effort to distribute narcotics-related intelligence to Washington consumers. According to a 1991 department evaluation of foreign service narcotics reporting, titled 'Dept. of State Special Report – Special Evaluation of Foreign Service Reporting, Oct. 1990–Feb. 1991', most consumers surveyed, including INM, did not believe they were getting sufficient information of counter-narcotics intelligence, especially from CIA and DEA.

In addition, the CIA's National Humint Collection Plan stated that DEA is collecting a significant and expanding body of raw intelligence due to increasing drug seizures, arrest and interrogation of drug traffickers. However, according to the plan, DEA is not fully using the information and it is not being disseminated to the narcotics analytic community. The nature of DIA's intelligence collection function is overt and had traditionally been focused on military issues, although we believe that DIA could provide valuable information on the war on drugs, especially regarding the host military's involvement in trafficking and related corruption.

DAO's have not been effective in collecting and sharing narcotics intelligence information. At embassy Bangkok for example, little information existed in the DAO's files on host military involvement in trafficking. This information was in DEA's files. We found this unusual. Although DIA has been in Thailand for decades, it has little to show in documenting the extent of Thai military corruption, especially as it relates to narcotics. The CIA's National Humint Collection Plan also states that DAO reporting from Burma and Thailand had diminished in recent years and was too narrowly focused on issues already covered by other agencies.

In Thailand, for example, narcotics-related intelligence collection analysis . . . by US govt agencies in Thailand continued to be adversely affected by the divergent requirements and responsibilities of mission elements. For example, at DEA – Chiang Mai – official stated that the CIA provides little tactical (actionable) intelligence. He stated that in his recollection, intelligence received from CIA resulted in 2 cases in the past 5 years. The CIA official stated that the station provides DEA and other action elements with all the tactical intelligence it collects, but the CIA primarily focuses on strategic intelligence and its policy is to avoid direct involvement in the law enforcement process. Consequently this limits the volume of tactical intelligence it can furnish.

The fact that the intelligence community can argue for a larger mission in the drug war, and that Congress has accepted their arguments and agreed the resources, and the same old shambles continues is a national disgrace. The State Department report will not be published, and there is no evidence that any action has been taken on its recommendations.

But South East Asia is a traditional threat, an enemy which is largely known and understood. The collapse of communism in Eastern Europe has led to a change in drug patterns potentially profoundly disturbing for other European countries as well as for America. Three different threats have been identified: cocaine smuggled from Colombia to Eastern Europe and then shipped to the West; opium grown in the former Soviet Union, manufactured into heroin and then shipped overland or through the Baltic ports to other European countries; amphetamines manufactured in countries such as Poland and sold in the West.

The consumption of drugs in all the former communist countries is increasing rapidly with the development of well-organized criminal gangs who used to specialize in smuggling Western goods to the East and who have now switched to drugs. As one classified report prepared in 1992 for the US State Department puts it: 'The Polish drug distribution scene used to be characterized by the lack of black market production and dealing because the producers were usually the addicts themselves, producing primarily for their own purposes. There was also a lack of smuggling into the country of illicit drugs because of currency exchange problems. The situation now appears to be changing into one more resembling that of Western Europe. Both the production and distribution of kompot (a local heroin substitute) is reported to be becoming more organized with a network of laboratories being set up exclusively for the purpose of selling kompot. Some informants have linked this process to the increasing use of Poland as a transit country of illicit drugs from Asia to Europe.'[5]

The Colombian barons have switched their smuggling routes from Spain and Portugal, moving the drugs west from the former communist bloc by land, sea and air. The Colombians are not turning away from the American market because of effective law enforcement activities but because they believe the market is saturated. They are confident they can continue to penetrate the border screen and the police in the cities by changing smuggling routes and methods regularly. But there are new opportunities in Europe which they are anxious to exploit.

The first indications that the Colombians were moving into Europe came in 1986 when Diego Sanchez, a Colombian national, was given a permit by the then communist government to set up an import-export business in Prague. The Jaros company had three members of the Czech intelligence service on its board which is one of the reasons it first came to the attention of Western intelligence. At that stage, it looked as if it was just one of a number of businesses involving Czech intelligence agents, some of which had an intelligence function but most of which were set up as sidelines so that the agents could boost their salaries.

Then in late 1988, British customs stopped a Czech emigré living in London who was trying to smuggle fourteen kilos of cocaine into the country. At the request of the customs service, SIS agreed to look into the matter to see if the man was acting alone or as part of an organized smuggling operation. SIS tracked the company and its staff over a period of months. They learned that over the previous three years, the company had established a regular pattern of shipping around twelve containers a month from Colombia to Poland and then overland by truck to a new warehouse in the town of Hradec Kralove, north of Prague. Once there, the goods would be loaded into new containers, redocumented as freight which had originated in Prague, then shipped to Germany, Holland and the UK. By various means, SIS managed to learn who Sanchez had been contacting in England and elsewhere in Europe. They also learned that a new shipment of cocaine was due to arrive in September 1991. The Czech police were alerted and they told the border posts to keep on the lookout. Unfortunately, two over-enthusiastic border guards spotted the container and immediately arrested the occupants.

The Czech authorities found documents in the warehouse that pointed to a second container still in Poland. As the Czechs and the Poles do not talk to each other on such matters, it was the British who alerted the Polish authorities. Polish customs searched the 4,000-ton container ship *Polonia*, which is registered to Polish Ocean Lines, when it docked on September 20, 1991 at the port of Gdynia with a cargo of beans and tea from South America. Inside one of the containers were a number of wooden pallets and inside their cross members had been hidden 546 metal containers with 109.2 kilos of cocaine inside. It was a classic Colombian smuggling operation. The pallet beams had been specially built with hollowed-out cores into which the drugs could be slipped. The pallets were identical in size and weight to all the other pallets in the cargo and would never have been spotted by Polish customs without outside help.[6]

Later investigation revealed that the smuggling ring was run by two Czechs resident in Holland who used a number of friends all of whom had attended the same school in Czechoslovakia and who had spread across Western Europe to take up a life of crime. Two members of the gang lived in Britain and are now in jail. They had hooked up with the Colombian drug cartels as a way of expanding their operations.

That particular criminal ring began operations before the collapse of communism. Since then, drug smuggling has become a major industry.

According to the US State Department, 'South American cocaine traffickers are also beginning to gain a foothold on the continent through Poland. At Gdansk, Polish authorities seized some 100 kg of cocaine transported from Colombia on a Polish ocean liner. A similar 100 kg cocaine seizure made in Czechoslovakia is believed to have been part of an earlier shipment through Gdansk.'[7]

There is also evidence that the Colombians are using the drug money to buy up businesses in the former communist countries, causing concern that the drug barons may come to play an increasingly powerful role in the new countries, as they have done in Central and South America. As an illustration of the scale of this new problem, intelligence sources say that 8,500 Colombians visited Prague in 1992, 15,000 citizens from the Indian subcontinent living in Warsaw and 10,000 Iranians living in Sofia, many of whom are trying to exploit the opportunities presented by the collapse of communism.

The criminals have found a welcome among mobsters of the former Eastern bloc. Several countries have a history of drug abuse – always denied by the regimes – and an entrenched Mafia underworld which has survived operating against some of the most ruthless secret police forces in the world. Countries such as Bulgaria have long been used by smugglers, money launderers, terrorists and gun runners. Officials were frequently bribed or took a share of profits, and now the drug smugglers are able to plug straight into this network. Recently, police seized about 100 kilos of heroin in Bulgaria. In the first two months of 1992 alone they found 135 kilos, suggesting a tenfold increase.

Although all countries involved have said they want Western help to combat the problem, they remain ambivalent about what should be done. Romania, for example, is still shipping marijuana seeds into Czechoslovakia, where they are sold in garden centres. Between 1990 and 1991, Poland, a major conduit for illegal drugs, cut its police budget by 13%, and the use of police cars was limited to sixty kilometres a day while plans to modernize their vehicles and communications equipment were abandoned. In the whole country, only thirty policemen were on full-time assignment to anti-drug operations.[8]

Perhaps the most serious threat is posed by the emergence of the Asian republics of the former Soviet Union as big heroin producers. Most heroin in Europe comes from the Golden Crescent of Turkey, Iran,

Pakistan and Afghanistan. But that will soon change as the new sources are farmed.

The Soviet Union always possessed a large base of raw materials for the production of narcotics: millions of hectares of mostly wild hemp, including as many as 4 million hectares in Kazakhstan alone, and expansive poppy fields in Central Asia, Kazakhstan, Azerbaijan, the Ukraine and southern European Russia. According to the United Nations, more than 3 million acres of marijuana are being cultivated in the former Soviet Union with about 100,000 poppy fields in Russia alone.[9]

A small window into the potential of the problem is given in the State Department's 1993 International Narcotics Control Strategy Report:

'Azerbaijan. Narcotics trafficking and abuse in Azerbaijan increased markedly in the past year as its location and open borders make it an increasingly attractive transshipment point. Azerbaijan has promoted cross-border trade and travel with Russia and Central Asia and has opened its border with Iran to encourage contact with the 12 to 20 million Azerbaijanis resident in Northern Iran. Information on the drug trafficking groups in Azerbaijan is limited but there are NIS press reports that Azerbaijani criminal networks, headquartered in Baku and other key cities, control 80% of the drug distribution operations in Moscow. Before the USSR's collapse, all anti-drug efforts were orchestrated from Moscow. Azerbaijan has signed anti-drug agreements with Iran, Georgia, and Russia.'[10]

Although exact statistics are impossible to obtain, customs and intelligence officials warn that up to 150,000 hectares in the former Soviet Union are being planted with opium poppies, equivalent to 30% of the existing world supply. Many ex-spies have turned to smuggling, using their training and networks to move drugs across borders.

Potentially, this is as worrying a development as the problem of Soviet nuclear scientists emigrating or the proliferation of conventional or unconventional weapons, yet almost no resources are being devoted to the issue.

The fight against the drug traffic has been hampered by the refusal of several countries to acknowledge the problem. Often governments claim that drugs were only passing through, so stopping the traffic was a low priority – a problem that has become known as the 'European carousel'. In late 1992, the EC established the European Drug Intelligence Unit with a staff of several hundred which is designed to stem the flow of illegal drugs into Europe and devise new methods for combating the problem inside the EC's borders. But another layer of bureaucracy, particularly EC bureaucracy, is unlikely to do much to control the profound changes that are occurring in the trafficking patterns outside Western Europe.

The Clinton administration has responded to the past failures and the changing nature of the threat by attempting to deal with the problem at home rather than abroad. The President's 1993 budget allows $13.14 billion for the drug war, with new emphasis placed on the prevention of smuggling combined with improved law enforcement and treatment programmes within America's borders. The President reduced financing for some international operations in South America and Asia by 8%, cutting $44 million from the previous budget of $536 million. But he added $19 million for fighting smuggling. Nothing of significance was done to address the growing problems in the former communist bloc.

US Attorney General Janet Reno has made it clear that she thinks the emphasis placed by the Reagan-Bush administrations on crop substitution and cultivation control on supplier countries was wrong, pointing out that it appears to have had little effect on the overall pattern of trafficking.[11]

But if the drug producers are allowed to grow what, where and when they want, the supply of illegal drugs, already difficult to control, will grow to such an extent that borders will be impossible to patrol effectively. Each year, 430 million people, 120 million cars, 8 million containers, 720,000 jets and small planes and 290,000 ships and small boats cross the American border. Amidst all that traffic are the thirteen tractor-trailer trucks filled with cocaine that are needed to feed the American habit for a year.[12]

Law enforcement agencies claim to seize a maximum of 25% of the illegal drugs entering the south-eastern part of the US. They know that they need to seize at least 75% of all illegal drugs to have any serious effect on trafficking, a task which is clearly impossible.

Pouring money into drug control at home while ignoring production abroad plays into the hands of the traffickers, who have developed imaginative and flexible methods of smuggling. As law enforcement agencies are almost always reacting to these new initiatives, they will be constantly behind the interdiction curve, being reactive rather than proactive.

Much of the success against terrorism can be attributed to developing a better understanding of the methods terrorists use, and the devotion of resources for gathering intelligence about their training, financing and arming in and around their home base. Every law enforcement agency in the Western world understood, after a decade when the terrorists held the initiative, that the key to counter-terrorist success was to take the fight to the terrorists' home ground. The social issues that allowed the terrorists to flourish were addressed by some governments, the financial infrastructure of all terrorist organizations was attacked by a number of intelligence agencies and those countries which sponsored terrorists were gradually isolated. While terrorism has not been removed as a threat, it has been brought under control.

The same problems exist with the drug war. Aside from the apparently endless bickering among agencies, it has to be understood that if the war is being fought on the streets of New York or Los Angeles or London it has already been lost. The war needs to be taken to the poppy fields and the coca plantations so that the drugs and the traffickers can be stopped at source.

It is probably not realistic to rely on crop substitution as a solution. In those countries where marijuana or opium is grown, it is a significant cash crop and no amount of bribery by local governments with subsidies from abroad is going to have a significant effect. The emphasis needs to be on the production facilities and the smuggling routes.

At present, each nation tends to view the drugs problem from a narrow, national perspective. For the trafficker, the business is international. The producers tend to be flexible and responsive to market needs, while consumers are inflexible and largely unresponsive to changing demands.

America has to take the lead in the drug war. It is by far the largest consumer and has the biggest budget for combating the problem. But to date, America has tended to view the problem from the narrowest perspective and this introspective approach is going to get worse in the Clinton administration. During the Reagan and Bush years, considerable resources were allocated to the drug war in Central and South America, in particular to combat the Colombian barons. That mission was seen as important because what happened in those countries was considered as a potential threat to the security of the United States.

Today, those same Colombian drug barons, who have almost destroyed their own society, have shifted their attention to the former communist countries. They are using their profits to buy up privatized companies and industries in countries like Poland and Hungary, establishing new smuggling networks through Eastern Europe and the former Soviet Union and forging links with the gangs that control much of the trade between the new democracies and Western Europe. If the Colombian drug barons do for Poland or Hungary what they achieved in Colombia, that will affect the security of the United States in two ways. First, a destabilized and lawless country in central Europe will be a focus for proliferation and terrorism. Second, the amount of money the new drug business will generate will be enough to control some of the countries and destabilize others.

The international intelligence community is beginning to understand the dimension of this problem but has yet to devise any coherent policy to deal with it. It is up to the US to take the initiative and provide leadership that will cut through the old rivalries and produce a single, coherent policy setting out the roles and mission for the community to fight an enemy that is common to all.

CONCLUSION:
THE NEW SPY

CHAPTER TWENTY-THREE

WELCOME BACK, MR BOND

The Reagan years gave the operators a brief glimpse of what many felt were the halcyon days of the CIA. Under DCI Bill Casey there was a freewheeling attitude to Congress, the law and covert action, with active operations being encouraged all over the world from Afghanistan to Angola, from Lebanon to Libya. But these operations were out of step with the new generation that had grown up with the modern intelligence community. If promoted from within, DCIs had tended to come from the Operations Directorate, but, following the Turner cuts during the Carter presidency, it was the technocrats who had gained in authority and influence. The people end of the business was seen as the somewhat shabby and often unnecessary province of the cowboys. There were not the inherent skills left in the community to do the kind of job that Casey wanted, so enthusiastic amateurs like Colonel Oliver North stepped into the breach and set the cause of covert action back years.

But the new threats that have been identified require someone's eyes and ears on the ground gathering information. There remains room for improvement with the technology that listens to conversations or breaks codes or snaps photographs from space. Increasingly, the targets of such activity have some understanding of the systems deployed against them and take the necessary precautions to make them deaf and blind.

For example, in the lengthy hunt in Lebanon for the hostages held by the Hizbollah, the Iranian-backed terrorist organization, it proved extraordinarily difficult to gather any useful intelligence by technical means. The terrorists never spoke to each other on the telephone, rarely travelled outside their small area of operations, kept every activity in a tight cell structure based around a number of families and did nothing of interest outside the protection of buildings. In that instance, every intelligence agency wanted to infiltrate an agent and this proved impossible, demonstrating the limitations of both human and technical intelligence.

No country, including Israel, had sources inside Iraq able to give any intelligence at all about Saddam's intentions during the Gulf War. The allies were routinely hoovering up all his radio traffic and deciphering his codes, but this only provided some tactical intelligence and gave no picture at all of the state of morale in the Iraqi high command, or what effect the allied bombing campaign was having on Saddam himself. This was a serious failure, made all the more extraordinary given the intelligence relationship that had been established between the US and Iraq during that country's war with Iran in the 1980s.

There was a similar situation in Iran. Despite a long and close relationship with the Shah, despite the fact that the American armed forces had trained hundreds of Iranian officers and men, when the Ayatollah Khomeini came to power in 1979 there was no effective HUMINT apparatus in place. Even when the CIA did manage to establish a network in the Iranian military after the failure of the Desert One rescue mission, it was eventually rolled up in its entirety and all the agents executed.[1]

To combat the modern terrorist, drug trafficker or arms dealer, it is the spies on the ground who are going to make the difference and it is here that there is a new worldwide effort to recruit and train the agents of tomorrow. For some intelligence organizations, the recruiting and running of agents has always been a strength. The British have access to the vast amount of information produced by the American intelligence community for two reasons. First, as a legacy of the British colonial era, Britain has some important GCHQ listening posts in countries like Cyprus and Hong Kong which cover parts of the world not covered by the Americans. Second, SIS has always placed a high priority on recruiting and running agents and has a good record of success in critical countries like Russia and China.

The American intelligence community has been less successful for a number of reasons. First, the relatively recent switch away from human to technical intelligence has meant that the ambitious career intelligence officer will not focus on the relatively unproductive area of recruiting and running agents if he can progress faster in other areas. At the same time, the amount of money devoted to HUMINT has declined significantly in proportion to that available for ELINT and SIGINT, or even for analysis, so the smart operators have followed the money.

There is, too, a cultural difference between America and its European allies or even Russia. In the US, society is afflicted with 'short termism', a sense of urgency that means things need to be fixed today or, at the very latest, tomorrow. The culture tends to encourage not management by strategy but management by crisis, with each new drama requiring the full attention of everyone involved. But HUMINT is a very long term business which requires great patience, and often produces very little reward for many years. To recruit an agent may take five or ten years of gentle seduction, and nine times out of ten all the wooing will produce nothing but a rejection. So, the culture and the structure of an intelligence organization has to be designed to allow for that kind of success (or failure) rate. If promotions are won simply by recruiting HUMINT sources, then an agency will never build up a successful network. There has to be a ten-year investment in a comprehensive recruitment network targeted at key areas.

These shortcomings were recognized by both Congress and the DCI. In the 1992 intelligence budget, Congress authorized an additional $50m over and above the sums requested by the DCI for HUMINT.[2] The fact that Congress earmarked such an increase at a time when almost every other area of the intelligence budget was being cut is a measure of the importance the legislators attach to the improvement in the gathering of that type of intelligence.

According to a senior Western intelligence official, 'We are talking about a growing number of problems that demand more human intelligence as a means of finding out what is going on. When we focused huge percentages of our resources on the Soviet Union, our satellites could provide us with an extraordinary amount of information about Soviet forces, the capability of their military equipment, their R and D program, and a host of other issues. But now as we look at problems that increasingly are occupiers like proliferation, terrorism, counter-narcotics, certain kinds of technology theft and so on, these are problems where human intelligence has a unique contribution to make. On chemical and biological weapons, I think we're almost wholly dependent on human intelligence.'[3]

In June 1992, Gates established the National Human Intelligence Tasking Center, designed to coordinate the tasking and performance of all American intelligence agencies involved in HUMINT. For the first time, there will be some attempt to eliminate duplication and provide a set of priorities that will affect everyone from the 2,500 operators in the CIA's DO to the recruiters in the DIA or the navy.[4]

This change will for the first time bring some coherence to an area of American intelligence which has experienced mixed fortunes since the end of World War II. At that time, covert action in all its forms was recognized as a vital instrument of foreign policy. Many of those who had worked with the OSS during the war crossed over to help found the CIA, and they were used to pursue an aggressive covert action policy with little oversight or control.

Gradually, that freedom has been eroded, in part by a series of highly publicized mistakes such as the Bay of Pigs, and in part because technology has provided easier, safer and more reliable methods of achieving the same objectives. But with the end of the Cold War, the role of covert action as an instrument of foreign policy and a tool of the intelligence community has come full circle.

For some professionals, this change in philosophy and operating style brings with it the need to alter the concepts that lie behind covert action. Dick Kerr, a former deputy director of Central Intelligence, argues that the whole definition and approval process for covert action needs to be reviewed. He divides covert action into three different categories with different approval procedures for each.

1. Activity intended primarily to assist a foreign government to improve its capability to counter terrorists, be more effective in counter-narcotics programs or protect its leadership should be taken out of the covert action category. (This does not mean that there should be no oversight of these activities by Congress. Such activities should be reported to Congress and defended as part of the normal process.) Attempts to help a country improve its ability to assist in areas that the United States believes are important to its interest should not be seen as sinister.

2. Activity aimed at supporting well established policy such as countering illegal trafficking or terrorism should be placed into a new category that allows executive action without going through the current finding process. Many actions involving US intelligence and law enforcement should be done on the basis of executive authority. Review of these activities by Congress is necessary but committees are not good risk-taking organizations and are not capable of making operational decisions. If Congress does not have a role in approving operations and only reviews performance, it is imperative that the Executive have effective internal control procedures.

3. Activity aimed at changing governments, behavior of governments and other such politically sensitive actions require some type

of 'finding' process, but the current process must be improved. Over the past dozen or so years, the Congress has used the covert action approval process as the way to debate foreign policy decisions by the Executive. On some issues the Congress was opposed to the policy but did not have or choose to use another forum to debate the issue. Sometimes policy has not been well articulated or did not exist. There is no simple solution to this problem and all of the above will occur again. But some of the more destructive fights can be avoided by better communications and better procedures.[5]

It is very unlikely that any of the current restrictions on covert action will be relaxed in any country as a result of the new emphasis. There has never been a relaxation of oversight once a policy is in place, and one is not likely in the future. No politician will allow for any change in the oversight system, in case those new rules are abused and there is a search for someone to blame. The trend is to increase oversight both internally and externally in every intelligence agency. This will make attempts to increase HUMINT extremely difficult. By its very nature, covert action is the most dangerous end of the intelligence business, and brings with it the highest personal and political risk. There will undoubtedly be mistakes in the years to come but mistakes should not be used as an excuse to scale down what is going to become one of the most important of the intelligence community's efforts in the future.

It is difficult to imagine just how this new game will be played. The new James Bonds will find that before donning their Walther PPK and setting off for the late night assignation, they will first have to get the approval of a Congressional oversight committee. Then, every step they take will be monitored by in-house lawyers. Finally, the results will be pored over to ensure that no national or international laws have been broken while gathering the information.

CONCLUSION:
THE REFORMS

CHAPTER TWENTY-FOUR

ENOUGH IS NOT ENOUGH

Intelligence, as it has been understood since the end of World War II, is a dying business. The end of the Cold War brought with it the destruction of a world where each intelligence agency had clear targets, broadly understood the nature of the threat and had a clear role and the technical means to combat it. Today there is no such security. The conflict between the superpowers and their allies is over, with the West having achieved a clear victory over the communist bloc.

Whatever they may say now, the overwhelming amount of work carried out by the main intelligence agencies in the Nato and Warsaw Pact countries was in support of the Cold War. It was aimed either at gathering intelligence about the enemy or trying to prevent the enemy's spies from gathering information about us. This wilderness of mirrors brought with it both paranoia (reds under the bed) and security (know your enemy). In the former communist countries, such as East Germany, Poland and Hungary, the arrival of democracy gave the people the opportunity to shrug off the repressive chains of the police state and sweep away the old intelligence agencies. These have vanished forever and will never return in their old form.

Every country needs an intelligence service which can play a part in guaranteeing national security. In those countries where new agencies are emerging from the old, they are doing so with the help of their former enemies in the West. Being born with all the safeguards of a modern Western intelligence agency should ensure that they do not become political tools, but are used only for the collection and analysis of information vital to the security of the state (as opposed to individual governments of whatever political complexion).

The end of the Cold War also brought with it calls for cutbacks in both the military and intelligence communities. The elimination of the main threat, it was argued, meant that a 'peace dividend' could be extracted from both areas. As a result, every intelligence agency has suffered budget cuts in the past four years – but some less than others. In 1993, for example, SIS reduced its staff by only fifty out of around 1,900 while the Security Service maintained its existing staff. The American and Russian intelligence agencies were not so fortunate. While the 'dividend' may have proved elusive, the cuts were justified. Indeed, they might have been much deeper had the intelligence services been subject to more outside scrutiny. As it is, the intelligence community has devised its own role for the future and decided how the requirements should be met.

It was Bob Gates as DCI who charged the American intelligence community with bringing the new world into view, examining the potential threats, consulting with consumers in the American government and presenting a list of what the community can do for the money available. The FBI designed its National Security Threat List, the SVR produced theirs, SIS organized something similar and so did the British Security Service. It was hardly surprising that the lists were all remarkably similar. Indeed the language used by the heads of agencies in America, Russia and Britain could be spoken from the same script. Military threats to the state, proliferation, counter-espionage, drugs, terrorism and international financial crime are the new priorities. The new world order is so unstable that each of these areas requires additional resources if the challenges are to be met effectively.

The collapse of the retaining structure of the superpower confrontation and the authoritarian control of communist states over their people has freed ethnic tensions that go back hundreds of years and are only now finding expression. In the early part of this century, many of these ethnic tensions were limited in their influence because of a lack of technology or weaponry. Now modern weapons are readily available. It is certain that there will be a proliferation of small wars in the future; witness Bosnia and Somalia. When the problem appears relatively 'easy' (Somalia) the international community can agree a common policy. Where it is more complex (Bosnia) it is virtually impossible to have a common policy adopted and acted upon. Even in such apparently 'simple' situations as Somalia, it is clear that international consensus can swiftly fragment under the pressures of the realities of low intensity conflict on the ground. What governments are swiftly learning is that there are no simple problems. They are all difficult, and all will involve unique

317

challenges for the intelligence community to generate reliable information for the commanders and policy makers to act upon.

This is going to be a recurring problem and the role of the intelligence community will be to provide sufficient early warning and sound analysis that will allow policy makers to respond before the crisis gets out of hand. This will require the intelligence community to be more forthright in its analysis than it has been in the past. The more ambiguous the intelligence presentations, the more room the policy makers have to take the option of minimum pain, and the more likely a crisis is to get out of hand.

In terms of terrorism, arms control and drugs, the evolution of the problems now poses unique challenges to the intelligence community. Each is a concern and a threat to national security in the same way that a nuclear exchange was during the Cold War. By the end of this century, a number of Middle Eastern countries are likely to have ballistic missiles which can carry chemical or nuclear warheads and will have the range to reach most of Western Europe. As the intelligence failures in Iraq demonstrated, unless there is a determined effort to gather the information and act upon it, the proliferation has become a fact by which time it may well be too late to act.

Drugs and terrorism are more insidious, but their impact can be enormous. The cost of fighting the drug war in America is currently over $13 billion a year and rising, without a commensurate reduction either in the amount of drug use or the profits made by the drug barons. The new patterns of trafficking that are emerging out of the former communist countries mean that Western Europe, the new democracies in Eastern Europe and the US can all expect new sources of supply and an increased number of illegal drugs reaching a new range of buyers. To date, the combating of the drug problem only plays into the hands of the traffickers.

In theory, the reorganization of the international intelligence effort should improve this situation but there is little sign that the changes already in place or the much vaunted new effort by the intelligence agencies in this area are actually going to alter anything.

In terrorism, too, the reforms have not produced new thinking, merely additional resources. The nature of the problem is evolving rapidly, in part through the rise of Islamic fundamentalism, which has produced a new brand of terror. There is no grand conspiracy to replace the illusion of a grand conspiracy of the Marxist-Leninist terrorists of the 1970s. Then it was convenient to think of Moscow as the architect of the bombings and the killings, the single hand controlling the explosion of revolutionary fervour that erupted almost simultaneously all over the world.

Today the focus has shifted to Tehran as the source of everything from the civil war in Algeria to the bombing of the World Trade Center. Iran may be a convenient culprit, but the evidence does not support the concept of some kind of worldwide Iranian-sponsored terrorist conspiracy. Iran has supplied cash, arms and training to terrorist groups and continues to do so. But this seems to be on an ad hoc basis and Tehran appears to exercise little control over most of the cells now entrenched in many developed countries. That being the case, it is important that a new strategy be developed.

The intelligence community has the resources to gather the raw data on the different groups and movements, to direct law enforcement to catch the perpetrators and to direct the policy makers to the issues that can be tackled to undermine the terrorists' power base within the community.

The reforms that have taken place as a result of various studies have changed the way intelligence is conducted, not least because the focus has shifted from the previous emphasis on East-West confrontation. There has also been a general recognition that there needs to be a greater emphasis on human sources, an area which has fallen into disfavour in the United States in recent years. Only eyes on the ground can bring back intelligence on terrorists, on underground arms networks, on the release of nuclear materials onto the black market. The illegal operators, be they terrorists or arms dealers, now understand the capabilities of the technical means of gathering intelligence, and have developed methods of combating them. Terrorists no longer talk on the telephone (unless they are amateurs like those who blew up the World Trade Center); drug dealers don't communicate by fax, or arms merchants through a single front company via telex.

It is clear that no nation should have to rely entirely on open sources for its national security needs. Satellites, signals intelligence and human sources can all play their part in dealing with proliferation and terrorism as well as potential military threats. The major objection to an intelligence service working in a democratic society is that the right to operate in secrecy can bring with it abuses of power and freedoms which can be hidden from the public and the government. There have been enough examples of this in recent years   from Iran-Contra to the operation of psychiatric units for dissidents in the Soviet Union – for this to be a legitimate fear. But in recent years steps have been taken to

319

address these issues, particularly in the major Western agencies. Oversight is now more effective than it has ever been; the all-pervasive influence of lawyers within agencies has grown even stronger; above all, the culture of the cowboy has all but vanished. Of course there will still be abuses because the system is run by people and people make mistakes. But overall, that is a small price to pay if the general effect is to produce greater stability in the world.

Despite all these changes and the certainty that the intelligence community does have a role in the new world, there is ample reason to believe that the reforms implemented so far do not go far enough. The changes in the United States have been ones of emphasis rather than substance. There are new targets and each agency has faithfully switched targets to deliver a different product to cope with the identified threats. There is no argument about the nature of the threats, but the raw information gathered is only as good as the people and the methods used to process it. Despite the reforms, every single American intelligence organization has survived the end of the Cold War. By the end of this decade, the US intelligence budget will have fallen by around 25% in real terms, a massive reduction which the bureaucracy has absorbed not through radical change but by an overall cut, a salami-slicing of the capability of individual agencies.

During the Cold War, every intelligence professional was aware of the unnecessary duplication that existed between intelligence agencies – for example, the CIA, DIA, NRO, NSA, INR and all four armed services were gathering information on terrorists. Competitive analysis and the rivalries between agencies were divisive, costly and inefficient. Yet nothing has been done to change the basic methods used to process intelligence and to ensure a timely and accurate product. Bob Gates did what he could to improve the analytical process (NIEs tend to be shorter, sharper and more timely) and Woolsey has continued that process by trying to break down some of the barriers between the DO and DI in the CIA. But these are superficial changes.

The climate of secrecy that has saturated every aspect of the intelligence world for the past forty years should have changed forever. Espionage threats are posed by Russia and China, which still retain a major intelligence gathering capability and could pose a military threat to the US. But the other areas that now are seen as threats to national security – proliferation, drugs and terrorism – are not in the same class. No drug baron operates the kind of intelligence apparatus that is going to try and recruit sources inside the NSA and such an attempt would be unlikely to succeed. No terrorist organization in the world runs an aggressive spying effort and certainly none tries, on a regular basis, to gather secrets (as opposed to carrying out active reconnaissance missions) in foreign countries. So whole areas that used to be regarded as secret are hidden no longer and information once jealously guarded can be freed from the restrictions that kept it from the public gaze.

But there has been no real relaxation of the old secrecy rules. Instead, the intelligence agencies continue to guard the information they gather jealously and hold equally close the analytical process by which judgements for policy makers are made. This is not a freedom of information issue. There should be secrets that protect both sources and methods, but within that constraint a great deal more can be done. There is no logical reason why the intelligence community holds to itself the vast majority of the information it gathers. Most of it comes from open sources (the press, government publications, etc.) or from overt human sources (government officials, the press, lobbying groups). Only a very small percentage of information is gathered by technical means (satellites, listening posts) or by agents (spies).

In the United States there has been a long and healthy tradition of employing outside consultants such as the Rand Corporation to produce reports on specific projects for government departments. Those who work on such projects are generally given security clearances that allow them to see classified material. The reports have additional value because they are produced by outside contractors who operate free of the politics and bureaucracy of the department which hires them. That system, which seems to be unique to the US, is rarely used by the intelligence community. They rely on their own people to do their analysis, which is frequently duplicated not once but several times, creating not just a huge and inefficient bureaucracy but a product that is often the result of endless argument and compromise, and so full of caveats as to be of little value to the policy maker.

This structural inertia has hardly been addressed by the reforms, in part because the problem is so large that it would involve an extremely aggressive approach to a system that would oppose any change. Yet it is logical that in a time of budget constraints money should be saved on the tail (the analytical process) and devoted to the teeth (the information gatherers). It is generally acknowledged that the British process of analysis is both more effective and more efficient than the American version. It is a fraction of the size – twenty people compared with thousands.

Instead of the present massive duplication and waste, the analytical process could be gathered into one Central Analytical Agency which would be responsible only for producing the classified studies that involve highly sensitive sources and methods. Other studies would be put out to competitive tender in the same way that consultants work for other departments. The intelligence community would argue that such a system would compromise sources and methods, but this need not necessarily be so. An analysis on, say, the political situation in Bolivia, could be prepared using open sources which could be made available by the intelligence community and others. Then, when the paper is delivered to the Central Analytical Agency, additional information could be added if it materially affected the judgements that had been made. Already any intelligence professional would readily acknowledge that the majority of assessments produced by the intelligence community are affected only marginally by the addition of top secret information. In any event, when such assessments are made, the analytical process that currently exists ensures that different agencies are forced to justify their judgements, which leads to some seepage of sources and methods.

As part of this different approach, the community should make available most of the economic data assembled for political and economic analyses of countries and trading relationships. This is a national resource which, in for example Japan, is treated as such, and made available to industry and business leaders as a matter of course. Once again, the counter argument would be that such a process would compromise sources and methods, but a Central Analytical Agency could sift through the information to make sure that top secret data was not released. A second counter argument would suggest that the released database would benefit our trading competitors. However as countries like Japan, China, Russia and France routinely steal such information anyway, it makes sense to allow the American business community to have the same opportunities as the competition abroad.

It is difficult to gauge just how much money this concept would save as there is no detailed breakdown of the intelligence community's budget available for examination. But a more competitive (in the business sense) system would save money and allow resources to be devoted to the gathering of intelligence rather than the analysis. At the same time, a valuable national resource which has been hidden behind veils of secrecy can be opened to a wider audience.

As the KGB fell apart after the second Russian revolution, a new era began which divided the old monolith into a number of parts, all subject to a form of parliamentary oversight. The old First Chief Directorate, which was responsible for foreign spying, became the SVR, with altered responsibilities. According to Yevgeni Primakov, the head of the SVR, in future there will be no spying for political rather than national security purposes. Attempts to subvert foreign governments through covert support of terrorist organizations, opposition groups or even agents in place will not be tolerated. This new pragmatism is driven in part by changing political circumstances, but also because the SVR simply does not have the cash to pay for such extravagance.

Amidst these changes, Primakov has tried to open a door between the SVR and Western intelligence agencies. Bob Gates visited Moscow in 1992 and Primakov came to Washington to talk with Jim Woolsey in June 1993. These visits stressed the common ground that now exists between the former enemies. Primakov would like to see greater sharing of intelligence on such matters as drugs, organized crime and proliferation. In principle this makes good sense. To emphasize how different their world has become, the KGB archives have been opened to allow publication in the West of books and articles based on previously classified documents. The former KGB now has an efficient public relations office which answers questions from the media and has become adept at leaking stories which place the organization in a good light. These are changes for the good and set the KGB ahead of the game, when compared with the SIS or the DGSE. But it is not simply altruism or a Damascus-like conversion that has prompted this new openness. All the information released so far has contributed to an image of the former KGB as a successful organization that frequently managed to defeat the West. The message is that it was the KGB that provided the intelligence that kept the Soviet Union strong. By implication, the KGB should be retained to keep Russia strong in the new world.

The same cannot be said for the GRU, the intelligence arm of the Russian military. There has been little reduction in their activities. They continue to try and steal Western scientific and technological secrets to help the struggling Russian industrial base. They are also active in trying to recruit spies in the major industrial countries. A number of attempts have been made to persuade Boris Yeltsin to curb their activities but he has been unwilling or, more likely, unable to do anything. Clearly, the military is too powerful in the new Russia for Yeltsin to rein in the GRU. While that remains the case, there is little hope for a new relationship between Russia and the West. A serious new relationship would mean that one country does not spy on the other.

Also, the Russians have refused to provide any intelligence they may have about terrorist organizations or clandestine arms procurement networks in countries like Iraq and Libya. There is little reason for such reticence if the Russians are in earnest about combating the problems they share with other countries. If they actually began to share some intelligence, this might convince the sceptics that they were not simply paying lip service to cooperation as a way of winning plaudits at home.

There are other reasons for caution. Public protestations aside, many of the old KGB have simply donned new uniforms and overnight become staunch democrats. It is difficult to believe that all these thousands of men and women are genuine converts, and there is ample evidence that at many levels in the current Russian political system the levers are still being pulled by ex-KGB operators. At the wish of their political masters, most Western spy agencies, such as those in America, Germany and France, have been forced publicly to embrace the new KGB, exchanging delegations and declaring their chief spies in each other's capitals. The single holdout has been Britain where the country's obsession with secrecy has given the politicians greater freedom to act on evidence rather than impulse.

The revelations about the current state of Russia's biological weapons programme suggests that Britain is right to be careful. Instead of obeying the orders of the democratically elected Russian President and shutting the programme, senior Russian military officers have continued to research and develop new genetically engineered weapons that can only be used in offensive operations. Yet Russia has officially disavowed any offensive military operations. Clearly, both the military and the intelligence services wish to retain independent options separate from political leaders. That suggests they retain military ambitions which have yet to be revealed.

Aside from Russia, the end of the Cold War has had the most dramatic effect in Britain. In the space of four years, the secrecy that surrounded the three principal intelligence organizations, SIS, the Security Service and GCHQ, has ended. Two new acts of parliament have brought the agencies out into the light, complete with a visible parliamentary oversight system. For a country like Britain, where the overwhelming majority are tolerant of a secret society in a way that would be illegal and unacceptable in America, these changes have been little short of revolutionary. They have been driven not by the political process, but by the intelligence agencies themselves, who believed that by being shut away they were losing touch with political reality. They recognized that if public confidence in what they do was to be maintained, they must be visible to defend themselves. There was a pragmatic side to this argument in that there was serious concern that if parliament had no understanding of their work and, presumably, no appreciation of how valuable that work is for the national interest, then the appetite for continuing to vote more than £800m a year for their budget would disappear. Rather than be emasculated in the shadows, the intelligence services preferred to come out and fight their corner in the public gaze.

Some adjustments have been made to make all the British intelligence organizations more effective. The night of the long knives in SIS in December 1992 brought to power a new generation of younger leaders not so imbued with the rigidities of the Cold War era. SIS hopes that this younger blood will produce a more dynamic organization, better able to deal with the challenges of the future. SIS has adopted the same set of new priorities as the CIA or the SVR, but in Britain the Security Service has managed to gain more power and influence while SIS has been forced to reduce the scale of its operations.

Twenty years ago, the divisions were simple: SIS would gather intelligence abroad, including Ireland, while the Security Service would counter espionage and subversion at home. Today, MI5 is responsible for countering terrorism in Ireland and the rest of the world which involves actively gathering intelligence. The Security Service is also trying to gain a share of the proliferation action from SIS. Underlying these arguments is Box's (MI5's) conviction that where there is overlap, the Security Service should have precedence.

In the past, SIS had an enormous operation spread across the globe with a presence in nearly all the embassies the Foreign Office kept open. This was justified in part by the argument that SIS could recruit Eastern bloc spies in these far away places. In part, too, the British were anxious to maintain knowledge and influence in the remnants of the British Empire. Today, neither of these arguments holds true. There is still some need to recruit Russian spies but there is arguably more opportunity to do that in Russia itself or in the industrialized nations than in the developing world.

Interest in the former British Empire is declining as the countries that were once close to Britain go their ways and British dependence on traditional trading links is replaced by new relationships, particularly with the EC.

Inevitably, the influence of SIS will reduce, with officers being withdrawn from countries of marginal interest and redeployed to gather intelligence on the new threats. Already, SIS has shut stations in South

Asia, Central and North Africa, Latin America and the Far East, and concentrates almost entirely on Europe, Southern Africa, the Middle East, China and Hong Kong.

This declining role means the divisions that currently exist between SIS and the Security Service will become ever more meaningless. With MI5 controlling the counter-terrorist effort, and the world of money laundering and drug trafficking becoming increasingly intermingled with terrorism, it makes sense for a single agency to control those three areas. Counter-espionage has always been an MI5 strength and, despite recent mistakes, continues to be so.

It seems clear that there are strong arguments to merge the two organizations. At a stroke, this would bring immediate economies of scale, eliminate the rivalry that still bedevils both organizations and produce a more efficient intelligence apparatus tuned to the needs of tomorrow rather than those of yesterday. The question then is, which organization survives. There are strengths in both operations. SIS has an outstanding record in recruiting and handling sources in the Eastern bloc; MI5 has a good record in countering Soviet espionage in Britain but has been much less effective against the modern IRA; neither body has done well against drugs or proliferation, but that is in part the fault of the policy makers.

The solution is to abolish both organizations and to create the British Intelligence Organization, a single body responsible to the cabinet office. This suggestion will be strongly resisted. The SIS worries that a merger with MI5 would bring with it all the counterculture of that organization. They argue, with some justification, that the Security Service tends to be plodding and unimaginative while SIS is allowed considerable latitude in its operations abroad. A merger, they say, would stifle the initiative that is the lifeblood of a successful spying agency. Both agencies also argue that they employ very different people for different tasks.

For their part, the Security Service would prefer to take over SIS by stealth rather than lose its identity. But a new organization would be a sensible use of the smaller amount of money available from the taxpayer, would produce a coherent organization to combat the threats into the next century and would eliminate an inefficient and often incompetent bureaucracy which remains embedded in a culture of secrecy that should have been buried with the Cold War.

Such blueprints, whether they be for Britain, America, Russia or anywhere else are a tough call, if action is really expected on any of them. Whatever legal barriers or oversight systems are in place, the only people who understand intelligence are the people who work inside the intelligence services. To the outsider it remains a mysterious world, where a few extraordinary individuals armed with strange gadgets and often great courage can achieve miracles. This is a myth that has been perpetuated over the years by the community who, by careful leaking of the odd exciting tidbit to the politicians, have embraced the policy makers into their world. It is hardly surprising that it is the intelligence community that has inspected itself, pronounced itself in need of minor surgery and then given itself a clean bill of health. No outside body or group of individuals really understands what goes on in the closed world and so the intelligence community has been able to allow the end of the Cold War (an end none of them predicted) to slide by as if it was a small blip in their otherwise ordered lives.

The end of the Cold War should have produced a massive upheaval in the intelligence community, not just a shifting of priorities or a scaling back of budgets. The rationale behind whole areas vanished along with the Soviet Union and with their disappearance, such agencies or directorates should have been swept away as well. It is not too late, particularly under the impetus of a Democratic administration in Washington. True reform will produce a leaner, more efficient and responsive intelligence community which will enable the policy makers to take the right decisions based on the right information. The status quo leaves too many of the old practices intact with little evidence that the intelligence community is ready to face the fast changing, frightening world that lies ahead.

NOTES

DEFINING INTELLIGENCE

1 *The Random House Dictionary of the English Language*, Random House, New York, 1987.
2 William A. Arkin, Joshua M. Handler, Julia A. Morrissey and Jacquelyn M. Walsh, *Encyclopedia of the US Military*, Harper & Row, New York, 1990, p.335.
3 Bruce W. Watson, Susan M. Watson and Gerald W. Hopple, eds, *United States Intelligence, an Encyclopedia*, Garland, New York, 1990, p.296.
4 Abram Shulsky and Jennifer Sims, *What is Intelligence*? Consortium for the Study of Intelligence, April 29, 1992, p.2.
5 Institute for the Study of Diplomacy, School of Foreign Service, Georgetown University, *The Foreign Service in 2001*, August 1992, p.5.

CHAPTER 1

1 The material gathered for this section comes from two trips to Moscow in June and September 1992. The second visit was as a guest of the former KGB when I was the first journalist – Russian or Western – to interview Yevgeni Primakov, the current head of the SVR, the former First Chief Directorate of the KGB. During the week, I was given unprecedented access to current and former KGB officials and saw at first hand their facilities and their working methods.
2 Western intelligence source, October, 1993.
3 Western intelligence source, February, 1993.
4 Interview, Washington, December, 1992.
5 Western intelligence source, February, 1993.
6 Information supplied by Western intelligence officials, October, 1992.
7 *Evening Standard*, March 20, 1991, *The Times*, March 21, 1991, *Sunday Telegraph*, March 24, 1991 and intelligence sources.
8 Interview, January 19, 1992.
9 Information for this section comes from an interview with Bob Gates on April 28, 1993 and interviews with Russian intelligence officials in January and February, 1993.
10 William Colby and Peter Forbath, *Honorable Men: My Life in the CIA*, Simon & Schuster, New York, 1978, pp.416–418. See also John Ranelagh, *The Agency: the Rise and Decline of the CIA*, Simon & Schuster, New York, 1986, pp.602–3.
11 British Broadcasting Corporation, *Summary of World Broadcasts/The Monitoring Report*, October 19, 1992, reporting a broadcast by ITAR-TASS.

CHAPTER 2

1 *US News and World Report*, May 3, 1993, p.37.
2 Press conference at Department of Justice, January 9, 1992.

CHAPTER 3

1 Detailed accounts of Operation Ryan appear in Christopher Andrew and Oleg
   Gordievsky, *KGB: the Inside Story*, Hodder & Stoughton, London, 1990, pp.488–507;
   Andrew and Gordievsky, *Instructions from the Centre*, Hodder & Stoughton, London,
   1991, pp.67–90; Gordon Brook-Shepherd, *The Storm Birds*, Weidenfeld & Nicolson,
   London, 1988, pp.267–269.
2 *New York Times*, February 2, 1993.
3 *Soviet Forces for Intercontinental Conflict through the Mid-1980s*, National Intelligence
   Estimate 11-3/8/76 (Team A); *Soviet Strategic Objectives: An alternative view*, Report
   of Team B; See also, Ranelagh, *The Agency, op. cit.*, pp.622–624; *Washington Post*,
   October 12, 1992.
4 *Newsweek*, May 14, 1990.
5 Interview July 10, 1991.
6 *New York Times*, February 1, 1993.
7 *New York Times*, February 7, 1992.
8 *ibid.*
9 Interview, June 1, 1993.
10 *Financial Times*, January 19, 1983.
11 James Q. Wilson, *Thinking About Reorganization*, a paper for the Working Group on
   Intelligence Reform, a project organized by the Consortium for the Study of
   Intelligence, June 10, 1992, pp.8–9.
12 Interview, April 24, 1993.

CHAPTER 4

1 Interview, January 17, 1992.
2 *Washington Post*, December 2, 1991.
3 Interview, September 1, 1992.
4 Ben Brown and David Shukman, *All Necessary Means*, BBC Books, London, 1951,
   p.112.
5 *Intelligence Successes and Failures in Operations Desert Shield/Desert Storm*, US House of
   Representatives Committee on Armed Services 103rd Congress, August 1993, p.4.
6 *Army Times*, December 9, 1991.
7 Interview, January 14, 1992.
8 A detailed account of just what the CIA knew and when appears in Jonathan Beaty
   and S.C. Gwynne, *The Outlaw Bank: A Wild Ride in the Secret Heart of BCCI*,
   Random House, New York, 1993, pp.297–319.
9 Interview, January 14, 1992.
10 Associated Press, March 13, 1992.

11 Statement of the Director of Central Intelligence before the House Armed Services Committee Defense Policy Panel, December 10, 1991.

12 Hearing on Intelligence Reorganization, Senate Select Committee on Intelligence, March 21, 1991.

13 Testimony before Senate Select Committee on Intelligence, March 12, 1992.

14 *New York Times*, February 6, 1992; *Washington Times*, February 6, 1992; *Washington Post*, February 6 and March 24, 1992.

15 Joint Hearing of the House and Senate Select Committees on Intelligence, April 1, 1992.

16 Interview, January 17, 1992.

17 *Defense News*, June 15, 1992; *Aviation Week and Space Technology*, June 8, 1992; *Los Angeles Times*, October 16, 1992.

18 Hearing of the Senate Select Committee on Intelligence, February 2, 1993.

19 Statement of James Woolsey, Director of Central Intelligence, before the Permanent Select Committee on Intelligence, US House of Representatives, March 9, 1993.

20 Interview with senior intelligence official, June 3, 1993.

21 *Wall Street Journal*, February 26, 1993.

CHAPTER 5

1 Interview, June 8, 1992.

2 For a detailed study of the KGB see John Barron's, *KGB Today: The Hidden Hand*, Reader's Digest Press, New York, 1983.

3 Different structures are given in different sources. I have drawn on Barron (see above) pp.443–453; Jeffrey T. Richelson, *Sword and Shield: Soviet Intelligence and Security Apparatus*, Ballinger, Cambridge, Mass., 1986, p.33; and Andrew and Gordievsky, *KGB: The Inside Story, op. cit.*, pp.550–551. I have relied on Andrew and Gordievsky more than the others as it is the most recent and draws from primary source material.

4 *New York Times*, November 24, 1991.

5 Interview, February 1992.

6 Interview, September 23, 1992.

7 *US News and World Report*, February 8, 1993, pp.42–44.

8 *Washington Times*, April 13, 1992; *Izvestia*, April 13 and 14, 1992; *New York Times*, May 12, 1992; Agence France Presse, April 23, 1992.

9 *Washington Times*, January 1, 1993 and intelligence sources.

10 Interview, November 19, 1992.

11 Interview, July 14, 1993.

CHAPTER 6

1 Mark Almond, *Still Serving Silently*, Institute for European Defence and Strategic Studies, London, December 1992, pp.18–19.

2 Interview, July 14, 1993.

3 Interviewed in *Nezavisimaya Gazeta* quoted in *Washington Times*, August 22, 1993.

4 *The Sunday Times*, July 4, 1993.

5 *The Sunday Times*, August 14, 1993; *Los Angeles Times*, August 7, 1993; *Washington Times*, August 11, 1993; *BBC Summary of World Broadcasts*, August 10, 1993 and intelligence sources.

CHAPTER 7

1 Interview, April 12, 1989.

2 Brook-Shepherd, *The Storm Birds*, *op.cit.*

3 Security Service Bill, HMSO number 300793, November 23, 1988.

4 Interview, June 17, 1992.

5 *The Security Service*, Her Majesty's Stationery Office, London, 1993, p.12.

6 Reuters, December 17, 1991.

7 *The Times, Daily Telegraph, Guardian*, July 17, 1993.

8 Speech by Bob Gates to the Standing Committee on Law and National Security of the American Bar Association on February 18, 1993.

9 *ibid.*

10 *Independent*, January 19, 1993.

11 *The Sunday Times*, January 19, 1992.

12 *The Times*, July 28, 1993; *Guardian*, July 27, 1993; *Daily Telegraph*, July 28, 1993.

13 Alan Clark, *Diaries*, Weidenfeld & Nicolson, London 1993, pp.17–18.

14 *Washington Post*, May 13, 1993.

CHAPTER 8

1 *Los Angeles Times*, July 2, 1989; *New York Times*, July 24, 1988; *Chicago Tribune*, July 22, 1988; *Time*, July 10, 1989, p.40 and July 17, 1989, p.105; *Washington Post*, July 2, 1989; and *The Sunday Times*, July 2, 1989; and intelligence sources.

2 The most detailed account of this view appears in Ronald Kessler, *The Spy in the Russian Club*, Scribners, New York, 1990.

3 Ladislav Bittman, *The KGB and Soviet Disinformation*, Pergamon-Brassey's, London, 1985, p.58.

4 Interview, September 23, 1992.

5 *Los Angeles Times*, January 15, 1990.

6 *New York Times*, January 23, 1990; *Washington Times*, January 15, 1990.

7 Jerrold Schecter and Peter Driabin, *The Spy who Saved the World*, Scribners, New York, 1992.

8 Andrew and Gordievsky, *KGB: The Inside Story*, *op. cit.*

9 Tom Bower, *The Red Web*, Aurum, London, 1989.

10 John Costello and Oleg Tsarev, *Deadly Illusions*, Crown Books, New York, 1993.

CHAPTER 9

1 Interview with Clinton administration official, April 7, 1993; *Sunday Times* April 11, 1993.

2 Although *The Sunday Times* first reported the story, the Knight-Ridder news service obtained the actual document anonymously through the mail. This list is taken from their report.
3 Interview April 29, 1993.
4 *Washington Post*, April 27, 1993.
5 *Wall Street Journal*, April 26, 1993.
6 *Defense Week*, April 26, 1993, p.3.
7 *International Herald Tribune*, September 14, 1991. Marion appeared on the NBC program, *Expose*, on September 13, 1991.
8 Interview, April 14, 1993.
9 *Daily Telegraph* January 24, 1992; *L'Express*, May 18, 1990.
10 Reuters, October 22, 1991.
11 Interview, April 3, 1993.

CHAPTER 10

1 Brook-Shepherd, *The Storm Birds, op. cit.*, pp.253–265. This book, which was prepared with the help of a number of intelligence agencies, gives excellent and accurate accounts of a number of people who spied for the West during the Cold War.
2 *ibid.*, pp.260–261.
3 *The Sunday Times*, May 28, 1989.
4 Interview, June 6, 1992.
5 Interview, May 25, 1989.
6 *Chicago Tribune*, May 10, 1992.
7 Interview with Bob Gates, April 28, 1993.
8 *Washington Post*, June 27, 1993.
9 *Washington Times*, March 23, 1993.
10 *Washington Times*, February 9, 1992.
11 *New York Times*, April 30, 1993.
12 Interview, April 27, 1993.
13 Interview, January 14, 1992.
14 Hearing of the Select Committee on Intelligence, February 2, 1993.

CHAPTER 11

1 The most detailed account of the Munich massacre appears in Rolf Tophoven, *GSG9: German Response to Terrorism*, Bernard and Graefe Verlag, Bonn, 1984; for an Israeli perspective see Yossi Melman and Dan Daviv, *The Imperfect Spies*, Sidgwick & Jackson, London, 1989, pp.202–4; see also James Adams, *Secret Armies*, Century Hutchinson, London, 1987, pp.77–78.
2 Henry Kissinger, *Years of Upheaval*, Weidenfeld & Nicolson, London, 1982, p.629.
3 *Wall Street Journal*, February 10, 1983; John and Janet Wallach, *Arafat*, Lyle Stuart, New York, 1990, pp. 344–350; Andrew Gowers and Tony Walker, *Behind the Myth: Yasser Arafat and the Palestinian Revolution*, W.H. Allen, London, 1990, pp.165–168.

4 Patrick Seale, *Abu Nidal: A Gun for Hire*, Random House, New York, 1992, p.168.

5 Wallach, *Arafat, op. cit.*, p.346.

6 George Shultz, *Turmoil and Triumph*, Scribners, New York, 1993, p.50.

7 David Martin and John Walcott, *Best Laid Plans*, Harper & Row, 1988, p.105.

8 Edward F. Mickolus, *Transnational Terrorism*, Aldwych Press, London, 1980, p xxi

9 Stansfield Turner, *Secrecy and Democracy*, Houghton Mifflin, New York, 1985, pp.91–92.

10 Richard Marcinko, *Rogue Warrior*, Pocket Books, New York, 1992, pp.194–195. See also, Paul Ryan, *The Iranian Rescue Mission*, Naval Institute Press, Annapolis, 1985, pp.31–33.

11 Colonel Charles Beckwith (retd.), *Delta Force*, Harcourt Brace Jovanovich, New York, 1983, pp.199–200.

12 Martin and Walcott, *Best Laid Plans, op. cit.*, pp.6–7.

13 A detailed account of the Desert One affair appears in James Adams, *Secret Armies*, Atlantic Monthly Press, New York, 1987, pp.110–134.

14 Quoted in Jeffrey Richelson, *The US Intelligence Community*, Ballinger, Cambridge, Mass., 1989, p.64.

15 Alexander M. Haig Jr., *Inner Circles*, Warner Books, New York, 1992, p.542.

16 *ibid*, p.540.

17 Martin and Walcott, *op. cit.*, p.53.; Ranelagh, *The Agency, op. cit.*, pp.698–699.

CHAPTER 12

1 Interview with British intelligence officials, December 14, 1990.

2 *Independent on Sunday*, September 8, 1991.

3 A detailed breakdown of state sponsorship of terrorist organizations can be found in *Terrorist Group Profiles* published by the US Defense Department, 1988.

4 Bruce W. Watson, ed., *Military Lessons of the Gulf War*, Greenhill Books, London, 1991, p.177.

5 *New York Times*, February 1, 1991.

6 *The Times*, January 8, 1991.

7 *Evening Standard*, January 30, 1991.

8 *Los Angeles Times*, February 18, 1991.

9 *Dispatch*, US Department of State, Bureau of Public Affairs, Vol.2, No. 26.

10 Interview, December 16, 1991.

11 Information on the Nidal funding came from meetings with Western intelligence officials in October, 1991.

12 *The Times*, June 7, 1991.

CHAPTER 13

1 The information on the World Trade Center blast comes from interviews with CIA, FBI and New York City officials as well as the following published documents: *New York*, March 15, 1993, pp.30–33; *Newsweek*, March 8, 1993, pp.18–29; *Time*, March 8, 1993, pp.24–35; *Washington Post*, April 5, 1993; and daily news reports in the

New York Times, *Washington Post*, *Washington Times* and *Newsday* at the time of the blast.

2 Testimony before the US Senate Committee on Environment and Public Works, Subcommittee on Clean Air and Nuclear Regulation, *March* 19, 1993.

3 Indictment issued by the US District Court, Eastern District of Missouri, Eastern Division, April 1, 1993; *Washington Post*, April 2, 1993.

4 *New York Times*, May 26, 1993.

5 *New York Times*, April 25, 1993.

6 Details on Rahman's experiences with the Immigration and Naturalization Service come from *US News and World Report*, March 22, 1993, p.36 and *Time*, May 24, 1993, p.44.

7 *US News and World Report*, March 22, 1993, p.31.

8 Yossef Bodansky, *Target America: Terrorism in the US Today*, S.P.I. Books, New York, 1993.

9 A number of articles appeared immediately after the attack: *Newsday*, June 26, 1993; *New York Times*, June 26, 1993; *The Sunday Times*, June 27, 1993; *Time*, July 5, 1993; in addition the indictment issued by the southern district of New York on June 23, 1993 gives a useful chronology.

10 *Washington Post*, August 26, 1993.

11 Patrick Brogan, *World Conflicts*, Bloomsbury, London, 1989, pp.117–129. A more detailed account of the covert supply network can be found in James Adams, *Engines of War*, Atlantic Monthly Press, New York, 1990, pp.65–80.

12 *New York Times*, April 11, 1993.

13 *The Sunday Times*, May 9, 1993.

14 *Washington Post*, December 16, 1989; *Washington Times*, December 4, 1989.

15 The first details of Iran's new support for terrorists came from a briefing supplied by Western intelligence to the author on October 30, 1991.

16 *Newsday*, April 11, 1993.

17 *ibid*.

18 *Washington Post*, May 19, 1993.

19 *New York Times*, April 18, 1993.

20 Interview, August 28, 1992.

21 *New York Times*, May 12, 1993.

22 AP report, May 17, 1993.

23 *The Sunday Times*, May 9, 1993.

CHAPTER 14

1 Kevin Kelley, *The Longest War*, Zed Books, London 1982, p.189.

2 Quoted in James Adams, Robin Morgan and Anthony Bambridge, *Ambush: The War Between the SAS and the IRA*, Pan, London, 1988, p.54.

3 A detailed account of this initial deployment can be found in Michael Paul Kennedy, *Soldier 'I' SAS*, Bloomsbury, London, 1989, pp.114–131.

4 Information about the intelligence-gathering structure in Northern Ireland comes from interviews with a number of those involved in operations in the past twenty years. For obvious reasons they cannot be named. Some details on structure and

activities appear in Mark Urban, *Big Boys' Rules*, Faber & Faber, London, 1992, pp.94–98; Tony Geraghty, *Who Dares Wins*, Little, Brown, New York, 1992, pp.222–231.

5 Details on the German operations come from the *New Statesman*, October 20, 1989 and *Republican News*, which published the documents in full on October 19, 1989.

6 Interview with British intelligence official, January 18, 1992.

7 Interview with senior British intelligence official, January 18, 1992.

8 *Independent*, January 9, 1992; *Guardian*, January 23, 1992 and February 2, 1992; *The Times*, January 30, 1992; and interviews with army intelligence sources.

9 Interview, December 7, 1993.

CHAPTER 15

1 *The Sunday Times*, March 26, 1989.

2 *Daily Telegraph*, October 4, 1990 and January 25, 1992; *Guardian*, April 6, 1993; *Independent*, October 4, 1990; *The Times*, October 4, 1990.

3 *The Sunday Times*, October 11, 1992 and intelligence sources.

4 *The Sunday Times*, September 6, 1992.

5 *The Sunday Times*, May 2, 1993.

6. Statement made to the House of Commons by Sir Patrick Mayhew, November 29, 1993. Other details were supplied by Sinn Fein the same day.

7. *The Sunday Times* and *The Sunday Telegraph*, December 12, 1993; *The Times*, December 13, 1993.

8. Interview with British intelligence official in London, March, 1993.

9. These broad points were confirmed in an interview with Sir Patrick Mayhew, May 4, 1993.

CHAPTER 16

1 Indictment issued by the US District Court for the District of Columbia, November 14, 1991.

2 Further details on Libya's relations with the IRA in the early years can be found in Adams, *Engines of War*, *op. cit.*; and Adams, Morgan and Bambridge, *Ambush*, *op. cit.*

3 *The Sunday Times*, May 10, 1992.

4 Some details of the meeting appeared in *The Sunday Times* on June 14, 1992 and June 21, 1992. Other details come from American and British intelligence sources.

CHAPTER 17

1 David Long, *The Anatomy of Terrorism*, The Free Press, New York, 1990, p.143.

2 *Independent*, April 13, 1992.

3 Claire Sterling, *The Terror Network*, Weidenfeld & Nicolson, London, 1981.

4 Interview, May 17, 1993.

5 *Los Angeles Times*, April 6, 1993.
6 Interview, April 14, 1993.
7 Interview, April 28, 1993.
8 US Department of State, *Patterns of Global Terrorism 1992*, April 1993; AP file, May 1, 1993.
9 *Newsweek*, July 5, 1993, p.22.

CHAPTER 18

1 *Jane's Defence Weekly*, February 1, 1992, p.158.
2 *Washington Times*, June 10, 1993.
3 *Washington Times*, May 11, 1993. This was a reprint of an article which originally appeared in the London *Observer*.
4 *Newsday*, April 11, 1992.
5 *Washington Times*, April 22, 1992.
6 *New York Times*, November 30, 1992.
7 The International Institute for Strategic Studies, *The Military Balance, 1992–1993*, Brassey's, London, 1993, pp.102–126.
8 *New York Times*, March 6, 1992.
9 *Los Angeles Times*, March 11, 1993.
10 *The Press Democrat*, March 17, 1992; Tass, March 16, 1992, quoted in Betsy Perabo, *A Chronology of Iran's Nuclear Program*, Monterey Institute of International Studies, September 25, 1992, p.19.
11 *The Times*, May 22, 1992.
12 *Washington Post*, November 17, 1992.
13 *ibid.*
14 *Jerusalem Post*, February 24, 1993.
15 *Houston Chronicle*, March 28, 1992.
16 Interview, May 28, 1992.
17 *Business Week*, June 14, 1993, p.31.
18 *New Statesman and Society*, June 11, 1993, p.12.
19 Interview with Charlie Allen, August 28, 1992.
20 Mark Perry, *The Eclipse*, William Morrow, New York, 1992, p.383.
21 Interview with Charlie Allen, August 28, 1992.
22 Interview, June 3, 1993.
23 *Washington Post*, October 4, 1992.
24 Associated Press, March 24, 1992.
25 *Washington Post*, January 6, 1993.
26 *Washington Post*, December 6, 1992.
27 Interview, May 29, 1992.
28 *New York Times*, June 10, 1993.
29 *Washington Post*, May 23, 1993; *New York Times*, May 27, 1993.
30 *Iraq Rebuilds its Military Industries*, a staff report by the Subcommittee on International Security, International Organizations and Human Rights, of the Committee on Foreign Affairs of the House of Representatives, June 29, 1993; *Los Angeles Times*, June 30, 1993.

CHAPTER 19

1 *Washington Post*, June 24, 1993. In addition, this section on Libya has been prepared with assistance from Western intelligence sources.
2 Hearing of the Senate Governmental Affairs Committee on Weapons Proliferation in the New World Order, January 15, 1992.
3 *The New York Times*, November 10, 1993; *The Times*, October 16, 1993.
4 Interview, July 15, 1993.

CHAPTER 20

1 Unless otherwise stated, information in this chapter comes from interviews with Vladimir Pasechnik and Western intelligence sources. The interviews were conducted in September, 1993.
2 *Washington Post*, June 16, 1992.
3 *Newsweek*, February 1, 1993, p.40.
4 *Washington Post*, August 31, 1992.
5 *Washington Times*, July 4, 1992.
6 *Nezavisimaya Gazeta*, December 2, 1992.
7 *The Sunday Times*, October 1, 1989.
8 *Izvestiya*, December 3, 1992.
9 *Baltimore Sun*, October 23, 1992.
10 *Novoye Vremya* No. 6, February 1993.
11 Interview, September 1993.

CHAPTER 21

1 *Washington Post*, June 13, 1993.
2 *Washington Times*, July 7, 1993.
3 *US News and World Report*, August 9, 1993, p.19.
4 Speech at the Nixon Library Conference, Four Seasons Hotel, Washington DC, March 12, 1992.
5 *New York Times*, July 20, 1993; *Washington Post*, July 21, 1993.
6 *Daily Telegraph*, July 19, 1993.
7 *Washington Post*, June 21, 1992, *Washington Times*, December 3, 1991, *Wall Street Journal*, December 13, 1991.
8 Testimony by James Woolsey on Proliferation Threats of the 1990s before the Senate Committee on Governmental Affairs, February 24, 1993.
9 Testimony before the House Appropriations Committee quoted by Gabriel Schoenfeld, *Post-Soviet Prospects*, Center for Strategic and International Studies, No. 18, March 1993.
10 Jeffrey Richelson, *Can the Intelligence Community Keep Pace with the Threat?*, a paper for the Woodrow Wilson Center for International Scholars Conference on Nuclear Proliferation in the 1990s: Challenges and Opportunities.
11 Joseph Pilat, *Responding to Proliferation: A Role for Nonlethal Defenses*, a paper presented at the Woodrow Wilson Center in Washington DC, June 1993.
12 Rick Atkinson, *Crusade*, Houghton Mifflin, New York, 1993, pp.30 and 38.

CHAPTER 22

1 John Dilulio Jr., *The Next War on Drugs*, The Brookings Review, Summer 1993, p.28.
2 *Newsday*, February 5, 1992.
3 *US Efforts to Reduce Heroin Traffic in South East Asia*, Office of the Inspector General, US Department of State, Report of the Auditor, March, 1993, p.8.
4 *ibid., passim.*
5 Paper prepared for the US State Department in early 1992 following a fact-finding mission to Poland.
6 *Prawo I Zycte*, October 12, 1991, p.1.
7 *International Narcotics Control Strategy Report*, Bureau of International Narcotics Matters, US Department of State, April 1993, p.374.
8 *The Transnational Drug Challenge and the New World Order*, Center for Stragic and International Studies, Washington DC, January 1993, p.11.
9 *Financial Times*, June 9, 1992.
10 *International Narcotics Control Strategy Report, op. cit.*, p.26.
11 *New York Times*, May 8, 1993.
12 Stephen Flynn, *Worldwide Drugs Scourge: The Response*, The Brookings Review, Spring 1993, p.38.

CHAPTER 23

1 *Daily Telegraph*, August 9, 1989.
2 Interview, December 15, 1991.
3 Interview, January 14, 1992.
4 *Washington Times*, May 11, 1992.
5 Richard Kerr, *Covert Action in the 1990s*, Working Group on Intelligence Reform, Consortium for the Study of Intelligence, December 1992, p.65.

APPENDIX I
Intelligence Agencies

GERMANY

Militärischer Abschirm Dienst (MAD)

5000 Köln 1
Postfach 10 01 06
Telephone: 0221 37 00 26 57
Facsimile: 0221 34 13 61

Director   Dr Rudolf von Hoegen

Staff of approximately 1,500. MAD is in charge of internal security of the armed forces and is under the control of the Federal Ministry of Defence.

BundesNachrichten Dienst (BND)

Bonn
82-042 Pullach
Postfach 120
Telephone: 089 793 0190
Facsimile: 089 793 0620

President   Konrad Porzner
Vice President   Dr Paul Munstermann

Staff of approximately 6,000. BND collects information on international developments outside of Germany. It is supervised by the Federal Chancellery and under parliamentary control.

BundesKriminal Amt

PF 18 20
Thaerstrasse 11
6200 Wiesbaden

Telephone: 0611 511
Facsimile: 0611 552323

President   Hans Ludwig Zachert
Spokesman   Brunhilde Spies-Mohr

Bundesamt fur Verfassungsschutz (BfV)

Merianstrasse 100
W-5000 Köln 71
Telephone: 0221 7920

President   Dr Eckart Werthebach

Staff of approximately 2,000. The BfV (Office of the protection of the Constitution) is an internal intelligence organization which is subordinate to the Minister of the Interior.

CHINA

International Liaison Department (ILD)

Head	Zhu Liang
Deputy Head	Li Shuzheng
Deputy Head	Jiang Guanghua
Deputy Head	Zhu Shanqing
Deputy Head	Li Chengren
Secretary General	Li Beihai
Advisor	Tang Mingzhao
Advisor	Zhang Zhixiang
Advisor	Ou Tangliang
Advisor	Liu Zinquan
Advisor	Zhang Xiangshan
Advisor	Tian Yiming
Spokesperson	Wu Xingtang
Asian Bureau Director	?
Deputy Director	Duan Yuanpei
African Bureau Director	Xu Qingshan
European Bureau Director	Zhu Dacheng
Research Centre Director	Wu Xingtang

Develops relationships with communist revolutionary groups and

340

Socialist labour parties worldwide. Engages in both overt and covert activities.

Military Intelligence Department (MID)

Subordinate to General Staff. Emphasis on order of battle, foreign military capabilities, foreign weapons systems. Politico-military and military-strategic emphasis. Photographic reconnaissance.

Ministry of State Security (MSS)

14 Dongchangan Jie, Dongcheng Dist.
Beijing
Telephone: 01 553871

Minister   Jia Chunwang
Director (Foreign Affairs Division)   Guan Ping

Emphasis on counter-espionage, prevention of 'leaks' to foreign press. Founded in 1983, is known to be overzealous, conspicuous, and has had several setbacks.

New China News Agency (NCNA)

Collects and disseminates news in China and abroad. Also used as cover for espionage.

Science and Technology Department

Director   Wang Tongye

Signals intelligence from ships, submarines and stations. Department is subordinate to Ministry of Defence.

FRANCE

Direction des Affairs Stratégiques (DAS)

Director   Jean Claude Mallet

Staff of approximately 25. Follows international negotiations related to defence and also carries out defence planning work.

Direction du Protection et de la Sécurité de la Défense (DPSD)

Deputy Director   Claude Menard

Emphasis on military intelligence, formerly Sécurité Militaire.

Direction du Renseignement Militaire (DRM)

Director   General Jean Heinrich

Staff of approximately 500. Emphasis on military and space intelligence. The DRM is supposedly based in Creil (Oise), where the Satellite Imaging Interpretation Centre is located. Structurally, the DRM is divided into 5 subdirectorates: Research, Operations, Arms Proliferation, Techniques, and Human Resources/Administration.

Directorate for Strategic Evolution

Director   Jean Claude Cousseran

Most likely located in the prime minister's office, but not sure. The Directorate is responsible for DRM's political forecasting.

Directorate for Surveillance of the Territory (DST)

7 rue Nelaton
75015 Paris
Telephone 45 71 49 42

Director	Jacques Fournet
Director of Cabinet	Jean Pierre Pochon
Adjunct Director	Raymond Nart
Vice Director	Jean Pierre Alba
Vice Director	Jean François Clair
Vice Director	Fernand Colin
Vice Director	Jacky Debain
Vice Director	Michel Guiral

Staff of approximately 2-5 thousand (1988 figure). Emphasis on counter-espionage, counter-intelligence, surveillance of embassies, protection of classified information. The DST is subordinate to the Ministry of the Interior.

Direction Générale de la Sécurité Extérieure (DGSE)

141, Boulevard Mortier

75020 Paris
Telephone 40 65 30 11

Director General   Jacques Dewatre
  (Appointed recently following a débâcle in Central Africa)
Director of Cabinet   André Boix
Director   Michael la Carrière
Director   Jean Claude Tressens
Director   Jerome Ventre

Staff of approximately 3,500. Emphasis on industrial/economic intelligence, terrorism, human intelligence.

Secretariat Général de la Défense Nationale (SGDN)

51, bd de Latour-Maubourg (7e)
75700 Paris
Telephone 45 55 30 11

SGDN is a military intelligence agency that serves the prime minister, and is in charge of civil defence.

Traitement du Reseignement et Action contre les Circuits Financiers Clandestins (Tracfin)

Created in 1990, Tracfin is responsible for the fight against drug money laundering. Hopes to increase powers to include working against organized crime. Not responsible for legal operations or making arrests. The office is most likely located in the Ministry of Interior, but not sure.

JAPAN

Cabinet Research Office (Naicho)

1-6-1 Negate cho
Chiyoda-ku
Tokyo 100

Telephone: (81 3) 3581 2361 (number for the prime minister's office)

Staff of approximately 122 (1986 figure). Naicho provides the prime minister with analyses and studies to aid in making foreign and defence policy. Budget in 1986: $25 million.

Information Analysis, Research and Planning Bureau

Ministry of Foreign Affairs
2-2-1 Kasumigaseki
Chiyoda-ku
Tokyo 100

Telephone: (81 3) 3580 3311 (number for Foreign Ministry)

The Bureau collects, distributes and analyzes information on foreign affairs.

Ministry of International Trade and Industry (MITI)

1-3-1 Kasumigaseki
Chiyoda-ku
Tokyo 100

Telephone: (81 3) 3501 1511

Minister: Yoshiro Mori

MITI has a staff of approximately 15,000 (1983 figure). Collects and analyzes information on trade, commerce, markets and technological developments; it has management, organizational and technical knowledge. Also, Japanese External Trade Organization (JETRO) is part of MITI, and collects information worldwide. It has 270 employees in 81 cities, 59 countries, 1,200 analysts, and a budget of $130 million annually (1986 estimate).

Japan Defence Agency (Boeicho)

9-7-45 Akasaka
Minato-ku
Tokyo 107

Telephone: (81 3) 3408 5211

Bureau of Defence Policy

Director, 1st Defence Intelligence Division: Shigeaki Ishikawa
   Extension 2044
Director, 2nd Defence Intelligence Division: Takehiko Shimaguchi
   Extension 3175

Joint Staff Council

JSC is equivalent to a Defence Staff in other countries' MODs with the chairman of the JSC reporting directly to the Minister of State for Defence.

Director, Intelligence: Rear Adm. Tadashi Satoh

Ground Self-Defence Force (Nibetsu)

7-45 Aksada 9-chome
Minato-ku
Tokyo 107
Telephone: (81 3) 3408 5211

Intelligence Department

Director: Maj. Gen. Mitsuhiro Saino
Chief, 1st Intelligence Division: Col. Shuzo Hiyama
Chief, Foreign Liaison: Col. Hidematsu Koga
Chief, 2nd Intelligence Division: Col. Makoto Kagata

Japan Maritime Self-Defence Force

9-7-45 Akasaka
Minato-ku
Tokyo 107
Telephone: (81 3) 3408 5211

Intelligence Department

Director: Rear Adm. Makoto Ikari
Chief, 1st Intelligence Division: Capt. Yasuo Wakabayashi
Chief, 2nd Intelligence Division: Capt. Gentaro Hiraga

Produces naval intelligence on countries of regional importance. May supervise monitoring of naval movements near Japan.

Japan Air Self-Defence Force

9-7-45 Akasaka
Minato-ku
Tokyo 107

Telephone: (81 3) 3408 5211

Intelligence Department

Director: Maj. Gen. Goroh Kondo
Chief, 1st Intelligence Division: Col. Norimasa Nishida
Chief, 2nd Intelligence Division: Col. Tegsusaku Takechi

Produces intelligence on air forces or regional powers. May supervise imaging for Japanese military. Airborne operations conducted by 501 Flight Squadron (Hyakuri Air Base).

Public Security Investigation Agency (PSIA)

Staff of approximately 2,000. PSIA concentrates on counter-espionage and counter-terrorism, and gains cooperation through economic incentives.

RUSSIA

Glavnoye Razvedyvatelnoye Upravlenie (GRU)

Ministry of Defence Press Centre
11 Znamenka Street
Moscow

Telephone: 095 296 03 65

Director: Lt. Gen. Feodor Ladygin
Contact: Vladimir Nikonorov

Responsible for military intelligence.

Federal Counterintelligence Service

Lubiank 2
Moscow

Director: Viktor Golushko

PR Centre: Oleg Tsarev
               22 Kuznetsky Most Street
               10100 Moscow
Contact: Andrei Chernenko: 095 224 50 97

Staff of approximately 136,000. Emphasis is on border control, counter-intelligence and secret police.

Sluzhba Vneshnie Razvedaki (SVR)
(External Intelligence Service)

Yasenevo 11 Kolpachny
Moscow, 101000

Telephone: 095 923 62 13

Director:	Yevgeni Primakov
First Dep. Director:	Lt. Gen. Vyacheslav Trubinkov
Dep. Director:	Gen. Ivan Gorelovsky (former head of Azerbaijan KGB)
PA:	Yuri Kobaladze
Primakov's PAO:	Tatiana Samolis
Contact:	Robert Martaryan

SVR concentrates on economic, industrial and commercial intelligence; political intelligence; and covert and clandestine activities.

ISRAEL

Israeli Defence Forces

Chief Intelligence Officer: Brig. Gen. Doran Tamir

Has overall responsibility for coordinating intelligence for the General Staff. It is assumed that he has a close working relationship with Maj. Gen. Uri Saguy, the Director of AMAN.

Israeli Defence Forces Intelligence Branch (AMAN)

Director: Maj. Gen. Uri Saguy

Collects, produces and disseminates military, geographic, and economic intelligence, especially about the Middle East.

Air Force Intelligence

Conducts intelligence activities to support air activities, and coordinates collection efforts with the director of AMAN. Aerial reconnaissance, signals intelligence.

Border Police

Parliamentary unit of Israeli police. BP operates under police supervision when in Israel, and under direction of Israeli Defence Force in occupied territories.

Central Institute for Intelligence and Special Duties (MOSSAD)

Human intelligence collection, covert action, counter-terrorism. Conducts operations against Arab organizations and nations worldwide. Seeks to acquire military equipment.

General Security Services (Shin Beth or SHABEK)

Counter-espionage, internal security.

Naval Intelligence

Naval order of battle, foreign capabilities, sea borne threats. Not subordinate to director of AMAN, except to provide consultative assistance in naval matters.

Research and Political Planning Centre

Prepares intelligence analysis for policy makers.

UNITED KINGDOM

Government Communications Headquarters (GCHQ)

Cheltenham
Gloucestershire
or
2–8 Palmer Street
London SW1

Director: Sir John Adye

Staff of approximately 6,500. Monitors, decodes radio, telex and telegram communications in and out of Britain.

Secret Intelligence Service (SIS or MI6)

Century House
Vauxhall Cross
London

THE SECURITY SERVICE

CENTRAL UK INTELLIGENCE ORGANIZATION

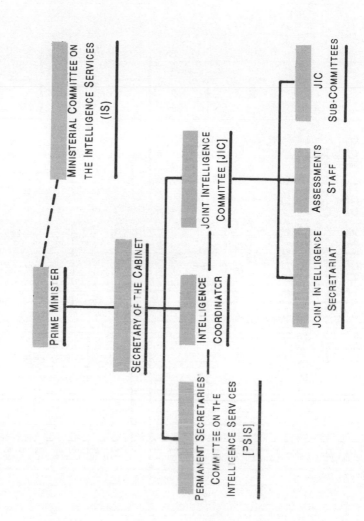

PRIME MINISTER

MINISTERIAL COMMITTEE ON THE INTELLIGENCE SERVICES (IS)

SECRETARY OF THE CABINET

PERMANENT SECRETARIES' COMMITTEE ON THE INTELLIGENCE SERVICES [PSIS]

INTELLIGENCE COORDINATOR

JOINT INTELLIGENCE COMMITTEE [JIC]

JOINT INTELLIGENCE SECRETARIAT

ASSESSMENTS STAFF

JIC SUB-COMMITTEES

THE SECURITY SERVICE

THE UK INTELLIGENCE ORGANIZATION: MINISTERIAL RESPONSIBILITY

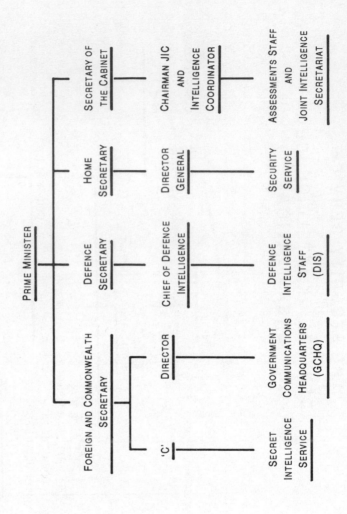

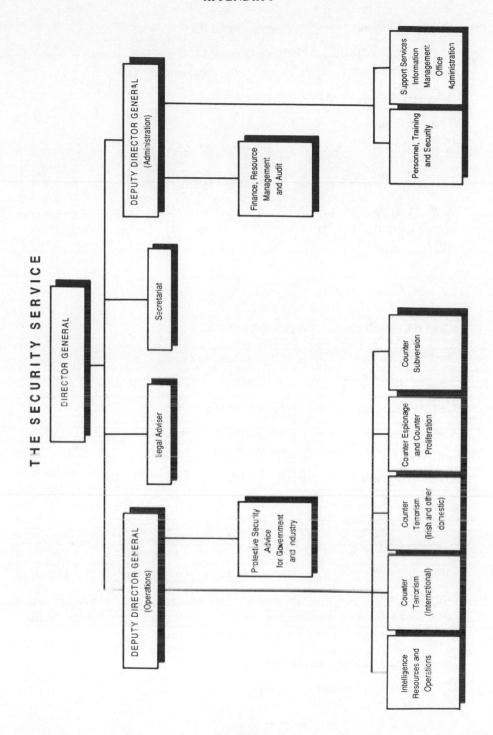

THE SECURITY SERVICE

DIRECTOR GENERAL

Legal Adviser

Secretariat

DEPUTY DIRECTOR GENERAL (Administration)

Finance, Resource Management and Audit

Personnel, Training and Security

Support Services
Information Management
Office Administration

DEPUTY DIRECTOR GENERAL (Operations)

Protective Security Advice for Government and Industry

Intelligence Resources and Operations

Counter Terrorism (International)

Counter Terrorism (Irish and other domestic)

Counter Espionage and Counter Proliferation

Counter Subversion

Director General: Sir Colin McColl

Staff of approximately 1,850, budget of $210 million. Recruits agents, counter-intelligence, clandestine operations, intelligence collection.

Security Service (MI5)

Thames House
Millbank
London

Director: Stella Rimington

Staff of approximately 2,000. Internal functions: counter-espionage, counter-intelligence, monitors subversives, surveillance of foreign nations.

UNITED STATES

Central Intelligence Agency (CIA)

Washington DC 20505

Telephone: 703 482 1100

Director: DCI James Woolsey

Covert and clandestine activities and operations. Intelligence analysis, primarily broken down geographically.

Defense Intelligence Agency (DIA)

Boling Air Force Base
Washington DC 20340

Telephone: 703 695 0071

Director: Lt. Gen. James R. Clapper (US Air Force)

Military intelligence, foreign military and military related requirements, coordinates defence intelligence, component of the Joint Chiefs of Staff. Funded through both the Defense and Intelligence budgets.

Intelligence and Research (INR)

US Department of State
Washington DC 20520

Telephone: 202 647 5050

Director: Secretary of State Warren Christopher

Staff of approximately 330 (1991). Plays minor role, has little impact on policy. On EC matters, its analyses do play a part.

National Imagery Office (NIO)

The Pentagon
Arlington, VA 20301

Coordinates all US satellite intelligence activities. Established by directive signed by Secretary Chaney on May 6, 1992. Unclassified office.

National Reconnaissance Office (NRO)

The Pentagon
Arlington, VA 20301

Acquires and deploys satellites, highly classified.

National Security Agency (NSA)

Fort George G. Meade
Maryland, 20755 6000

Telephone: 301 688 6311 or 301 688 6524 (Public Affairs)

Director: Vice Adm. J.M. McConnell (US Navy)

Signals intelligence, satellite intelligence, cryptography.

National Reconnaissance Office
New Structure - 1993

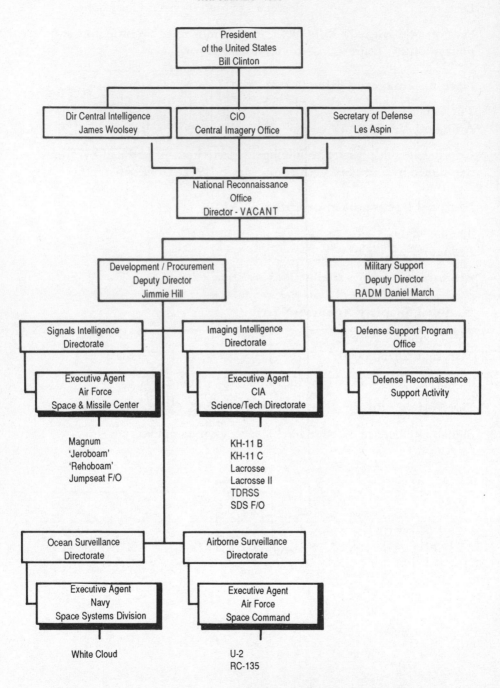

President
of the United States
Bill Clinton

Dir Central Intelligence
James Woolsey

CIO
Central Imagery Office

Secretary of Defense
Les Aspin

National Reconnaissance
Office
Director - VACANT

Development / Procurement
Deputy Director
Jimmie Hill

Military Support
Deputy Director
RADM Daniel March

Signals Intelligence
Directorate

Imaging Intelligence
Directorate

Defense Support Program
Office

Executive Agent
Air Force
Space & Missile Center

Executive Agent
CIA
Science/Tech Directorate

Defense Reconnaissance
Support Activity

Magnum
'Jeroboam'
'Rehoboam'
Jumpseat F/O

KH-11 B
KH-11 C
Lacrosse
Lacrosse II
TDRSS
SDS F/O

Ocean Surveillance
Directorate

Airborne Surveillance
Directorate

Executive Agent
Navy
Space Systems Division

Executive Agent
Air Force
Space Command

White Cloud

U-2
RC-135

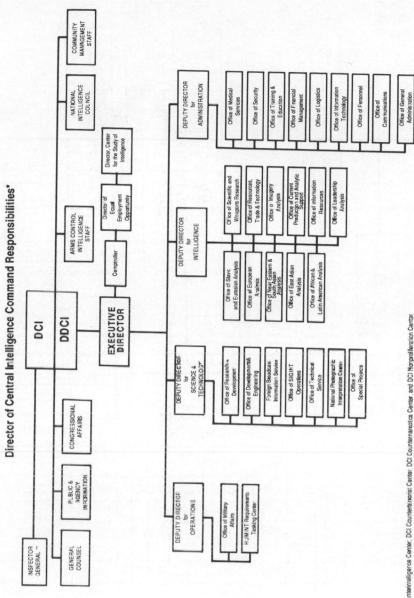

Director of Central Intelligence Command Responsibilities*

* DCI Counterintelligence Center; DCI Counterterrorist Center; DCI Counternarcotics Center; and DCI Nonproliferation Center
** Statutory Inspector General—nominated by the President; confirmed by Congress
*** Also serves as Special Assistant to the DCI for Equal Employment Opportunity

FBI Headquarters Functional Organizational Chart

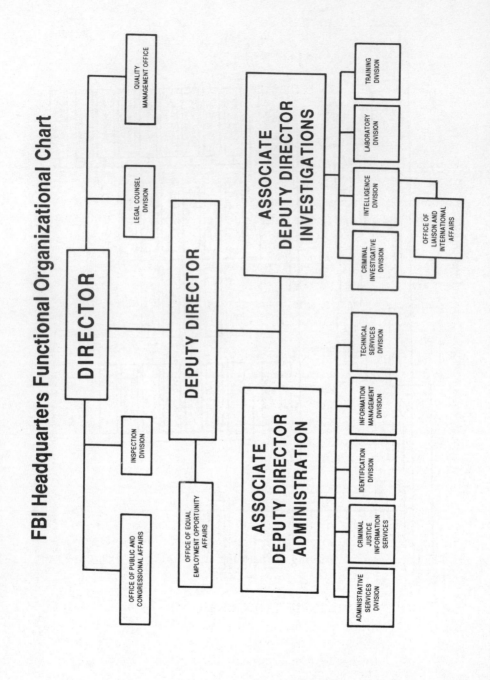

APPENDIX II
Nuclear Status

NUCLEAR WEAPON STATES:
United States, Russia, Great Britain, France, China (have declared their nuclear status; are recognized under Nuclear Non-Proliferation Treaty as nuclear weapon states because detonated first tests prior to January 1, 1967; Russia succeeding to status of the former Soviet Union.)

FORMER SOVIET REPUBLICS WITH NUCLEAR WEAPONS ON THEIR TERRITORY:
Belarus, Kazakhstan, Ukraine (have pledged to join Nuclear Non-Proliferation Treaty as non-nuclear weapon states at the soonest possible time; not able to use nuclear weapons independent of central command in Russia; Ukraine gradually increasing control over nuclear weapons on its territory and backing away from de-nuclearization pledges.)

DE FACTO NUCLEAR-WEAPON STATES:
Israel, India, Pakistan (able to deploy nuclear weapons rapidly, but have not acknowledged possessing them. Israeli arsenal probably 100+ devices; Indian arsenal probably 60+; Pakistani arsenal probably 10-15.)

RENOUNCING NUCLEAR WEAPONS:
South Africa (joined NPT in 1991; after years of ambiguity, has acknowledged manufacturing six nuclear weapons during late 1970s and 1980s, which it claims to have destroyed; International Atomic Energy Agency (IAEA) in process of verifying dismantling and inspecting weapons-grade materials.)

RENOUNCING PRESUMED NUCLEAR-WEAPONS EFFORTS:
Argentina, Brazil (possess facilities needed for nuclear weapons, but agreed to implement comprehensive IAEA and bilateral inspections in 1990–1991; mutual inspection regime in place, but Brazil has yet to ratify formal IAEA agreement.)

COUNTRIES TO MONITOR:

Algeria, Iran, Iraq, Libya, North Korea, Syria (nuclear weapon ambitions currently checked by international controls and technological constraints. North Korea closest; resisting full application of IAEA inspections under NPT; may have produced enough weapons-grade material for a nuclear device, but US intelligence community divided on issue. Iran thought eight years from nuclear weapons, but could accelerate programme if nuclear assets leak from former Soviet Union. Iraqi nuclear programme dismantled under UN/IAEA post-Gulf War inspections; subject to continuing monitoring.)

Source: Leonard Spector, Carnegie Endowment for International Peace, June, 1993

APPENDIX III
Planning an Intelligence Operation in Northern Ireland

The Meetings:

1. Assistant Chief Constable (ACC) (Special Branch) meets with Deputy Chief Constable (Operations)
2. ACC (GB) meets with Chief Constable
3. ACC (GB) meets with MI5's Director and Coordinator of Intelligence (DCI)

PURPOSE:

a. Meetings 1,2,3
i.   Full disclosure of all information
     Discussion of outline plan or ideas already jammed in box or wherever
     No limitations on questions
     Caveat set on dissemination of information

ii. Decision making would include:
     Resources available, access to them, and how they should be tasked
     Operational parameters being set
     Timings and location being discussed and if possible agreed if they had not already been set

4. ACC (GB) will meet Det. Chief Superintendent for the region

PURPOSE:

b. Meeting 4
i.   Information passed will be more operationally based
     Less political information, less strategic information
     Consultation and discussion on resources – availability, how used

Discussion on wider applications
Passing on decisions already made

ii.   Decisions made will include:
Operational outline
Parameters of operating
Dissemination of information
Planning deadlines
Reporting and accountability structures
Points of coordination

5. Det. Chief Supt. (SB) region will meet Det. Supt. (SB) for those divisions of areas affected and Det. Supt. Tasking and Coordinating Group (TCG) SAS 14 Int. E4A commander also may be present at these meetings but unlikely.

PURPOSE:

c. Meeting 5
This meeting will be where serious operational planning will take place.
i.   Information will depend to some extent on 2 things:
1) Trust and relationship
2) Information already known

Full picture will not be given but a broad outline will be passed. Personalities not discussed. Location not identified in detail.
More detail will be given if information is specific to the area/region? individuals identified, locations detailed.
Pass on decisions made.

ii.   Operations discussed and decisions made:
Operational resources
Tasks needed
Tasks desired
Troops to task and how briefed by whom
Planning deadlines
Operational timings and parameters
Reporting and accountability structure
Coordinating points – timings
               routes and areas
               means of identification of different agencies
               communications

control and operations location
limits of exploitation – geographically
– operationally (e.g. hot
pursuit compromise)

Operations will be split between information gathering and securing/ protection.

6. Det. Chief Supt. Region will meet with Commanders/LOs of SAS, E4A–14 Int. (less likely) if not met in 5.

PURPOSE

d. Meetings 6 onwards
i. The information passed in these will definitely be 'need to know'. This does not necessarily include background information, i.e. the 'reason why' the operation is being carried out.

Meetings 1–5 inclusive have involved all the planners, decision makers and controllers of the operations. These people will not be involved on the ground or reacting directly to situations occurring. Therefore, in order for them to direct effectively, they need a decent amount of background information on the 'reasons why'.

Meetings 6 onwards are the operational people – those responsible for carrying out the plans. 'Need to know' is a protective measure – protective of those going on the ground. The operators are denied much of the 'reasons why' and are only told the plan of 'what' the operation is, 'who' is involved that will affect their operating (so they probably do not know everybody involved) and 'how' they will carry out their task. They are protected by only being able to act on the operational information given in orders, and to react to a situation as they see it. i.e. less room for confusion, less room for personal agendas and prejudices, less room for judgements being made with old information (if all info is passed at the start of operation then the burden is to update constantly – this is usually difficult to achieve whilst remaining secure in a covert operation).

Too many commanders do not see the 'protective' nature of 'need to know' and believe it is only fair that the men know the reasons behind an operation. Others are caught in the trap where they describe every operation as 'very important' and 'very secret' – using these as a means of motivation. Trust has to be established so that if a task is given, it is important without question, and is secret without question.

ii.   Decisions made in these meetings were operational:
      Planning deadlines
      Operational perimeters
      Operational timings and duration
      Equipment
      Dress – limitations on re supply
      Means of identification
      Boundaries
      Routes
      Communication plans
      Chain of command
      Documentation necessary

7. Det. Supt. TCG will meet with Det. Inspectors and probably MIO TCG (RUC and army may have separate meetings as information given tends to be different). The Det. Sgt.s may also be involved.

8a. Det. Inspectors TCG meet Unit Commanders – those responsible for the operations on the ground. These include E4A and 14 Int. and SAS LO.

8b. MIO TCG will meet army covert unit commanders. Definitely COPs (close observation platoon) probably NIGS (Northern Ireland Surveillance Section). Possibly 14 Int. LO depending on relationship.

9. Det. Supt. Divisions will meet with local SB commanders (inspectors) to gather intelligence or for them to task handlers to obtain specific information.

Meanwhile

10. Tasking meetings:
    a. Bde Commander to Commanding Officer
    b. CLF to ACOS G1 (Assistant Chief of Staff, Intelligence + Sy)
    c. ACOS G1 to SMIU and FRU (Field Research Unit if army sources are involved)
    d. Agency commanders to operators.

BIBLIOGRAPHY

Adams, James, *Secret Armies, Inside the American, Soviet and European Special Forces*, Atlantic Monthly Press, New York, 1987.

Adams, James, Robin Morgan and Anthony Bambridge, *Ambush: The War between the SAS and the IRA*, Pan, London, 1988.

Adams, James, *Bull's Eye: The Assassination and Life of Supergun Inventor Gerald Bull*, Times Books, New York, 1992.

Adams, James, *The Financing of Terror*, Simon & Schuster, New York, 1986.

Adams, James, *Trading in Death: Weapons, Warfare and the New Arms Race*, Hutchinson, London, 1990.

Allen, Thomas B. and Norman Polmar, *Merchants of Treason: America's Secrets for Sale*, Robert Hale, London, 1988.

Allison, Graham, Ashton B. Carter, Steven E. Miller and Philip Selikow, eds., *Co-operative Denuclearization: From Pledges to Deeds*, Harvard University, Cambridge, 1993.

Andrew, Christopher and Oleg Gordievsky, *Instructions from the Centre: Top Secret Files on KGB Foreign Operations 1975–1985*, Hodder & Stoughton, London, 1991.

Andrew, Christopher and Oleg Gordievsky, *KGB: The Inside Story*, Hodder & Stoughton, London, 1990.

Arkin, William M., Joshua M. Handler, Julia A. Morrisey and Jacquelyn M. Walsh, *Encyclopedia of the US Military*, Harper & Row, New York, 1990.

Asher, Michael, *Shoot to Kill: A Soldier's Journey through Violence*, Viking, London, 1990.

Atkinson, Rick, *Crusade: The Untold Story of the Persian Gulf War*, Houghton Mifflin, New York, 1993.

Ball, Desmond, *Soviet Signals Intelligence (SIGINT)*, Strategic and Defence Studies Centre, Research School of Pacific Studies, Canberra, Australia, 1989.

Bamford, James, *The Puzzle Palace: America's National Security Agency and its Special Relationship with Britain's GCHQ*, Sidgwick & Jackson, London, 1982.

Barron, John, *KGB Today: The Hidden Hand*, Reader's Digest Press, New York, 1983.

Beaty, Jonathon and S.C. Gwynne, *The Outlaw Bank: A Wild Ride into the Secret Heart of BCCI*, Random House, New York, 1993.

Beckwith, Col. Charlie A., USA (Ret.), and Donald Knox, *Delta Force: The US Counter-Terrorist Unit and the Iran Hostage Rescue Mission*, Harcourt Brace Jovanovich, New York, 1983.

Bell, J. Bowyer, *The Secret Army: The IRA 1916–1979*, Academy Press, Dublin, 1970.

Beschloss, Michael R., and Strobe Talbott, *At the Highest Levels; The Inside Story of the End of the Cold War*, Little, Brown, Boston, 1993.

Bishop, Patrick, and Eamonn Mallie, *The Provisional IRA*, Corgi, London, 1987.

Bittman, Ladislav, *The KGB and Soviet Disinformation*, Pergamon-Brassey's, Washington, 1985.

Blake, George, *No Other Choice*, Jonathan Cape, London, 1990.

Blum, Howard, *I Pledge Allegiance . . . The True Story of the Walkers: An American Spy Family*, Weidenfeld & Nicolson, London, 1988.

Bower, Tom, *The Red Web: MI6 and the KGB Master Coup*, Aurum Press, London, 1989.

Boyle, Andrew, *The Climate of Treason*, Hodder & Stoughton, London, 1979.

Breckinridge, Scott D., *The CIA and the US Intelligence System*, Westview Press, Boulder, 1986.

Brogan, Patrick, *World Conflicts: Why and Where they are Happening*, Bloomsbury, London, 1989.

Brook-Shepherd, Gordon, *The Storm Birds: Soviet Post-War Defectors*, Weidenfeld & Nicolson, London, 1988.

Brown, Ben and David Shukman, *All Necessary Means: Inside the Gulf War*, BBC Books, London, 1991.

Brzezinski, Zbigniew, *Power and Principle, Memoirs of the National Security Advisor 1977–1981*, Farrar, Straus & Giroux, New York, 1985.

Cavendish, Anthony, *Inside Intelligence*, Collins, London, 1990.

Clark, Alan, *Diaries*, Weidenfeld & Nicolson, London, 1993.

Corson, William B., Susan B. Trento and Joseph J. Trento, *Widows: Four American spies, the wives they left behind and the KGB's crippling of Western intelligence*, Macdonald, 1989.

Costello, John and Oleg Tsarev, *Deadly Illusions*, Crown Publishers, New York, 1993.

Crowe, Admiral William J., Jr. with David Chanoff, *The Line of Fire: From Washington to the Gulf, the Politics and Battles of the New Military*, Simon & Schuster, New York, 1993.

Dailey, Brian D. and Patrick J. Parker, eds., *Soviet Strategic Deception*, Lexington Books, Lexington, 1987.

de Grazia, Jessica, *DEA: The War against Drugs*, BBC Books, 1991.

Deacon, Richard, *The Chinese Secret Service*, Grafton Books, London, 1974.

Deriabin, Peter and T. H. Bagley, *The KGB: Masters of the Soviet Union*, Robson Books, London, 1990.

Earley, Pete, *Family of Spies: Inside the John Walker Spy Ring*, Bantam Books, New York, 1988.

Emerson, Steven, *Secret Warriors: Inside the Covert Military Operations of the Reagan Era*, G. P. Putnam's Sons, New York, 1988.

Epstein, Edward Jay, *Deception: The Invisible War between the KGB and the CIA*, W. H. Allen, London, 1989.

Faligot, Roger and Pascal Krop, *La Piscine: The French Secret Service since 1944*, Basil Blackwell, Oxford, 1989.

Freemantle, Brian, *KGB*, Michael Joseph, London, 1982.

Gann, Ernest K., *The Black Watch: The Men who Fly America's Secret Spy Planes*, Random House, New York, 1989.

Gelb, Norman, *The Berlin Wall*, Michael Joseph, London, 1986.

Geraghty, Tony, *Who Dares Wins: The Special Air Service, 1950 to the Gulf War*, Little, Brown, London, 1992.

Godson, Roy, ed., *Intelligence Requirements for the 1980s: Covert Action*, National Strategy Information Center, Inc., Washington DC, 1981.

Godson, Roy, ed., *Intelligence Requirements for the 1980s: Clandestine Collection*, National Strategy Information Center, Inc., Washington DC, 1982.

Godson, Roy, ed., *Intelligence Requirements for the 1990s: Collection, Analysis, Counterintelligence, and Covert Action*, Lexington Books, Lexington, 1989.

Haig, Alexander M. Jr., with Charles McCarry, *Inner Circles: How America Changed the World, A Memoir*, Warner Books, New York, 1992.

Hayden, Lt. Col. H. T., USMC, *Shadow War: Special Operations and Low Intensity Conflict*, Pacific Aero Press, Vista, CA, 1992.

Higgins, Trumbull, *The Perfect Failure: Kennedy, Eisenhower, and the CIA at the Bay of Pigs*, W. W. Norton, New York, 1987.

Hyde, H. Montgomery, *George Blake, Superspy*, Constable, London, 1987.

The International Institute for Strategic Studies, *The Military Balance 1992–1993*, Brassey's, London, 1992.

Jeffreys-Jones, Rhodri, *The CIA & American Democracy*, Yale University Press, New Haven, 1989.

Johnson, Loch K., *America's Secret Power: The CIA in a Democratic Society*, Oxford University Press, New York, 1989.

Kelly, Kevin, *The Longest War: Northern Ireland and the IRA*, Zed, London, 1982.

Kennedy, Michael Paul, *Soldier 'I' SAS*, Bloomsbury, London, 1989.

Kessler, Ronald, *Inside the CIA: Revealing the Secrets of the World's Most Powerful Spy Agency*, Pocket Books, New York, 1992.

Kessler, Ronald, *The Spy in the Russian Club*, Scribners, New York, 1990.

Kwitny, Jonathon, *The Crimes of Patriots: A True Tale of Dope, Dirty Money, and the CIA*, W. W. Norton, New York, 1987.

Leigh, David, *The Wilson Plot: The Intelligence Services and the Discrediting of a Prime Minister 1945–1976*, Heinemann, London, 1988.

Leppard, David, *On the Trail of Terror: The Inside Story of the Lockerbie Investigation*, Jonathan Cape, London, 1991.

McClintock, Michael, *Instruments of Statecraft: US Guerrilla Warfare, Counterinsurgency, and Counterterrorism, 1940–1990*, Pantheon Books, New York, 1992.

McGehee, Ralph W., *Deadly Deceits: My 25 Years in the CIA*, Sheridan Square Publications, New York, 1983.

Mangold, Tom, *Cold Warrior, James Jesus Angleton: The CIA's Master Spy Hunter*, Simon & Schuster, London, 1991.

Marchetti, Victor and John D. Marks, *The CIA and the Cult of Intelligence*, Dell Publishing, New York, 1974.

Marcinko, Richard, with John Weisman, *Rogue Warrior*, Pocket Books, New York, 1992.

Martin, David C., and John Walcott, *Best Laid Plans: The Inside Story of America's War against Terrorism*, Harper & Row, New York, 1988.

Melman, Yossi and Dan Raviv, *The Imperfect Spies: The History of Israeli Intelligence*, Sidgwick & Jackson, London, 1989.

O'Toole, G. J. A., *Honorable Treachery: A History of US Intelligence, Espionage, and Covert Action from the American Revolution to the CIA*, Atlantic Monthly Press, New York, 1991.

Perry, Mark, *Eclipse, The Last Days of the CIA*, William Morrow, New York, 1992.

Persico, Joseph E., *Casey: From the OSS to the CIA*, Penguin, New York, 1990.

Philby, Kim, *My Silent War: The Autobiography of Kim Philby*, Grafton Books, London, 1989.

Pincher, Chapman, *The Secret Offensive, Active Measures: A Saga of Deception, Disinformation, Subversion, Terrorism, Sabotage and Assassination*, Sidwick & Jackson, London, 1985.

Power, Thomas, *The Man Who Kept the Secrets: Richard Helms and the CIA*, Alfred A. Knopf, New York, 1979.

Prados, John, *Keepers of the Keys: A History of the National Security Council from Truman to Bush*, William Morrow, New York, 1991.

Prados, John, *President's Secret Wars: CIA and Pentagon Covert Operations since World War II*, William Morrow, New York, 1986.

Ranelagh, John, *The Agency: The Rise and Decline of the CIA, from Wild Bill Donovan to William Casey*, Simon & Schuster, New York, 1986.

Raviv, Dan and Yossi Melman, *Every Spy a Prince: The Complete History of Israel's Intelligence Community*, Houghton Mifflin, Boston, 1990.

Richelson, Jeffrey T., *The US Intelligence Community*, 2nd ed., Ballinger, Cambridge, Mass., 1988.

Richelson, Jeffrey T., *Foreign Intelligence Organizations*, Ballinger, Cambridge, Mass., 1988.

Richelson, Jeffrey T., *Sword and Shield: Soviet Intelligence and Security Apparatus*, Ballinger, Cambridge, Mass., 1986.

Richelson, Jeffrey, *American Espionage and the Soviet Target*, William Morrow, New York, 1987.

Robertson, K. G., *British and American Approaches to Intelligence*, Macmillan, London, 1987.

Romerstein, Herbert and Stanislav Lavchenko, *The KGB Against the 'Main Enemy': How the Soviet Intelligence Service Operates against the United States*, Lexington Books, Lexington, 1989.

Rositzke, Harry, *The KGB: The Eyes of Russia*, Sidgwick & Jackson, London, 1981.

Rositzke, Harry, *The CIA's Secret Operations: Espionage, Counterespionage, and Covert Action*, Westview Press, Boulder, 1977.

Runde, Carl Peter and Greg Voss, eds., *Intelligence and the New World Order: Former Cold War Adversaries Look toward the 21st Century*, International Freedom Foundation, Buxtehude, BRD, 1992.

Ryan, Paul B., *The Iranian Rescue Mission: Why it Failed*, Naval Institute Press, Annapolis, 1985.

Ryder, Chris, *The Rug: A Force Under Fire*, Methuen, London, 1989.

Schecter, Jerrold L. and Peter S. Deriabin, *The Spy Who Saved the World: How a Soviet Colonel Changed the Course of the Cold War*, Scribners, New York, 1992.

Schultz, George P., *Turmoil and Triumph: My Years as Secretary of State*, Scribners, New York, 1993.

Seale, Patrick, *Abu Nidal: A Gun for Hire*, Random House, New York, 1992.

Shulsky, Abram N., *Silent Warfare: Understanding the World of Intelligence*, Brassey's, Washington, 1991.

Skillen, Hugh, *Spies of the Airwaves*, Hugh Skillen, Middlesex, 1989.

Sterling, Claire, *The Terror Network: The Secret War of International Terrorism*, Weidenfeld & Nicolson, London, 1981.

Steven, Stewart, *The Spymasters of Israel*, Ballantine Books, New York, 1980.

Stockwell, John, *In Search of Enemies: A CIA Story*, W. W. Norton, New York, 1978.

Suvorov, Viktor, *Soviet Military Intelligence*, Hamish Hamilton, London, 1984.

Suvorov, Viktor, *Aquarium: The Career and Defection of a Soviet Military Spy*, Hamish Hamilton, London, 1985.

Treverton, Gregory F., *Covert Action: The Limits of Intervention in the Postwar World*, I.B. Tauris, London, 1989.

Tuck, Jay, *High Tech Espionage: How the KGB Smuggles NATO's Strategic Secrets to Moscow*, Sidgwick & Jackson, London, 1986.

Turner, Stansfield, *Secrecy and Democracy: The CIA in Transition*, Houghton Mifflin, Boston, 1985.

Urban, Mark, *Big Boys' Rules: The Secret Struggle against the IRA*, Faber & Faber, London, 1992.

Wallach, Janet and John Wallach, *Arafat: In the Eyes of the Beholder*, Carol Publishing Group, New York, 1990.

Watson, Bruce W., Susan M., Watson and Gerald W., Hopple eds., *United States Intelligence: An Encyclopedia*, Garland, New York, 1990.

Watson, Bruce W., Bruce George, MP, Peter Touras and B. L. Cyr, *Military Lessons of the Gulf War*, Greenhill, London, 1991.

West, Nigel, *The Friends: Britain's Post War Secret Intelligence Operations*, Weidenfeld & Nicolson, London, 1988.

West, Nigel, *GCHQ: The Secret Wireless War 1900–86*, Weidenfeld & Nicolson, London, 1986.

West, Nigel, *Games of Intelligence: The Classified Conflict of International Espionage*, Weidenfeld & Nicolson, London, 1989.

Whitney, Craig R., *Spy Trader: Germany's Devil's Advocate & the Darkest Secrets of the Cold War*, Times Books, New York, 1993.

Wilkinson, Paul and A. M. Stewart, eds., *Contemporary Research on Terrorism*, Aberdeen University Press, Great Britain, 1987.

Willan, Philip, *Puppet Masters: The Political Use of Terrorism in Italy*, Constable, London, 1991.

Wilson, Harold, *Final Term: The Labour Government 1974–1976*, Weidenfeld & Nicolson and Michael Joseph, London, 1979.

Wise, David, *The Spy Who Got Away*, Collins, London, 1988.

Wise, David, *Molehunt: The Secret Search for Traitors that Shattered the CIA*, Random House, New York, 1992.

Woodward, Bob, *Veil: The Secret Wars of the CIA 1981–1987*, Simon & Schuster, London, 1987.

Wright, Peter, *Spy Catcher: The Candid Autobiography of a Senior Intelligence Officer*, Viking, New York, 1987.

INDEX